DISTRIBUTION COSTS

By

J. BROOKS HECKERT

Professor of Accounting
The Ohio State University

ROBERT B. MINER

Assistant Professor of Business Organization
The Ohio State University

SECOND EDITION

THE RONALD PRESS COMPANY ⸗ NEW YORK

Library of Congress Catalog Card Number: 52–11307

PRINTED IN THE UNITED STATES OF AMERICA

PREFACE

In a country characterized by private enterprise, the hope of reducing the effort necessary to transfer goods from producers to consumers rests chiefly on the ingenuity and efficiency of business executives in directing marketing effort and controlling distribution costs. Despite the opportunities in this field, the methods and techniques by which the distribution outlay has been given direction and control have too often received inadequate attention from executives. In many concerns the information pertaining to selling operations is meager, and the cost of distribution is subjected to far less rigid tests than is the cost of production operations. While this problem must admittedly be attacked on many fronts and in different ways by individual concerns, there is probably a greater opportunity for savings and improved efficiency from this than from any other source.

This book has been written to aid accountants and marketing executives in the difficult task of the analysis, supervision, and control of selling costs. It offers a basic plan and suggestions of illustrative methods which will help those who have to work out and use procedures suitable to specific situations. In presenting each topic the authors outline the fundamental problems to be solved and describe the methods and techniques which have been successfully used by different types of concerns. The material is drawn from companies in manufacturing, wholesaling, and retailing as well as from authoritative published sources.

The book consists of two parts. In Part I the subject of analysis of distribution costs is examined. Here different bases of allocation are suggested under varying circumstances, and there is a thorough treatment of the net profit and contribution margin approaches to distribution cost analysis. In Part II methods and procedures for controlling such costs are covered in detail; in addition, significant legislation relevant to the marketing field is summarized and appraised. The authors have attempted, particularly in Part I, to make each chapter a reasonably complete unit so that "leafing back" to items covered in earlier chapters is minimized.

The authors wish to express their deep appreciation to numerous friends and professional acquaintances for generous assistance, as well as to users of the first edition who have made valuable suggestions for improvement. A particular debt of gratitude is due Miss Josephine

iii

Lowrie, C.P.A., formerly Research Director of F. & R. Lazarus and Co., who originally prepared much of the text material relating to department stores in the chapter on analysis by organization and operating divisions.

J. Brooks Heckert
Robert B. Miner

Columbus, Ohio
    December, 1952

CONTENTS

PART I

ANALYSIS OF DISTRIBUTION COSTS

PART II

CONTROL AND PLANNING OF DISTRIBUTION COSTS

v

CONTENTS

APPENDIX

ILLUSTRATIONS

PART I

ANALYSIS OF DISTRIBUTION COSTS

CHAPTER 1

INTRODUCTION

Distribution Functions Are Essential.—Distribution costs are the costs of all business activities necessary to effect transfers in the ownership of tangible goods and to provide for their physical distribution. In other words, distribution costs are the costs of performing the distribution functions.

That such functions are vital to society is a statement that should require no elaboration; nevertheless, there still persists in some quarters a suspicion that distribution costs are not costs of the same character or caliber as production costs. This is apparently a heritage of the past, particularly of the time when economists were loath to regard anyone as productive except direct labor engaged in form utility production. Actually, of course, distribution is truly as much a part of *economic* production as is manufacturing or farming. This assertion assumes significance when it is realized that, in its economic sense, production consists of the addition of utilities of all kinds to goods.

Changing the form of goods obviously adds one kind of utility—form utility—to the goods, but distribution activities are correspondingly instrumental in the addition or creation of time, place, and ownership utilities. By reason of these utilities, consumer needs and wants are satisfied. Groceries and drugs of all description are at hand in the corner store, packaged in convenient size and ready for the asking, even though they must be gathered from the ends of the earth. Moreover, consumers demand an infinite variety of services as well as goods, services such as charge accounts, free deliveries, returned goods privileges, and merchandise guaranties. Provision of these services lies within the province of distribution. But these and other services cannot be provided without cost.

Are Distribution Costs Too High?—The statement is frequently made that distribution costs are too high. This in itself is not a highly significant statement. We may as well say that production costs are too high, or that all costs are too high—a statement that is true only in that our productive and distributive processes have not attained perfection. Costs are too high only if they can be reduced without loss in quantity and quality of goods and services consumed. Yet, when the farmer receives as little as one-sixth of the price per pound paid by the housewife for a cabbage, the critics are likely to rise up and condemn the marketing structure, either with or without justification. Likewise, when the individual manufacturer finds that his cost of distribution is constituting a relatively higher, and his cost of production a relatively lower, portion of his total cost, he is likely to raise the question as to whether or not his distribution activities are being efficiently directed. What is forgotten all too often is that our complex distributive structure is the natural complement of a productive system characterized by mass production and specialization.

Still, in the long run, the costs of marketing must be justified economically. The public is interested in the best balance between the costs of production and distribution. It has been variously estimated that distribution costs account for from 50% to 60% of the consumer's dollar.[1] Regardless of what the value of the true percentage may be, it is evident that it costs about as much to market goods as to produce them. In the intricate recirculation of goods, rushing this way and that in the labyrinth of modern commerce, there must lie large opportunities for simplification, increased efficiency, economic savings, and increased profits.

Public Interest in Distribution Policies.—Public interest in distribution policies, particularly in respect to marketing methods and price setting, is evidenced by the growing volume of federal and state regulatory legislation. The Federal Trade Commission Act and the Clayton Act, both passed in 1914, were general enactments directed toward fair trade practice. The Robinson-Patman Act of 1936 and numerous recent state laws have been directed more specifically to price policies and the justification of price differentials. Whether such legislation is of a permanent nature or reflects only current political and economic trends may be questioned; but it is certain that compliance with such regulatory measures is rendered most difficult without the use of effective distribution cost accounting technique. Further consideration of this legislation is given in Chapter 22.

Business Executive's Viewpoint.—It is not the function of this book to consider matters of general economic policy relating to our marketing system, but, rather, the problems of the business executive who must direct his distribution activities in the economic environment as he finds it. The immediate problem of the business executive is to discover the necessary means of reducing and controlling distribution

---

[1] Variations in cost estimates are traceable to (1) the scope of cost data selected for study, (2) the manner of separating distribution costs from production costs, and (3) differences in meaning ascribed to the consumer's dollar as a basis for expressing total dollar distribution costs in percentage form.

costs in such manner as to make a profit. Ultimately, however, he must develop an economical method of getting his goods into the hands of consumers or he will be supplanted by competitors. The manufacturer, for example, must look not only to his own immediate and individual distribution costs but also to those of wholesalers, retailers, and other middlemen who assist him in distributing his goods to the ultimate consumer. If the services of these agencies become too costly, the manufacturer who uses them will find his products forced out of the market.

Increased Importance of Distribution Cost as a Business Factor. —Most business executives are finding the cost of distribution a factor of increasing importance. In many concerns it constitutes the major cost and in most industries it is a factor of major proportion. If a business is to succeed it must exert no less effort toward the efficient direction and control of distribution cost than toward production cost. While such a statement appears obvious, it is significant in that much greater emphasis has, in the past, been directed to production efficiency.

Accounting and Marketing Executives Must Join Forces.—Just as accounting and production executives have joined forces in developing methods of production cost control, so must the accounting and marketing executives work jointly in the control of the distribution costs. Intelligent sales direction depends largely upon cost analysis. Sales executives must learn to use statistical and accounting data and accounting executives must become better students of marketing principles and methods. The accountant must study intensively the sales problems of his particular concern. He must learn how to translate sales and distribution cost statistics into trends, relationships, and useful signals for the guidance of sales effort. No mere tabulation of figures will suffice. There must be accurate and intelligent interpretation of the data by means of which sales executives can act with confidence and certainty.

Distribution Functions.—Distribution (or marketing) functions,[2] viewed broadly, include all those business activities necessary to effect transfer of ownership in goods, and to provide for their physical distribution. These activities may be outlined as follows:

1. Buying
2. Selling
3. Transportation
4. Storage
5. Standardization and grading
6. Financing
7. Risk bearing
8. Collection, analysis, and interpretation of market information

[2] Throughout this book the terms "distribution" and "marketing" are used synonymously.

Buying is concerned with the determination of what, where, when, and in what quantity goods are to be procured. In a given business unit, it may involve the accumulation of large quantities of one kind of goods, as in the case of cotton merchants; or it may require the accumulation of thousands of different items, as in the case of a wholesale druggist. Selling involves the influencing of prospective customers to buy the goods. Buying and selling constitute the two primary functions of marketing. The remaining functions are, in a sense, facilitative. Transportation and storage have to do with the physical factor; they add place and time utility. Standardization involves the establishment of certain criteria to which the goods must conform. Grading is the process of classifying the goods according to the standards prescribed. These two activities make marketing easier.

Financing has become an important part of the scheme of distribution. Consumers are now accustomed to purchasing on credit. Manufacturers extend credit to wholesalers, wholesalers extend credit to retailers, and so on. Again, when a distributor invests in inventories, he is financing an operation. The distributor also takes many risks: possible losses due to changes in style or price and nonpayment of debts are examples. Finally, the collection, analysis, and interpretation of market information must serve as a basis for determining what the trade wants, what they will pay, and what the costs will be of securing and distributing the goods.

It should be noted that certain of these activities are not usually considered as a part of distribution. Purchasing, for example, may be considered as a separate function or as related to production. In trading concerns, however, it is usually included with other distribution activities.

Distribution Cost Components.—In the analysis of costs for purposes of managerial control, there is much to be said in favor of resolving all costs into two general functional groups—production and distribution, or the cost to make and the cost to sell. General administrative and financial expenses are incurred, in final analysis, for the facilitation of production or distribution. Distribution costs may then be considered to include all costs other than the cost of the goods purchased or produced. The distribution costs may be conveniently classified as follows:

1. Direct selling expense—all direct expense of salesmen, sales offices, sales supervision, and service connected therewith
2. Advertising and sales promotional expense—all advertising; sales promotional, publicity, educational, and market development activity; and expense incident thereto

3. Transportation expense—all transportation charges on outbound goods, returned sales, and local deliveries; maintenance and operation of outward transportation facilities; and the distribution share of traffic service expense

4. Warehousing and handling expense—the total expense of warehousing, storing, and handling finished goods beyond the point of production

5. Credit and collection expense—all expenses of maintaining a credit and collection department, expense of accounts receivable records, collection expense, and loss from bad debts

6. Financial expense—the cost of carrying accounts receivable and finished inventories, cost of fixed and working capital for distribution activities, and cash discounts allowed on sales

7. General distribution expense—the expense of distribution accounting and market research, the distribution share of general administrative expense, and all other expenses related to distribution activities not included above

Even though it is theoretically desirable to resolve the financial and general administrative expenses into their distribution and production components for internal control purposes, management frequently visualizes them as distinct expenses to be analyzed and controlled separately.

In wholesaling and retailing concerns where the purchasing and selling functions are closely related and frequently performed by the same persons, the purchasing expense is generally included with the distribution costs as a part of the total cost of doing business.

Distribution Channels.—The distribution channels through which goods pass from producer to consumer are numerous and varied.[3] An individual producing concern may distribute one product through one channel, another product through a different channel. Again, the same product may be distributed partly through one channel and partly through another. Although few rigid patterns exist for either similar concerns or similar products, the usual trade channels are:

    A. Consumer goods
        1. Producer to consumer
        2. Producer to retailer to consumer
        3. Producer to wholesaler to retailer to consumer
    B. Industrial goods
        1. Producer to user
        2. Producer to wholesale middleman to user

[3] Strictly interpreted, a "channel of distribution" is the course taken in the transfer of title to a commodity. Title to some commodities may be transferred several times while the goods themselves are in transit or stored. Ordinarily, however, both goods and title take the same path.

Some of the factors which enter into the determination of the channels to be used in distributing products may be noted as follows:

1. The size of the producing concern. A large producer requires a high degree of dependability in distribution. This may necessitate the use of trade channels which can be closely controlled.
2. The financial strength of the producer. A strong company may be able to finance the distribution program through to the consumer; a weak company may not.
3. The completeness of the line of goods produced. An incomplete line may require the services of middlemen who can profitably combine it with other related goods.
4. The nature of the commodity. Highly perishable products, such as fresh meat, require a shorter marketing process than nonperishable products.
5. The nature of the market. Where the market consists of a comparatively few industrial users, the producer may sell direct to consumer; where the goods are for personal use with consumers numbering millions this may be impracticable.

The foregoing are only suggestive of the numerous factors affecting the selection of trade channels. For more complete statements, the reader is referred to the numerous studies of marketing.

Distribution Agencies.—The producer may sell direct to the consumer in order to control prices and selling methods, or to protect his market from the inroad of competitors. Or he may sell direct to retailers in order to command a closer control over his market than he can secure through wholesalers. If he sells to large retail units such as chain stores, his purpose may be to obtain a low selling cost. Again, he may find his most profitable channel to be through established wholesalers. Many producers have found it desirable to operate their own wholesale or retail outlets.

The wholesaler of consumer goods is a middleman who purchases goods, usually in large quantities, and resells them in smaller lots to the retailer. He is used as an agency in distribution when he can perform certain services better or more economically than can the producer. The services performed by the regular or full-function wholesaler may be summarized as follows:

1. He assembles and warehouses. The wholesaler assembles and warehouses in a convenient place both a quantity and variety of merchandise. This involves investment, risk, and judgment as to consumer demand.

2. He contributes to the stability of production. Since the wholesaler places his orders in advance of consumer demand, he must anticipate wants. In this manner he aids the manufacturer in the regulation of production.

3. He reduces transportation costs. By buying in large quantities, frequently in carload lots, the wholesaler reduces the transportation costs from producer to retailer.

4. He provides delivery service. The wholesaler usually provides a delivery service for his own city and surrounding territory. This may be more economical than that which could be provided by individual producers.

5. He grants credit. The wholesaler usually operates in a limited area and, through intimate knowledge of his customers, may be able to grant credit more intelligently than could the manufacturer.

6. He renders advice. The wholesaler is very often in a position to advise and help the retailers whom he serves.

7. He specializes in distribution. The wholesaler is a specialist in distribution. He can study intensively the problems of a more or less permanent list of customers and thereby provide for their needs.

The function of the retailer is to supply individual consumers with the goods desired for personal consumption. The retailer performs all of the marketing functions such as anticipating the needs of consumers, assembling and storing goods, financing, risk bearing, and demand creation.

There are numerous other types of wholesale middlemen who have developed to meet particular marketing needs of sellers and buyers. Brokers, for example, serve to bring buyer and seller together. They do not take title to, or handle, the goods. Their only place of business is an office. They receive a commission as compensation for their services. Selling agents are important in some lines, such as textiles. They often sell the entire output of several mills, style the goods for the manufacturer, extend financial aid to him, and perform the credit and collection function. More restricted than selling agents as to territory of operations and terms of sale, manufacturers' agents dispose of but part of the output of the manufacturers represented. This form of selling representation permeates nearly all manufacturing lines. The commission man is a familiar figure in the marketing of farm products. He receives the goods on consignment, sells them, and remits the proceeds, less his commission.

The ultimate problem of the individual business is to select that combination of trade channels and marketing agencies which will be most profitable in the long run.

CHAPTER 2

PROBLEMS OF DISTRIBUTION COST ANALYSIS

Basic Purpose of Distribution Cost Analysis.—The basic purpose of distribution cost analysis is to supply marketing executives with the information needed in the planning, direction, and control of distribution effort. Questions must be answered as to what, when, where, and how to sell, and at what prices. Sales effort must be pointed in the most profitable direction and unproductive effort eliminated. Programs for the future must be developed which bear promise of reasonable profit and the execution of such programs must be closely watched for adverse trends. In so far as possible, standards must be established for the measurement of distribution performance and costs, and actual operations measured thereby. While the analysis of costs will not supply all of the information necessary for effective direction of distribution activities it is an essential factor.

Production and Distribution Costs Contrasted.—Production costs are analyzed for the purpose of cost determination and cost control. Costs must be determined in order to establish inventory values, prepare financial and operating statements, and guide production and price policies. More important still, the production costs must be analyzed for the purpose of holding the production performance and costs to what they should be. Production costs are analyzed chiefly by operations and products and cost variances are resolved into efficiency, volume, and price factors.

Distribution costs are analyzed for the purpose of cost determination, cost control, and direction of effort. While it is not the practice to absorb distribution costs in inventory values, the costs must be determined for purposes of establishing distribution policies; setting prices; and preparing divisional operating statements, such as those for territories, commodities, and branches. As in the case of production, the most important purpose of distribution cost analysis is the control of costs and the intelligent direction of effort.

While in production the cost analysis is restricted chiefly to operations and products, it must usually be extended much further in distribution. Many analyses and cross analyses are required to supply the necessary information for marketing guidance.

Distribution costs must be analyzed by functions, functional operations, territories, commodities, channels of distribution, methods of sale, classes of customers, size of orders, operating divisions, methods of delivery, terms of sale, etc. Cost variances must be analyzed not only as to volume and price factors, but also with respect to the relationship between distribution effort and result, i.e., efficiency of performance.

In production, the cost analysis is largely of internal operating data; in distribution, not all of the necessary information can be obtained from an analysis of internal operations. To this must be added the intelligence of market research, pertaining to such factors as the nature, strength, and location of consumer demand; products desired; and effective methods of sale. Both internal and external data must be analyzed, related, and jointly interpreted as a basis for marketing strategy.

Two Approaches to Distribution Cost Control and Direction of Effort.—Several statements contained in the foregoing paragraphs suggest that there are two approaches to the problems of controlling distribution costs and directing marketing effort properly. These approaches are, however, closely related in terms of dependence upon one another.

The first approach may well be termed the "marketing management" approach. In order to ascertain the most effective means of achieving maximum marketing results, marketing research methods and procedures are employed in the determination of market and sales potentials and in the selection of effective distribution methods and facilities. Illustrative of studies encompassed by this approach are the following: sales records analyses, field studies of salesmen's performance, measurement of advertising effectiveness by areas, studies of warehouse location and layout, and studies leading to forecasts of consumer demand.

The second approach, the one emphasized in this book, is distribution cost analysis. It is immediately concerned with the principles and procedures of determining and controlling the costs of segments of marketing effort, such as functions, territories, and commodity groups. Since accounting records necessarily provide the bulk of the data for analysis, this approach has sometimes been called the "accounting" approach.[1] Such a designation is not accurate, however, because accounting procedures need not play an important role in the analysis. In fact, distribution cost analysis lays greater stress on statistical procedures than on accounting techniques.

[1] For example, see Richard D. Crisp, *How to Reduce Distribution Costs* (New York: Funk & Wagnalls Co. in association with *Modern Industry* magazine, 1948), pp. 382–83. This book is an excellent presentation of the marketing management approach, although it is concerned primarily with the *sales* manager's point of view.

Actually, as was suggested above, the two approaches are so inter-related that proper analysis requires the use of both if good cost control and effective direction of marketing effort are to be achieved.

Distribution Problems.—As a basis for further consideration of distribution cost analysis and control, it is desirable to suggest the nature of the problems faced by executives in the planning and direction of distribution effort. Illustrative of such problems are the following:

1. *Commodities to be sold.* What goods should be handled; how extensive the lines; staple or fancy goods; standard or special items; high, medium, or low quality; branded or unbranded products? Innumerable such questions arise, the answers to which depend largely upon cost analysis.

2. *Prices to be charged.* Prices are not, as a rule, immediately and directly determined by costs, but the establishment and maintenance of a sound price policy are impossible without a knowledge of both production and distribution costs. In concerns which approach a monopolistic or semimonopolistic position, prices are set (barring governmental regulation) as nearly as possible at the point which will yield the greatest total profit; but this can be determined only by knowing the total cost at different volume levels. In the so-called free markets, where the forces of supply and demand are in complete freedom, immediate prices are set by the market. Here the cost has no immediate effect on the price. Between these extremes the degree of closeness of relationship between cost and price varies. Where goods are sold on a cost-plus basis or where prices are set by a fairly uniform rate of markup over costs, the relationship is close. Where prices are changed frequently to meet competition, the relationship is more remote and more difficult of perception.

Regardless of the immediate relationship of costs and prices, the costs must be used as a basis for ultimate price policy. Goods may be sold today at less than cost because competitive prices are less; but over any considerable period, such a policy would obviously lead to ruin. When it is apparent that prices will continue below costs, costs must be lowered, or the products must be discontinued.

Moreover, regulatory legislation relative to discriminatory prices may necessitate full cost information as a basis for defending pricing practices.[2]

3. *Extent of territory to be served.* A concern should know the limits of its natural and profitable territory; that is to say, the territory in which it can, in the long run, sell at a cost as low or lower than that

---

[2] See discussion of the Robinson-Patman Act in Chapter 22.

of any substantial competitor. Even before reaching such limits, questions will arise as to the relative profitability of expanding in various directions, as to whether or not territories should be thoroughly covered, as to the desirability of developing foreign markets, etc.

4. *Classes of trade to be cultivated.* Few concerns cover every class of trade; usually a choice must be made. A concern selling to retailers may elect to cultivate only regular retail stores in its line or it may extend its effort to department stores, variety stores, mail order houses, etc. Questions will arise as to the cost of selling to each class and the trend of such costs.

5. *Distribution channels and agencies to be used.* In addition to the problem of selection of classes of trade on one level of distribution, there is frequently a choice to be made of distribution channels and combinations of distribution agencies. Here again the cost is one of the major factors in the decision.

6. *Profitable size of order.* The question often arises as to the profitableness of small orders. An analysis of costs may reveal that many orders are handled at a loss. While it may not be good policy to reject all such orders, an intelligent decision cannot be made without knowledge of the cost and the extent of the loss.

7. *Profitable size of unit of sale.* If the goods are packed by the gross, the distribution cost of a single item may equal or exceed the cost of a gross. It may be necessary to limit the size of the unit below which sales will not be made except at a higher price.

8. *Credit terms to be granted.* A decision as to the credit terms to be offered and enforced requires, among other factors, a knowledge of the cost of operating under various credit plans.

9. *When to expand.* Any proposal of expansion in production facilities must be carefully tested by the estimated cost of extending the distribution facilities and effort into new markets and the probable effect of such extension on competition. Can the new markets be secured and held at a cost which offers reasonable profit opportunity over the long term?

10. *Inventories to be carried.* One important factor in determining the amount of finished inventory to be carried and the rate of turnover to be maintained is the cost of carrying the inventory.

11. *Control of individual distribution operations and cost items.* Standards must be set by which to control the cost of distribution operations and individual cost items; and a comparison of actual costs with such standards must serve as the primary means of distribution cost control.

12. *Results to be obtained from costs.* Selling effort is particularly susceptible to maladjustments in relation to sales volume secured; yet,

a proper effort-result relationship must be maintained. The cost analysis must be such as to quickly reveal any such maladjustment.

The foregoing is by no means a comprehensive outline of distribution problems, but it suggests the nature of the problems to which cost analysis must be directed. The accounting and marketing executives, working together, must select the type of cost analysis adapted to the problems of their particular concern.

Difficulties of Distribution Cost Analysis.—Certain difficulties arise in the analysis of distribution costs. Particularly are these apparent in contrast with the analysis of production costs, with which accountants and executives have become more familiar. Before proceeding with the consideration of methods of distribution cost analysis, it is desirable to have a clear understanding of these difficulties.

DISTRIBUTION AGENCIES NUMEROUS AND VARIED. The agencies employed in distribution are numerous and varied in character. Particularly is this apparent in contrast with production. A concern manufacturing washing machines, for example, will machine its castings in a manner similar to that employed by all other such manufacturers. There are fairly definite limits to the methods which may be employed. But in the distribution of the product, the concerns may employ entirely different agencies and combinations of agencies. One concern may sell its product to large mail order houses through the agency of a few salesmen; another may spend vast sums on advertising and rely upon house-to-house salesmen, dealers, agents, branches, department stores, foreign agents, etc. The problem as to which agency or combination of agencies should be employed is one to which the cost analysis must lend help.

DISTRIBUTION METHODS MORE FLEXIBLE THAN PRODUCTION METHODS.—Again, the agencies of distribution may be and frequently are quickly readjusted or shifted from one combination to another. Policy commitment need not be projected as far in the future as in the case of production. The manufacturer of washing machines would meet some difficulty in quickly shifting to the production of cosmetics. He would, in fact, find it difficult to quickly change his methods of production of the same product. He may, however, rather quickly shift to other agencies and methods of distribution. This situation calls for a greater degree of flexibility and versatility in distribution cost analysis than is usually required for production costs.

PSYCHOLOGICAL FACTORS IN DISTRIBUTION PRESENT DIFFICULTIES.—Moreover, the human element is more pronounced in distribution than in production activity. Factors are more largely psychological and less mechanical. In distribution the action of the buyer as well as the salesman must be considered, whereas in production the worker alone supplies the human element and his actions may be directly limited by the mechanics of the task. To be sure some distribution activity such as delivery of goods may be fully as mechanical as production, but the effort of a salesman of steam fittings to persuade a customer to place a $5,000 order with the salesman's concern rather than with a competitor, when prices and specifications are identical, is by no means a purely mechanical task. There are far more variables in marketing than in production. These are due to the lack of control over customers and competitors. These variables complicate the task of analyzing distribution costs.

DISTRIBUTION ACTIVITIES DIFFICULT TO STANDARDIZE.—In view of the psychological element and continuous readjustment of distribution agencies, the distribution activities are more difficult to standardize than production activities. This implies further that distribution performance is more difficult to measure. The chief task of the accountant in the control of costs is to measure performance but this is impossible without standards of measurement. An engineer can determine with a fair degree of accuracy the number of tools of a certain specification which can and should be sharpened in a sand blast in one hour. This is a definite unit of measurement—a standard. It may be used to measure production performance. But how much business should be secured by the driver-salesman of a bakery wagon in a certain industrial section of the city in which a competitor is making price concessions in a drive to secure a foothold? The standard here is difficult to set and performance hard to measure.

BASIC INFORMATION DIFFICULT TO OBTAIN.—Another difficulty is that of securing basic information. Marketing activities may be widely scattered. No timekeepers and inspectors are at hand when a salesman calls on a customer.[3] Sales executives and employees are not always accustomed to records and reports of activity. They are sensitive to anything resembling espionage. Sales activities are largely of an intangible character and not easily related to specific results. Danger of error or unfairness requires caution on the part of the accountant.

DISTRIBUTION COSTS DIFFICULT TO INTERPRET.—Moreover, the information once secured is difficult to interpret. Distribution costs are largely indirect costs, not readily assignable to specific and imme-

[3] Time and duty analysis of salesmen has been attempted with gratifying success in a few recorded instances. For example, see James H. Davis, *Increasing Wholesale Drug Salesmen's Effectiveness* (Columbus, Ohio: Bureau of Business Research, Ohio State University, 1948).

diate results. These indirect costs have been troublesome in production; they are even more so in distribution, where they constitute a larger proportion of the total cost. The interpretation of these costs requires intensive study and exacting analysis.

DIFFERENT COSTS ARE NEEDED.—Another problem is to determine what costs will be useful. For example, where there are large elements of indirect costs, the analysis may advantageously be directed to the measurement of the *additional* costs incurred under various prescribed circumstances. Thus it may be desired to find the additional cost of sending a salesman on into some adjacent territory not otherwise covered; or the cost of handling Line X without Line Y and Line Z without Line X; or the cost of handling a certain class of customers and the minimum volume necessary to cover this cost.

Task Not Impossible.—While numerous difficulties are encountered in any attempt to analyze distribution costs, the opportunities for profitable results justify the effort. Sales management can be made more scientific, intelligent, and efficient. Much wasteful sales and advertising effort can be eliminated. There is little room left in modern sales management for the rule-of-thumb or the rabbit's-foot executive. Ways must be found to ferret out the facts and properly interpret them. While the field is comparatively new and little standardized practice has been developed, the accounting and marketing executives must direct the full force of their training, experience, and ingenuity to the intelligent analysis of distribution costs. Production costs are fairly well controlled in well-managed companies; distribution costs can be subjected to much the same type of control. The task is by no means impossible, as is evidenced by the successful experience of firms in many lines of business.

CHAPTER 3

METHOD OF DISTRIBUTION COST ANALYSIS

Types of Analyses.—Distribution costs may be analyzed:

1. By the nature of cost items or object of expenditure
2. By functions or functional operations performed
3. By the manner in which the distribution effort is applied (i.e., by territories, customers, or other segments of the business)

In most concerns it is necessary to apply all methods, at least to some extent, in order to supply marketing executives with the information necessary for the efficient direction and control of distribution effort.

Analysis by Nature of Cost Items.—The first analysis made of distribution costs is usually by nature of cost items or object of expenditure. Thus salaries, advertising, supplies, taxes, traveling expense, etc., are recorded separately. Such a classification of cost items is usually made a part of the ledger accounts themselves and forms the basis of subsequent analysis. For example, in the classification of accounts on pages 34 to 39 separate accounts are provided for each cost item falling within a general functional group.

An analysis by nature of cost items provides some general information for cost control purposes. If, for example, traveling expense is recorded in a separate account, it will be possible to compare the expense with previous periods and determine the ratio of the expense to sales volume. Such comparisons and relationships may reveal weaknesses if they are extreme; but they will not reveal the fact that the cost per mile of operating salesmen's automobiles is excessive or that many calls are being made on customers whose business, actual or potential, cannot possibly justify the traveling expense involved. Again, it is possible, by such analysis, to ascertain the percentage of advertising cost to sales; but, if this appears excessive, it is not possible to tell what adjustments should be made to effect a satisfactory relationship. Analysis by nature of cost items is sufficient only when there are no problems as to the efficiency of particular distribution operations; or as to what territories to cover, what commodities to sell, what sales methods to employ, etc. There are few concerns in which these conditions prevail.

By this type of analysis it is possible only to ascertain the cost of the distribution function as a whole. But too many executives know merely how much it costs to *carry on business as a whole,* without knowing the cost of performing specific operations or securing particular results. A sales manager may be told that his selling costs are too high but such a statement is of no great help in reducing them. Before they can be reduced they must be analyzed to the point where it is known just what operations are too costly or unproductive and who is responsible. An executive cannot base intelligent action on generalities, he must have specific facts.

Analysis by Functions.—The analysis of distribution costs by functions and functional operations is particularly valuable as a means of cost control. It is also useful in making subsequent analyses of the costs by manner of application of distribution effort.

For purposes of analysis a function may be defined as a major distribution activity for which costs are assembled.[1] Throughout this text seven activities are so distinguished, although the selection should be regarded as illustrative rather than authoritative. The list of functions includes (1) direct selling, (2) advertising and sales promotion, (3) transportation, (4) warehousing and handling, (5) credit and collections, (6) distribution finance, and (7) general distribution activity. Functional operations, in turn, are subsidiary to the functions and provide for more detailed cost classification. For example, the direct selling function might in some companies be further classified as salesmen's personal calls and telephone solicitations; transportation might similarly be divided into delivery to branches, delivery to break-bulk points, and delivery to customers.

The *first* step in functional analysis for any company is accordingly to outline clearly the functions and functional operations being performed. As a corollary to this step an internal organization must be perfected whereby the responsibility for performance is definitely fixed. If responsibility accounting is used,[2] a group of costs assembled under a single responsibility—an arrangement comparable to the cost centers used in manufacturing—may often include more than one operation; hence caution is necessary in interpreting the figures assembled. To illustrate, a prominent manufacturing concern designates its distribu-

---

[1] The distribution functions referred to are functions of the individual firm; hence, a list of such functions may differ considerably from the list (see page 5) of basic distribution functions inherent in the entire marketing process.

[2] Responsibility accounting is a term used to describe the synchronization of a company's accounting control system and its organization planning. True responsibility accounting is achieved "when organization units have been created in such a way that their costs can be collected and reported on to produce an evaluation of performance and intelligent action toward improving performance." (Harry B. Ailman, "Basic Organizational Planning to Tie in with Responsibility Accounting," *N.A.C.A. Bulletin*, May, 1950, p. 1116.)

tion personnel and training section as a center of responsibility. This section, however, performs services benefiting several functional operations.

The *second* step in the analysis is to classify the individual cost items according to functional groupings. For the major functions this may be effected through the ledger accounts, as illustrated on pages 34 to 39. For functional operations it is usually impossible to assemble all of the costs directly; certain costs common to two or more operations must be apportioned in an equitable manner. For control purposes, however, not all costs applicable to a function or functional operation are pertinent. This important qualification is considered at length following a brief résumé of the remaining steps in functional analysis.

The *third* step is to establish, in so far as possible, units of measurement of functional service. Thus the operation of order writing may have as a unit of measurement the individual order; the handling of sales by salesgirls in the drug sundries department of a department store may have, as a unit of measurement, the sales transaction. While units of measurement as specific as these cannot be found for all functional operations, some reasonable measurement of the service can be found for a considerable part of the distribution activity. Some additional examples of functional operations and units, as provided by the service wholesale drug trade, may be listed as follows:

Functional Operation	*Functional Unit*
Typing country orders	Copied country order
Registering country orders	Country order registered
Supervision of order assembling	Order line
City shipping	City order delivered
Country shipping	Country order shipped
Packing, weighing, and stamping parcel posts	Parcel post order
Invoicing	Order line
Statistical coding and tabulating	Order line
Accounts receivable posting	Individual posting
General filing	Active customer account
Claim investigation and correspondence	Return and adjustment credit memo
Buying	Item stocked

The *fourth* step is to divide the total cost of an operation by the number of units of service performed, to arrive at a unit operation cost. This opens the way for the establishment of standard unit costs and the control of the costs by the application of such standards.

Classification of Costs for Control Purposes.—Functional analysis has utility as a means of cost control only when variable, controllable costs are considered. The full import of this statement cannot be appreciated until careful distinctions are drawn between the types of costs encompassed in the following two groups: (1) variable, semivariable, and fixed costs; (2) controllable and noncontrollable costs.

Variable costs of distribution are those which vary in approximately direct ratio to changes in volume; basically, money or physical volume of sales. For example, commissions to salesmen are a variable cost of the direct selling function, when commissions are calculated as a percentage of sales. An increase of $1,000 in sales would, for instance, occasion a proportional increase of $30 in commission cost, assuming a 3% commission rate. In cost control work, however, volume should be expressed in units which best measure fluctuations in the activity which causes costs to vary, even though such activity is something other than sales *per se*. Thus, salesmen's traveling expenses may be found to vary more closely with the number of calls on prospects than with sales volume. Again, the variable cost items making up the operation of assembling stock for orders are variable chiefly because they are directly related to the volume of items assembled.

Semivariable costs are those which vary with volume but not in direct ratio because such costs contain some fixed as well as variable elements. For example, warehousing clerical and office expense ordinarily bears some relation to storage and handling activity as measured by the weight or cubic content of goods handled; however, the relationship is scarcely proportional. The same conclusion may be reached in the case of salesmen's compensation which is a combination of salaries and commissions. The commission element, as noted above, is largely variable, whereas the salary element is usually fixed within a prescribed range of time and sales volume. In combination, the compensation is best regarded as a semivariable cost. It is obvious that semivariable costs exist only because classification is not sufficiently detailed. If it were, analysis of cost items would disclose only fixed and variable elements.

Fixed costs are those which remain approximately the same in amount throughout a specified period of time, even though fairly substantial changes occur in the volume of operations. Occupancy expense of sales facilities is usually a fixed cost of the direct selling function because associated with a given investment in such facilities are certain irrecoverable expenditures and contractual obligations that continue irrespective of the level of operations. Another example of a fixed cost is the portion of office supervision assigned to the functional operation of preparing and mailing invoices. This cost has little relation to the volume of activity as measured by the number of invoices or invoice lines.

It should be apparent from the discussion of cost terms that in the "long run" all costs are variable, whereas in the "short run" (say one year or less) some costs are variable and others are fixed because entrepreneurs tend to use only a given combination of productive services. "There is nothing in a cost itself that makes it variable or fixed; it is the period of time in relation to use of the factors that gives rise to the distinction." [3] For cost control a short range point of view is taken with budgets and standards commonly established for periods which do not exceed a year. Consequently variable costs are primarily dealt with in functional analysis for control purposes because the value of such analysis is dependent on a reasonable correspondence of changes in volume and costs. Fixed costs must be excluded if such correspondence is to be attained. "This does not mean, of course, that functions and units can be so devised that the cost can be expected to vary completely and perfectly with the difference in the number of service units, and it may be in some cases that the only solution will be 'sliding scale' unit cost standards—that is, standard costs which are adjustable to changes in volume." [4]

Attention must now center upon the second group of cost terms mentioned previously. In this group are controllable and noncontrollable costs. *Controllable costs* are those which are subject to control by persons whose performance is being measured. For example, the payroll of salesclerks employed in a unit of a chain store system is controllable by the store manager. Again, salesmen's traveling expense is controllable by the salesmen themselves as well as by the sales manager. Controllable costs are usually variable costs, nevertheless it is desirable to make separate use of the former as a term because it focuses attention on the responsibility of individuals. Some controllable costs are not variable, however. If a territorial manager were to be given the authority to lease a warehouse, the rent paid would be a fixed cost; yet it would still be controllable by the manager.

Noncontrollable costs are, of course, not subject to control by those whose performance is being measured. Salesmen have no control over the share of sales administration expense for which they may be assessed. Similarly, the transportation superintendent does not control the amount paid for various licenses on equipment. Most noncontrollable costs are fixed costs; however, some items can be distinguished as variable. For example, a variable cost of direct selling is clerical order handling expense. From the standpoint of the individual sales-

[3] John G. Blocker, *Cost Accounting* (New York: McGraw-Hill Book Co., Inc., 1948), p. 667.
[4] Herbert F. Taggart, *Distribution Cost Accounting for Wholesaling*, Domestic Commerce Series No. 106, U. S. Department of Commerce (Washington, D. C.: Government Printing Office, 1939), p. 12.

man, this expense, although it may be charged as a flat amount per order, is not controllable.

On the premise, then, that functional analysis should be designed to measure the cost of activities for which given individuals are responsible, only those variable costs which are controllable should be included in the analysis. This restriction on the composition of functional costs, as far as cost control is concerned, is valid whether firm-wide costs or costs of particular segments of the business are in question.

Illustration of Cost Control Through Functional Analysis.—The use of functional analysis as a control device may be made clearer by a simple illustration. Assume, for example, that a certain concern has five sales territories, each having a separate sales force. Standard unit costs have been established in each territory for various functional operations, including the one at issue here, namely, salesmen's calls on prospects. Only variable, controllable costs comprise the standard and actual figures determined. Plans for a given month called for the following volume and cost objectives:

Territory	Planned Number of Calls	Standard Cost per Call	Budgeted Total Cost
1	10,000	$4.00	$40,000
2	5,000	4.50	22,500
3	15,000	4.20	63,000
4	20,000	4.00	80,000
5	8,000	5.00	40,000

Assume further that the actual results for the month in question were as follows:

Territory	Actual Number of Calls	Total Actual Cost	Actual Cost per Call
1	10,200	$41,820	$4.10
2	6,000	26,400	4.40
3	14,300	60,060	4.20
4	20,500	80,975	3.95
5	8,000	44,000	5.50

Such a comparison of planned and actual figures enables management to make a preliminary evaluation of the performance of this functional operation in each territory. In Territory 1 the actual number of calls exceeded the planned number, but at the standard unit cost of $4.00 the total cost should have been $40,800 (10,200 actual calls × $4.00). Actually, the total cost was $41,820, or $4.10 per call; hence there was an efficiency loss of $1,020 ($41,820 less $40,800). That is, the quality of salesmen's performance—as measured by cost—was below standard to the extent of 10 cents per call. An even more serious situation characterized operations in Territory 5 which showed an efficiency loss of $4,000 ($44,000 less $40,000). None of the increases in cost in this territory, moreover, resulted from greater volume of activity as measured by calls. Territories 1 and 5 are, thus, immediately marked for further scrutiny by management. On the other hand, volume gains and efficiency savings were scored in Territories 2 and 4. Actual costs per call in both territories were above standard. Finally, salesmen's calls on prospects in Territory 3 were made exactly at standard, i.e., $4.20 per call. Volume, however, was under the planned figure by 700 units, a difference requiring satisfactory explanation to sales executives.

Functional analysis, it will be recalled, not only serves as a control device but also facilitates the analysis of costs by manner of application. Thus if an analysis is being made by classes of customers, it is necessary only to record the number of units of a certain functional service applied to a particular class of customers, and multiply this number by the functional unit cost, to determine the share of the functional cost applicable to that class of customers.

It must be remembered, however, that the share so applied will include only the variable, controllable costs of the functional operation. Since control is not the principal objective of analysis by manner of application, the functional costs need not be so limited in scope. Separate provision must therefore be made for the distribution of fixed and noncontrollable costs, if their inclusion in the analysis is deemed desirable. Furthermore, some of the cost items assembled in a given functional operation will be direct costs, as defined on page 25, in so far as particular segments of sales are concerned. Hence, assignment of functional costs on a composite basis, as is true of the method described above, is likely to be less accurate than would be the case if direct costs were separately applied. Finally, even if the method of utilizing units of functional service is held to be expedient in view of the above qualifications, a single measurement unit may not be best for all types of analysis. For example, costs associated with salesmen's calls on prospects may, as has been illustrated previously, have the call as the measurement unit for control purposes. This same unit or basis of allocation (to use the term customarily employed in segment analysis) may be the best choice for applying these costs to groups of customers; for application to groups of commodities, however, time studies may prove a superior basis.

Analysis by Manner of Application.[5]—While analyses of distribution costs by nature of items and functions are valuable for cost control purposes, they do not aid greatly in the direction of the distribution

[5] Other commonly used terms having a similar meaning include analysis by segments of the business, analysis by segments of sales, and analysis by categories of sales.

effort. Distribution effort, even though efficiently exercised, will be unproductive unless given proper direction. Ultimately it is necessary to extend the cost analysis to a point which reveals the manner in which the distribution effort is being applied. This is necessary in order to relate effort and cost to results obtained, to adjust the effort to sales possibilities, and to properly balance the distribution factors.

The steps in such an analysis are as follows:

1. Determine which analyses should be made.
2. Classify the costs as to those which are direct and indirect, in relation to each analysis used.
3. Select suitable bases of allocation to be applied to the indirect cost items.
4. Apply the bases selected.
5. Prepare the final analyses and their interpretation for executive use.

Determination of Analyses to Be Made.—The analysis of distribution costs according to the manner in which the distribution effort is applied may take numerous forms depending upon the nature of the problem of the individual concern. The analyses most frequently needed are as follows:

1. By territories—for example, districts, branch areas, salesmen's territories, trade centers, states, counties, or cities
2. By commodities—for example, individual commodities or related groups of commodities
3. By channels of distribution—for example, to wholesalers, retailers, or ultimate consumers
4. By methods of sale—for example, through salesmen, mail order, company stores, house-to-house solicitation, etc.
5. By classes of customers—for example, customers with large and small annual purchases
6. By size of orders—for example, the cost applied to securing, handling, and filling orders of varying size, measured in money
7. By organization and operating divisions—for example, branches, departments, stores, etc.
8. By salesmen—that is, the cost applied to the work of individual salesmen or groups of salesmen
9. By method of delivery—for example, over-the-counter, delivery-on-request, store-door delivery, peddler trucks, etc.
10. By size or number of physical units—for example, full and broken cases, gross and fractions of a gross, carload and less than carload lots, etc.
11. By terms of sale—for example, cash, short-term credit, instalment, etc.

It should be understood that not all of these analyses are usually necessary in any one concern; and that such analyses as are used need not all be made continuously. Certain of them, such as analysis by channels of distribution may be found necessary only once a year. Others may be the subject of special studies, to be utilized only when it is necessary to localize weakness. In some instances it is desirable to make cross-analyses. Thus, sales and costs may be analyzed by territories; and the cost of each territory then further subdivided according to commodities or size of customer order.

Classification of Cost Items in Relation to Analyses Used.—After selecting the cost analyses to be made, the next step is to classify the individual cost items in accordance with the directness of their relationship to each particular analysis. If, for example, an analysis is to be made by territories, then it must be known which costs obviously and directly relate to individual territories and which ones bear only an indirect or remote relationship. This is an important step. Unless some close relationship can be established for the major part of the costs, the validity of the results will be questioned by executives and they will be reluctant to use them.

For the purpose of analysis by application, distribution costs may be divided into three major groups; direct costs, semidirect costs, and indirect costs. *Direct costs,* as the term implies, are those which can be definitely charged or allocated. Thus, in an analysis by territories, the salaries of salesmen, who work exclusively in individual territories, are direct costs of those territories. The classification of accounts in itself usually expresses this direct relationship in some one direction. Thus, in the classification of accounts given on pages 34 to 39, separate account sections could be provided for the direct costs of each branch. The accounts can be similarly classified for territories or other desired analyses.

Semidirect costs are those which are related in some measurable way to a particular category. The charges cannot be made immediately and directly, but a dependable basis of measurement is available. For example: the cost of packing may be distributed on the basis of physical volume; the cost of billing, on the basis of number of orders or number of lines of billing; or the cost of credit supervision, on the basis of the number of customers.

Indirect costs are those costs which admit of no measurable relationship with any one territory, product, or channel of distribution, as distinguished from any other. They are recognized as a general charge on the total business; and, therefore, if they are apportioned, some arbitrary basis must be used. Examples of this type of expense are the salaries of general executives, and institutional advertising. There may be, for example, no well-defined relationship between institutional advertising and the sale of Product A as contrasted with Product B. While there are some indirect cost items for which no measurable relation can be found, the amount of such costs is usually small. A diligent search into effort and result relationships will reveal that most distribution cost items have some ascertainable basis of apportionment.

Selection of Bases of Allocation.—In practically all analyses of distribution costs there are semidirect costs for which bases of allocation must be selected. Likewise the indirect costs, if apportioned, require bases of distribution. The procedure of selecting such bases has been introduced in the preceding discussion of the steps in functional cost analysis. Establishment of units of functional service is, however, fundamentally a problem in choosing factors of variability useful in control of costs. Such factors may or may not serve equally well as bases of allocation of costs to categories of sales effort.

The problem of selecting appropriate bases is simple in theory. If, for example, it is desired to distribute the cost of preparing and mailing monthly statements to customers; and if it is found that the work entailed is practically the same for each customer; and if an analysis of cost by territories is under consideration; then the basis selected may well be the average number of customers in each territory. Such figures are easily secured, simple of application, and accurate in results. They constitute a satisfactory basis. In practice, the problem is often more difficult. Considerable judgment and common sense are necessary in striking the proper balance between accuracy of results, cost of securing the data, and complexity of application. The greater the amount involved, the greater the justification for the cost of securing the needed data. Where large amounts are concerned, great pains must be taken to secure an accurate and dependable basis.

Two criteria govern the choice of suitable bases of allocation. First, the choice should be made on logical grounds; that is, a basis should either be the obvious numerical expression of fluctuations in the activity or activities giving rise to the cost, or it should bear a demonstrable relationship to such fluctuations. For example, in an analysis by commodities the share of salaries and traveling expense of general line salesmen applicable to each commodity group might logically be a function of the amount of time devoted to each. If this is the case, the appropriate basis of allocation is the percentage of total time spent. As a second criterion, the basis should be selected on practical grounds to the extent that it should be measurable without undue expense. With regard to the example just offered, the expense of collecting reliable data for time measurement might be prohibitive in relation to the value of the results. This criterion should not, however, be permitted to overshadow the first-named one in importance; otherwise the allocation process becomes an exercise of convenience with misleading information its end product.

Methods of Selection.—Selection of the most logical basis to use in allocating a particular cost item often may be aided by simple graphic analysis. Construction of scatter diagrams in which cost is plotted against a succession of possible factors of variability will permit the analyst to determine the factor most closely related to changes in cost. Graphic analysis is also of value as a means of effecting a rough separation of fixed and variable elements of cost. As an illustration, the hypothetical relationship between the number of salesmen's calls and total direct selling expense for a given period of time is shown by the dots in Figure 1. The diagonal line represents a freehand estimate

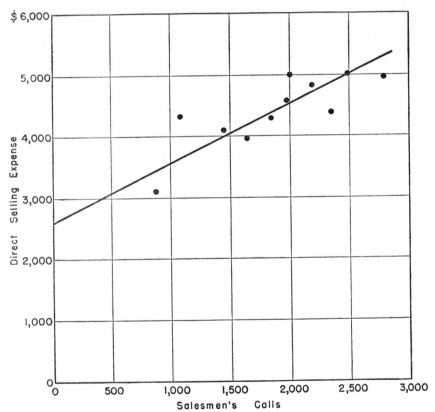

FIGURE 1. Relationship Between Number of Salesmen's Calls and Direct Selling Expense

of the linear tendency exhibited by the paired values. With a sufficient number of observations correlation techniques may be used to develop such a line (straight or curved) mathematically.

It is apparent that greater expense is associated with an increased number of calls. Even with no calls, however, there is a substantial amount of expense, namely, $2,500. This figure may be considered an approximation of the fixed element in direct selling expense. The slope of the line in turn indicates the amount of variable expense incurred per call. In this case the amount is about $1. Thus, with 2,500 calls the total expense can be read from the chart as $5,000, consisting of $2,500 in fixed and $2,500 (2,500 calls at $1 each) in variable expense.

For those costs to which such methods are applicable, time studies and job analyses of the activities of distribution personnel are being used to an increasing extent in selection of bases of allocation. A commentary on current practice with respect to the nature and qualifications of these methods is provided by the Committee on Research of the National Association of Cost Accountants: [6]

Detailed measurements are made for a test period or on a sampling basis to determine what factors influence costs and what the relationships are. Such methods are more readily applicable to repetitive activities (e.g., packing, loading and shipping, billing) than they are to the more varied activities such as direct selling and administration. However, such methods must be used with discrimination. To illustrate, one of the companies interviewed found that time of sales executives was almost wholly devoted to new products, to sales territories where performance was unsatisfactory, and to similar problems which were non-routine and highly variable in nature. Allocation of executive salary and office costs according to the distribution of the executive's time therefore produced erratic results which were considered unsatisfactory. On the other hand, another company follows the practice of having divisional executives such as the sales manager estimate the ratios in which their time is divided among product lines and in this case the ratios are found to be stable and are viewed as satisfactory bases for allocating the costs in question. Some companies also allocate salesmen's salaries and expenses on bases established by studies to ascertain how salesmen spend their time while other companies consider such studies to be of no value.

The purpose which management has in mind in authorizing expenditures should be thoroughly appreciated by those charged with selection of bases. As a matter of fact, many analysts are convinced that planned distribution of effort provides a better basis for allocation than does either actual distribution or results achieved. Salesmen's salaries and traveling expenses thus might be allocated according to

---

[6] Research Series No. 19, "Assignment of Nonmanufacturing Costs for Managerial Decisions," *N.A.C.A. Bulletin,* May, 1951, p. 1153. Throughout this section of the chapter liberal use is made of the content of this excellent report.

the judgment of the sales executive who is responsible for the planning and direction of the salesmen's efforts. It is doubtful whether actual effort would depart greatly from the planned pattern.

Bases of allocation which do not permit costs of marketing effort to be determined independently of the results obtained from such effort are ordinarily unsatisfactory. As observed in the committee report already cited: [7]

Such commonly used bases of allocation as actual sales dollars violate this principle, for here costs of marketing are made to depend in part on sales realized. Use of such costing methods for pricing amounts to reasoning in a circle since the cost which is supposed to determine the price is also determined by the price. The real cause of a change in cost would seem to be a decision to vary the marketing effort applied to the segment and hence a good basis of allocation should reflect this decision without being affected by extraneous influences.

In so far as possible, a single factor of variability should be employed as a basis for an individual cost item. This not only simplifies the work of analysis but also makes the procedure clearer to executives and salesmen against whom the cost elements may be charged. There are some instances, however, in which several factors must be combined. Thus, in allocating storage expense to products, the number of units handled may be considered the primary variable factor. However, a more accurate basis of cost allocation may result if the number of units handled is factored both by the average rate of stock-turn of the product and by an average measure of product bulk or weight.

Sources of Allocation Data.—Most of the data needed for selecting and utilizing bases of cost allocation are contained in the regular records and reports of a company. The problem facing the analyst is principally that of determining what techniques to employ in economically summarizing the data. Accounting techniques are most commonly used; however, statistical sampling methods have important applications. For example, in the course of a study of costs by lines of merchandise handled in the wholesale mill supply business it was found practicable, for those houses not having adequate sales analysis records, to obtain figures on the number of invoice items, sales volume, and cost of sales by sampling every fifth invoice for the study period. Special cost analyses of various types frequently necessitate use of sampling methods for reasons of economy. A manufacturer of consumer goods limited the territorial coverage of a product analysis to a few areas selected as typical in terms of total sales volume, proportion of rural and urban population, and product mix of goods sold. In view of the seasonal nature of the business, however, the analysis covered

[7] *Ibid.*, p. 1155.

an entire year rather than a sample of weeks or months within a year. As part of this same analysis, sampling studies also were used to lessen the amount of work involved in allocating salesmen's salaries and expense among product groups not uniformly distributed to all dealers.

Not all the data required for allocation purposes are available from regular internal records. As mentioned above, time studies and job analyses are sometimes necessary, as are other studies which utilize either internal or external data developed observationally and/or experimentally. Clearly, the combined efforts of the accountant and the marketing researcher are essential to success in the allocation process.

Two notes of caution should be entered at this point. Because of differences in conditions, an allocation basis found useful in one company is not necessarily a proper basis for the same cost in another company. For this reason, numerous illustrations are given, in the next several chapters, of bases suitable for use with the various types of analyses in differing circumstances. As a second warning, it is wise to document the selection of bases of allocation. A record showing the reasons for choosing a particular basis not only is helpful to management in understanding the decision made but is useful in the evaluation of subsequent proposals to adopt a new basis.

Allocation of Cost Items.—Once the foregoing steps have been taken, the remaining procedure of cost allocation is comparatively simple. Thus, if an analysis is being made by commodities, the direct costs are first assigned to each commodity group. Semidirect and indirect costs are next allocated in accordance with the various bases selected. To illustrate, assume that bad debt losses are to be allocated to commodities on the basis of credit sales. The calculation would then be as follows:

Commodity Group	Credit Sales	Per Cent of Total	Distribution of Bad Debt Losses
A	$ 450,000	30	$2,250
B	300,000	20	1,500
C	750,000	50	3,750
Total	$1,500,000	100	$7,500

A similar procedure must be followed for each semidirect and indirect cost item to be allocated.[8]

[8] From a theoretical standpoint there may be certain objections to making cost allocation a problem of simple proportions. R. Parker Eastwood in *Sales Control by Quantitative Methods* (New York: Columbia University Press, 1940), pp. 272–81, observes that if any part of the cost to be allocated is fixed, the proportional method distributes it in the same fashion as the variable part. Moreover, the method assumes that the interclass variations in each item of cost can be explained in terms of a single variable. Eastwood suggests two alternative methods—simultaneous equations and correlation analysis—that possess theoretical advantages over the proportional method. These statistical methods are quite technical

There is always a question as to the desirability of allocating indirect costs. The results obtained down to the point of these costs may be more useful for managerial purposes than an attempt to make a complete allocation. Such costs may simply be considered as a residual group and management informed accordingly. Such a plan does not permit of final profit and loss determination for individual divisions, but such results, even if secured, are frequently of little value. If a complete analysis of all costs is required, executives must be warned of the extent to which arbitrary allocation has been necessary. There are instances, however, in which the analysis must be complete, as for example, in the preparation of certain defense material for hearings before the Federal Trade Commission. Field study indicates, furthermore, that assignment of all distribution costs in analyses by products or product groups, as well as by territories, is a majority preference among firms active in analysis work.

Net Profit vs. Contribution Margin Approach.—Among those professionally interested in the field of distribution costs, a controversy—at times quite heated—has been in progress for some years. The focal point of the arguments is essentially the topic of the preceding paragraph, namely, the extent to which allocation should be carried. There is, however, a basic divergence in views concerning the purpose of cost analysis which is not clearly revealed above. On one side of the controversy are those who hold that analysis by manner of application should be designed so as to provide for full allocation of costs and, hence, for the determination of a net profit figure. This view is commonly called the "net profit approach" to cost analysis. On the opposing side are those who decry the net profit objective and urge in its stead the objective of a figure that measures merely the contribution made by the particular segment (territory, department, etc.) to unallocated costs and net profit. The only costs considered in arriving at the contribution margin are those which would be saved if a segment were to be eliminated or, conversely, those which would be incurred if a segment were added. This view may be designated the "contribution margin approach." [9]

It is important to emphasize that much of the argument on either side rests upon the misconception that one or the other approach must *always* be used. In reality each approach has its own area of usefulness, in most cases clearly indicated by the nature of the decision management must make on the basis of cost and income data. The net

in character and are not likely to gain widespread usage. The reader will note, however, that the graphic analysis discussed above is an initial phase of the correlation approach to cost allocation.

[9] No consideration need be given here to the extreme position sometimes taken that gross margin is the only useful figure for determining the profitableness of segments.

profit approach is singularly well adapted to the determination of segment costs in four well-defined instances. These are:

1. For regular and systematic reporting of historical costs. From the profit (or loss) information obtained, management can evaluate the relative strength or weakness of each segment by means of one or more comparisons of the following kind: [10]

   a) Other segments of the same class (i.e., one product with another)

   b) Expected or budgeted profit for the same segment

   c) Desired or standard profit for the same segment

   d) Profit on the same segment in previous periods

2. For special, long-range studies of the relative profitableness of individual segments

3. For budgeting costs in the manner in which management wishes them to be borne by each segment

4. For long-range pricing policies and the determination of markup policies

The contribution margin approach is the logical choice in problems involving alternative courses of action of short run duration. Specifically, this approach is useful:

1. For special studies of limited scope designed to aid management in making decisions in current tactical problems, such as pricing special orders and meeting competition in particular areas.

2. For periodic reporting of data which management can utilize for immediate remedial action purposes

More detailed consideration of the marginal approach is reserved for Chapter 12. Comparative references to this approach are made, however, in the section which follows.

Evaluation of Net Profit Approach.—As a thesis, the net profit approach views each sales segment as a separate business that should be required to assume its share of the indirect costs needed for its continued operation. A sales territory, for example, "does not exist alone as a separate business activity but . . . depends for its existence upon other activities of the business, the costs of which are therefore charged to it on the most equitable and reasonable bases which the accountant can select." [11] The net profit approach thus possesses the great advantage of being a guide to management in centering attention upon problem areas calling for long-run remedial action.

---

[10] "Assignment of Nonmanufacturing Costs for Managerial Decisions," *op. cit.*, p. 1158.
[11] John A. Beckett, "The Art and the Science of Distribution Costing," *N.A.C.A. Bulletin*, April, 1951, p. 901.

The fact that this approach cannot show the expected behavior of costs under assumed conditions imposed by various alternative decisions relative to direction of marketing effort does not detract from the advantage. "Those who perform this sort of cost analysis with their eyes open know that this is not a picture of cost behavior and that it would be exceedingly dangerous to take revolutionary action on the basis of its findings." [12] In other words, the fact that a particular product group or territory shows a net loss after allocation of all or most indirect costs does not mean that it should be summarily eliminated. Many of the allocated costs are fixed costs for short periods and hence abandonment of a segment would leave such costs unabsorbed. As the period of time under consideration is extended, however, the fixed costs tend to vary with some measure of volume. Accordingly, as these costs move into the realm of controllable costs, management has a real need for net profit information by segments. Armed with such knowledge, management can take the necessary steps toward making a given segment

yield a more satisfactory margin or toward finding something else to replace it which will both absorb its share of allocated fixed costs and show an adequate net profit. This is apt to be a gradual process in the course of which a number of proposed courses of action are evaluated by special studies to determine the effect they may be expected to have on profit from the segment. These special studies need to take account of the over-all effect which a decision will have on indirect costs and profits of the company as a whole.[13]

The net profit approach is emphasized throughout the analysis chapters of this text. It is felt that, as a general case, this approach has more to recommend it than has the contribution margin approach. The authors admittedly are influenced in this belief by their desire to stress the value of cost analysis as a regular and systematic procedure leading to the control of costs and the direction of marketing effort. It should be noted, nevertheless, that the plan suggested for each type of analysis by manner of application of effort provides for profit determination after each of three cost levels. For example, the method of territorial analysis outlined on pages 44 and 45 provide for (1) profit after direct costs, (2) profit after semidirect costs, and (3) the final territorial net profit (after indirect costs). Having three sets of profit figures at his disposal, the executive is enabled to form judgments with much greater facility than would be the case if only one profit figure were available. Although profit after direct costs is not the same as contributed margin,

---

[12] *Ibid.,* p. 902. This and the preceding quotation from the same source should not be read out of context as indorsements by Mr. Beckett for the net profit approach. His article is a thoroughly objective appraisal of both approaches.
[13] "Assignment of Nonmanufacturing Costs for Managerial Decisions," *op. cit.,* pp. 1158–59. The same precaution voiced in footnote 12, *supra,* is applicable to this source.

there is likely to be a close correspondence in the values of the two items in many instances. The "modified" net profit approach is thus capable of yielding approximate information as to the cost implications of alternative proposals affecting a given segment.

In terms of the mechanics of analysis the two approaches entail the same problems, but with different degrees of complexity. Since allocation is held to a minimum in the contribution margin approach, procedural technique is highly simplified in comparison with the net profit plan.

Preparation and Use of Final Analysis.—With the analysis completed, costs must be summarized according to their direct, semidirect, and indirect elements; related to corresponding sales and gross profit; compared with standards and budgets; interpreted as to causes of and responsibility for variances; and reported to executives as a basis for future planning, direction, and control of distribution effort. Such procedure is considered in subsequent chapters.

Illustrative Classification of Distribution Cost Accounts.—There is given below an illustrative classification of distribution costs accounts for a manufacturing concern with branches. Here the classification is developed on a functional basis with separate account groups, under each function, for home office and branches. Where the accounts become too numerous, control accounts can be substituted with corresponding subsidiary ledgers.

CLASSIFICATION OF ACCOUNTS

DISTRIBUTION COSTS

100–199   DIRECT SELLING EXPENSE
  100–149   Home Office Expense
      101   Salaries—Administration and Supervision
      102   Salaries—Clerical
      103   Salaries—Special Salesmen
      104   Commissions—Special Salesmen
      105   Commissions—Agents and Brokers
      106   Traveling Expense
      107   Entertainment
      108   Education and Training
      109   Insurance—Property, Life, Liability, Etc.
      110   Insurance—Workmen's Compensation
      111   Taxes—Property
      112   Taxes—Social Security
      113   Heat, Light, Power, and Elevator Expense
      114   Repairs and Maintenance
      115   Depreciation—Fixtures

116 Depreciation—Building
117 Telephones
118 Telegraph
119 Postage
120 Office Supplies
121 Miscellaneous Home Office Direct Selling Expense

150–199 Branch Expense
151 Salaries—Administration and Supervision
152 Salaries—Clerical
153 Salaries—Salesmen
154 Salaries—Special Salesmen
155 Commissions—Salesmen
156 Commissions—Special Salesmen
157 Commissions—Agents, Brokers, and Consignees
158 Traveling Expense—Salesmen
159 Traveling Expense—General
160 Operation and Maintenance of Automobiles
161 Depreciation—Automobiles
162 Entertainment
163 Spoiled Work Chargeable to Salesmen
164 Insurance—Property, Life, Liability, Etc.
165 Insurance—Workmen's Compensation
166 Taxes—Property
167 Taxes—Social Security
168 Taxes—Sales and Excise
169 Taxes—License, Privilege, Etc.
170 Heat and Light
171 Rent
172 Repairs and Maintenance
173 Depreciation—Fixtures
174 Telephones
175 Telegraph
176 Postage
177 Office Supplies
178 Miscellaneous Branch Direct Selling Expense

200–299 ADVERTISING AND SALES PROMOTION
200–249 Home Office Expense
201 Salaries—Administration and Supervision
202 Salaries—Clerical
203 Salaries—Advertising Production
204 Space—General Publications
205 Space—Trade Journals
206 Mailing List Expense
207 Radio Time
208 Advertising Copy and Artwork
209 Advertising Production Materials and Supplies

210   Printing
211   Broadcasting Expense
212   Radio and Television Tests
213   Advertising Agency Commission
214   Advertising Agency Expense
215   Contest Expense
216   Conventions and Exhibitions
217   Contributions
218   Traveling Expense
219   Insurance—Property, Life, Liability, Etc.
220   Insurance—Workmen's Compensation
221   Taxes—Property
222   Taxes—Social Security
223   Heat, Light, and Power
224   Repairs and Maintenance
225   Depreciation—Fixtures
226   Telephones
227   Telegraph
228   Postage
229   Office Supplies
230   Miscellaneous Home Office Advertising Expense

250–299   Branch Expense
251   Salaries—Administration and Supervision
252   Salaries—Clerical
253   Salaries—Demonstrators
254   Space—Newspapers
255   Direct Mail
256   Catalogs
257   Dealer Helps and Displays
258   Billboards and Car Cards
259   Advertising Allowances
260   Sample Distribution
261   Demonstrations
262   Contest Expense
263   Contributions
264   Traveling Expense
265   Insurance—Property, Life, Liability, Etc.
266   Insurance—Workmen's Compensation
267   Taxes—Property
268   Taxes—Social Security
269   Communications and Postage
270   Office Supplies
271   Miscellaneous Branch Advertising Expense

300–399   TRANSPORTATION
300–349   Home Office Expense
301   Salaries—Administration and Supervision

302   Salaries—Clerical
303   Salaries—Truck Drivers
304   Salaries—Mechanics
305   Operation and Maintenance—Motor Trucks
306   Depreciation—Motor Trucks
307   Transportation Supplies
308   Tariffs
309   Insurance—Property, Life, Liability, Etc.
310   Insurance—Workmen's Compensation
311   Taxes—Property
312   Taxes—Licenses
313   Taxes—Social Security
314   Heat, Light, and Power
315   Repairs and Maintenance
316   Depreciation—Fixtures
317   Depreciation—Building
318   Office Supplies
319   Miscellaneous Home Office Transportation Expense

350–399   Branch Expense
351   Salaries—Administration and Supervision
352   Salaries—Clerical
353   Out-Freight—Factory to Warehouses and Customers
354   Out-Freight—Warehouses to Customers
355   In-Freight—Returned Goods
356   Purchased Trucking—Outward Deliveries
357   Salaries—Truck Drivers
358   Salaries—Mechanics
359   Operation and Maintenance—Motor Trucks
360   Depreciation—Motor Trucks
361   Transportation Supplies
362   Rent
363   Insurance—Property, Life, Liability, Etc.
364   Insurance—Workmen's Compensation
365   Taxes—Property
366   Taxes—Social Security
367   Heat, Light, and Power
368   Repairs and Maintenance
369   Depreciation—Fixtures
370   Office Supplies
371   Miscellaneous Branch Transportation Expense

400–499   WAREHOUSING AND HANDLING
400–449   Home Office Expense
401   Salaries—Administration and Supervision
402   Salaries—Clerical
403   Salaries—Warehouse
404   Shipping and Warehouse Supplies

405 Storage Charges
406 Insurance—Property, Life, Liability, Etc.
407 Insurance—Workmen's Compensation
408 Taxes—Property
409 Taxes—Social Security
410 Heat, Light, Power, and Elevator Expense
411 Repairs
412 Maintenance
413 Depreciation—Fixtures and Equipment
414 Depreciation—Building
415 Communication
416 Miscellaneous Home Office Warehouse Expense

450–499 Branch Expense
451 Salaries—Administration and Supervision
452 Salaries—Clerical
453 Salaries—Warehouse
454 Shipping and Warehouse Supplies
455 Breakage and Reconditioning
456 Storage Charges
457 Rent
458 Insurance—Property, Life, Liability, Etc.
459 Insurance—Workmen's Compensation
460 Taxes—Property
461 Taxes—Social Security
462 Heat, Light, and Power
463 Repairs
464 Maintenance
465 Depreciation—Fixtures and Equipment
466 Communication
467 Miscellaneous Branch Warehouse Expense

500–599 CREDIT AND COLLECTIONS
500–549 Home Office Expense
501 Salaries—Administration and Supervision
502 Salaries—Clerical
503 Bad Debt Losses
504 Credit Services
505 Legal Expense
506 Traveling Expense
507 Insurance—Life, Liability, Etc.
508 Insurance—Workmen's Compensation
509 Taxes—Intangibles
510 Taxes—Social Security
511 Heat and Light
512 Repairs and Maintenance
513 Depreciation—Fixtures
514 Telephones

515 Telegraph
516 Postage
517 Office Supplies
518 Miscellaneous Credit Expense

600–699 FINANCE
  600–649 Home Office Expense
    601 Salaries—Financial Executives
    602 Salaries—Clerical
    603 Interest
    604 Cash Discount on Sales
    605 Financial Services
    606 Trustee, Registrar, and Transfer Agent's Fees
    607 Legal Fees
    608 Accountants' Fees
    609 SEC Expense
    610 Insurance—Workmen's Compensation
    611 Taxes—Social Security
    612 Depreciation—Fixtures
    613 Communication
    614 Office Supplies
    615 Miscellaneous Financial Expense

700–799 GENERAL DISTRIBUTION EXPENSE
  700–749 Home Office Expense
    701 Distribution Accounting
    702 Market and Sales Research Expense
    703 Personnel Expense
    704 Pensions
    705 Dues and Subscriptions
    706 Taxes—Franchise and General Corporation
    707 Insurance—Use and Occupancy
    708 Public Relations Expense
  (All other expenses applicable to distribution)

In the foregoing classification of accounts only one set of accounts is indicated as "Branch Expense" under each function. It should be understood that a similar set of accounts would be required for each branch or division. The classification as given suggests certain basic functions. These would, of course, vary with individual concerns. In some instances special activities, on which considerable emphasis is placed, should be classified separately. For example, some concerns may require separate accounts for such functions as market research or customer service.

A Further Illustration of Classification of Expense Accounts.— The "tailor-made" nature of account classification may well be appreciated by reference to the plan of organization of expense accounts in a general merchandise wholesale concern. This concern is organized along divisional lines and operates branch establishments in several market centers. The same system of account classification is used in the main house and in the branches. Expenses are divided into seven functional groups as follows:

    6100   Selling, Service, and Advertising
    6200   Operating
    6300   Merchandising
    6400   Administrative
    6500   Occupancy
    6600   Redistributed Headquarters Charges

All these accounts are carried in the general ledger in one control account (#6000). The functional groups are divided into subfunctions according to the following plan:

    6100   Selling, Service, and Advertising
        6110   Direct Selling
        6120   Direct Service
        6130   Field Supervision
        6140   Sales Management
        6150   Employees' Store
        6160   Home Furnishings Specialty Selling
        6170   Advertising

    6200   Operating
        6210   Direct Operating
        6270   Building Operating and Maintenance
        6280   Traffic and Delivery

    6300   Merchandising
        6310   General Merchandising
        6390   Home Furnishings Merchandising

    6400   Administrative
        6410   Accounting
        6420   Credit and Adjustments
        6430   Management
        6440   General
        6450   Other Income or Deductions
        6460   Restaurant
        6480   Provision for House Executive Incentive Compensation

    6500   Occupancy
        6510   Occupancy

    6600   Redistributed Headquarters Charges
        6610   Redistributed Headquarters Charges

Each subfunction is further divided into natural expense categories. The following account titles are used for this purpose:

01	Payroll	40	Traveling
08	Provision for Incentive Compen-	43	Telephone and Telegraph
	sation	44	Postage
09	Payroll Contra	45	Repairs
10	Rent	48	Depreciation
16	Taxes	55	Miscellaneous
17	Social Security Taxes	58	Charges Between Houses and Di-
23	Supplies		visions
28	Light, Heat, Power	60	Charges to Customers
33	Sampling		

Headquarters expenses are separately handled and are divided into seven functional divisions:

7100	Executive Management
7300	Financial Control Division
7400	Merchandise Division
7500	Wholesale Division
7600	Retail Division
7700	General Personnel Division
7800	Advertising

Certain expenses not chargeable to any of the above are included in nondepartmental (#7900). Headquarters divisional expense is treated as an overhead charge to the respective branch counterparts of the headquarters organization. Headquarters nondepartmental expense, and executive management expense, are prorated to branches on the basis of the sum of branch functional expenses.

CHAPTER 4

ANALYSIS BY TERRITORIES

Definition of Territory.—By territory is meant a geographical area such as a state, county, city, trading area, sales district, or other arbitrary area used by a concern as a basis for sales planning and direction. In a particular concern, different territorial arrangements may be employed for different purposes; thus, entirely different territorial divisions may be used for different products.

The territorial analysis, to be complete, must extend to sales, cost of goods sold, and distribution costs. The analysis should follow the physical goods rather than the point of sale. That is, goods sold to a customer, whose home office is in Chicago but who has the goods shipped to some point in Ohio, would be considered as an Ohio sale.

Purpose of Territorial Analysis.—The gross profit of a given product, assuming the same price and a central production point, is not affected by the geographical distribution of the goods. Whether the article is sold in New York or Los Angeles, the gross profit is the same. Yet, the net profit may be influenced greatly by the territorial factor. Geographical sections differ widely in respect to transportation charges; customer density; competitive conditions; and customs, needs, and desires of the population. All of these have their effect upon the cost of distribution. It is because of these dissimilar conditions, with their consequent influence on costs, that sales executives need an analysis of distribution costs by territories.

Broadly speaking, there are two purposes for the analysis of distribution costs by territories: first, to control the distribution expenditures within a territory or on its behalf; and, second, to direct sales effort into the most profitable areas.

The satisfactory control of costs depends largely upon the establishment of cost standards. We must know what the costs should be. But the same standards will not be applicable in different territories. Different standards must be set for different territories. The detailed analysis of costs will assist in the development of the proper standards and in their use as a control device. To illustrate, the cost of a salesman's call in a sparsely populated district may be much higher than in a metropolitan area. To control this item effectively, different standards must be set, actual costs must be determined, and adverse variances corrected.

Moreover, the territorial cost analysis serves as a basis for developing the territorial sales policy. Coupled with market analysis, the cost study enables management to direct the sales effort to those areas which, in the long run, can be made most profitable. No territory should be covered which does not return its *additional* costs unless potential profit clearly justifies the present loss. Even a small profit above the *additional* costs is not sufficient if other territories offer greater possibilities.

The territorial cost analysis serves not only as a basis for long-run policy, but also as a basis for immediate territorial plans. The costs may reveal the fact that it is too expensive to sell, let us say, in Arizona and New Mexico, at least under present methods. The territory may then be dropped or different methods employed. Unless the executive knows what expenditure is made for a territory, and with what results, it is impossible to develop intelligent plans. Again, the territorial investigation will reveal not only the most profitable and logical territories to be covered, but also the manner in which the sales districts should be revised to give the most effective results.

In many instances, the territorial analysis will be only the starting point from which to proceed to still more detailed study of the costs within the territories. Such further analyses are discussed in subsequent chapters.

When Should Territorial Analysis Be Made?—A territorial analysis of distribution costs is unnecessary in certain types of concerns. Most retail concerns with only one establishment, such as department stores, do not require such an analysis. On the other hand, manufacturers, wholesalers, and chains of retail stores, covering any considerable area find such analysis of great value.

The usual concept of a recurrent territorial analysis is one by districts or branches with territorial managers in direct charge of the individual areas. Here again, the value of a territorial analysis for cost control purposes may be somewhat limited if the major part of the costs is controlled by the central executives. In such cases the analysis may be more useful if it takes the direction of trading areas, salesmen's routes, or towns and cities of like population and sales potentialities. On the other hand, if territorial executives are charged with responsibility for sales and cost direction and control, an analysis of the territorial costs and results is essential.

As noted above, different territorial divisions must, in some instances, be made for different products. For example, certain special products may be sold by special salesmen whose district or territorial divisions do not coincide with those of the regular line of products. There may be, in effect, two different sales organizations operating in different territorial divisions and requiring separate analysis.

Selecting the Territorial Unit.—Several considerations enter into the selection of the territorial unit. In the first place, the unit must not be so large that high costs in one section may be offset by low costs in another, thereby failing to reveal to management the true conditions. A state, for example, is ordinarily too large a unit. It usually consists of several types of markets which require individual study and control.

In the next place, territorial units should be selected which lend themselves naturally to sales and cost analysis. The smaller the unit, the larger the proportion of indirect costs; the larger the unit, the larger the proportion of direct costs. If the area is too large, the answer is of little value, because it does not reach the specific points of sales effort and result. If the area is too small, the high proportion of indirect costs which must be allocated renders the results of doubtful value. A satisfactory balance must be achieved.

As a further consideration, the territorial unit selected should be one which is expressive of sales potentialities. Selling effort should be directed to those areas where the sales possibilities are greatest and the territorial analysis of sales and costs should make such direction of effort possible. It is beyond the scope of this book to consider methods of measuring market potentialities.[1] It is sufficient to note here that territorial units must be selected which lend themselves to the analysis of quantitative and qualitative market data expressive of sales possibilities; and that such territorial units must be capable of intelligent cost analysis.

Method of Territorial Analysis.—Having selected satisfactory territorial units, the next consideration is the proper method to follow in making the territorial analysis. This procedure may be outlined as follows:

1. Determine gross profit by territories.
2. Accumulate the direct territorial distribution costs and deduct these from the gross profit to determine territorial *profit after direct costs.*
3. Distribute to the territories their respective shares of the semidirect costs and deduct these to arrive at territorial *profit after semidirect costs.*

---

[1] For information on this subject see, for example, H. H. Maynard and H. C. Nolen, *Sales Management* (rev. ed.; New York: The Ronald Press Co., 1950), Part III; and L. O. Brown, *Marketing and Distribution Research* (New York: The Ronald Press Co., 1949), chap. ix.

4. Allocate to the territories their respective shares of the general or indirect costs and deduct these to arrive at the final territorial *net profit*.
5. Make such subanalyses of the results of individual territories as may be deemed useful (e.g., by products, channels, salesmen, etc.)

The determination of territorial gross profit is secured through the usual accounting procedure of analyzing sales and cost of goods sold. Such information may be provided by the subsidiary accounts or by a direct analysis. The direct territorial costs needed for the second step may also be revealed by the subsidiary ledger accounts. If, for example, the territories are synonymous with branch organizations, such as illustrated in the classification of accounts on pages 34 to 39, the direct costs will be available in the accounts. If the account classification is based upon some other arrangement, as for example, by products, then a special analysis procedure will be required for the territorial costs. It will be necessary in such cases to reclassify the cost items by territories, assigning to each territory its direct charges. Semidirect and indirect territorial costs will be listed on analysis sheets suitable for allocation to territories. Such procedure is illustrated in Figures 9 to 15 (pages 75–81).

Which Expenses Should Be Allocated?—The extent to which the distribution costs should be allocated to territories depends primarily on the use to be made of the results. If the analysis is made chiefly for cost control purposes, then each territory should be charged only with those expense items over which the district executives have direct control. These include such items as salaries and expense of salesmen operating in a territory, local advertising, and district operating expense. Where the analysis is used not only for cost control but also for policy determination and the guidance of sales effort, the indirect expenses must be allocated even though they cannot be charged directly against the territorial executives. These include national advertising, sales supervision, and similar items.

When indirect costs are included in the analysis, the executives should be informed as to the bases of allocation used, particularly for the larger items; as the bases used may have an important bearing upon the interpretation of the results.

Bases of Allocation.—Two different methods may be employed in selecting bases of allocation. The semidirect and indirect cost items may be grouped into major divisions such as direct selling expense, advertising and sales promotional expense, warehousing, etc.; and some one basis of allocation selected for the entire group as a whole. Or each individual expense item may be distributed separately. The methods differ only in the matter of degree. Generally speaking, a separate basis should be selected for each expense item of importance, with minor items grouped and allocated on a single basis.

A modification of these methods is to group the costs of a particular distribution function, establish a standard charge for units of functional service and thereby distribute the cost of the function to territories on the basis of the functional units used. Such a plan is frequently useful for such costs as order filling, transportation, and delivery.

It is impossible to set forth particular bases of allocation of general applicability to all concerns. The selection of proper bases requires an intimate knowledge of local conditions, internal organization, and methods of operation. It is possible here only to suggest various bases which have been found useful in particular instances. Each company presents a problem in itself which must be solved through the ingenuity of its accounting and marketing executives who are intimately familiar with its operations.

On the following pages there is given an illustrative analysis in which the costs are grouped, first, by major functions; and, secondly, into direct, semidirect, and indirect costs as explained on page 25. Whether or not a cost is semidirect or indirect in a particular case depends upon the individual circumstances and the possibility of finding a satisfactory basis of allocation. The same cost item may be considered as semidirect in one concern and indirect in another, where circumstances are different.

Allocation of Direct Selling Expense to Territories.—

DIRECT COSTS. The following items of direct selling expense can usually be charged directly against the individual territories to which they pertain, no bases of allocation being necessary:

1. Salaries and expense of sales administrators and supervisors within the individual territories
2. Clerical salaries and office expense of territorial sales offices
3. Salaries, commissions, and traveling expense of salesmen working in individual territories
4. Commissions to agents, brokers, and consignees
5. All automobile expense on cars used exclusively in individual territories
6. Entertainment expenditures within individual territories or for customers identifiable with individual territories
7. Spoiled work chargeable against territorial salesmen
8. Property insurance and taxes on sales equipment and facilities within individual territories

9. Liability insurance related to territorial operations
10. Workmen's compensation insurance on territorial direct sales payroll
11. Social security taxes on territorial direct sales payroll
12. Sales and excise taxes on territorial sales
13. License and privilege taxes necessary for territorial operations
14. Heat, light, rent, maintenance, depreciation, and general occupancy expense for territorial sales facilities (such as district sales offices)
15. Communication, supplies, and general expense of territorial sales offices

If, as is generally the case, a number of functions in addition to direct selling are performed in territorial sales offices, many of the above expenses will have required prior apportionment among the several functions.

SEMIDIRECT COSTS.

1. *Salaries, commissions, and traveling expense of special salesmen.* The salaries and expense of specialty and missionary salesmen, working from the home office should be allocated on the basis of the working time spent in each territory. Where such salesmen direct their efforts primarily to securing immediate orders on which a commission is paid, a territorial analysis of such sales or commissions will provide the means of allocation.

Where it is impracticable to analyze the time of special salesmen, the allocation may be made on such bases as the number of regular salesmen or number of customers in each territory, or the number of calls made in each territory by special salesmen.

2. *Commissions to agents and brokers.* This item cannot always be charged directly to territories. Commission is sometimes paid to an agent or broker for executing a sale to a large purchaser who will ultimately require the goods to be shipped into various territories. The cost may be distributed on the basis of ultimate shipments, the charge being deferred in the meantime; or on the average territorial distribution of such sales. The former method is, of course, preferable, if it can be conveniently applied.

3. *Sales clerical expense.* This item includes sales clerical salaries, office supplies, and insurance and tax charges related to clerical payroll.

Where the sales clerical expense, such as the cost of order writing, maintenance of price and discount files, filing, billing, adjustments, and communication, constitutes a relatively important cost, special clerical departments will be maintained for these activities. Such departmental costs can then be distributed to territories on the basis of the number of orders, sales transactions, billing lines, customers, or units sold. In some instances, different bases must be applied to different parts of the cost. Where such departmental analysis is not practicable, the cost must be distributed as an indirect item as noted below.

4. *Entertainment expenditures of home office.* Where this item is small it may be considered as an indirect cost, as noted below. Where it constitutes an important item, it should be directly analyzed and ultimately distributed to the territories whose buyers profit (or dis-profit) thereby. Where such direct analysis is not feasible, it must be considered as an indirect cost.

INDIRECT COSTS.

1. *Salaries and expense of general sales executives and supervisors.* The proper basis for the distribution of this item to territories is the time, thought, and effort devoted by executives to the various territories. This can never be known with exactness and often it can only be approximated. Where it is impossible to secure a reasonably accurate analysis of the time and effort spent, resort must be made to such general bases of distribution as number of salesmen, number of customers, number of orders, gross profit, or, finally, if no other basis is suitable, the total of direct and semidirect costs.

2. *Sales clerical expense.* As noted above, this item may be distributed on a semidirect basis; that is, by measurable units of service used. Where the cost is of insufficient importance to justify such analysis, some one general basis may be used for the entire cost as, for example, number of sales transactions, number of orders, number of shipments, number of invoices, or number of billing lines. It is usually possible to select some one basis which reasonably measures the territorial costs.

3. *Entertainment expense of home office.* When this item is of insufficient importance to justify its distribution on a semidirect basis, as noted above, some general basis must be used, such as number of salesmen or total budgeted direct distribution cost for each territory. If such bases are not satisfactory, the sales executives must estimate the amount chargeable to each territory.

4. *Education and training of sales force.* This item consists of the preparation of training manuals, maintenance of schools, preparation and distribution of "salesmen's helps," convention expense, etc. If the program is a continuous one for all salesmen, the proper basis of distribution is salesmen's earnings in each territory. If the training effort is restricted chiefly to new men, the territorial charge may be made on the basis of new men employed or number of salesmen in each territory. Where the training is done chiefly by men who go out into the territories, time spent in each territory may be used as a basis.

5. *Home office communication.* This includes the cost of telephones, telegraph, postage, special stenographic departments, dictating equipment, etc., in so far as these relate to distribution. Where the cost of communication is large, the more important items, such as long-distance calls and telegrams, may be tabulated by territories and distributed as direct charges. Usually, however, some general basis can be used, such as number of accounts, number of orders, number of sales transactions, or number of salesmen.

6. *General home office direct selling expense.* This includes a number of home office items which are not of sufficient importance to distribute individually as, for example, insurance and taxes on home office sales facilities, occupancy expense, payroll taxes and insurance on general sales office, not otherwise distributed, miscellaneous supplies, etc. The largest items here usually relate to the sales clerical expense, mentioned in Item 2 above, and can be equitably distributed on the same basis as used for that item. Another basis which may be used is total direct and semidirect costs.

Allocation of Advertising and Sales Promotional Expense to Territories.—

DIRECT COSTS. The following items of advertising and sales promotional expense can usually be charged directly against the individual territories to which they pertain, no bases of allocation being necessary:

1. Salaries and expense of advertising executives and supervisors within the individual territories
2. Clerical salaries and office expense of territorial advertising offices
3. Salaries and expense of demonstrators
4. Local newspaper space
5. Outdoor advertising space (billboards, signs, etc.)
6. Advertising allowances to customers
7. Local contest expenses
8. Local contributions
9. Property insurance and taxes on advertising equipment and facilities within individual territories
10. Insurance and taxes on territorial direct advertising payroll
11. Communication, supplies, and general expense of territorial advertising offices

SEMIDIRECT COSTS. The advertising and sales promotional expense which usually cannot be charged directly to territories may be classified into four divisions:

1. Advertising administration and overhead, such as advertising executives' salaries

2. Cost of copy preparation, such as copywriting and artwork
3. Cost of physical production, such as printing of catalogs and circulars
4. Direct cost of advertising media of general coverage, such as radio and television time and magazine space

The first step in the territorial analysis is to resolve these costs into individual medium costs. The second step is to allocate the costs of individual media to territories benefiting thereby. Such procedure may be illustrated as follows:

1. *Advertising administration and overhead.* This includes such expense items as:

1. Administration and supervision salaries
2. Clerical salaries of general advertising office
3. Traveling expense
4. Insurance and taxes relating to general advertising office, particularly those on payroll
5. Occupancy expense of general advertising office, such as heat, light, maintenance, and depreciation
6. Communication expense of general advertising office, such as telephones, telegraph, postage, and dictation
7. General expense of central advertising office

This overhead expense must be distributed in four directions as follows:

1. To the preparation of advertising copy
2. To the physical production of advertising material
3. To supervision of individual media
4. To territorial supervision

There is no one basis by which such allocation can be made. Conditions vary so widely in individual concerns as to make any intelligent generalization difficult. In some concerns the preparation of advertising copy is done almost entirely by outside agencies; in others, the work is largely done within the organization. Some concerns have their own production facilities for printing, etc.; others depend upon outside purchases. Some concerns closely supervise the selection of media; others depend upon advertising agencies. Some concerns localize much of their advertising effort in territories and direct their general supervision to these territorial activities; others center practically all activity at the home office. In a particular concern, however, it is possible to make a reasonable estimate of the direction which the overhead takes and to arbitrarily apportion it to the four divisions accordingly. The total amount of the overhead apportioned to territorial supervision can, in turn, be allocated to individual territories on the basis of direct territorial advertising cost.

2. *Preparation of advertising copy.* This includes the cost of copywriting, artwork, preparation of catalog copy, radio and television script and entertainment (when provided by advertiser), and a share of the general advertising overhead as noted above. With the exception of the overhead, these costs relate directly to individual media. The overhead can be distributed to media on the basis of direct media costs.

3. *Cost of physical production of advertising material.* This includes the entire cost of all purchases and physical production of advertising material, such as printing of direct mail pieces and catalogs; also a share of the general advertising overhead. This is usually costed on a production job order basis and charged to asset accounts. The material is then expensed as used. Distribution of this cost can always be made directly to individual media, such as direct mail, outdoor signs, dealer helps, and displays.

4. *Total advertising media costs and their allocation.* The direct costs of individual advertising media consist of:

1. Space in general publications
2. Space in trade journals
3. Radio and television time
4. Broadcasting expense
5. Radio and television tests
6. Advertising agency commissions
7. Direct contest expense

To the direct cost of each individual advertising medium must be added its charges for overhead, copy preparation, and physical production, in so far as these apply, to ascertain the total advertising medium cost. In this manner the total cost is secured for such media as:

1. General publications	6. Demonstrations
2. Trade journals	7. Dealer helps and displays
3. Radio and television	8. Catalogs and circulars
4. Contests	9. Outdoor advertising
5. Direct mail	10. Sample distribution

Once the total media costs are secured they can be distributed to the territories on such bases as the following:

General and trade publications
    Circulation
    Circulation weighted by purchasing power
    Marked inquiries

Radio and television
Territorial coverage as determined by commercial agencies and company tests
Territorial coverage weighted by purchasing power
Contest and sales feature returns
Inquiries received

Contests
Returns received

Direct mail
Direct charge for pieces sent into territories

Demonstrations
Direct charge per demonstration
Time spent by demonstration crews or staffs

Dealer helps and displays
Direct charge for pieces used

Catalogs and circulars
Direct charge for pieces sent into territories

Outdoor advertising
Direct charge for displays within territories

Sample distribution
Direct charge for samples distributed

INDIRECT COSTS. There are some types of advertising and sales promotional effort which probably bear little relationship to any territorial division. They are primarily of an institutional and goodwill nature. The sponsoring of great musical broadcasts, impressive displays and exhibits at fairs, and pure scientific research are illustrative. Such expenditures may be kept separate from the regular advertising program and classified as indirect costs. If such items are distributed at all to territories, the basis must be quite arbitrary. Such expenditures are usually made only by very large concerns with national coverage. Territorial buying power has been suggested as a suitable basis for distributing such costs.

Allocation of Transportation Expense to Territories.—

DIRECT COSTS. The following items of transportation expense can usually be charged directly against the individual territories to which they pertain, no bases of allocation being necessary:

1. Salaries of transportation supervisors within the individual territories
2. Clerical salaries and office expense of territorial transportation offices
3. Out-freight, express, and purchased trucking—factory to warehouse (if not included in cost of goods), factory to customers, and warehouse to customers
4. In-freight on returned goods
5. All cost of operation and maintenance of trucking facilities used exclusively within individual territories, including wages of drivers and mechanics, depreciation, supplies, garage rent, taxes, licenses, insurance, heat, light, power, repairs, and maintenance

SEMIDIRECT COSTS. Transportation costs of the home office consist of: (1) general transportation administration and (2) the cost of maintenance and operation of the company's own trucking facilities used in transporting goods to the territorial warehouses and direct to the customers within the territories.

The former item is in the nature of general overhead. Where transportation offices and facilities are maintained both in the territories and at the home office, this overhead can be divided as between the home office on the one hand and the territorial offices on the other, on some one of the following bases:

1. Total direct costs
2. Direct costs exclusive of purchased transportation
3. Number of transportation units used, such as number of delivery trucks
4. Number of men employed

If no one of these bases gives an equitable distribution, transportation executives must arbitrarily divide the overhead as between the part which pertains to the home office operations and the part which should be charged to territorial supervision. The latter part should then be distributed to individual territories on some one of the above bases.

Where trucking facilities are maintained at the home office and used for distributing goods to the territories, standard unit transportation costs should be established. As goods are transported to the territories, they (the territories) should be charged the regular standard transportation rates in the same manner as though the transportation services were purchased.[2] Such charges should be accumulated through the

---

[2] Although transportation to territories is considered here as an element of distribution cost, it should be observed that under certain conditions transportation cost might better

month and, at the close of the month, debited to individual territories and credited to a "Transportation Absorbed" account. In the long run this account should offset the home office transportation costs. Such standard costs should also include the home office share of transportation overhead.

Standard transportation costs should be expressed in some such unit as:

1. Ton-mile.
2. 100 lbs.-mile.
3. Product unit-mile. Where the product is of such a nature that it can be resolved into comparable units, this measure can be used. For example, it may be possible to resolve barrels, half-barrels, kegs, and cases into some standard unit measure.
4. Individual delivery. Where distances to the various territories are not great and where deliveries to customers are fairly uniform in size, this unit of measure will sometimes serve.
5. Product unit. This unit of measure may be used where distance is not an important factor but where the size of deliveries varies.

Standard Transportation Costs Applied on Sales.—The desirability of establishing standard unit transportation costs which permit apportionment of the two elements of home office transportation costs —i.e., general overhead and cost of home office trucking facilities—to territories on the basis of shipments into the various territories has been recognized by many companies. A number of concerns have found it even more desirable to establish *over-all* standard transportation costs for each unit of product to each territory. Such territorial standards include not only the transportation costs of the home office but also the direct transportation costs of the individual territories. Consequently, the standards must be applied on territorial sales rather than on deliveries from factory to warehouses or from factory to individual customers.

This plan has many advantages and is capable of wide application. Even where a concern has hundreds of products, they can usually be grouped in such a way as to present a comparatively few product classes for transportation purposes. A standard unit must then be established for each product class. This can be done by a proper weighting of bulk and weight factors. Since most concerns find it desirable to make a product analysis by territories, the number of standard product

---

be treated as an addition to the production cost of the goods. Thus, if transportation is an important cost factor and if the flow of goods in and out of territories is not rapid, the cost of transportation to warehouses or other break bulk points can be included in inventory values and, hence, in cost of sales.

transportation units going into each territory can be determined with very little clerical effort. These units can then be factored by the standard territorial costs of the various product groups and the total standard transportation charge determined. This plan has the very great advantage of making the cost uniform for each product in each territory and removes the frequent objection of territorial executives that they are being overcharged for transportation. Moreover, it brings the transportation charge into the same period with the corresponding sales.

To reduce this plan to a very simple illustration, assume that a certain concern has six products which can be grouped conveniently for transportation purposes into three groups—A, B, and C. The individual products are weighted as follows:

	Product Equivalent in Transportation Units	
Group A		That is, one unit of Product
Product 1	5	1 is equivalent to five trans-
Product 2	2	portation units; one unit of
Product 3	1	Product 2 is equivalent to
Group B		two transportation units; etc.
Product 4	3	It is assumed that the trans-
Product 5	2	portation unit would be dif-
Group C		ferent for each group of
Product 6	1	products.

Assume next that the products are sold in three territories—X, Y, and Z, and that standard transportation costs have been established as follows:

Products	Cost of One Transportation Unit to Territories		
	X	Y	Z
Group A	$0.10	$0.15	$0.20
Group B	.20	.30	.40
Group C	.03	.04	.05

Assume next that the analysis of sales (not shipments) by products for a particular month reveals the following:

Product	Units Sold in Territories		
	X	Y	Z
1	1,000	2,000	6,000
2	5,000	8,000	20,000
3	2,000	5,000	10,000
4	7,000	12,000	20,000
5	4,000	8,000	5,000
6	100,000	150,000	300,000

The determination of the standard transportation cost for Territory X would then be as follows:

Products	Units Sold	Transportation Unit Equivalent	Standard Transportation Units	
Group A				
1	1,000	5	5,000	
2	5,000	2	10,000	
3	2,000	1	2,000	
			17,000 at 0.10 per unit =	$ 1,700
Group B				
4	7,000	3	21,000	
5	4,000	2	8,000	
			29,000 at .20 per unit =	5,800
Group C				
6	100,000	1	100,000 at .03 per unit =	3,000
Total Standard Transportation Cost for Territory X				$10,500

The same procedure would be followed for each territory.

The standards should be applied in every case, regardless of the actual route of the goods. A customer may be supplied from the factory; a branch warehouse; or, in an emergency, from some other branch warehouse outside his own territory. Figure 2 illustrates such a situation. Here Customer M would normally be supplied from Ware-

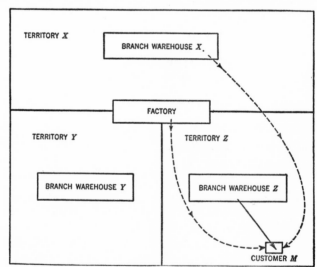

FIGURE 2. Possible Transportation Routes to Customers

house Z, but large shipments might be made direct from the factory. In an emergency he may be supplied from Warehouse X. In every instance the same standard cost would be applied.

By this method charges are made to the territories monthly with corresponding credit to the Transportation Absorbed account, as noted above. The excess of actual transportation costs over the amount absorbed should represent the transportation value of products en route and in branch warehouses and should be included in inventory values. One large concern using this plan finds it necessary to revise the standards only once a year.

Once the proper standards are established for this method, comparatively little clerical work is required for its execution.

It should be noted that in territorial analysis of transportation costs, the concept of additional or marginal costs should not enter. Particularly is this true where there are no branch warehouses. If a load of goods is delivered partly in Territory X and the balance of the load, carried only a few miles farther, into Territory Y, then Territory Y should bear not merely the cost of the additional few miles but its regular standard cost.

Allocation of Warehousing and Handling Expense to Territories. —The warehousing plan varies so greatly in different concerns as to make it difficult to generalize on cost analysis procedure. For example, the following plans may be followed:

1. Goods may go, upon completion, to:
   Central warehouse
   Branch warehouses
   Direct to customers

2. Goods may go from the central warehouse to:
   Branch warehouses
   Direct to customers

3. Goods may go from branch warehouses to:
   Other branch warehouses (in emergency)
   Direct to customers

Moreover, a particular product may sometimes take different routes. Thus, Product A, if sold in large orders, may go direct from factory to customer; but, when sold in small orders, it may go through central and branch warehouses. A particular concern may be employing a number of different routes at the same time.

In complex situations of this kind the best procedure is to establish standard warehousing and handling costs for each product or product group. Such standard costs should include all central and branch warehouse and handling expense and should be applied as the goods are sold, regardless of the route taken from factory to customer.

The items which should be included in the standard cost are:

1. Salaries of warehouse and shipping department executives and supervisors
2. Clerical salaries and office expense of warehouse and shipping offices
3. Warehouse and shipping labor
4. Supplies
5. Outside storage charges
6. Insurance and taxes on finished inventories
7. Insurance and taxes relating to warehouse and handling operations, such as liability insurance and payroll taxes
8. Occupancy expense including rent, insurance, taxes, heat, light, power, elevator, and depreciation
9. Communication
10. Miscellaneous warehouse, handling, and shipping expense

All costs should be included whether incurred at the central or at the branch warehouses.

Standards must be expressed in units of product or product groups. Where products are grouped it is usually necessary to weight the individual items within the group to arrive at their equivalent in warehouse units. A similar plan is explained on page 55 for standard transportation units. Once the products are classified into proper groups, and suitable units established, the standard unit costs for each group must be determined by a study of such factors as:

1. Average time such goods are in storage
2. Space required
3. Labor and machine hours required in handling
4. Supplies required
5. Clerical work required
6. Value of product

All of the costs noted above, except general administration, relate to some one of these factors and can be classified accordingly. The general administration will usually follow the labor hours and can be allocated to the other costs accordingly. With the costs so classified and with the relationship of the various products to these factors known, standard unit costs can be established with a high degree of accuracy.

Under this plan, there is no distinction of direct, semidirect, and indirect costs. All costs may be considered as direct. To secure the territorial warehouse and handling expense it is necessary only to make a territorial analysis of products and apply the standard costs to the units sold.

In some concerns where there is considerable regularity in the flow of goods from factory to central warehouse to branch warehouses, it is desirable to establish separate standard costs for each warehouse. If, then, a unit of Product A is sold in Territory X, that territory must be charged with two standard unit costs—the central warehouse cost and its own branch warehouse cost. This localizes the standards and increases their value for control purposes.

Where warehousing and handling costs are of comparatively little importance, the distribution to territories may be made on some very general basis such as:

1. Product weight shipped
2. Units of product shipped
3. Number of orders
4. Cost of goods sold

Such blanket bases, however, are seldom equitable and should be used with caution. Storage and handling costs are usually a considerable item and the standard cost method is much to be preferred.

Allocation of Credit and Collection Expense to Territories.— The credit and collection expenses usually group themselves into five natural divisions as follows:

1. Credit approval and administration
2. Clerical cost of handling receivables
3. Collection costs
4. Bad debt losses
5. Taxes on receivables

Were all customers alike in regard to credit risk and were the purchases of all customers alike in quantity and frequency, the entire credit and collection expense could be equitably distributed to territories on the basis of credit sales. Obviously, such similarity does not often exist; and, unless it is closely approximated, this basis is not satisfactory. Suppose, for example, that in Territory X, a sale of $200,000 is made to a strongly financed mail order house; and, at the same time in Territory Y, a sale of $2,000 is made to a weakly financed jobber. If the credit and collection expense were distributed on the basis of sales, Territory X would receive 100 times the amount charged to Territory Y when in reality the actual costs (with the exception of taxes on receivables) would probably be much less for the mail order concern than for the jobber. Less time would be required for credit investigation and approval and the risk of loss would be less. Consequently, more equitable bases must be found. Suggestions as to suitable bases for the individual cost groups are as follows:

1. *Credit approval and administration.* This includes the expense of maintaining the central credit office, administrative salaries, clerical salaries, credit services, credit files, general traveling expense, communication, office supplies, incident insurance and taxes, and occupancy expense. Where credit offices are maintained within the territories, the expense of such offices is, of course, a direct cost. Where credit approval and administration is centered at the home or in district offices (assuming a district to cover several territories), the most equitable bases are usually the average number of accounts, the number of sales transactions, or the number of credit approvals.

2. *Clerical cost of handling receivables.* In a broad sense, credit and collection expense includes the cost of keeping accounts receivable records, the posting of all charges and credits, and the sending of monthly statements. While this work is usually done by the accounting department, for purposes of accurate analysis, it should be distributed as a part of the credit and collection activity. It consists chiefly of clerical salaries, supplies, and such part of the accounting department administrative and occupancy overhead as may be applicable. Such accounting overhead usually follows closely the clerical labor cost.

The cost of posting charges follows closely the number of invoices; the issuing of monthly statements and the posting of credits follow more closely the number of accounts; and miscellaneous adjustments and references may follow either the number of invoices or the number of accounts. Where these costs are considerable in amount and the work highly departmentalized with different clerical divisions for different parts of the work, each of these bases may be used. Usually, however, a standard clerical cost per invoice or per account can be established; or the entire clerical cost can be equitably distributed on one of these bases. Where the clerical work is done within the territory, the costs are, of course, direct and require no allocation.

3. *Collection costs.* This includes the cost of continuous review of the receivable records, adjustment of credit limits, collection letters, salary and expense of collectors, and legal expense. Such costs usually follow most closely the number of accounts and should be allocated to territories accordingly. Where the work centers in territorial offices, the charges are direct.

4. *Bad debt losses.* Where bad debt losses are taken as realized, they should be analyzed by territories and charged directly. Where reserves are provided, the charges should be allocated on the same basis as that used in determining the amount to be credited to the reserve. Thus, if a reserve is provided amounting to 0.1% of credit sales, the territorial charges should be on the basis of 0.1% of their credit sales. It is frequently desirable to apply a different percentage for different

classes of business. Thus, one percentage may be used for sales to jobbers and another for large industrial consumers. Such percentages must be determined from past experience.

Bad debts recovered, if taken as income, should be credited directly to territories. While such recoveries may be small in the aggregate, territorial executives usually expect credit for them.

5. *Taxes on receivables.* Most governmental jurisdictions impose an intangible tax on receivables of sufficient importance to justify its consideration as a separate item in the territorial analysis. Frequently the tax is imposed on the excess of receivables over payables. As a rule this tax as finally computed can be equitably distributed, within each jurisdiction, on the basis of average amount of receivables outstanding.

Allocation of Financial Expense to Territories.—The usual financial expenses of industrial and commercial concerns consist of the following items:

1. Salaries and expense of financial executives
2. Clerical salaries and expense of central finance office including communication, supplies, occupancy, and incident insurance and taxes
3. Trustee, registrar, and transfer agent's fees
4. Legal fees
5. Accountants' fees
6. SEC expense
7. Cash discounts allowed
8. Interest paid
9. Interest on investment

Financial executive activity has to do with the determination of financial policies and the administration of the financial program pertaining to capital issues, bonds, short-term loans, banking relations, dividends, interest payments, etc. Clerical activity includes the detailed procedure incident to such a program. Professional and fiscal fees are those incident to mortgage indebtedness and security issues and their listing. Cash discounts are those allowed for prompt payment of receivables, presumably for the purpose of reducing investment and credit losses. Interest paid includes all interest actually paid or accrued on borrowed funds.

Interest on investment contemplates an arbitrary interest charge on invested capital aside from any borrowed funds. Businessmen generally, and accountants in particular, are familiar with the fact that interest on investment is ordinarily not included as a cost of production and to so include it violates generally accepted accounting practice. The chief reason for this rule is the danger of inflating inventory values and thereby reflecting unrealized profit in the accounts. Since distribution costs are not ordinarily included in the inventory values, the force of the rule does not apply against the inclusion, in such costs, of interest on that part of the investment which is required for distribution activities.

The financial requirements of distribution activities arise from the following:

1. Physical facilities used
2. Finished goods and merchandise inventories carried
3. Receivables carried
4. Working funds needed for distribution payroll and current distribution expenses

If such requirements were uniform in all territories or if they bore a uniform and constant relationship to territorial net profit, it would be unnecessary to allocate the financial costs. Obviously, such cases are rare indeed. In one territory, the warehouse may be rented, with no investment requirements; in another, it may be owned, subject to bonded indebtedness; in still another, it may be owned subject to no direct indebtedness. Inventories may vary considerably in territories, depending upon distance from the factory. Receivables may likewise vary, depending upon the classes of customers in the various territories. Working capital requirements will also vary depending upon sizes of orders, amount of handling required, etc.

No intelligent determination of territorial profit can be made without an analysis of financial costs, including interest on invested capital.

The first step in the analysis of financial costs by territories is to determine the total financial cost of the entire business. To illustrate this step, assume that a particular concern has the following *average* financial position for the period under consideration.

Assets

Cash	$ 200,000
Investments of current funds (temporarily idle but required for operating purposes)	100,000
Receivables	700,000
Inventories:	
Production—Materials, work in process, and supplies	400,000
Distribution—Finished goods and supplies	600,000
Plants and equipment:	
Production	2,000,000
Distribution	800,000
Investments of surplus funds (not required for operating purposes)	150,000
Miscellaneous (operating assets)	50,000
Total Assets	$5,000,000

Borrowed and Invested Capital

Non-interest-bearing indebtedness	$ 400,000
Interest-bearing indebtedness	600,000
Capital and surplus	4,000,000
Total Capital	$5,000,000

Assume next that the financial expenses for the period are as follows:

Salaries and expense of executives	$ 20,000
Clerical salaries and expense	5,000
Trustee, registrar, and transfer agent and professional fees	2,000
Cash discounts allowed	60,000
Interest paid on indebtedness	30,000
Interest on investment of $4,000,000 at a rate of 5% (as decided by management)	200,000
Total financial expense	$317,000

The second step is to divide the financial expense as between production, distribution, and nonoperating activities. To do this it is necessary first to determine the manner in which the funds are used. Physical facilities, inventories, receivables, and nonoperating items can be separated directly by reference to the accounting records. A special calculation and apportionment is usually necessary for working funds. In the case at hand, this calculation might be made as follows:

Cash used for operating purposes	$200,000
Investments of current funds considered necessary for operating purposes	100,000
Miscellaneous operating assets such as accrued and deferred items not directly identifiable with production or distribution	50,000
Total	$350,000
Deduct current indebtedness on which no interest is paid	400,000
Net working funds	($ 50,000)

In this instance the net working funds result in a minus quantity. Regardless of whether the net amount is a plus or minus quantity, it must be divided between production and distribution. This apportionment can usually be made equitably on the basis of annual direct expenditures for the two functions. For the purpose of this illustration it may be assumed that the company spends $3,000,000 annually for production labor, materials, and services; and $2,000,000 for distribution payroll, advertising, and other direct services. The apportionment of the working funds would then be 60% to production and 40% to distribution.

The final division of the funds would then be as follows:

	Total	Production	Distribution
Physical facilities	$2,800,000	$2,000,000	$ 800,000
Inventories	1,000,000	400,000	600,000
Receivables	700,000		700,000
Working funds	(50,000)	(30,000)	(20,000)
	$4,450,000	$2,370,000	$2,080,000
Nonoperating assets	150,000		
	$4,600,000		

It is apparent from the above that $4,600,000 of capital has been more or less permanently provided (non-interest-bearing indebtedness is excluded) and that its cost may be divided as follows:

	Amount	Per Cent of Total
For production	$2,370,000	51.5
For distribution	2,080,000	45.2
For nonoperating purposes	150,000	3.3
Total	$4,600,000	100.0

If then the total financial expense is $317,000, the share properly chargeable to distribution activity is 45.2% of $317,000 or $143,284.

The third step is the allocation of the distribution share of the financial expense to territories. To continue the illustration, assume the following data relative to territorial financial requirements:

			Territories	
	Total	X	Y	Z
Percentage of territorial direct distribution expenditures to total as a basis for allocating working funds	100%	50%	30%	20%
Financial requirements:				
Working funds (as per above percentages)	($ 20,000)	($ 10,000)	($ 6,000)	($ 4,000)
Receivables (direct allocation)	700,000	200,000	300,000	200,000
Inventories (direct allocation)	600,000	280,000	200,000	120,000
Physical facilities (direct allocation)	800,000	450,000	200,000	150,000
Totals	$2,080,000	$920,000	$694,000	$466,000
Percentage of total	100.0%	44.3%	33.3%	22.4%
Allocation of distribution financial expense	$ 143,284	$ 63,475	$ 47,713	$ 32,096

In this illustration it is assumed that data are available for a direct territorial analysis of receivables, inventories, and physical facilities.

This may or may not be the case. Where each territory has its own warehouse and keeps its own inventories and receivables locally, the data are of course available. Where inventories are centered at the home office, the inventory requirements of territories can be determined by analyzing the territorial cost of goods sold by products and dividing by average rate of turnover for each product. There is usually little difficulty in securing the average receivables by territories regardless of where the records are kept.

While it is usually desirable to include interest on investment as a financial cost, it should be noted that the foregoing method can be used whether or not such interest is included.

Allocation of General Distribution Expense to Territories.—In addition to the functional costs mentioned in the preceding topics, there are various other distribution costs of a general nature which are likely to arise in particular concerns. In some instances these items, or certain of them, are of sufficient importance to require individual bases of territorial allocation. Usually, however, they are of such a general nature that it is impossible to relate them to individual territories, or they may be of insufficient importance to merit such analysis. In such cases they must be assigned to a general group and allocated as a whole on some general basis; or merely added to total costs as a residual item. Illustrative are:

1. *Distribution accounting.* The most important elements of distribution accounting, such as order handling and accounts receivable, are included in the above functional expense groups. Other distribution accounting, such as a part of the payroll expense, accounts payable, analysis, tabulating, reporting, etc., may be allocated as a whole. Some fair basis of allocation to territories can usually be found, such as number of sales transactions, number of orders, number of shipments, or number of employees. Where this is not practicable the cost should be assigned to the general group.

2. *Market and sales research.* When this activity is directed toward the examination of particular territorial markets the charge may be made directly to territories. Where the study is directed primarily to particular products or methods, or is of a very general nature, the allocation must follow the sales of individual territories by products or channels. If the cost is insufficient to justify such analysis, it must be grouped with other general items.

3. *Personnel expense.* The distribution share of this expense, except for education and training, which are considered above as a direct selling expense, may be distributed to territories on the basis of number of employees, or assigned to the general group.

4. *Pensions.* This item may be allocated on the basis of territorial payroll, or, if unimportant, assigned to the general group.

5. *Dues and subscriptions.* This item includes membership in various trade associations, chambers of commerce, professional and semi-professional organizations; and subscriptions to various journals and services relating to distribution or commercial activities. It is usually a general expense item.

6. *General taxes.* The distribution share of such general taxes as domestic and foreign franchise fees and general corporation taxes are usually assessed on a basis of net worth, gross income, or both, within the taxing jurisdiction. If sufficiently important they may be allocated to territories on similar bases. If not, they must be assigned to the general group.

7. *General insurance.* Such general insurance items as use and occupancy, fidelity, etc. are usually of minor consequence and may be assigned to the general group.

8. *Public relations.* In some concerns, a considerable expenditure is made to promote satisfactory public relations. Where these concern particular territories they should be charged directly; otherwise, assigned to the general group.

9. *General executive salaries and expense.* The salaries and expense of general executives must be divided between production and distribution and the latter share assigned to the general group of distribution expenses. The proper division between production and distribution should be determined by the general executives themselves.

It will be noted that all such items as the above, which directly relate to individual territories, should be so charged. Only those items which cannot be directly related or equitably and conveniently allocated should be left for general apportionment.

There is no one basis suitable for allocating the general distribution expenses to territories which would apply to all concerns. One method which has been found useful is that of weighting several factors to form a composite basis. To illustrate, assume the following data:

Factors Selected	Total	Territories		
		X	Y	Z
Number of sales transactions	20,000	10,000	4,000	6,000
Number of customers	1,000	600	100	300
Number of distribution employees ..	400	240	60	100
Budgeted gross profit	$2,000,000	$600,000	$1,000,000	$400,000

Assume next that the four factors are estimated to have a weight of 3, 2, 1, and 4 respectively in determining the relationship of general expense to territories. These ratios would then be applied as follows:

	X			Y			Z		
	Per Cent of Total	Weight	Product	Per Cent of Total	Weight	Product	Per Cent of Total	Weight	Product
Transactions ..	50	3	150	20	3	60	30	3	90
Customers	60	2	120	10	2	20	30	2	60
Employees	60	1	60	15	1	15	25	1	25
Gross profit ...	30	4	120	50	4	200	20	4	80
		10	450		10	295		10	255

$$450 \div 10 = 45.0 \qquad 295 \div 10 = 29.5 \qquad 255 \div 10 = 25.5$$

The territorial division of the general expense would be:

X 45.0%
Y 29.5%
Z 25.5%

Total 100.0%

Where a method such as the above is not feasible, the general distribution expenses may be distributed on the basis of all other distribution costs.

Territorial Costs by Synthesis.—In the preceding discussion it has been assumed that the territorial analysis of distribution costs will proceed largely by taking individual expense items and distributing them to the various territories benefiting thereby. The share of all such expense items distributed or allocated to a particular territory would then constitute the territory's cost. Another method of arriving at territorial distribution cost is sometimes used where there are a considerable number of distribution units, such as stores and branches, in each territorial division; and where the major part of the costs are direct. Here the territorial costs may be secured by accumulating the cost of individual stores or branches. Home office costs may be allocated to stores or branches or to territories as a whole, but these are usually of minor consequence. In some instances such home office costs are added to the cost of goods sold.

This procedure may be illustrated through the method used by several large rubber manufacturing concerns in handling commercial sales at stores and branches. The general plan is illustrated in Figures 3 to 8.

Figure 3 illustrates an operating report for an individual store. Here there is given a complete analysis of sales and gross profit by individual items with the total gross profit. From this is then deducted the total store controllable expense to arrive at the controllable profit

STORE OPERATING REPORT

Store _____ City _____ State _____ District _____ Month _____

Line No.	CLASSIFICATION	Dept. No.	CURRENT MONTH					FISCAL YEAR TO DATE				
			Estimated		Actual			Estimated		Actual		
			Quota and Budget 2	% 3	Sales 4	Gross Profit 5	% 6	Quota and Budget 7	% 8	Sales 9	Gross Profit 10	% 11
1	Auto Tires—Dealer	164										
2	Auto Tires—Retail	164										
3	Truck Tires—Dealer	165										
4	Truck Tires—Retail	165										
5	Retread Tires	166										
6	Batteries—Dealer	169										
7	Batteries—Retail	169										
8	Gasoline	167										
9	Oil	06										
10	Radio—Dealer	01										
11	Radio—Retail	01										
12	M. & A. Spec.—Dealer	02										
13	M. & A. Spec.—Retail	02										
14	Heaters—Dealer	03										
15	Heaters—Retail	03										
16	Bicycles—Dealer	04										
17	Bicycles—Retail	04										
18	Summer Spec.—Dlr.	05										
19	Summer Spec.—Ret.	05										
20	Wheels	08										
21	Winter Spec.—Dlr.	09										
22	Winter Spec.—Ret.	09										
23	Access.—Dlr.	41										
24	Access.—Ret.	41										

25	Total Spec.—Dlr.	
26	Total Spec.—Ret.	
27	Gross Sales & Margins	100
28	Sales Tax	172
29	Volume Rebate	174
30	Cash Discount	173
31	Transportation	175
32	Total Deductions	
33	N. M. Sales & Margins	100
34	Lubrication	180
35	Brake	181
36	Vulcanizing	182
37	Battery	183
38	Washing	184
39	Storage	185
40	Misc. Service	186
41	Total Service Income	101
42	Total Sales & Ser. Income	
43	Cost of Sales	200
44	Gross Profit	
45	Grand Total Exp.	
46	Misc. Income	600
47	Net Total Exp.	
48	Controllable P. or L.	
49	Uncontrollable Exp.	414
50	Net Opr. P. or L.	

FIGURE 3. Store Operating Report for Rubber Manufacturing Concern

DETAIL OF STORE EXPENSE

Line No.	ACCOUNT	A/C No.	CURRENT MONTH — Estimated Emp. 2	Budget 3	% 4	CURRENT MONTH — Actual Expense 5	% 6	Emp. 7	FISCAL YEAR TO DATE — Estimated Budget 8	% 9	Actual Expense 10	% 11	ANALYSIS OF UNCONTROLLABLE EXPENSE PER ABOVE
51	Service Cost												
52	Labor (Units)	300											1 Excess Rent
53	Commission Labor	300A											2 Empl. Repr. Pl
54	Light, Heat and Power	301											3 Moving Exp.
55	Materials	302											
56	Trk. Opr.(Incl. Depr.)	303											Total
57	Depr.—Other Equip.	304											RETAIL TIRE AND TUBE SALES EXCLUDE DEALER SALES
58	Serv. Tools & Supplies	306											Commission Crew % Mo. % Yr. to Date
59	Maint.&Misc.Ser.Exp.	307											Auto Tire & Tube Sales
60													Truck Tire & Tube Sales
61	Total Service Cost												Total Tire & Tube Sales
62	Store Expense												House Sales
63	Salaries, Sales	400											
64	Salaries, Office	400A											Auto Tire & Tube Sales
65	Auto. Tr. & Depr.	401											Truck Tire & Tube Sales
66	Advertising	402											Total Tire & Tube Sales
67	Com. to Employees	403											Commercial Salesmen
68	Com. to Others	404											
69	Bad Debt. Exp.	405											Auto Tire & Tube Sales
70	Employees' Bonus	406											Truck Tire & Tube Sales
71	Tel. and Tel.	407											Total Tire & Tube Sales
72	Rent	408											
73	Ins. and Taxes	409											TOTAL STORES § SALES Month Year to Date
74	Misc.Sales & Opr.Exp.	410											
75	Mercantile Expense	411											Commission Crew
76	Cash Over and Short	412											Commercial Slsm.
77	Whse. Salaries	413											House Sales
78	Coll. & Legal Exp.	415											Store Mgr.
79	Total Store Exp.												Total
80	Grand Total Expense												

FIGURE 4. Detail of Store Expense for Rubber Manufacturing Concern

UNIT SALES DATA

81	Unit Sales Comparison	This Month 14	% to Quota 15	% of Incr. 16	Year to Date 17	Quota Sales Year 18	Sales Last Year To Date 19
82	Pneu. Cases Auto and Truck						
83	Truck Tires						
84	Imp. & Tractor Tires						
85	Retreaded Tires						
86	All Tubes						
87	Gasoline (Gallons)						
88	Batteries						
89	Used Tire Sales ($ only)						
90							
91							

FIGURE 5. Unit Sales Data Report for Retail Store of Rubber Manufacturing Concern

DISTRICT PROFIT AND LOSS STATEMENT
GENERAL LINE BUSINESS ONLY

DISTRICT..   DIV.....................
PERIOD..

ACCOUNTS	DISTRICT TOTAL		%	WHOLESALE		%	STORES		%
SALES									
AUTO TIRES & TUBES									
TRUCK TIRES & TUBES									
RETREADED TIRES									
ACCESSORIES - REPAIR MATERIAL									
MECH. GDS. SOLD BY L. S.									
BATTERIES									
TOTAL COMPANY PRODUCTS									
OTHER MERCHANDISE									
SERVICE INCOME									
TOTAL SALES									
LESS SALES DEDUCTIONS									
SALES TAXES									
VOLUME REBATES									
TRANSPORTATION									
CASH DISCOUNT									
TOTAL DEDUCTIONS									
NET SALES									
COST OF SALES									
GROSS PROFIT									
DISTRICT EXPENSES									
SELLING									
OPERATING									
RENTS, TAXES, INS. & BLDG. EXP.									
STORES-DEPOTS EXPENSES									
TOTAL DISTRICT EXPENSES									
LESS MISCELLANEOUS INCOME									
NET DISTRICT EXPENSES									
NET OPERATING PROFIT OR LOSS									

FIGURE 6. District Operating Report for Rubber Manufacturing Concern

71

or loss. Next the uncontrollable expense is deducted to arrive at the net operating profit or loss. Both budget and actual figures are provided and the comparisons are shown for both the current month and the year to date. Figure 4 is a continuation of Figure 3. Here the detail is shown for both controllable and uncontrollable expenses with additional analysis of sales data. Figure 5 is a further continuation of Figures 3 and 4. Here data are provided relative to unit sales as

DISTRICT STATEMENT OF EXPENSE
GENERAL LINE BUSINESS ONLY

DISTRICT_____ DIV._____

PERIOD_____

ACCOUNTS	DISTRICT TOTAL		WHOLESALE		STORES	
		%		%		%
SELLING EXPENSES						
1-A MANAGER'S AND SALESMEN'S SALARIES, COMMISSIONS AND BONUSES						
2 MANAGER'S AND SALESMEN'S TRAVELING EXPENSE INCLUDING DEPRECIATION						
3-B ADVERTISING (LOCAL ONLY)						
3-A MISC. SELLING EXPENSE						
"C" STORE SUPERVISION						
TOTAL SELLING EXPENSES						
OPERATING EXPENSES						
4-A OFFICE SALARIES						
4-C OFFICE TRAVEL						
4-D BAD DEBTS						
5-A MISC. OFFICE EXPENSE						
5-B CREDIT AND COLLECTION EXPENSE						
5-C TELEPHONE AND TELEGRAPH						
5-D POSTAGE						
3-C COMMISSIONS - DEPOTS, STORES, WAREHOUSES AND AGENTS						
6-A LABOR-SHIPPING, STOCKING, WATCHMEN						
7-A TRUCK DRIVERS' SALARIES						
8-D LIGHT, HEAT, POWER, WATER						
10-A DEPRECIATION, EX. AUTOS AND TRUCKS						
TOTAL OPERATING EXPENSES						
8-A RENTS, TAXES, INSURANCE, BLDG. EXP.						
8-E BUILDING ATTENDANTS						
TOTAL RENTS, TAXES, INS. & BLDG. EXP.						
STORES-DEPOTS EXPENSES						
TOTAL DISTRICT EXPENSES						
6-C MISCELLANEOUS INCOME						
NET TOTAL DISTRICT EXPENSES						

UNIT SALES DATA — NOVEMBER 1st TO DATE

	THIS YEAR TO DATE	% QUOTA	LAST YEAR TO DATE	% QUOTA	% INCR.
QUOTA, ALL PNEUMATIC TIRES (FULL YEAR)					
TOTAL PNEU. TIRE SALES & PERCENT TO QUOTA					
ALL TUBES					
ALL PNEU. TRUCK TIRES SALES & PERCENT TO QUOTA					
OVER 6" PNEU. TRUCK TIRES					
FARM IMPLEMENT TIRES					

FIGURE 7. Detail of District Expenses for Rubber Manufacturing Concern

contrasted with dollar sales in the previous figures. Figures 6 and 7 illustrate the summarization of the individual store operations into territorial (district) operating statements. Figure 7 provides the detail of expense and Figure 6 the summarized district profit or loss. These final summaries include both wholesale and retail types of business. Figure 8 illustrates a further summarization of sales and expenses by branches.

BRANCH OPERATING REPORT

BRANCH   MONTH OF   19

AMOUNT THIS MONTH		DESCRIPTION	AMOUNT THIS YEAR TO DATE	AMOUNT LAST YEAR TO DATE	
$		SALES—TIRES, TUBES	$	$	
		—MERCHANDISE			
$		—TOTAL SALES	$	$	
		—LESS RETURNED GOODS			
$		SALES LESS RETURNED GOODS	$	$	
		DEDUCTIONS FROM SALES			
		—REBATES AND ALLOWANCES			
		—FREIGHT			
		—ADJUSTMENTS			
		—EXCISE AND SALES TAXES			
		—CASH DISCOUNT ON SALES			
$		TOTAL DEDUCTIONS	$	$	
$		NET SALES	$	$	
		BRANCH OPERATING EXPENSE			
		RENT			
		OFFICE SALARIES			
		OFFICE TRAVEL			
		DRAYAGE			
		POSTAGE			
		OVERTIME MEALS			
		SHIPPING EXPENSE			
		TAXES			
		OFFICE EXPENSE			
		BUILDING REPAIRS—MAINTENANCE			
		MEMBERSHIPS—DUES—SUBSCRIPTIONS			
		HEAT—LIGHT—POWER—WATER			
		TELEPHONE			
		TELEGRAPH			
		INVENTORY ADJUSTMENT			
		CREDIT AND COLLECTION EXPENSE			
		STATIONERY AND PRINTING			
		DEPRECIATION			
		INSURANCE			
		BAD DEBTS			
		MISCELLANEOUS UNCLASSIFIED EXPENSE			
$		TOTAL BRANCH OPERATING EXPENSE	$	$	
		BRANCH OPERATING PROFIT OR LOSS			

Figure 8. Branch Operating Report for Rubber Manufacturing Concern

Subanalyses of Territorial Costs.—While considerable emphasis has been placed upon a territorial analysis of distribution costs and operating results, it is not to be expected that such an analysis will reveal the solution to all distribution problems. It should localize the weaknesses and point the direction of corrective action. The analysis must, however, often go further. A territorial analysis may, for example, reveal that selling costs are too high in Territory X but it may be necessary to extend the investigation to the individual salesmen within the territory, to the products sold, or to the channels of distribution used in order to finally arrive at the point of needed correction. In brief, various subanalyses of the costs of individual territories may be necessary. The method of such analyses is considered in subsequent chapters.

Corrective Action.—To find the points of weakness is not enough. Once these are discovered they must be promptly corrected. Corrective action may take such form as:

1. Rearrangement of territorial boundaries
2. Better balance of territorial effort to sales potentialities
3. Changes in methods and channels used in certain territories
4. Changes in physical facilities of territories
5. Shifting of salesmen
6. More emphasis on neglected lines
7. Abandonment of territories

It should be understood that the territorial analysis and related subanalyses of distribution costs may be made regularly each period or such analyses may be the object of occasional special studies to be made only when some weakness is apparent or suspected. In fact, the territorial analysis may itself be a subanalysis which follows some other major investigation as, for example, the cost and results by products.

Illustrative Procedure.—The procedure for analyzing distribution costs by territories is briefly illustrated in Figures 9 to 15. It must be understood, of course, that any such illustrations can suggest only the general method applicable to a theoretical case and must be greatly condensed. Such illustrations should be useful, however, in suggesting the method of approach. In the illustrations given, the following assumptions are made:

1. Sales and advertising offices are maintained both at the home office and in the territories.
2. Most salesmen operate within individual territories but a few special salesmen operate from the home office and cover several territories.

DIRECT SELLING EXPENSE	Total Expense	Basis of Allocation	Territorial Percentage X	Y	Z	Territorial Distribution X	Y	Z
Direct Territorial Costs								
Salaries and expense of territorial sales administration and supervision....	$ 50,000					$ 25,000	$15,500	$ 9,500
Territorial clerical salaries and office expense.............	15,000					7,000	5,500	2,500
Salaries and expense of territorial salesmen.................	200,000					95,000	67,000	38,000
Property insurance and taxes.........	2,000					1,000	600	400
Workmen's compensation insurance......	600					300	200	100
Social security taxes...............	12,000					6,100	3,500	2,400
Occupancy.........................	7,500					4,000	2,000	1,500
Communication, supplies, and general expense........................	2,900					1,600	700	600
Total direct territorial costs......	$290,000					$140,000	$95,000	$55,000

These costs relate to individual territories and are charged directly through the accounting procedure.

Semi-Direct Territorial Costs	Total Expense	Basis of Allocation	Territorial Percentage Expressive of Basis of Allocation X	Y	Z	Territorial Distribution X	Y	Z
Salaries and expense of special salesmen.	$ 15,000	Working time spent............	40	40	20	$ 6,000	$ 6,000	$ 3,000
Order writing...................	6,000	Number of orders.............	35	37	28	2,100	2,200	1,700
Billing.........................	3,000	Number of billing lines*......	33	37	30	1,000	1,100	900
Other sales clerical expense......	2,000	Number of invoices...........	33	37	30	600	800	600
Entertainment—home office........	4,000	Direct analysis†.............				2,000	1,900	100
Total semi-direct territorial costs...	$ 30,000					$ 11,700	$12,000	$ 6,300
Indirect Territorial Costs								
Sales and expense of general sales executives....................	$ 20,000	Number of salesmen........	40	36	24	$ 8,000	$ 7,200	$ 4,800
Education and training...........	5,000	Salesmen's earnings........	40	34	26	2,000	1,700	1,300
Home office communication........	5,000	Number of orders...........	35	37	28	1,700	1,900	1,400
General home office expense......	10,000	Direct and semi-direct costs.....	47	33	20	4,700	3,300	2,000
Total indirect territorial costs......	$ 40,000					$ 16,400	$ 14,100	$ 9,500
Total direct selling expense........	$360,000					$168,100	$121,100	$70,800

* By number of billing lines is meant the number of individual lines written on invoices. For example, an invoice written for the following items would be considered as two billing lines:

200 No. 682 ½" nipples at $4.00..............	$ 8.00
300 No. 683 ¾" nipples at $5.00..............	15.00
	$23.00

† "Direct analysis" means that the distribution of the charges is not made directly through the accounts but that some auxiliary records are kept whereby a substantially accurate direct distribution can be made.

FIGURE 9. Analysis of Direct Selling Expense by Territories

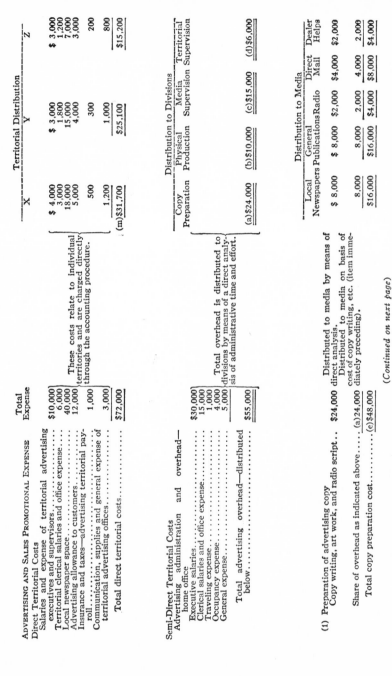

ADVERTISING AND SALES PROMOTIONAL EXPENSE	Total Expense	Territorial Distribution		
		X	Y	Z
Direct Territorial Costs				
Salaries and expense of territorial advertising executives and supervisors	$10,000	$ 4,000	$ 3,000	$ 3,000
Territorial clerical salaries and office expense	6,000	3,000	1,800	1,200
Local newspaper space	40,000	18,000	15,000	7,000
Advertising allowance to customers	12,000	5,000	4,000	3,000
Insurance and taxes—advertising territorial payroll	1,000	500	300	200
Communication, supplies and general expense of territorial advertising offices	3,000	1,200	1,000	800
Total direct territorial costs	$72,000	(m)$31,700	$25,100	$15,200

These costs relate to individual territories and are charged directly through the accounting procedure.

Semi-Direct Territorial Costs	
Advertising administration and overhead—home office	
Executive salaries	$30,000
Clerical salaries and office expense	15,000
Traveling expense	1,000
Occupancy expense	4,000
General expense	5,000
Total advertising overhead—distributed below	$55,000

Total overhead is distributed to divisions by means of a direct analysis of administrative time and effort.

	Distribution to Divisions			
	Copy Preparation	Physical Production	Media Supervision	Territorial Supervision
	(a)$24,000	(b)$10,000	(c)$15,000	(d)$6,000

(1) Preparation of advertising copy
Copy writing, art work, and radio script.. $24,000 — Distributed to media by means of direct analysis.

Share of overhead as indicated above..... (a)24,000 — Distributed to media on basis of cost of copy writing, etc. (item immediately preceding).

Total copy preparation cost...........(e)$48,000

	Distribution to Media				
	Local Newspapers	General Publications	Radio	Direct Mail	Dealer Helps
	$ 8,000	$ 8,000	$2,000	$4,000	$2,000
	8,000	8,000	2,000	4,000	2,000
	$16,000	$16,000	$4,000	$8,000	$4,000

(Continued on next page)

FIGURE 10. Analysis of Advertising and Sales Promotional Expense by Territories

(2) Cost of physical production of advertising material

Direct production costs	$ 40,000	
Share of overhead, as indicated above, is included with production cost	(b)10,000	} This production is costed on a job order basis and distributed to media by direct charge.
Total cost of physical production	(f)$ 50,000	

(3) Direct media costs

Space in general publications	$ 60,000	
Radio time	80,000	} These are charged directly to media.
Advertising agency commission	10,000	
Total direct media costs	(g)$150,000	

Summary of media costs (distributed to media)

	Total	Local newspapers	General publications	Radio	Direct mail	Dealer helps
(1) Preparation of copy as above	(e)$ 48,000	$16,000	$16,000	$ 4,000	$ 8,000	$ 4,000
(2) Physical production as above	(f)50,000	1,000	None	None	31,000	18,000
(3) Direct media costs as above	(g)150,000	None	$60,000 / 8,000 = $68,000	$80,000 / 2,000 = $82,000	None	None
Share of overhead as above	(c)15,000	1,000	5,100	5,200	2,400	1,300
Total media costs	$263,000	(h)$18,000	(i)$89,100	(j)$91,200	(k)$41,400	(l)$23,300

Distributed to media on basis of three above costs, or by estimate.

Distribution of media and overhead costs to territories

		Basis of Allocation	Territorial Distribution		
			X	Y	Z
Local newspapers	(h)$ 18,000	This does not include newspaper space cost which is included above under direct territorial costs. The distribution of this item is made on the basis of the space cost.	$ 8,100	$ 6,800	$ 3,100
General publications	(i) 89,100	Circulation weighted by purchasing power. Territorial coverage weighted by purchasing power.	49,000	27,100	13,000
Radio	(j) 91,200		53,000	28,200	10,000
Direct mail	(k) 41,400	Charged directly.	14,000	9,400	18,000
Dealer helps	(l) 23,300	Charged directly.	11,000	8,300	4,000
Share of overhead for territorial supervision as above	(d) 6,000	Territorial direct cost. See (m) on preceding page for ratio.	2,600	2,100	1,300
Total semi-direct territorial costs	$269,000		$137,700	$ 81,900	$49,400
Total advertising and sales promotional expense (direct cost of $72,000, plus semi-direct cost of $269,000)	$341,000		$169,400	$107,000	$64,600

FIGURE 10. (*Continued*)

TRANSPORTATION EXPENSE	Total Expense	Territorial Distribution		
		X	Y	Z
Direct Territorial Costs				
Salaries of transportation supervisors within territories..........................	$ 12,000	$ 5,000	$ 4,000	$ 3,000
Territorial clerical salaries and office expense..	4,000	2,000	1,000	1,000
Out-freight (Purchased).................	40,000	21,000	14,000	5,000
Operation and maintenance of trucking facilities within territories............				
Total direct territorial cost..............	24,000	12,000	7,000	5,000
	(a)$ 80,000	(d)$40,000	$26,000	$14,000
Semi-Direct Territorial Costs				
Operation and maintenance of trucking facilities at home office.....................(a)$ 50,000				
Transportation administrative expense of home office.................................	27,000			
Total............................	$ 77,000	$30,000	$24,000	$11,000
Home office cost (a)$50,000 + (b)$15,000]	$ 65,000	6,000	3,900	2,100
Territorial share of home office administration expense............................	(c)12,000			
Total semi-direct territorial cost...........	$ 77,000	$36,000	$27,900	$13,100
Total transportation expense..............	$157,000	$76,000	$53,900	$27,100

These costs relate to individual territories and are charged directly through the accounting procedure.

Divided between territorial operations and home office operations on the basis of direct costs exclusive of purchased transportation, as follows:

	Cost	Per Cent	Division
Territories ($80,000— $40,000).........	$40,000	44.4	(c)$12,000
Home office............	(a)50,000	55.6	(b) 15,000
Total..............	$90,000	100.0	$27,000

Charged to territories on standard cost basis as explained on pages 53 to 57.

Distributed to territories on basis of direct territorial costs. See (d) above for ratio.

FIGURE 11. Analysis of Transportation Expense by Territories

WAREHOUSING AND HANDLING EXPENSE

	Total Expense	Basis of Allocation	Territorial Distribution		
			X	Y	Z
Direct Territorial Costs					
Standard warehousing and handling cost........	$20,000	Charged to territories on standard cost basis as explained on pages 57 to 59.	$ 9,000	$ 7,000	$ 4,000

CREDIT AND COLLECTION EXPENSE

	Total Expense	Basis of Allocation	Territorial Percentage Expressive of Basis of Allocation			Territorial Distribution		
			X	Y	Z	X	Y	Z
Semi-Direct Territorial Costs								
Credit approval and administration........	$ 7,000	Number of accounts........	40	40	20	$ 2,800	$ 2,800	$ 1,400
Clerical cost of handling receivables........	8,000	Number of invoices........	30	40	30	2,400	3,200	2,400
Collection costs........	2,000	Number of accounts........	40	40	20	800	800	400
Bad debt losses........	4,000	Net sales........	51	27	22	2,000	1,100	900
Taxes on receivables........	4,000	Average receivables........	30	52	18	1,200	2,100	700
Total credit and collection expense........	$25,000					$ 9,200	$10,000	$ 5,800

FINANCIAL EXPENSE (Including Interest on Invested Capital at 5%)

	Total Expense	Basis of Allocation	Territorial Distribution		
			X	Y	Z
Semi-Direct Territorial Costs					
Distribution share of total financial cost as explained on pages 61 to 65	$150,000	Distributed to territories on basis of financial requirements as illustrated on page 64.	$65,000	$55,000	$30,000

FIGURE 12. Analysis of Warehousing, Credit, and Financial Expenses by Territories

GENERAL DISTRIBUTION EXPENSE	Total Expense	Basis of Allocation	Territorial Percentage Expressive of Basis of Allocation			Territorial Distribution		
			X	Y	Z	X	Y	Z
Semi-Direct Territorial Costs								
Distribution accounting (other than included above)	$20,000	Number of sales transactions.	36	36	28	$ 7,200	$ 7,200	$ 5,600
Indirect Territorial Costs								
Market and sales research	$20,000							
Personnel expense	4,000							
Pensions	8,000	Allocated on composite basis as illustrated on pages 66 and 67.						
Dues and subscriptions	1,000							
General taxes	1,000							
General insurance	2,000							
Share of general executives' salaries and expense	30,000		45	40	15	$29,700	$26,400	$ 9,900
Total indirect territorial costs	$66,000							
Total general distribution expense	$86,000					$36,900	$33,600	$15,500

FIGURE 13. Analysis of General Distribution Expense by Territories

TERRITORIAL EXPENSE	Total Expense	Territorial Distribution		
		X	Y	Z
Summary of Territorial Costs by Functions				
Direct selling	$ 360,000	$168,100	$121,100	$ 70,800
Advertising and sales promotional	341,000	169,400	107,000	64,600
Transportation	157,000	76,000	53,900	27,100
Warehousing and handling	20,000	9,000	7,000	4,000
Credit and collection	25,000	9,200	10,000	5,800
Financial	150,000	65,000	55,000	30,000
General	86,000	36,900	33,600	15,500
Total distribution costs	$1,139,000	$533,600	$387,600	$217,800
Summary by Directness of Territorial Relationship				
Direct	$ 462,000	$220,700	$153,100	$ 88,200
Semi-Direct	571,000	266,800	194,000	110,200
Indirect	106,000	46,100	40,500	19,400
Total distribution costs	$1,139,000	$533,600	$387,600	$217,800

FIGURE 14. Summary of Territorial Expense by Functions and Relationship

STATEMENT OF PROFIT AND LOSS BY TERRITORIES

	Total	X	Territories Y	Territories Z
Gross Sales	$3,050,000	$1,540,000	$830,000	$680,000
Less Sales Deductions	40,600	18,000	12,100	10,500
Net Sales	3,009,400	1,522,000	817,900	669,500
Cost of Goods Sold	1,800,400	908,400	490,300	401,700
Gross Profit	1,209,000	613,600	327,600	267,800
Direct Territorial Distribution Costs	462,000	220,700	153,100	88,200
Profit Remaining after Direct Costs	747,000	392,900	174,500	179,600
Semi-Direct Territorial Distribution Costs	571,000	266,800	194,000	110,200
Profit Remaining after Semi-Direct Costs	176,000	126,100	(19,500)	69,400
Indirect Territorial Distribution Costs	106,000	46,100	40,500	19,400
Profit Remaining after All Distribution Costs (including interest on invested capital at 5%)	$ 70,000	$ 80,000	$(60,000)	$ 50,000
Percentages of Gross Sales				
Sales Deductions	1.3	1.2	1.5	1.5
Percentages of Net Sales				
Gross Profit	40.1	40.3	40.0	40.0
Direct Distribution Costs	15.4	14.5	18.7	13.1
Semi-Direct Distribution Costs	19.0	17.5	23.7	16.5
Total Direct and Semi-Direct Distribution Costs	34.4	32.0	42.4	29.6
Indirect Distribution Costs	3.5	3.0	5.0	2.9
Total All Distribution Costs	37.9	35.0	47.4	32.5
Percentages of Gross Profit				
Direct Distribution Costs	38.2	36.0	46.7	32.9
Total Direct and Semi-Direct Distribution Costs	85.4	79.4	106.0	73.8
Total All Distribution Costs	94.2	87.0	118.3	81.3

Figure 15. Statement of Profit and Loss by Territories

3. All order writing, billing, credit, and accounts receivable procedures are carried on at the home office.
4. Trucking facilities are maintained within the territories and also at the home office.
5. General transportation administration centers at the home office.
6. Warehouses are maintained in some, but not all, territories and also at the home office.

Figures 9 to 14 show the plan of distributing the various functional expenses to the individual territories. Figure 15 shows the final determination of profit or loss by territories with various significant percentages. It should be emphasized that a report, such as shown in Figure 15, serves only as a starting point in the analysis and control of the distribution costs. It provides signals as to the direction which further examination and investigation should take. In this case, for example, it appears that the distribution cost of Territory Y is entirely out of line with results in sales and gross profit. By comparison with cost and performance standards and operations in other territories the specific points of weakness must be discovered and corrected. This may require further analysis into products, channels, methods, salesmen, etc. Such analyses are discussed in subsequent chapters.

CHAPTER 5

ANALYSIS BY COMMODITIES

Purpose of Commodity Cost Analysis.—Most concerns are faced with the question—what goods to sell. The answer must come from two sources—a study of the market and an analysis of costs. From a study of the market, it must be ascertained what goods consumers want and what prices they will pay; from an analysis of costs, it must be determined which of these goods can be made (or purchased) and sold at a profit. This requires an analysis of costs by commodities.

The major selling emphasis should be placed on those commodities which offer the greatest profit opportunities. Since conditions change rapidly, costs must be constantly at hand to guide the effort in the direction of greatest profit.

It not infrequently happens that a concern keeps adding to its line of products until it has many items which, through slow movement, fail to pay their way. In many concerns a comparatively few items provide the bulk of the sales volume, with hundreds or thousands of others supplying a small portion. Such a situation is not bad in itself, but it does present a danger that many items are no longer profitable. If products are carefully classified and costed, this danger can be avoided. Moreover, when new lines are under consideration, the probable costs, based largely on past experience, should be carefully examined before the decision is made.

It is quite true that a concern cannot always drop a low-profit item or line. Some products must be carried to satisfy the convenience of the trade or to utilize what might otherwise be idle productive capacity; however, such situations must be closely watched and held within limits.

The fact that a particular commodity or group of commodities does not yield a satisfactory profit may not indicate that the commodities should be dropped, but rather that the costs are higher than they should be; hence, a commodity cost analysis may also serve as a basis for cost control. Distribution methods employed may be too costly or individual cost items, directly relating to particular products, may be excessive. Distribution costs relating directly to products are usually fewer than those relating directly to territories; however, a considerable part of the costs can often be related to products. This is particularly true when the sales organization is set up on a product or commodity basis.

83

Finally, a product cost analysis may be useful in setting selling prices. Where no immediate expression of market price is at hand, the price may be fixed to cover total production and distribution costs, plus reasonable profit. This is frequently the situation in bidding and in the computation of markup in retail stores. Moreover, as a concern approaches a monopolistic position, either through direct control of the source of supply or by advertising or branding, costs become an essential factor in price setting.

A special significance attaches to the analysis of commodity costs for price-setting purposes as a result of fair price legislation. This is exemplified by the Robinson-Patman Act, which is discussed in detail in Chapter 22. Here it may be found necessary to demonstrate the cost of particular commodities to particular customers in order to establish reasonable price differentials as between customers, or to defend such differentials when questioned as to their fairness.

When to Use a Commodity Analysis.—An analysis of distribution costs by commodities should be made when the characteristics of the commodities or their methods of distribution are such that a uniform basis of cost apportionment would not correctly relate the cost to results. If the total distribution cost can be correctly apportioned to the various commodities on some such uniform basis as sales volume, units, or physical weight, then obviously, no analysis is required. It is seldom that such a uniform basis can be used. Circumstances which prevent the use of such apportionment may be noted as follows:

1. *Differences in the amount or kind of selling effort required.* Some products may require the services of a missionary salesman for introductory purposes. Again, specialty salesmen may be used continuously to sell a given article, while other items receive only the time of the general line salesmen. Certain of the products may be advertised extensively; others not at all. These varying conditions of selling emphasis result in unequal costs of products.

2. *Differences in physical and money volumes per unit sold.* The physical volume of a 25-cent ash tray and a $25 watch do not differ considerably, but the money volume of the latter is 100 times as large. Here the handling and delivery costs may not vary considerably. On the other hand, there is considerable difference in the physical volume and weight of a fur coat and a refrigerator, although the money value may be identical. Obviously, some of the distribution costs will differ widely as a result of these differences in physical and money volumes per unit.

3. *Differences in size of orders.* A certain paper concern sells one of its leading products almost entirely in carload lots; whereas it has other products sold chiefly by the ream. The money value of an order

of the former is often 200 times the value of the ream products. Clerical costs are practically the same for both types of orders.

4. *Differences in trade channels used.* A certain small tool manufacturing concern sells one of its products exclusively to a few automobile manufacturers; other products are sold to jobbers throughout the entire United States. The money volumes of industrial and jobber products are about equal, but by no stretch of the imagination could the distribution costs be considered equal.

The above differences are only illustrative; many others could be sighted which demonstrate beyond doubt that distribution costs can seldom be distributed to products by any uniform basis.

Classification of Commodities.—While many commodities are dissimilar in regard to distribution costs required, it is conversely true that many different commodities are quite similar in regard to such costs. This requires a proper classification of the products for costing purposes. Few concerns have a single product. The majority have one or more "lines," containing from a few to several hundred items. The typical wholesale hardware concern, for example, has about 60,000 items, and the ordinary wholesale drug company from 30,000 to 40,000 items. In such cases, it would be exceedingly difficult to secure a measure of the sales effort required for each item, and such procedure would be highly impracticable. Only those businesses which sell a few dissimilar products need analyze costs by individual items. Other concerns will find it possible to group their products into classes according to distribution similarity. There are several factors which will be found useful in making such classifications; for example:[1]

1. Nature of the product—e.g., a manufacturer of rubber goods has separate classifications for tires and tubes, footwear, mechanical goods, and chemicals. Each of these groups is divided into subgroups according to size, grade, kind, and other characteristics.
2. Method of packaging—e.g., packaged goods and goods sold in bulk.
3. Brand name—all items carrying the same brand grouped together.
4. Use made of product by customer—e.g., a number of companies classify separately products which customers buy for their own use and those which they buy for resale.
5. Volume of sale—e.g., a company groups its products into classes according to sales volume.
6. Organizational responsibility—products for which a single divisional executive is responsible are grouped together.

By a proper selection of such factors as the above, it is possible to classify the products intelligently for distribution cost analysis purposes. For example, a large producer of soap and shortening classifies

[1] N.A.C.A. Research Series No. 20, "The Assignment of Nonmanufacturing Costs to Products," *N.A.C.A. Bulletin*, August, 1951, p. 1560.

its products as (1) case goods and (2) industrial goods. Case goods are sold primarily to retailers and wholesalers, whereas the industrial items are sold to such customers as manufacturing plants, bakeries, hotels, and governmental institutions. Separate sales organizations are maintained for major commodity groups within each of the two primary classifications. Commodity costing is thus easily accomplished as a part of regular distributive operations.

It should be noted that a commodity classification for distribution cost analysis purposes will frequently differ from that selected as a basis for production cost analysis where the primary consideration is similarity of production operations required. Moreover, it is often desirable to eliminate from the former type of classification a few individual commodity items of outstanding importance, which can be costed separately. This frequently gives individual costing to a substantial part of the sales volume.

Current Practice in Commodity Analysis.—The Committee on Research of the National Association of Cost Accountants has summarized the findings of interviews conducted among 70 industrial concerns in an effort to learn—among other things—the nature of the commodity analyses employed by leading business organizations. A portion of the committee's report is presented below.[2]

Practices of the companies interviewed were found to differ in frequency, method of procedure, and completeness with which nonmanufacturing costs are assigned to products. Many of the companies used more than one method. The principal differences observed are summarized in the following paragraphs.

Periodic Margin Reports by Product Lines

In most of the companies, assignment of nonmanufacturing costs to product lines is made periodically, as part of the regular accounting routine, and by following standardized accounting procedures. The result is generally a monthly profit and loss statement by product groups or lines. Such statements are not prepared for individual items within the product lines except in companies which produce only a few products. Assignment deals principally with historical costs since the objective is to determine actual profit or loss on each product line.

The field study showed that periodic reports of product margins are prepared by 56 of the 70 companies interviewed. A tabulation of the intervals at which product margins are reported follows.

Interval at Which Product Margins Are Reported	Number of Companies
Monthly	47
Quarterly	4
Irregularly (but oftener than once a year)	3
Annually	2
Total number of companies having periodic product margin reports	56

[2] "The Assignment of Nonmanufacturing Costs to Products," pp. 1561–65.

In 45 companies these product margin reports carry assignment of nonmanufacturing costs to the point where net profit by product line is ascertained. The remaining 11 companies do not report net profit by product classification, but do determine other margins. In 5 of these companies, no nonmanufacturing costs are assigned to products and the information with respect to product profitability is limited to gross margin after manufacturing cost. The other 6 companies assign some but not all nonmanufacturing costs to products. The nature of the resulting product margins is shown below.

"Selling margin," i.e. gross margin less direct selling costs (2 companies).
"Secondary revenue," i.e. gross margin less costs of order filling and delivery (one company).
Gross margin less advertising (one company)
Gross margin less salesmen's commissions (one company)
Margin after deducting home office costs from selling commissions charged to factories (one company).

Product Margins by Special Study

Assignment of nonmanufacturing costs to individual products as distinguished from product lines is made infrequently and often by special study rather than by standardized repetitive procedures. In costing individual items within lines, the large number usually makes it impractical to assign costs frequently. Moreover, when cost data are wanted for specific decisions which involve modification of present conditions, routine methods may not be applicable. Complete coverage of all products at any one time is often not attempted where special studies are used.

Companies interviewed commonly employ a combination of regular reports and special studies in determining product costs. The specific methods chosen in each case have been developed to supply the kind and amount of information wanted by management. Where products are numerous, periodic studies take the place of regular reports for determining costs of individual products because frequent reports are unduly expensive in terms of clerical effort. However, costs are usually assigned to groups or lines at regular intervals. Since there is no general pattern in such company practices, the following case examples are given to illustrate some of the different practices.

Company No. 1: This company has six operating divisions, each of which produces a separate type of product. Each division prepares a monthly profit and loss statement covering its operations. The divisions in turn have a number of product lines which are composed of numerous items and varieties. A monthly statement of profit or loss is prepared for each product line and gross profit is determined for individual products within the lines.

Company No. 2: The great number of individual products, most of which represent a very small fraction of total sales volume, makes it impractical to calculate costs for all products at frequent intervals. For those individual products which comprise the major portion of the volume, costs are determined annually; for the other products, costs are determined when the information is wanted. Product line costs are determined annually. This company makes no monthly calculation of historical product costs. Instead, product costs are determined in preparing the budget and hence they represent anticipated operating expenses and forecasted volume.

Company No. 3: A monthly net income statement is prepared for each of the company's 35 brands. Each brand has several package sizes for which no separate nonmanufacturing costs are determined.

Company No. 4: Product costs are determined only by special studies and no periodic assignment of historical costs to products is made. Cost of an individual item is refigured when a change in design, methods of manufacturing or marketing, or other conditions indicate the need for revision. This company's products are classified into 135 types with about 1000 different models.

Company No. 5: A monthly statement is prepared showing (1) sales, (2) manufacturing cost, (3) gross margin, (4) costs of order filling and transportation, and (5) margin after deducting the latter costs from gross margin. Statements give the above information for product lines and for products within each line, but not for individual product sizes, colors, and other varieties. This company does not make a routine monthly allocation of selling, advertising, and administrative costs to products.

Company No. 6: Actual profit or loss for each individual product is determined by annual study in which all costs are assigned. At the same time budgeted profit by products is determined for the coming year.

Method of Commodity Analysis.—The basic procedure for commodity analysis of distribution costs is similar to that suggested in the preceding chapter for territorial analysis. The particular steps may be outlined as follows:

1. Determine the gross profit by products or groups of products.
2. Accumulate the direct product distribution costs and deduct these from the gross profit to determine product *profit after direct costs.*
3. Distribute to the products their respective shares of the semidirect costs and deduct these to arrive at product *profit after semidirect costs.*
4. Allocate to the products their respective shares of the general or indirect costs and deduct these to arrive at the final product *net profit.*
5. Make such subanalyses of the results by products as may be deemed useful (e.g., by territories, channels, customers, etc.)

The gross profit by products will be available through the usual direct analysis of sales and cost of goods sold; or, as in the case of some mercantile concerns, by the retail inventory method.[3] In some concerns, where the sales organization and activities are based upon a product classification, the ledger classification of distribution cost accounts is set up on a product basis. In such cases, the direct product costs will be available in the general or subsidiary ledger accounts. Where a different basis of classification is employed, as, for example,

---

[3] The method is explained in Chapter 10.

in the illustration on pages 34 to 39 (there the basic classification is by territories rather than products), a special analysis procedure is necessary. Each item of distribution cost must be considered separately in its relation to products. If it relates directly to a particular product it will be charged to that product; if it has a semidirect relationship, some basis must be found for measurement of that relationship; if it has only an indirect relationship it must be apportioned on some arbitrary basis or assigned to a residual cost group for which no satisfactory method of allocation can be found.

Bases of Allocation.—The reliability of a cost analysis by commodities is particularly dependent upon the suitability of the bases of allocation selected. To a considerable extent the selection of bases will depend upon the nature of the internal organization. Thus, where the sales organization is developed on a product plan, many distribution cost items may be of a direct nature. Moreover, under such conditions, more accurate bases will be available for the semidirect and indirect items than would otherwise be the case. As a rule, the same bases will apply to the costs of both the home office and the branches.

In the following pages there are suggested various bases frequently suitable for the commodity analysis. These must be taken as purely illustrative. As in the case of a territorial analysis, suitable bases will vary widely in different concerns and with different local conditions existing in the same types of concerns. Moreover the classification of cost items as *direct, semidirect,* and *indirect* will be found to vary under different circumstances.

Allocation of Direct Selling Expense to Commodities.—

DIRECT COSTS. Commodity analysis of distribution costs is of value particularly in those concerns where the sales effort is directed along commodity lines. In such cases a considerable amount of the direct selling expense can usually be charged directly against individual commodities or commodity lines to which they pertain, no bases of allocation being necessary. Illustrative of such items are:

1. Salaries and expense of administrators and supervisors of individual commodity lines
2. Salaries, commission, traveling, and automobile expense of individual commodity salesmen
3. Commissions to agents, brokers, and consignees
4. Entertainment expenditures identifiable with individual commodities
5. Education and training of individual commodity salesmen
6. Insurance and taxes related to payroll of individual commodity sales personnel

7. Spoiled work chargeable to salesmen
8. Sales and excise taxes
9. Communication, supplies, occupancy, and general expense of commodity sales departments

SEMIDIRECT COSTS.

1. *Salaries, commissions, and traveling expense of general salesmen.* This is frequently the most important single item of direct selling expense and it is often difficult accurately to apportion it to commodities. Meat-packing concerns, as an illustration, experience such difficulty because of the wide line of related products sold to individual buyers.

Where there are only a few products or product groups, it is sometimes possible to determine the relative amount of time which salesmen devote to each. This may be secured by occasional studies or by salesmen's daily time reports. The cost is then distributed on the basis of time spent. The following cases from the N.A.C.A. research report illustrate procedures used in determining the manner of distributing salesmen's time to classes of products.[4]

Company No. 1: This company's procedure was described in the steps listed below:

1. Product lines are carefully defined and coded. It is essential to have all members of the sales and order handling staff familiar with these codes.
2. Orders received are coded to product lines.
3. Each sales and service man is provided with time cards on which he records weekly the customers he has visited, the amount of time he spent with each customer, and what line he was selling or servicing. When a single visit covers two or more lines, the amount of time spent on each is estimated.
4. The above reports are tabulated by product lines monthly. Working time not reported spent in presence of customers is prorated between lines in the same ratios as time reported spent with customers.

Company No. 2: In contrast with the preceding case, this company found it impractical to use reports of time spent by salesmen on different product lines. It therefore developed a rating sheet on which salesmen rated the company's product lines as to the relative amount of effort necessary to sell them. The essential form of these rating sheets is shown below:

Product Lines	Rating on Basis of Effort Required to Sell
A	x%
B	x%
C	x%
etc.	x%
	100%

---

[4] "The Assignment of Nonmanufacturing Costs to Products," pp. 1572–73.

Successive samples of ratings given the lines by salesmen, supervisors and executives were taken until several hundred replies had been obtained. While individual rating sheets showed wide variations, when combined a quite consistent pattern was found. It was concluded that this was a reasonably good measure of the relative amounts of effort required to sell the various lines and that it accordingly should serve as a good basis for allocating salesmen's salaries and expenses to product lines.

Company No. 3: This company sells industrial equipment which requires extensive use of consulting and application engineering services in addition to the usual sales work. Cost of time spent by engineering and other specialists is recorded, and charged directly to product lines. On the other hand, costs of general salesmen are allocated on the basis of the number of scheduled hours each salesman is expected to spend with each customer. An individual customer buys only those items in a specific line and hence costs by lines as well as by customers are obtained.

Again, where all customers are potential buyers of all products in some fixed proportion, this item of cost may be distributed to the products in that proportion. For example, if each customer normally distributes 50% of his purchases to Product A, 30% to Product B, and 20% to Product C, then the salesmen's costs may be distributed accordingly. This plan has the advantage of an incentive to product department heads to see that salesmen do not neglect their goods. The executive in charge of Product A, knowing that he will be charged with 50% of the cost, will insist that the salesmen secure the proper share of orders for his goods. The authors are familiar with cases in which this plan has worked successfully.

Another basis sometimes useful is that of the number of items ordered (or lines billed). Thus, assume that Salesman O'Day calls on five customers; three customers order only Product A, and two order Products A and B. Then Product A would bear five-sevenths of the cost. While such bases sometimes result in a fair apportionment of the cost, they should be used with caution. For numerous companies the number of items ordered per commodity gives no clue as to unit value, physical volume, or selling effort required.

2. *Sales clerical expense.* This item includes sales clerical salaries, office supplies, and insurance and tax charges related to clerical payroll.

Where the sales clerical expense, such as cost of order writing, maintenance of price and discount files, filing, billing, adjustments, and communication, constitutes an important element of the selling cost, special clerical departments are usually maintained for these activities. If different order forms are used for each commodity and if the different commodities are billed on separate invoices, as is sometimes the case, the various sales clerical department costs can be allocated to commodities on the basis of number of orders, number of invoices, etc. Where this is not the case, test studies must usually be made to ascertain the basis for distributing the clerical costs to commodities or commodity lines. If the cost is of insufficient importance to justify such studies, it must be considered as an indirect cost as noted below.

3. *Education and training of sales force.* This item consists of the cost of preparing training manuals, maintenance of sales training schools, preparation and distribution of "salesmen's helps," sales conventions, etc.

Where this training is directed primarily to the salesmen of individual commodities, the cost can be distributed directly as indicated under direct costs. Where the training is directed to general line salesmen, the cost may be distributed on the same basis as that used for general line salesmen's salaries or in accordance with executives' estimates as to the commodities which receive the major emphasis. Where this item of cost is relatively unimportant, it may be included with general selling expense and will then be distributed as an indirect cost.

4. *Insurance and taxes on payroll of general line salesmen.* These items, such as workmen's compensation, life, and fidelity insurance, and social security taxes on salesmen selling all commodities, can be distributed on the same basis as that selected for salesmen's salaries above.

INDIRECT COSTS.

1. *Salaries and expense of sales executives and supervisors.* Theoretically, at least, the proper basis for the allocation of this expense to commodities or commodity lines is the time and effort devoted by executives to each. This can never be measured with exactness, and often it can only be approximated. Where it is deemed impracticable or impossible to secure a reasonable approximation of the time and effort spent, resort must be had to some other basis of allocation. If the sales organization consists largely of specialty salesmen, selling one product or line, the supervision expense may be distributed according to the number of salesmen. The suitability of this basis rests on the assumption that each salesman requires about the same amount of supervision. Where the organization consists chiefly of general line salesmen, the most satisfactory plan is usually to apportion this item on the basis of total direct and semidirect costs or on the basis of salesmen's salaries, commissions, and traveling expense (Item 1 under Semidirect Costs). One of the leading manufacturers of packaged food products follows the last-named procedure, but also takes into account the number of invoice lines and the budgeted unit sales volume for each commodity group.

2. *Sales clerical expense.* As noted above, all or part of this cost may be distributed as a semidirect item. Where this plan is not suit-

able, some general basis must be used, such as total of direct and semidirect costs, number of units sold, or number of billing lines. If such bases are not suitable, periodic test studies should be made to ascertain the fair apportionment.

3. *Entertainment expense.* In some instances this item can be charged directly to commodities. Where this is not the case, it is usually best to apportion it on the same basis as salesmen's salaries or by executive estimate.

4. *Communication expense.* This item includes the cost of telephones, telegraph, postage, special stenographic departments, dictating equipment, etc., in so far as these charges are related to distribution activity. Where the sales organization is formed on product lines, much of the communication expense can be charged directly to products. In other cases, the best plan is to make periodic studies or tests to ascertain the proper apportionment. General bases, sometimes useful, are number of orders and number of customers, where these can be separated by products.

5. *General direct selling expense.* This group includes those items which are not of sufficient importance to distribute individually, such as general sales traveling expense, insurance and taxes on sales administrative payroll, miscellaneous supplies, etc. As a rule, this group can be equitably apportioned on the basis of total direct and semidirect costs.

Allocation of Advertising and Sales Promotional Expense to Commodities.—Advertising and sales promotional costs are usually directed to the benefit of particular commodities, company brands, or institutional strength. The procedure of analysis is to resolve all costs into those of particular media or methods and then to allocate the latter to commodities. The method by which the individual cost items are resolved into media costs is explained on pages 50 to 52. To the extent that media costs are directed to the benefit of individual commodities they can be charged directly to those commodities. Where the advertising is directed to brands and institutional benefit as well as to individual commodities, the sales and general executives must arbitrarily determine the proportion of the total cost to be assigned to brand and institutional benefit. The share of the cost assigned to a particular brand can then be distributed to the products carrying the brand identification on the basis of their sales. The share of the cost assigned to institutional benefit can be distributed to all products on the basis of sales or to such of the products as, in the judgment of executives, benefit thereby.

To illustrate this procedure, assume that a certain concern spends $500,000 for advertising in general publications. Of this amount

$200,000 is used for Brand A products and $300,000 for Brand B products. Under Brand A there are three products and under Brand B, two. Of the total general publications cost, 10% is considered as institutional. In advertising Brand A products, 10% of the Brand A cost is considered as benefiting the brand generally, and 90% the individual products advertised; in Brand B products, 5% is considered as applicable to the brand and 95% to the individual products. Sales have been as follows:

	Sales	Per Cent of Brand Total	Per Cent of Grand Total
Brand A			
Product A–1	$ 400,000	16.7	6.7
Product A–2	800,000	33.3	13.3
Product A–3	1,200,000	50.0	20.0
	$2,400,000	100.0	
Brand B			
Product B–1	$1,600,000	44.4	26.7
Product B–2	2,000,000	55.6	33.3
	$3,600,000	100.0	
	$6,000,000		100.0

The distribution of the cost would then be as follows:

		Distribution of Brand Share to Brand Products on Basis of Sales		Distribution of Institutional Share to All Products on Basis of Sales		Total Product Costs
ADVERTISING APPLIED TO BRAND A PRODUCTS:						
Total	$200,000					
Institutional (10%)	20,000			→$20,000		
	$180,000					
Brand A (10%)	18,000	→$18,000				
Balance distributed to products	$162,000	Per Cent Sales		Per Cent Sales		
Product A–1 ⎫ Basis of	$ 30,000	16.7	3,000	6.7	$ 3,333	$ 36,333
Product A–2 ⎬ space	50,000	33.3	6,000	13.3	6,667	62,667
Product A–3 ⎭ used	82,000	50.0	9,000	20.0	10,000	101,000
	$162,000	100.0	$18,000			
ADVERTISING APPLIED TO BRAND B PRODUCTS:						
Total	$300,000					
Institutional (10%)	30,000			→$30,000		
	$270,000					
Brand B (5%)	13,500	→$13,500				
Balance distributed to products	$256,500					
Product B–1 ⎫ Basis of	$100,000	44.4	6,000	26.7	13,333	119,333
Product B–2 ⎬ space used	156,500	55.6	7,500	33.3	16,667	180,667
	$256,500	100.0	$13,500	100.0	$50,000	$500,000

In the illustration above, the cost of the medium of general publications, other than the share allocated to brands and institutional, is distributed to individual products according to the space used. This method can be used for such media as newspapers, general and trade publications, direct mail, dealer helps and displays, catalogs and circulars, and outdoor advertising.

The cost of other media may be distributed to commodities as follows:

Radio and/or television—time basis
Contests—directly to commodities promoted
Demonstrations—directly to commodities demonstrated
Sample distribution—directly
Allowances to customers—commodity sales to customers

Modifications are sometimes necessary in the application of bases of distribution. For example, it is sometimes the judgment of executives that products benefit equally, although the space or time is unequal. Where good reason appears to support this view, the apportionment must be adjusted on the basis of benefit received.

Whether the advertising costs should be considered as a direct or semidirect cost of commodities depends upon the closeness of the relationship. Where the institutional aspect is predominant, the cost should be considered as semidirect or even indirect. Where the major emphasis is on the promotion of the sale of individual commodities, the cost may properly be classified as direct.

Allocation of Transportation Expense to Commodities.—Where transportation services are purchased and different commodities are transported in separate shipments or deliveries, the transportation charges can be made directly against individual products or product groups. In such cases the overhead costs such as traffic direction and supervision can be allocated to commodities on the basis of the number of shipments or the direct costs.

Where transportation services are purchased but commodities are mixed in the same shipments, where a concern operates its own trucking facilities, or where transportation services are partly purchased and partly provided by the concern's own facilities, the most satisfactory procedure is to establish standard product transportation rates as explained on pages 53 to 57, such rates to include all direct and overhead transportation, delivery, and traffic costs. Such costs should usually be considered as direct commodity costs.

Allocation of Warehousing and Handling Expense to Commodities.—The most satisfactory method of apportioning warehousing, storing, and handling expense to products is by means of a standard cost plan as described on pages 57 to 59.

If standard warehousing costs are not used, the most satisfactory plan is to classify the products relative to weight, size, or other warehousing and handling factors; and then to weight each group in a manner similar to that described on pages 55 and 56, with reference to transportation costs. In this manner all commodities are translated into their equivalent in warehousing units. If then the total warehousing cost is divided by the total units, an average unit cost is secured. This unit cost multiplied by the number of warehousing units of a particular commodity provides the commodity cost. This method differs from the standard plan only in that an average instead of a standard unit cost is determined. The standard plan is preferable where commodity lines are well standardized.

This cost should be considered as a direct commodity charge.

Allocation of Credit and Collection Expense to Commodities.— As indicated under territorial analysis, the credit and collection expenses group themselves into five natural divisions as follows:

1. Cost of credit approval and administration
2. Cost of clerical handling of receivables
3. Collection costs
4. Bad debt losses
5. Taxes on receivables

The cost of extending credit and making collections bears no direct relationship to individual products. Rather, it is dependent upon the financial responsibility of the customer, and upon the frequency and amount of his purchases. If all products are purchased by all customers in somewhat the same proportion, the credit and collection costs can be distributed to products on the basis of sales. Where this is not the case, and particularly where this item of cost is important, separate bases should be sought for each division of the cost. Suggestions as to such bases are as follows:

1. *Credit approval and administration.* This group of expenses includes the cost of maintaining the credit office or offices, administrative salaries, credit services, credit files, general traveling expense, communications, office supplies, incident insurance and taxes, and occupancy expense.

The products of certain companies are often of such a nature that a given customer will purchase but one product or one product line. Thus, a certain concern sells cottonseed oil in tank cars to paint manufacturers and other large users, but sells these customers no other products. Again it sells bulk soap chips largely to laundries. In general, its different products go to different classes of customers. Under such conditions, these costs may be distributed on the basis of the number of accounts of each class of customers or the number of orders.

Where different products are sold to the same customers, and billed together, tests may be made to determine the average number of billing lines for each product and this basis used to distribute the cost. To illustrate, assume that 1,000 invoices contain 6,000 lines of billing and that these lines run as follows:

Product	Number of Billing Lines
A	1,200
B	2,400
C	2,400
	6,000

The cost would then be apportioned to the various products as follows:

To Product A	20%
To Product B	40
To Product C	40

2. Clerical cost of handling receivables. The clerical cost of handling receivables includes the expenses of posting all charges and credits, and the sending of monthly statements. While this work is usually done by the accounting department, it constitutes a part of the function of credit, and should be so considered when determining functional costs. It consists largely of clerical salaries, supplies, and such part of the accounting department's administrative and occupancy expense as may be applicable.

The cost of posting charges follows closely the number of invoices; the issuing of monthly statements and the posting of credits follow the number of accounts; and miscellaneous adjustments, etc., may follow either the number of invoices or the number of accounts. Here again, the distribution should be on the basis of number of invoices or accounts where these are separated by products. Where the invoices and accounts cannot be so separated, the average number of billing lines should be used as indicated for credit approval and administration.

3. Collection costs. This includes the cost of continuous review of the receivable records, adjustment of credit limits, collection letters, salaries and expense of collectors, and legal expense. These costs usually follow the number of accounts, and should be so distributed where different products are sold to different groups of customers. Where this is not the case, the most equitable bases are the number of invoices or the average number of billing lines as noted above.

4. *Bad debt losses.* Where the sales of different products are made to different customer groups and the accounts are separated accordingly, the bad debt losses can be related directly to products. This can be done regardless of whether losses are taken as realized or whether a reserve is provided. Where all products are sold to the same customers, an analysis can be made of actual losses to determine what products were sold to the defaulting customers. To illustrate, assume that such an analysis of actual losses during the past three years reveals the following:

Products	Amount of Actual Losses Suffered
A	$10,000
B	20,000
C	30,000
Total	$60,000

The distribution of current bad debt losses would then be as follows:

Product	Per Cent
A	16.7
B	33.3
C	50.0
	100.0

If losses are being taken as realized, the amount currently realized should be distributed on the basis of this past experience rather than by current analysis, in order to avoid accidental charges to particular products. If a reserve is provided, the amount currently credited should likewise be charged to products on this basis of past experience.

When making an analysis of actual losses, it is not always possible to relate them directly to products. For example, if a customer owes $1,000 and a settlement is made whereby $400 is received, there may be a question as to the particular products on which the loss was realized. In such cases the apportionment of the $600 loss should be made to products on the basis of recent sales to that particular customer.

5. *Taxes on receivables.* Where the same credit terms are applied to all commodities, this item may be distributed on the basis of net sales. Where credit terms vary, the sales factor should be weighted by the number of days accounts are outstanding under the various terms; or the basis of distribution should be estimated by the controller.

Credit and collection expense may be considered as a direct or semi-direct cost of commodities, depending upon the extent to which the analysis is carried in making its distribution. Where losses are heavy as in the case of some instalment concerns, the cost may well be considered as direct. Where the credit costs are relatively unimportant and are distributed on some general basis such as net credit sales, the cost should be classified as semidirect.

Allocation of Financial Expense to Commodities.—The financial costs of the typical industrial and commercial concern are noted on page 61. There are three steps in the distribution of these costs to commodities; namely:

1. To determine the total financial cost of the entire business
2. To divide the financial cost as between production, distribution, and nonoperating activities
3. To allocate the distribution share of the financial costs to commodities

The first two of these steps were illustrated on pages 62 to 64. In that illustration, a total permanent investment of $4,600,000 was assumed and, of this amount, the share attributable to distribution activities was found to be $2,080,000. This consisted of the following items:

Working funds	($ 20,000)
Receivables	700,000
Inventories	600,000
Physical facilities	800,000
Total	$2,080,000

The distribution share of the total financial expense was found to be $143,284. This illustration may now be continued by assuming the following data relative to factors of distribution to commodities:

FACTORS OF DISTRIBUTION

	Total	Commodities		
		A	B	C
Percentage of commodity direct and semidirect distribution costs to total as a basis for allocating working funds	100%	20%	30%	50%
Percentage of commodity net sales (or credit sales) to total sales as a basis for allocating receivables	100	10	30	60
Percentage of average commodity inventories to total inventories	100	20	30	50
Weighted index (as explained below) as a basis for allocating physical facilities	100	20	40	40

Working funds are here allocated to commodities on the basis of average direct and semidirect distribution costs of the commodity groups. Costs of previous periods or those budgeted for current periods may be used.

Where receivables can be separated by products, the allocation should be on the basis of average actual receivables. Where all commodities are sold to all customers, net sales are usually a satisfactory basis for allocation. The latter assumption is made here.

The allocation of the investment in inventories should be made on the basis of average commodity inventories, which factor will be known.

Physical facilities are used for warehousing, transportation, display, and sales management occupancy purposes. The investment required for each of these purposes can be determined with little difficulty and these amounts may be used as weight factors in the allocation of this financial requirement. To illustrate, assume, in the case at hand, that three-fifths of the investment in physical facilities is used for warehousing and two-fifths for transportation, the use for other purposes being negligible. By weighting the warehousing and transportation costs, it is possible to secure a basis for allocation of the physical investment requirements of commodities as shown in the following computation:

Commodities	Commodity Costs Previously Determined (Figures assumed here)	Weight Factor		Percentage Distribution
A	Warehousing	$ 3,000 × ⅗ = $ 1,800		
	Transportation	32,900 × ⅖ = 13,160	$14,960	20
B	Warehousing	5,000 × ⅗ = $ 3,000		
	Transportation	67,300 × ⅖ = 26,920	29,920	40
C	Warehousing	12,000 × ⅗ = $ 7,200		
	Transportation	56,800 × ⅖ = 22,720	29,920	40
			$74,800	100
Total	Warehousing	$ 20,000 × ⅗ = $12,000		
	Transportation	$157,000 × ⅖ = $62,800	$74,800	

ALLOCATION OF INVESTMENT REQUIREMENTS FOR PHYSICAL FACILITIES

Commodities	Percentage Distribution as Above	Investment Requirements
A	20	$160,000
B	40	320,000
C	40	320,000
	100	$800,000

With all of the above factors of distribution known, it is now possible to determine the financial requirements of each commodity or commodity group and to allocate the financial expense to each accordingly. This may be illustrated as follows:

ALLOCATION OF INVESTMENT ON BASIS
OF ABOVE FACTORS

| | Total | Commodities | | |
		A	B	C
Working funds	($ 20,000)	($ 4,000)	($ 6,000)	($ 10,000)
Receivables	700,000	70,000	210,000	420,000
Inventories (direct allocation)	600,000	120,000	180,000	300,000
Physical facilities	800,000	160,000	320,000	320,000
Totals	$2,080,000	$346,000	$704,000	$1,030,000
Percentage of total	100%	16.6%	33.9%	49.5%
Allocation of distribution financial expense	$143,284	$23,785	$48,573	$70,926

It should be noted that the foregoing method of allocating financial cost to commodities may be used either with or without the inclusion of interest on investment as a part of the cost.

Allocation of General Distribution Expense to Commodities.— Reference is made on pages 65 to 67, concerning territorial analysis, to various distribution costs of a general nature which are either difficult to allocate or of insufficient importance to justify the work of individual analysis. This situation obtains also in a commodity analysis. Where particular items are important, individual allocation may be made. For example, market analysis, when directed primarily to particular products, may be charged to such products directly or on the basis of the sales of those products. Usually, however, such items can best be distributed on some general basis, such as the total of all other distribution costs, or on a composite basis, as explained on pages 66 and 67. These items should be classified as indirect commodity costs.

Subanalyses of Commodity Costs.—In those concerns where the basic organization of sales activity is on commodity lines, the commodity analysis of distribution costs will usually come first. However, this must frequently be followed with subanalyses by territories, branches, salesmen, channels, classes of customers, etc., in order to reach to specific points of weakness and to provide definite control. If the cost of selling a particular product or product group is out of proportion to the results in sales, then the investigation must naturally proceed to determine the individual responsibility and to ascertain where and why the product results are unsatisfactory. The method of territorial analysis was discussed in Chapter 4; other analyses are discussed in subsequent chapters. Where the organization of sales activity is on some other primary basis, as, for example, territory or channel of distribution, the commodity analysis may itself take the position of a subanalysis.

Frequency of Commodity Analysis.—Most concerns, which have separate and distinct lines of commodities or products, find it necessary to make continuous analysis of distribution costs by commodities. This is particularly true where the sales organization is based on commodity lines. With other concerns the analysis may take the form of periodic tests. Such tests must naturally be used with caution.

Corrective Action.—Once the points of weakness are discovered, corrective action must be taken. This may take such form as:

1. Elimination of nonprofit items
2. Additions of items to share fixed elements of distribution cost
3. Insistence that salesmen give proper attention to neglected lines
4. Correction in product quality, design, or appeal
5. Adjustments in prices
6. Adjustment of sales compensation plans
7. Changes in type, amount, and direction of advertising
8. Adjustments in amount of sales effort as between products

The corrective action may take many different directions, the above suggestions being only illustrative.

Illustrative Procedure.—The procedure for analyzing distribution costs by commodities is briefly illustrated in Figures 16 to 21. It must be understood, of course, that any such illustration can suggest only the general method applicable to a theoretical case. In the actual case, consideration must be given to matters of internal organization and local circumstances. In this illustration the following assumptions are made:

1. There are three commodities, designated as A, B, and C.
2. There is a sales administrative head for each commodity line.
3. The concern employs special commodity salesmen and also salesmen who sell all lines. There are more of the former.
4. The different commodities are entered by salesmen on separate orders and are billed to customers on separate invoices.
5. Advertising is done primarily for the direct promotion of individual commodities; however, the executives arbitrarily allocate 10% of the cost of general publications to the trade name. Five advertising media are employed.
6. Standard transportation and warehouse costs are used.

Such a situation may be exemplified, for example, by a manufacturer of carpets who sells three major lines—carpets, rugs, and automobile carpets.

	Total Expense	Basis of Allocation	Commodity Percentage Expressive of Basis of Allocation			Commodity Distribution		
			A	B	C	A	B	C
DIRECT SELLING EXPENSE								
Direct Commodity Costs								
Salaries and expense of administrators and supervisors of individual commodity lines........	$ 60,000					$ 25,000	$ 20,000	$15,000
Salaries and expense of individual commodity salesmen.........	180,000					80,000	60,000	40,000
Commissions to agents, brokers, and consignees	10,000					8,000	2,000	none
Insurance and taxes related to individual commodity personnel.............	10,000					5,000	3,000	2,000
Communication, supplies, occupancy, and general expense of commodity sales departments........	12,000					5,000	4,000	3,000
Total direct commodity costs........	$272,000					$123,000	$ 89,000	$60,000

These costs relate to individual commodities and are charged directly through the accounting procedure.

	Total Expense	Basis of Allocation	Commodity Percentage Expressive of Basis of Allocation			Commodity Distribution		
			A	B	C	A	B	C
Semi-Direct Commodity Costs								
Salaries, commission, and traveling expense of general line salesmen.........	$ 60,000	Proportion of commodities purchased by customers from all sources.........	50	30	20	$ 30,000	$ 18,000	$12,000
Order writing..............	8,000	Number of orders.........	40	30	30	3,200	2,400	2,400
Billing................	4,000	Number of billing lines......	30	40	30	1,200	1,600	1,200
Other sales clerical expense.......	4,000	Number of invoices........	30	30	40	1,200	1,800	1,600
Education and training..........	6,000	Executive estimate........	60	30	10	3,600	1,800	600
Insurance and taxes on payroll of general line salesmen.........	3,000	Compensation of general line salesmen.........	50	30	20	1,500	900	600
Total semi-direct commodity costs........	$ 85,000					$ 40,700	$ 25,900	$18,400
Indirect Commodity Costs								
Salaries and expense of general sales executives and supervisors............	$ 25,000	Compensation of commodity and general salesmen	45	33	22	$ 11,250	$ 8,250	$ 5,500
Entertainment.............	4,000	Executive estimate........	60	30	10	2,400	1,200	400
Communication.............	9,000	Special studies..........	30	40	30	2,700	3,600	2,700
General selling expense.........	50,000	Direct and semi-direct costs	45.8	32.2	22	22,900	16,100	11,000
Total indirect commodity costs.......	$ 88,000					$ 39,250	$ 29,150	$19,600
Total direct selling expense.......	$445,000					$202,950	$144,050	$98,000

FIGURE 16.　Analysis of Direct Selling Expense by Commodities

ADVERTISING AND SALES PROMOTIONAL EXPENSE

	Total Expense	
Direct Commodity Costs		
Advertising administration and overhead		
Executive salaries	$ 30,000	
Clerical salaries and office expense	20,000	
Traveling expense	2,000	
Occupancy expense	4,000	
General expense	8,000	
Total advertising overhead—distrib. below	$ 64,000	Total overhead is distributed to divisions by means of a direct analysis of administrative time and effort.
(1) Preparation of advertising copy		
Copy writing and art work	$ 36,000	Distributed to media by direct analysis.
Share of overhead as indicated above	(a)30,000	Distributed to media on basis of copy writing, etc. (item immediately preceding).
Total cost of copy preparation	$ 66,000	
(2) Cost of physical production of Advertising material		
Direct production costs	$ 60,000	This production is costed on a job order basis and distributed to media by direct charge.
Share of overhead as indicated above	(b)20,000	
Total cost of physical production	$ 80,000	
(3) Direct media costs		
Space in general publications	$200,000	These are charged directly to media.
Advertising agency commission	25,000	
Total direct media costs	$225,000	
Overhead for media supervision	(c)$ 14,000	Distributed on basis of total of (1), (2), (3).
Total media costs	$385,000	

Distribution of media costs to commodities		Basis of Allocation
General publications	(d)$254,300	
Less 10% considered by executives as applicable to trade name	$ 25,430	
Balance allocated to commodities	228,870	Sales.
Direct mail	(e) 60,700	Space.
Catalogs and circulars	(f) 42,500	Space.
Dealer helps	(g) 20,700	Space.
Demonstrations	(h) 6,800	Charged directly.
Total adv. and sales promotional expense	$385,000	

Distribution of Overhead to Divisions

(1) Copy Preparation	(2) Physical Production	(3) Media Supervision
(a)$30,000	(b)$20,000	(c)$14,000

Distribution to Media

	General Publications	Direct Mail	Catalogs and Circulars	Dealer Helps	Demonstrations
(1)	$12,000	$ 9,000	$ 6,000	$ 6,000	$ 3,000
	10,000	7,500	5,000	5,000	2,500
	$22,000	$16,500	$11,000	$11,000	$ 5,500
(2)	None	$40,000	$30,000	$ 9,000	$ 1,000
(3)	$200,000				
	23,000	$ 2,000			
	$223,000	$ 2,000			
	$ 9,300	$ 2,200	$ 1,500	$ 700	$ 300
	(d)$254,300	(e)$60,700	(f)$42,500	(g)$20,700	(h)$ 6,800

Commodity Distribution

	A	B	C
General publications	$ 12,000	$ 7,630	$ 5,800
	208,000	8,470	12,400
	40,000	10,700	10,000
	20,000	2,500	20,000
		10,700	10,000
			6,800
	$280,000	$40,000	$65,000

FIGURE 17. Analysis of Advertising and Sales Promotional Expense by Commodities

	Total Expense	Basis of Allocation	Commodity Percentage Expressive of Basis of Allocation			Commodity Distribution		
			A	B	C	A	B	C
TRANSPORTATION EXPENSE								
Direct Commodity Costs								
Standard commodity transportation cost	$163,000	Analyze the prepaid shipments of each commodity by territories and apply territorial standard costs as explained on pages 53 to 57.				$77,000	$47,000	$39,000
WAREHOUSING AND HANDLING EXPENSE								
Direct Commodity Cost								
Standard warehousing and handling cost	$ 25,000	Charged to commodities on a standard cost basis as explained on pages 57 to 59.				$10,000	$ 9,000	$ 6,000
CREDIT AND COLLECTION EXPENSE								
Semi-Direct Commodity Costs								
Credit approval and administration	$ 8,000	Number of orders	40	30	30	$ 3,200	$ 2,400	$ 2,400
Clerical cost of handling receivables	9,000	Number of invoices	30	30	40	2,700	2,700	3,600
Collection costs	2,000	Number of invoices	30	30	40	600	600	800
		Actual product losses from past experience as explained on page 98						
Bad debt losses	4,000		20	30	50	800	1,200	2,000
Taxes on receivables	4,000	Controller's estimate	40	35	25	1,600	1,400	1,000
Total credit and collection expense	$ 27,000					$ 8,900	$ 8,300	$ 9,800
FINANCIAL EXPENSE (including interest on invested capital at 5%)								
Semi-Direct Commodity Costs								
Distribution share of total financial costs as explained on pages 61 to 65	$150,000	Distributed to commodities on basis of financial requirements as illustrated on pages 99 to 101.				$70,000	$50,000	$30,000

FIGURE 18. Analysis of Transportation, Warehousing, Credit, and Financial Expenses by Commodities

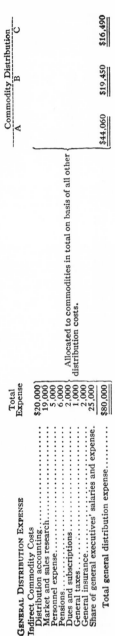

GENERAL DISTRIBUTION EXPENSE	Total Expense	Commodity Distribution		
		A	B	C
Indirect Commodity Costs				
Distribution accounting................	$20,000			
Market and sales research.............	19,000			
Personnel expense.....................	5,000			
Pensions..............................	6,000			
Dues and subscriptions................	2,000			
General taxes.........................	1,000			
General insurance.....................	2,000			
Share of general executives' salaries and expense.	25,000			
Total general distribution expense...........	$80,000	$44,060	$19,450	$16,490

Allocated to commodities in total on basis of all other distribution costs.

FIGURE 19. Analysis of General Distribution Expense by Commodities

COMMODITY EXPENSE	Total Expense	Commodities		
		A	B	C
Summary of Commodity Costs by Functions				
Direct selling.......................	$ 445,000	$202,950	$144,050	$ 98,000
Advertising and sales promotional...	385,000	280,000	40,000	65,000
Transportation......................	163,000	77,000	47,000	39,000
Warehousing and handling............	25,000	10,000	9,000	6,000
Credit and collection...............	27,000	8,900	8,300	9,800
Financial...........................	150,000	70,000	50,000	30,000
General.............................	80,000	44,060	19,450	16,490
Total distribution costs............	$1,275,000	$692,910	$317,800	$264,290
Summary by Directness of Commodity Relationship				
Direct..............................	$ 845,000	$490,000	$185,000	$170,000
Semi-direct.........................	262,000	119,600	84,200	58,200
Indirect............................	168,000	83,310	48,600	36,090
Total distribution costs............	$1,275,000	$692,910	$317,800	$264,290

FIGURE 20. Summary of Commodity Expense Analysis

STATEMENT OF PROFIT AND LOSS BY COMMODITIES

			Commodities	
	Total	A	B	C
Gross Sales	$3,450,000	$1,645,000	$1,020,000	$785,000
Less Sales Deductions	75,000	45,000	20,000	10,000
Net Sales	3,375,000	1,600,000	1,000,000	775,000
Cost of Goods Sold	2,000,000	1,050,000	585,000	365,000
Gross Profit	1,375,000	550,000	415,000	410,000
Direct Commodity Distribution Costs	845,000	490,000	185,000	170,000
Profit Remaining after Direct Costs	530,000	60,000	230,000	240,000
Semi-Direct Commodity Distribution Costs	262,000	119,600	84,200	58,200
Profit Remaining after Semi-Direct Costs	268,000	(59,600)	145,800	181,800
Indirect Commodity Distribution Costs	168,000	83,310	48,600	36,090
Profit Remaining after all Production and Distribution Costs (Including interest on invested capital at 5%)	$ 100,000	$ (142,910)	$ 97,200	$145,710

Percentages of Gross Sales

	Total	A	B	C
Sales Deductions	2.2	2.7	2.	1.3

Percentages of Net Sales

	Total	A	B	C
Gross Profit	40.7	34.4	41.5	52.9
Direct Distribution Costs	25.0	30.6	18.5	21.9
Semi-Direct Distribution Costs	7.8	7.5	8.4	7.5
Total Direct and Semi-Direct Distribution Costs	32.8	38.1	26.9	29.4
Indirect Distribution Costs	5.0	5.2	4.9	4.7
Total All Distribution Costs	37.8	43.3	31.8	34.1

Percentages of Gross Profit

	Total	A	B	C
Direct Distribution Costs	61.5	89.1	44.6	41.5
Total Direct and Semi-Direct Distribution Costs	80.5	110.8	64.9	55.7
Total All Distribution Costs	92.7	126.0	76.6	64.5

FIGURE 21. Statement of Profit and Loss by Commodities

Simplified Method of Analyses of Distribution Costs by Commodities.—Where the method of cost analysis as described in the foregoing pages involves more clerical effort than seems justified by the importance of the cost items, simpler procedures can be developed. As an illustration of a simpler plan, assume that a manufacturing concern classifies its distribution cost as follows:

Outside Sales Expense
  Jobber salesmen
  Dealer salesmen

Administrative and Office Expense
  Sales records
  Order and billing
  Traffic
  Transcribing
  Filing
  Statistical
  Accounting
  Credit and accounts receivable
  Administrative

Warehouse Expense
  Warehouse salaries
  Warehouse expense
  Trucking

Advertising

As a result of special studies, the concern establishes bases by which these expenses are to be distributed to the various lines of product. These are illustrated in Figure 22. It is determined, for example, that 50% of the cost of jobber salesmen should be distributed to lines of product in proportion to sales value, while the remaining 50% should be distributed in accordance with the number of jobbers to whom the products are sold. Figure 23 illustrates the analysis of the actual expenses by factors of variability. For example, there is $60,000 of expense of jobber salesmen. Of this amount, $30,000 is to be distributed to lines of product in proportion to sales value, and $30,000 according to the number of jobbers handling the various lines of product. Figures 24 and 25 illustrate the method by which the costs are finally distributed to classes of products. The factors of distribution and the percentages assigned are illustrative rather than representative of those applicable in any particular line of business.

The five factors of variability shown in Figures 22 and 23 are en-

	Direct	Sales Value	Number Dealers	Number Jobbers	Number Orders	Shipments Tonnage
Outside Sales Expense						
Jobber salesmen		50%		50%		
Dealer salesmen			100%			
Administrative and Office Expense						
Sales records			20	30	50%	
Order and billing					100	
Traffic					100	
Transcribing		50	20	30	75	
Filing				25	100	
Statistical		100				
Accounting				100		
Credit		50	20	30		
Administrative						
Warehouse Expense						
Warehouse salaries					100	
Warehouse expense					100	
Trucking						100%
Advertising	100%					

FIGURE 22. Chart of Allocation of Distribution Costs Showing Percentage of Each Cost Item to Which Particular Factors of Variability (bases) Are to Be Applied

FACTORS OF VARIABILITY

	Total	Direct	Sales Value	Number Dealers	Number Jobbers	Number Orders	Shipments Tonnage
Outside Sales Expense							
Jobber salesmen	$ 60,000		$30,000		$30,000		
Dealer salesmen	100,000			$100,000			
Administrative and Office Expense							
Sales records	3,000			600	900	$ 1,500	
Order and billing	15,000					15,000	
Traffic	2,500					2,500	
Transcribing	3,000		1,500	600	900		
Filing	1,500				375	1,125	
Statistical	3,000					3,000	
Accounting	9,000		9,000				
Credit	6,000				6,000		
Administrative	12,000		6,000	2,400	3,600		
Warehouse Expense							
Warehouse salaries	9,000					9,000	
Warehouse expense	11,000					11,000	
Trucking	15,000						$15,000
Advertising	150,000	$150,000					
Total	$400,000	$150,000	$46,500	$103,600	$41,775	$43,125	$15,000

FIGURE 23. Analysis of Distribution Costs According to Factors of Variability in Relation to Commodities

Bases of Allocation	Total	Commodities		
		A	B	C
Sales value..........	100%	50%	40%	10%
Number of dealers.......	100	40	40	20
Number of jobbers........	100	33	50	17
Number of orders.........	100	10	40	50
Shipments—tonnage.......	100	75	20	5

FIGURE 24. Bases of Allocation Expressed in Commodity Percentages (figures assumed)

Bases of Allocation	Amount of the Total Cost to be Allocated by the Individual Bases		Share of Cost Allocated to Each Commodity by Percentage Shown in Figure 23					
			A		B		C	
Sales value............	100%	$ 46,500	50%	$23,250	40%	$18,600	10%	$4,650
Number of dealers........	100	103,600	40	41,440	40	41,440	20	20,720
Number of jobbers........	100	41,775	33	13,925	50	20,888	17	6,962
Number of orders........	100	43,125	10	4,313	40	17,250	50	21,562
Shipments—tonnage.......	100	15,000	75	11,250	20	3,000	5	750
Charged directly (no basis is required; division is assumed)........	100	150,000		60,000		80,000		10,000
Total............	100%	$400,000	39%	$154,178	45%	$181,178	16%	$64,644

FIGURE 25. Distribution of Costs in Accordance with Selected Bases of Allocation

titled bases of allocation in Figures 24 and 25 to indicate more precisely their function in the process of assigning costs to commodity classes. The commodity percentages shown in Figure 24 express the relative importance of each commodity class with regard to a particular allocation factor. Thus, of the amount of total cost assignable to commodities on the basis of sales value, Class A will receive 50% because it is assumed that one-half of the total sales value is accounted for by this class. In like manner, Class B will bear 40% of the cost and Class C, 10%. Note that the percentages must be read horizontally by bases of allocation. The results of applying the percentages to the dollar amounts of cost developed in Figure 23 may be seen in Figure 25.

With reference to Figure 24, no difficulty is experienced in understanding the commodity percentage distributions of sales value and tonnage shipments. Some explanatory details, however, are necessary for proper interpretation of the percentages shown for the remaining allocation bases—numbers of dealers, jobbers, and orders. It may be safely assumed, for example, that some dealers handle only one class of commodities, whereas others handle two or even all three of the lines. Under such circumstances the sum obtained by adding together the number of dealers for each commodity class will exceed the true number of dealer accounts. In support of this statement let it be assumed that a breakdown of dealers by classes of commodities discloses the following information:

Commodities Handled	Number of Dealers
A only	25
B only	25
A and B	15
A, B, and C	40
Total accounts	105

The percentages shown in Figure 24 cannot be determined, however, until a segregation is made of the dealers handling each group of commodities. The necessary information is presented below.

Commodity A Dealers		Commodity B Dealers		Commodity C Dealers	
Handle A only ...	25	Handle B only ...	25	Handle A, B, and C	40
Handle A and B ..	15	Handle A and B ..	15		
Handle A, B, and C	40	Handle A, B, and C	40		
Total	80	Total	80	Total	40
	(40%)		(40%)		(20%)

The respective totals produce a grand total of 200 dealers, a figure in excess of the true dealer total by 95. The base of the desired percentages (shown in the parentheses) must be 200, nevertheless, if the percentages are to add to 100.

The procedure outlined above applies equally well to the determination of commodity percentages for the number of jobbers and the number of orders. In either case percentages are calculated, according to the assumption made in the dealer example, on bases which reflect a certain amount of duplication in the number of jobbers or orders.

CHAPTER 6

ANALYSIS BY CHANNELS OF DISTRIBUTION AND METHODS OF SALE

Definition.—By channel of distribution is meant the course taken in the transfer of title, irrespective of the route taken by the physical goods themselves. Thus, a producer may sell to consumers, retailers, wholesalers, or to any combination of these. Wholesalers sell typically to retailers but may sell also to manufacturers, other wholesalers, or large consumers. Retailers sell typically to consumers, but may sell also to wholesalers or other retailers. Again, any of the three typical marketing agencies may employ the services of brokers, commission men, or sales agents who assist in effecting sales, but do not take title to the goods. While almost every combination of agencies may be found in marketing practice, the usual channels of distribution for consumer goods are:

1. Producer to consumer
2. Producer to retailer to consumer
3. Producer to wholesaler to retailer to consumer

Closely allied to the subject of channels of distribution is the consideration of methods of sale. The following are typical of the methods of sale employed through the various channels:

Producer to consumer
    Salesmen who secure orders
    Salesmen who sell and deliver
    Mail order
    Company stores
    House sales—not delivered
    House sales—delivered

Producer to retailer
    Salesmen who secure orders
    Salesmen who sell and deliver
    Mail order
    House sales—not delivered
    House sales—delivered

Producer to wholesaler
  Salesmen
  Mail order
  House sales—not delivered

Wholesaler to retailer
  Salesmen who secure orders
  Salesmen who sell and deliver
  Mail order
  House sales—not delivered
  House sales—delivered

Retailer to consumer
  Over-the-counter—not delivered
  Over-the-counter—delivered
  Salesmen who secure orders
  Salesmen who sell and deliver
  Mail order

Purpose of Analysis by Channels.—It is apparent that a considerable choice of channels and methods is available and many concerns find it desirable to use a number of different combinations in order to reach different classes of customers or markets. The purpose of an analysis of distribution costs by channels is to direct the sales activity into the most profitable channels. Not only must initial selection of channels and methods be made, but also cost trends must be scrutinized for needed revision as circumstances change. In some concerns the sales activity is organized and directed on the basis of channels. For example, separate division of the sales organization may direct the work of selling to jobbers and large industrial consumers. If separate groups of salesmen are used in the different channels, much of the cost can be directly related to individual channels. An analysis of the costs, in such cases, assists greatly in correctly placing responsibility for the control of the costs.

Factors Involved in Selection of Channels.—While the cost is ultimately the most important factor in the selection of channels of distribution, other important factors must be considered. There is, for example, the problem of market control. A manufacturer may find that his business is most profitable for the moment if he sells exclusively to a few large industrial consumers, or to one or two mail order or chain concerns, rather than if he promotes a wide sale through jobbers or smaller industrial consumers; but if he selects the former channels, he runs the risk of a restricted market. In time his margin of profit may be reduced and his policy dictated by a few customers upon whom he is largely dependent.

Again, the character of the demand and nature of the market must be considered. For example, where buyers have little information concerning the product and where considerable amounts must be spent for advertising, demonstrations, missionary selling, and other special promotional effort, the producer may find it necessary to select channels and methods which carry him directly to the ultimate consumer. On the other hand, if buyers are widely scattered and if considerable outlays are required for transportation, storage, and financing, intermediate agencies may be more effective.

Likewise, the character of the product may be a factor. For example, if highly specialized installation and maintenance service is required, the manufacturer alone may be able to provide it. To some extent, the scale of production is a factor. Mass producers must have mass distribution and may find it necessary to employ several channels to secure the necessary sales volume. Moreover, the financial strength of a producer is often a factor. If the producer is financially strong, he may perform his own marketing functions; if he is weak, he may require the assistance of external agencies.

Among other factors which affect the choice of channels may be noted the following:

1. Size and frequency of orders
2. Regularity of demand
3. Extent to which products can be sold by advertising
4. Frequency of repeat sales
5. Weight of product in relation to price
6. Newness of product
7. Degree of standardization of products and frequency of changes in design
8. Degree of promptness in delivery required
9. Technical knowledge required in selling and servicing the product
10. Proximity of the market to producing plants
11. Importance of personal acquaintanceship with buyers

While it is beyond the scope of this book to consider in detail the application of such factors in the selection of distribution channels and methods, they should be thoroughly understood by both marketing and accounting executives in any attempt to analyze and interpret data relative to the cost and profitability of the various channels.

When an Analysis by Channels Should Be Made.—Some concerns use, and can use, only one method of distribution. Obviously, in such cases, no analysis of cost by channels is required. Where several channels and methods are employed, the cost should be periodically examined to ascertain any unfavorable trends. Where the sales organization and effort is formed largely on the basis of channels, a continuous analysis of cost and profit should be made for purposes of adequate cost control.

Method of Channel Analysis.—The basic procedure for an analysis of distribution costs by channels of distribution is similar to that suggested in the preceding chapters for territorial and commodity analysis. The specific steps may be repeated as follows:

1. Determine the gross profit by channels of distribution.
2. Accumulate the direct channel distribution costs and deduct these from the gross profit to determine the *profit after direct costs* for each channel.
3. Distribute to the channels their respective shares of the semidirect costs and deduct these to arrive at a channel *profit after semidirect costs*.
4. Allocate to the channels their respective shares of the general or indirect costs and deduct these to arrive at the final channel *net profit*.
5. Make such subanalyses of the results by channels as may be deemed useful (e.g., by territories, products, size of orders, customers, etc.).

Bases of Allocation.—As in the case of the analyses discussed in previous chapters, the bases of allocation, and the classification of costs as to directness of relationship, must vary widely with local conditions. No two concerns present an identical problem. The bases suggested in the outline immediately following must be taken as purely illustrative.

Allocation of Direct Selling Expense to Channels of Distribution.—

DIRECT COSTS. The following items of direct selling expense can usually be charged directly to particular channels:

1. Salaries and expense of sales administrators and supervisors whose efforts are directed to particular channels
2. Clerical salaries and office expense of sales offices related to particular channels
3. Salaries, commissions, traveling, and automobile expense of salesmen working in particular channels
4. Commissions paid to agents, brokers, and consignees
5. Entertainment expense directed to particular channels
6. Education and training of salesmen for particular channels

7. Insurance and taxes incident to payroll of individual channel sales personnel

8. Spoiled work chargeable to salesmen

9. Sales and excise taxes

10. Communication, supplies, occupancy, and general expense of sales offices related to particular channels

SEMIDIRECT COSTS.

1. *Salaries, commissions, and traveling expense of salesmen covering more than one channel.* This cost should be allocated on the basis of time spent by salesmen with the customers falling within each channel classification. If this is approximately the same with each type of customer, the cost may be distributed on the basis of the number of calls made. Where the time varies considerably, time sheets may be required showing the time spent with each type of customer. No general rule can be given as to the method of computing the time. Where approximately the same amount of traveling time is necessary to reach all types of customers, the distribution of the traveling expense to channels can be made on the basis of the actual calling time used with the customers representing the different channels. Where the traveling time varies considerably, the time sheet of each salesman must be analyzed for a fair apportionment.

2. *Sales clerical expense.* This group of expenses includes the cost of sales clerical salaries, office supplies, and insurance and tax charges related to the sales clerical payroll.

The sales clerical force performs the functions of order writing, maintenance of price and discount files, filing, billing, adjustments, communications, etc. If the sales clerical expense is relatively large, the work is usually departmentalized, and substantially accurate bases of allocation can then be found for each clerical function. Thus, the cost of order writing and billing may be distributed to channels according to the number of orders, the number of billing lines, or the number of invoices. When the work is not departmentalized, some one of these bases or the number of accounts will usually serve. Where such analysis is not practicable, the cost may be considered as an indirect item as noted below.

3. *Education and training of sales force.* This expense item includes the cost of preparing training manuals, maintenance of sales training schools, preparation and distribution of "salesmen's helps," sales conventions, etc.

Where the sales force of the different channels is trained separately, this cost can be charged directly. Where this is not the case, the cost may be allocated on the basis of salesmen's compensation (including both direct and semidirect charges for compensation). Where this item is relatively unimportant, it may be included with general selling expense and distributed as an indirect cost.

4. *Insurance and taxes on payroll of salesmen covering more than one channel.* These items, such as workmen's compensation, life and fidelity insurance, and social security taxes on salesmen covering several channels, should be distributed on the basis of salesmen's compensation (including both direct and semidirect charges for compensation).

INDIRECT COSTS. The following cost items must, as a rule, be classified as indirect costs in an analysis by channels of distribution.

Cost Items	Suggested Bases of Allocation
1. Salaries and expense of sales executives and supervisors	Number of salesmen Salesmen's compensation Total direct and semidirect costs
2. Sales clerical expense (when not considered as semidirect)	Number of sales transactions Number of shipments Number of invoices Number of billing lines Total direct and semidirect costs
3. Entertainment not identifiable with individual channels	Salesmen's salaries Executive estimate
4. Communication (that part not charged directly as noted above)	Number of accounts Number of orders Number of sales transactions Number of invoices
5. General selling expense—insurance and taxes on sales office facilities and general payroll, occupancy, and miscellaneous general sales office expense	Total direct and semidirect costs

Allocation of Advertising and Sales Promotional Expense to Channels of Distribution.—As in previous analyses, the advertising and sales promotional expense should first be resolved into individual media costs. (See pages 49 to 52.) Where particular media costs pertain to individual channels they should be charged directly to those channels. For example, dealer helps designed for the use of jobbers and advertising in trade journals which are read chiefly by jobbers should be charged to the wholesale channel. Demonstrations made to industrial consumers should be charged to the industrial trade. Where particular media pertain to several channels, one plan of analysis which may be used is first to allocate the cost to products (as explained on

pages 93 to 95), then to distribute the individual product costs to channels on the basis of product sales through the various channels. If this
plan is used, care must be exercised in the classification of products;
thus, if a certain product is sold under a brand name, widely advertised,
to jobbers and the identical product is sold to industrial consumers
without the brand identification, it must be classified as two separate
products.

To illustrate this procedure, assume that a concern has the following
advertising costs:

Media	Cost
General publications	$ 50,000
Trade journals	20,000
Dealer helps	20,000
Demonstrations	10,000
Total	$100,000

It may be assumed further that the company sells to jobbers and to
large industrial consumers. The dealer helps pertain only to jobbers,
the demonstrations only to industrial concerns, and the general publications and trade journals benefit sales through both channels. Four different products are sold as follows:

A   To jobbers only
B   To both jobbers and industrial consumers
C   To both jobbers and industrial consumers
D   To industrial consumers only

The distribution would then be as follows:

Media	Total Cost	Joint Channel Charges	Direct Channel Charges Jobbers	Industrial
General publications	$ 50,000	$50,000		
Trade journals	20,000	20,000		
Dealer helps	20,000		$20,000	
Demonstrations	10,000			$10,000
Total	$100,000	$70,000	$20,000	$10,000

DISTRIBUTION OF JOINT CHANNEL CHARGES TO PRODUCTS

(Figures assumed; method as explained in Chapter 5)

Media	Total	A	B	C	D
General publications	$50,000	$30,000	$20,000		
Trade journals	20,000		5,000	$5,000	$10,000
Total	$70,000	$30,000	$25,000	$5,000	$10,000

ANALYSIS OF PRODUCT SALES BY CHANNELS

Product	Total Sales	Jobber		Industrial	
		Sales	Per Cent of Total	Sales	Per Cent of Total
A	$ 500,000	$ 500,000	100	None	None
B	250,000	200,000	80	$ 50,000	20
C	1,000,000	800,000	80	200,000	20
D	1,000,000	None	None	1,000,000	100
	$2,750,000	$1,500,000		$1,250,000	

DISTRIBUTION OF PRODUCT CHARGES TO CHANNELS ON THE BASIS OF SALES

Product	Total	Jobber		Industrial	
		Per Cent	Amount	Per Cent	Amount
A	$30,000	100	$30,000	None	None
B	25,000	80	20,000	20	$ 5,000
C	5,000	80	4,000	20	1,000
D	10,000	None	None	100	10,000
	$70,000		$54,000		$16,000

	Total	Jobber	Industrial
Direct channel charges			
Dealer helps	$ 20,000	$20,000	None
Demonstrations	10,000	None	$10,000
Joint channel charges distributed first to products then to channels on basis of sales	70,000	54,000	16,000
Total	$100,000	$74,000	$26,000

In the above illustration, the product advertising charges are apportioned to channels on the basis of the product sales through each channel. It should be noted, however, that this pertains only to such advertising costs as actually benefit such channels. Obviously, some part of such product costs should be charged to each channel. A question may be raised as to whether or not sales is an equitable basis. If it appears not to be, the division must be left to the judgment of the executives.

Direct media charges should be classified as direct costs of channels; apportioned charges should be classified as semidirect.

Allocation of Transportation Expense to Channels of Distribution.—Where all products are sold through all channels, the allocation of transportation costs to channels may require an analysis of products sold by territories and a further analysis of the products sold in each territory by channels of distribution. If standard transportation costs are established for each product to each territory (as explained on pages 53 to 57), and it is known through what channels the products are sold in each territory, it is then possible to determine the cost by channels.

Where different channels are employed for different products, the problem is much simpler. Here it may be possible to allocate the charges directly. This is particularly true where the transportation services are purchased from various outside agencies.

In concerns which make local deliveries to customers, it is frequently necessary to divide the transportation costs between those entailed in moving the goods from factories to branch warehouses, and those required to make deliveries from warehouses to customers. This may require the development of two separate sets of transportation cost standards. In some instances the cost of transporting the goods to the warehouses will be added to the cost of the goods and not considered as a cost of distribution.

Transportation costs should be considered as either direct or semidirect costs of channels, usually the former.

Allocation of Warehousing and Handling Expense by Channels of Distribution.—The warehousing plan varies so greatly in different concerns as to make it difficult to generalize on cost analysis procedure. In some concerns, the warehousing cost relates entirely to jobber sales, industrial shipments being made direct upon completion in the factory. In other instances the warehousing is done to accommodate both jobber and industrial customers. Where the warehousing and handling costs relate to several channels, it is usually desirable to establish standard product warehousing costs, analyze products by channels, and apply the standard product costs by channels accordingly.

The warehousing cost should be classified as a direct or semidirect cost of channels, usually the former.

Allocation of Credit and Collection Expense to Channels of Distribution.—As indicated in the preceding chapters, the credit and collection costs group themselves into five natural divisions as follows:

1. Cost of credit approval and administration
2. Cost of clerical handling of receivables
3. Collection costs
4. Bad debt losses
5. Taxes on receivables

The cost of extending credit and making collections depends on the financial responsibility of each customer, and on the amount and frequency of his purchases. Since these factors are likely to vary in different channels, each division of the cost should be considered separately. The individual expense items entering into each division of cost are indicated on pages 96 to 98. Methods of allocating the costs to channels may be indicated as follows:

1. *Credit approval and administration.* This item of cost should be allocated on the basis of the number of accounts carried for each channel or the number of orders received through each channel.

2. *Clerical cost of handling receivables.* The cost of posting charges follows closely the number of invoices, the issuing of monthly statements and the posting of credits follows more closely the number of accounts, and miscellaneous adjustments and references may follow either the number of invoices or the number of accounts. Where these costs are considerable in amount and the clerical work departmentalized, these different bases may be used. Usually, however, a standard clerical cost per invoice or per account—for each channel—can be established to cover the entire cost; or the entire cost can be equitably distributed to channels on the basis of either the number of invoices or the number of accounts.

3. *Collection costs.* This cost usually follows the number of accounts and can be distributed accordingly.

4. *Bad debt losses.* Where bad debt losses are taken as realized, they should be analyzed by channels and charged directly. Where reserves are provided, the charges should be allocated to channels on the same basis as that used in determining the amount to be credited to the reserve. Where the credit to the reserve is based on net sales or net credit sales, it frequently happens that a different rate will be applied on sales through different channels.

5. *Taxes on receivables.* Where the same credit terms are applied to customers purchasing through all channels, this cost can be distributed on the basis of net sales. Where credit terms vary, the sales factor should be weighted by the average number of days accounts are outstanding under the various terms.

Credit and collection expense may be considered as a direct or semi-direct cost of channels, depending upon the extent to which the analysis is carried in making its distribution. Usually the relationship of the cost to channels will be sufficiently close as to consider it a direct cost.

Allocation of Financial Expense to Channels of Distribution.—

The allocation of financial expenses to channels of distribution should follow the same general plan as that outlined for territories on pages 61 to 65. The steps there suggested are:

1. To determine the total financial cost of the entire business.
2. To divide the financial cost as between production, distribution, and nonoperating activities.
3. To allocate the distribution share of the financial expense to the various channels of distribution.

The first two steps are fully explained on pages 62 to 64. With reference to the third step, the financial requirements of the individual channels may be ascertained in the following manner:

Working fund requirements may be based upon the total direct and semidirect distribution expenditures (other than financial).

Receivables incident to the various channels can be determined by direct inspection of receivable records.

Inventory requirements of the various channels are frequently difficult to determine. If the rate of inventory turnover is approximately the same, for particular products, through all channels employed, these requirements can be ascertained by analyzing the cost of goods sold first by channels and then by products within each channel. If then the product costs of a particular channel are divided by their respective average rates of turnover the inventory requirements of the channel can be determined. It is frequently the case, however, that the rate of inventory turnover for a particular product varies as between channels. In such cases, the inventory requirements of the various channels can best be determined by means of special studies made by the controller.

Physical facility requirements of channels may be ascertained by means of a weighted index as explained on pages 100 to 101.

Assuming the necessary figures, the foregoing method may be illustrated as follows:

FACTORS OF DISTRIBUTION

		Channels		
	Total	Jobbers	Direct to Large Retailers	Industrial Consumers
Percentage of direct and semidirect distribution costs of individual channels to total as a basis for allocating working funds	100%	20%	50%	30%
Percentage of average receivables to total as a basis for allocating receivables	100	30	40	30
Percentage of inventory requirements to total as determined by controller's estimate	100	20	40	40
Weighted index as a basis for allocating physical facilities	100	10	30	60

ALLOCATION OF INVESTMENT

	Total (Amounts Assumed)	Channels		
		Jobbers	Direct to Large Retailers	Industrial Consumers
Working funds	($ 20,000)	($ 4,000)	($ 10,000)	($ 6,000)
Receivables	700,000	210,000	280,000	210,000
Inventories	600,000	120,000	240,000	240,000
Physical facilities	800,000	80,000	240,000	480,000
Total	$2,080,000	$406,000	$750,000	$924,000
Percentage of total	100.0%	19.5%	36.1%	44.4%
Allocation of distribution financial expense (total amount assumed)	$ 143,284	$ 27,940	$ 51,726	$ 63,618

As in the case of other analyses, this method of allocating financial expenses to channels may be used either with or without the inclusion of interest on investment as a part of the cost. The financial expense should usually be classified as a semidirect cost.

Allocation of General Distribution Expenses to Channels of Distribution.—As in the case of previous analyses (see pages 65 to 67), these items are usually of insufficient importance to distribute separately. As a rule, they can be equitably distributed to channels on the basis of all other distribution costs. They should be classified as indirect costs.

Subanalyses of Costs by Channels of Distribution.—An analysis of costs by channels of distribution is usually only a beginning in an attempt to direct sales effort profitably. The cost of particular channels must frequently be further analyzed by territories, commodities, individual customers, etc., in order to reach to specific points of weakness and to provide a basis of definite action.

Corrective Action.—The analysis of distribution costs by channels of distribution will, in rare instances, demonstrate that certain channels should be abandoned. More often, however, the results of this and related subanalyses will be to direct attention to the desirability of certain changes in methods, products, territories, etc., within the various channels employed, to the end of making the sales effort more productive.

Illustrative Analysis.—In general, the procedure for analysis by channels of distribution will follow the same plan as that outlined for territories and commodities on pages 74 to 82 and pages 102 to 107, respectively.

Analysis by Methods of Sale.—As explained on page 114, an analysis of costs by channels of distribution is closely allied to that of methods of sale; in fact, the line of distinction between channels and methods frequently disappears in so far as practical operations are concerned. Moreover, there is a close relationship between the analyses by channels and methods on the one hand, and customers or classes of customers on the other. The latter is discussed more specifically in the following chapter.

The methods employed in selling and distributing goods are so numerous and varied as to make any generalization concerning the procedure of analysis virtually useless. A workable program for analyzing costs by methods of sale may, however, be suggested by an illustration drawn from the experience of a company engaged in the processing and marketing of a line of meats and packaged food products. This concern employs three methods of sale, described as follows:

1. *Route sales.* These are sales made to independent retailers by route salesmen who call on the retailers and take orders for subsequent delivery in company trucks from the plant.

2. *Plant sales.* These are sales made to customers (including independent retailers, chain store buyers, and wholesalers) who wish to inspect products at the plant and place orders for subsequent delivery in company trucks.

3. *F.O.B. sales.* These are sales made by telephone or by "house" salesmen to large buyers of all kinds who pick up the goods at the plant shipping platform and provide their own transportation service.

The distribution activities of the company which may be considered pertinent to the analysis by methods of sale are grouped into four categories or functions. These consist of:

1. Direct selling
2. Order filling and handling
3. Delivery
4. Sales accounting

In analyzing its costs this company believed that it would be highly useful to relate as many items of cost as possible to some factor of variability which could be used as a service factor for subsequent application of distribution costs to customers, orders, or products. Although no one factor seemed to influence all costs in the same way, experience tended to show that variations in the *number of orders* were of greatest significance in the amount of expense incurred in each of the functional cost groups. With reference to direct selling, the amount of expense incurred for plant salesmen was clearly affected by the volume of orders, and for route salesmen expense was closely tied to the number of calls, which bore a close identity to the number of orders obtained. Delivery cost was likewise directly related to orders through the medium of the number of stops made by company trucks. Although the number of order or invoice lines was a somewhat better measure of cost variability for order filling and handling and for sales accounting, nevertheless the number of orders processed was still an influential factor with regard to the costs of these two functions. Hence the company decided to separate the costs of each function into those expense items which were variable according to the number of orders and those which had no logical relationship to order activity. The former costs were termed "variable" and the latter were grouped as "overhead."

Function and Cost Item	Route Sales		Plant Sales		F.O.B. Sales	
	Variable	Overhead	Variable	Overhead	Variable	Overhead
DIRECT SELLING						
Salaries						
Route salesmen	$5,492	....	$ 436	....	....	....
Plant salesmen	....	....	1,700	....	$1,250	....
Travel and communication	2,380	....	228	....	166	....
Other selling expense ..	....	$1,628	....	$ 744	....	$ 668
Total	$7,872	$1,628	$2,364	$ 744	$1,416	$ 668
ORDER FILLING AND HANDLING						
Warehouse wages	$2,630	....	$ 838	....	....	$ 494
Containers	470	....	134	....	....	....
Loading expense	....	$ 638	....	$ 286	....	262
Total	$3,100	$ 638	$ 972	$ 286	....	$ 756
DELIVERY						
Drivers' wages	$3,662	....	$1,140	....	....	....
Vehicle operation	2,386	....	702	....	....	....
Maintenance	....	$1,234	....	$ 582	....	....
Total	$6,048	$1,234	$1,842	$ 582	....	....
SALES ACCOUNTING						
Billing and posting	$1,220	....	$ 384	....	$ 124	....
Supplies	170	....	54	....	12	....
Other clerical expense ..	....	$ 282	....	$ 90	....	$ 28
Total	$1,390	$ 282	$ 438	$ 90	$ 136	$ 28
Total distribution expense	$18,410	$3,782	$5,616	$1,702	$1,552	$1,452
Total number of orders ..	9,800		3,500		500	
Total hundredweight (cwt.)	11,200		5,200		4,700	

FIGURE 26. Illustrative Analysis of Distribution Costs by Methods of Sale

A representative month's operations were selected for analysis and the results for each method of sale were set forth in the form shown in Figure 26. It will be noted that route sales and plant sales required the performance of all the functions. F.O.B. sales necessitated no delivery expense and involved no order filling and handling expense identifiable as variable with the number of orders.

The information contained in Figure 26 was summarized by functions and reduced to a cost-per-order basis as follows:

Function	Variable Cost per Order		
	Route Sales	Plant Sales	F.O.B. Sales
Direct selling	$ .80	$ .68	$2.83
Order filling and handling	.32	.28	....
Delivery	.62	.53	....
Sales accounting	.14	.12	.27
Total variable cost per order	$1.88	$1.61	$3.10
Per cwt. cost:			
Total variable cost per cwt.	$1.64	$1.08	$ .33
Overhead cost per cwt.	.34	.33	.31
Total cost per cwt.	$1.98	$1.41	$ .64

Only the variable order costs were included in the per order cost computations. In addition, a cost per cwt. was determined for the total variable cost of each method of sale and for the overhead cost associated with each method. Per cwt. costs are useful in assessing the role which size of order (measured in physical volume) plays in the costs of each method of sale. For example, route sales and plant sales have fairly similar costs per order, but plant sales have a much lower cost per cwt. because of the larger size of order commonly received. F.O.B. sales have a high cost per order but an extremely low cost per cwt., a result attributable to the large orders arising from the quantity buying habits of, and the greater selling time and effort devoted to, the relatively few customers who purchase in this way.

CHAPTER 7

ANALYSIS BY CUSTOMERS

The Basis of Customer Analysis.—An analysis of distribution costs by channels of distribution, as discussed in the preceding chapter, is in reality an analysis by customers. Such analysis is, however, directed to large groups of customers and closely allied to methods of sale. It is desired here to discuss an extension of that analysis to smaller groups of customers or, alternatively, to typical customers within prescribed classes.

The need for this analysis is based on the fact that some customers require or receive more distribution effort, in proportion to sales and profit, than others. It costs more to sell to some types of customers than to others. Again, some customers require more distribution services than others, particularly in relation to such services as warehousing, delivery, financing, etc. Finally, different types of customers frequently demand different prices, particularly where the classification rests upon the amount of annual purchases or the size of individual orders.

Such differences may exist between customers located within the same territorial divisions or between customers who buy the same goods; hence, the profitability of their business is not revealed by territorial or commodity analyses.

Purpose of Customer Analysis.—The analysis by customers must proceed to a determination of the variation in distribution services required, the cost of such services, and the price differentials which are justified. More specifically, the purposes of analyzing distribution costs by customers are:

1. To aid in selecting profitable classes of customers
2. To intelligently adjust prices to the service required
3. To detect weakness and excessive costs in distribution methods

There is a natural tendency for sales executives to become volume-minded. Not infrequently they acquire the "empire conquest" idea—a desire to secure volume at any cost. An analysis of costs by classes of customers will temper this enthusiasm and assist in guiding it into profitable directions. Many concerns sell to classes of customers whose business they can never hope to make profitable.

If a concern performs its services efficiently and selects only those classes of customers which, in the long run, it can supply as well as or better than competitors, it is entitled to a profit on each customer. If the cost of supplying one customer is more than that of another, the price should vary accordingly. While the analysis of cost is seldom extended to each individual customer, it should extend to all classes or groups of customers between which any material difference in costs exists. In many concerns, little or no distinction is made between customers receiving the minimum and maximum of service rendered. Some customers obviously pay for more than they receive; others, less. This leaves the way open for alert competitors to "pick off" the profitable accounts which do not need the full service offered. While a customer should not, and in the long run cannot, be charged for marketing inefficiencies, he should be required to pay a fair price for the services demanded.

When an analysis of distribution costs by classes of customers reveals a high cost for a particular class or group it is entirely possible that the fault may lie with the company rather than with the extent of the services demanded by the customers. Unsuitable or expensive methods of distribution may be employed for particular customer groups. Salesmen may be calling more frequently than necessary, warehousing facilities may not be located properly geographically, or the sales effort to particular groups may be inefficiently directed. An analysis of costs by customer groups will detect such weakness and lead to its correction.

With the increasing trend in recent years toward unfair price and trade practice legislation, an additional reason is supplied for customer cost analysis. Such legislation and its requirements are discussed in Chapter 22.

Selecting Customer Classifications.—There is obviously no one method of customer classification suitable for all concerns; moreover, in some instances, more than one classification must be used. The basic considerations in selecting the customer groups for cost analysis purposes are: (1) the amount of distribution services required, and (2) the possibility of separation of distribution cost items. Two different groups of customers may vary widely as to their own operations, but, if they require practically the same distribution services, they should constitute one group for customer cost analysis purposes. On the other hand, where the distribution services required, by different customer groups, result to such a large degree in joint costs as to make any intelligent separation impossible, it may be necessary to restrict the analysis to those groups to which costs can reasonably be assigned. Classifications often useful are:

1. By amount of annual purchases
2. By frequency and size of orders
3. By credit rating of customers
4. By amount of advertising required
5. By location
6. By frequency of salesmen's calls
7. By nature of their operations—e.g., retailers, wholesalers, manufacturers, chain stores, mail order houses, governmental divisions, etc.

A concrete illustration of the need for customer analysis may be taken from a large office supply, book binding, and printing concern which deals in the following commodities:

1. Office stationery, forms, and supplies
2. Office furniture
3. Filing equipment and supplies
4. Legal publications
5. Legal blanks
6. Election supplies
7. Governmental records
8. Printing of bonds and stock certificates
9. Book binding
10. General commercial and legal printing

The first four items are purchased and resold, the last six are manufactured in its own plant. Some products are sold both to dealers and consumers; others, only to consumers. Its customers are classified as shown on the following page.

It will be noted from this outline that most classes of customers buy nearly all the commodities handled; however, the services performed for, and the prices granted to, the various classes of customers vary widely. A filing cabinet, for example, may be sent from the company's warehouse, by an individual delivery, to a commercial customer and carefully installed in the exact location desired; or 100 such cabinets may be ordered direct from the factory to be delivered to the office of a public utility company, the latter to make its own installation. Obviously, the price will vary as between the two customers. More than 40,000 different items are carried in stock to service all classes of customers. Many more items and much greater investment are required to provide for the needs of some classes of customers than others. Any

CUSTOMER CLASSIFICATION	COMMODITIES SOLD
C. Commercial	
C 1. Consumers	
C. 11 Large consumers	
C 111. Utilities	
C 112. Insurance companies	All items except numbers 6 and 7
C 113. Institutions	
C 114. Industrial and commercial concerns	
C 12. Small consumers	
C 2. Dealers	
G. Governmental divisions	All items
G 1. Federal	All items except numbers 6 and 8
G 2. State divisions	All items
G 201. Highway	
G 202. Liquor	
G 203. Unemployment insurance	All items except number 6
G 204. Industrial insurance	
G 205. Welfare and institutional	
G 206. All others	All items
G 3. Counties	All items
G 301. Auditors and Clerks	
G 302. Treasurers	
G 303. Recorders	
G 304. Clerks of Courts	All items except numbers 6 and 8
G 305. Probate judges	
G 306. Sheriffs	
G 307. Engineers	
G 308. Prosecuting attorneys	All items except numbers 6 and 8
G 309. Assessors	
G 310. Commissioners	All items except number 6
G 311. School superintendents	All items except numbers 6 and 8
G 312. Boards of election	All items except number 8
G 313. All others	All items except number 6
G 4. Municipal	All items except number 6
G 5. Townships	All items except number 6
G 6. School boards	All items except number 6

analysis of distribution costs in such a complex situation presents considerable difficulty.

A much simpler case is presented by a firm which manufactures pipe fittings. Here there are only two types of customers—jobbers and mail order houses. The jobbers are divided into large and small, based upon annual volume. Generally speaking, the distribution costs of all customers within each of the three groups bear a close relationship to volume.

As an illustration of the method of classifying customers for cost analysis purposes, the office supply company mentioned above analyzes distribution costs by the following customer groups:

Group 1. Large commercial consumers
Group 2. Small commercial consumers
Group 3. Large commercial dealers
Group 4. Small commercial dealers
Group 5. Federal and state divisions
Group 6. All county divisions except boards of election
Group 7. School superintendents, municipal, townships, and school boards
Group 8. Boards of election

To a considerable extent the direct selling costs and the advertising and sales promotional costs are separate for each group. Other distribution costs tend to be of a joint nature. Sales are analyzed in complete detail for all of the customer groups shown on page 132, but costs are separated only for the groups mentioned above. This situation illustrates the point that cost analysis may be more restricted than sales analysis where the factor of joint costs enters to a large degree. There is always the possibility, however, of extending the analysis within a selected cost group, when the profit of that group is unsatisfactory. This can be done by special studies directed to smaller groups or even to individual customers.

It should be noted also that a concern may use one customer classification for one product or class of products and a different classification for another product.

Customer Analysis Not Necessarily Continuous.—In most concerns it is unnecessary to continuously analyze distribution costs by classes of customers. Such analysis can be made occasionally or in the nature of special studies when changes are contemplated. A continuous analysis will usually be made of sales, and this is often sufficient to signal unprofitable accounts if occasional tests are made as to costs.

Method of Customer Analysis.—In general, two methods may be employed in analyzing distribution costs by customers. First, all customers may be classified into groups and all costs allocated either directly or by apportionment to these groups, thereby arriving at a total distribution cost for each group. Second, typical customers may be selected representing particular customer classifications and the cost ascertained for such customers.

First Method—Entire Cost by Customer Groups.—The first of these methods is illustrated in Figures 27 to 29. Here a concern manufacturing pipe fittings sells to three classes of customers—small jobbers, large jobbers, and mail order houses. The distinction between small and large jobbers is one of annual volume. Prices are uniform within each customer group, but vary as between groups. Different salesmen are employed for the different customer groups, hence their salaries, expense, and related costs can be directly allocated. Transportation services, for such goods as are delivered to customers, are purchased from outside transportation concerns; hence, this item of cost can be directly allocated. Advertising expenditures are small and pertain chiefly to descriptive catalogs.

The first step in the analysis is to separate the distribution cost items as between those which can be more or less directly related to customer groups and those which have only an indirect relationship to such groups. This separation is shown on Figures 27 and 28. These figures are illustrative only for this particular concern. Local conditions and circumstances will govern the classification to be made in each concern.

The second step is the allocation of the direct and indirect costs to customer groups. In Figure 27 the methods of allocating the direct cost items to customer groups are indicated. A somewhat different method is indicated for the indirect cost items, shown in Figure 28. Here factors of variability are established for each indirect item. Four such factors are suggested for this particular concern:

Average number of salesmen   Average number of customers
Sales volume (dollars)   Tonnage sold

Salaries and expense of sales administration and supervision are assumed to vary between customer groups as follows:

$\frac{1}{3}$ in accordance with number of salesmen
$\frac{1}{3}$ in accordance with sales volume
$\frac{1}{3}$ in accordance with number of customers

In like manner, factors of variability are assigned to each indirect expense item. The final distribution of the costs to customer groups is shown in Figure 29.

While any such procedure is somewhat arbitrary, it does provide a substantially accurate method of allocation which is useful for customer groups. As a rule it is unnecessary (and in some instances impossible or, at least, impracticable) to reduce the analysis of indirect customer costs to a high degree of accuracy. Certain approximations must be made and, for internal management purposes, such procedure is usually adequate.

Direct Customer Expense	Total Expense	Method of Allocation	Small Jobbers	Large Jobbers	Mail Order Houses
Salaries and expense of salesmen	$100,000	Allocated directly.	$ 82,000	$12,000	$ 6,000
Payroll insurance and taxes—salesmen and clerical	5,000	Allocated directly.	4,100	600	300
Clerical cost of writing and handling orders	10,000	Flat charge per order plus additional charge per item ordered.	6,000	3,000	1,000
Clerical cost of billing and bookkeeping	6,000	Flat charge per invoice plus additional charge per billing line.	3,000	2,000	1,000
Transportation	40,000	Allocated directly.	25,000	10,000	5,000
Direct cost of physical order handling	18,000	Flat charge per order shipped plus additional charge per pound.	10,000	5,000	3,000
Credit and collection expense	10,000	Allocated on percentage of sales based on past experience.	8,000	1,500	500
Financial expense (including interest on investment related to distribution activities)	10,000	Allocated by the same general plan as explained on pages 61 to 65 (for territories).	5,000	4,000	1,000
Total direct customer expense	$199,000		$143,100	$38,100	$17,800

FIGURE 27. Allocation of Direct Customer Expense

Indirect Customer Expense	Total Expense	Factors of Variability				Division of Expenses According to Factors of Variability			
		Average Number of Salesmen	Sales Volume	Average Number of Customers	Tonnage Sold	Average Number of Salesmen	Sales Volume	Average Number of Customers	Tonnage Sold
Salaries and expense of sales administration and supervision	$20,000	1/3	1/3	1/3		$ 6,667	$ 6,667	$ 6,666	
Sales administrative clerical expense	4,000	1/2	1/2			2,000	2,000		
Property insurance and taxes	6,000	1/3	1/3	1/3		2,000	2,000	2,000	
Payroll insurance and taxes other than salesmen and clerical	1,500	1/3	1/3	1/3		500	500	500	
Occupancy—sales administration	3,000	1/3	1/3	1/3		1,000	1,000	1,000	
Communication, supplies, and general expense	4,000	1/4		3/4		1,000		3,000	
Education and training	2,000	All				2,000			
Advertising and sales promotional cost	5,000			All				5,000	
Warehousing cost other than direct order handling	6,000				All				6,000
General distribution expense	6,000	1/3	1/3	1/3		2,000	2,000	2,000	
Total indirect customer expense	$57,500					$17,167	$14,167	$20,166	$6,000

Factors of Variability	Total		Small Jobbers		Large Jobbers		Mail Order Houses	
Average number of salesmen	23	100%	20	87.0%	2½	10.8%	½	2.2%
Sales volume	$1,500,000	100%	$800,000	53.3%	$400,000	26.7%	$300,000	20.0%
Average number of customers	2,045	100%	2,000	97.8%	40	2.0%	5	.2%
Tonnage sold	10,000	100%	5,000	50.0%	3,500	35.0%	1,500	15.0%

Factors of Variability	Total Expense from Above	Small Jobbers		Large Jobbers		Mail Order Houses	
Average number of salesmen	$17,167	87.0%	$14,935	10.8%	$1,854	2.2%	$ 378
Sales volume	14,167	53.3%	7,551	26.7%	3,783	20.0%	2,833
Average number of customers	20,166	97.8%	19,723	2.0%	403	.2%	40
Tonnage sold	6,000	50.0%	3,000	35.0%	2,100	15.0%	900
Totals	$57,500		$45,209		$8,140		$4,151

FIGURE 28. Allocation of Indirect Customer Expense

STATEMENT OF PROFIT AND LOSS BY CUSTOMER GROUPS

	Total	Small Jobbers	Large Jobbers	Mail Order Houses
Gross Sales	$1,530,000	$820,000	$408,000	$302,000
Less Sales Deductions	30,000	20,000	8,000	2,000
Net Sales	$1,500,000	$800,000	$400,000	$300,000
Cost of Goods Sold	1,193,500	550,900	364,400	278,200
Gross Profit	$ 306,500	$249,100	$ 35,600	$ 21,800
Direct Customer Distribution Costs	199,000	143,100	38,100	17,800
Profit Remaining after Direct Costs	$ 107,500	$106,000	($ 2,500)	$ 4,000
Indirect Customer Distribution Costs	57,500	45,209	8,140	4,151
Profit Remaining after All Distribution Costs (including interest on invested capital at 5%)	$ 50,000	$ 60,791	($ 10,640)	($ 151)
		Percentages of Net Sales		
Gross Profit	20.4	31.1	8.9	7.3
Direct Distribution Costs	13.3	17.9	9.5	5.9
Indirect Distribution Costs	3.8	5.6	2.0	1.4
Total Distribution Costs	17.1	23.5	11.5	7.3
Net Profit	3.3	7.6	(2.6)	0.0
		Average Discount		
Average Discount from List Prices	56.7%	50.0%	62.2%	62.9%

FIGURE 29. Statement of Profit and Loss by Customer Groups

Figure 29 illustrates a final profit and loss statement by customer groups. In this illustration, the "Profit Remaining after Direct Costs" is particularly significant. If a customer group does not cover its direct distribution costs (as indicated for "Large Dealers"), a serious question is raised either as to the ultimate profitability of the group, or as to the efficiency of the distribution effort directed to that group. If a customer group does cover its direct costs, but does not cover its total distribution costs (as indicated for "Mail Order Houses"), further analysis may be required. Since a part of the indirect cost is frequently of a fixed nature and since a part of the production cost is usually fixed, the question may be one of securing a similar volume elsewhere at a lower total distribution cost.

There are certain limitations to the foregoing procedure. It can be used successfully only where a substantial part of the distribution cost relates directly to customer groups. It does not localize the cost to individual customers. While a customer group may reveal a satisfactory profit, individual customers within the group may be unprofitable. Finally, it assumes a certain uniformity of operations whereby factors of variability can reasonably be established.

Second Method—Selection of Typical Customers.—In concerns where the major items of distribution cost are joint, as between customer groups, a direct analysis of the cost is difficult and frequently meaningless. A more fruitful method is to select typical customers representative of the various groups and direct the analysis to the costs of those particular customers. A condensed illustration of this procedure is given in Figures 30, 31, and 32. Here an office supply house which sells a large variety of products is interested in determining the profitability of customers with varying annual volume. Operations are restricted to a large city in which the concern is located and to a comparatively small surrounding industrial area. The same salesmen call on all classes of customers—large and small, and major costs are joint as between such groups. In general, all customers buy the entire line of products offered.

The following data present the basis for the analysis:

Volume groups selected	$1 to $75	$76 to $150	$151 to $350	$351 to $750	$751 up
Typical annual volume	$50	$100	$200	$500	$1,000
Number of customers represented by groups	2,000	2,000	1,500	1,000	500
Typical number of salesmen's calls per year	9	10	12	18	24
Typical number of orders received per year	8	11	14	20	30
Average dollar value of deliveries	$6	$9	$14	$25	$33

While few costs can be directly allocated to customers, some analysis of the relationship can be made. Figure 30 classifies the costs as between those which bear a close relationship to individual customers, those which can be reasonably apportioned to customers, and those which bear little or no relationship to individual customers. Obviously, the individual cost items which fall within such groups will vary with different concerns. The cost items within each group are then studied intensively to ascertain the amounts applicable to the individual customers selected as typical of particular volume groups. Here, again, the nature of the analysis and the methods of distribution must be suited to local conditions.

Figure 31 presents a statement showing the profit or loss of typical customers. Here it is apparent that a typical customer with an annual volume of $50 does not provide a gross profit sufficient to anyway near cover the costs which can be closely related to it; and when all costs are considered, such customers reveal a loss equal to 56% of their sales volume. This should lead the way to further study of such customers, of which the concern has 2,000. Some such customers may not be typical and their requirements in distribution effort may call for more or less cost; some may show promise of early improvement in volume; some should in all probability be eliminated, or retained by less costly distribution methods. In like manner, all customers whose annual volume falls below $150 should be subjected to scrutiny as none of these customers appears profitable.

Figure 32 presents a profit and loss summary based upon such typical customers. This is not an actual profit and loss statement, but it should closely approximate the actual statement. If it does not, some error has been made in the previous analysis. It provides a check on the accuracy of the work. This statement serves to emphasize the importance of proper customer selection. Here an enormous loss is revealed for low-volume accounts. This should awaken management to the importance of the problem. A grave danger is presented here in that alert competitors will "pick off" the profitable business.

The figures presented are only illustrative. Losses may be revealed in high rather than in low-volume accounts.

Instead of directing the analysis to the costs incurred in serving *a* typical customer within each annual volume class, a company may prefer to determine the costs of serving *every* customer within one or a few selected sales areas and for a representative time period. The results of the analysis may then be extended to other sales areas. In either case, a sampling of customers is made for analysis purposes.

The procedure followed in analyzing costs of customers within a limited area and period may be illustrated by reference to the ex-

	Method of Distribution	Typical Customers with Annual Volume of				
		$50	$100	$200	$500	$1,000
Expenses Which Can Be Closely Related to Individual Customers						
All direct costs of salesmen; including salaries, commissions, traveling expense, payroll taxes and insurance, education and training, etc..	Analysis of time required for calls, resulting cost per call, and typical number of calls per year (assumed cost of $3 per call).	$27.00	$30.00	$36.00	$54.00	$ 72.00
Delivery costs..	Average delivery cost weighted by money value.	3.20	4.93	7.39	14.08	24.96
Order handling—clerical..	Average cost per order.	1.20	1.65	2.10	3.00	4.50
Order handling—physical..	Average cost per order weighted by money value.	2.40	3.70	5.54	10.56	18.72
Credit and collection costs including clerical cost of handling receivables..	Cost per customer plus cost per order.	.90	1.05	1.20	1.50	2.00
Totals..		$34.70	$41.33	$52.23	$83.14	$122.18
Expenses which can be reasonably apportioned to individual customers						
All sales administration and supervision costs; including communication, general clerical, supplies, etc..	Percentage of direct cost of salesmen plus cost per customer.	$ 8.10	$10.00	$11.80	$17.20	$ 22.60
Financial and general distribution costs..	Percentage of total direct costs, as shown in above cost group, plus percentage of money volume.	3.78	5.31	8.18	16.65	29.77
Totals..		$11.88	$15.31	$19.98	$33.85	$ 52.37
Expenses which bear little or no relationship to individual customers						
All advertising costs..						
Warehousing, storing, and handling other than physical order handling..	Allocated on basis of sales volume.	$ 1.50	$ 3.00	$ 6.00	$15.00	$ 30.00
General sales occupancy expense..						

FIGURE 30. Allocation of Distribution Costs to Customers Typical of Annual Volume Groups

	Typical Customers with Annual Volume of				
	$50	$100	$200	$500	$1,000
Net Sales	$50.00	$100.00	$200.00	$500.00	$1,000.00
Cost of Goods Sold	30.00	60.00	120.00	312.50	650.00
Gross Profit	20.00	40.00	80.00	187.50	350.00
Expenses Closely Related to Customers					
Direct Selling	27.00	30.00	36.00	54.00	72.00
Delivery	3.20	4.93	7.39	14.08	24.96
Order Handling—Clerical	1.20	1.65	2.10	3.00	4.50
Order Handling—Physical	2.40	3.70	5.54	10.56	18.72
Credit and Collection	.90	1.05	1.20	1.50	2.00
Total	34.70	41.33	52.23	83.14	122.18
Profit or Loss	(14.70)	(1.33)	27.77	104.36	227.82
Apportioned Expenses					
Sales Administration and Supervision	8.10	10.00	11.80	17.20	22.60
Financial and General Distribution Expenses	3.78	5.31	8.18	16.65	29.77
Total	11.88	15.31	19.98	33.85	52.37
Profit or Loss	(26.58)	(16.64)	7.79	70.51	175.45
Other Distribution Costs	1.50	3.00	6.00	15.00	30.00
Net Profit	($28.08)	($ 19.64)	$ 1.79	$ 55.51	$ 145.45

FIGURE 31. Statement Showing Profit or Loss of Typical Customers Classified as to Annual Volume

STATEMENT OF PROFIT AND LOSS BASED ON TYPICAL CUSTOMERS

	Total	Customers with Annual Volume of				
		$50	$100	$200	$500	$1,000
Net Sales................	$1,600,000	$100,000	$200,000	$300,000	$500,000	$500,000
Cost of Goods Sold.......	997,500	60,000	120,000	180,000	312,500	325,000
Gross Profit............	602,500	40,000	80,000	120,000	187,500	175,000
Cost of Distribution......	567,020	96,160	119,280	117,315	131,990	102,275
Net Profit.............	$ 35,480	($ 56,160)	($ 39,280)	$ 2,685	$ 55,510	$ 72,725
	Percentages of Net Sales					
Gross Profit............	37.7	40.0	40.0	40.0	37.5	35.0
Cost of Distribution......	35.4	96.2	59.6	39.1	26.4	20.5
Net Profit.............	2.3	(56.2)	(19.6)	.9	11.1	14.5
Number of Customers......	7,000	2,000	2,000	1,500	1,000	500

Figure 32. Statement of Profit and Loss Based on Typical Customers

perience of a manufacturer of consumer goods selling direct to retail dealers.[1] The analysis in question applied to a typical sales area during an average week of the company's operations. The problem was to ascertain whether small dealers were unprofitable and whether shifting of marketing effort to large dealers would increase sales and profits. At the outset a distinction was made between fixed and variable expenses, and the latter were allocated to customers on the principle that gross profit should at least cover out-of-pocket costs.

As an illustration, the various out-of-pocket expenses, the bases of allocation, the average expenses per unit, and the expenses incurred in serving customer Smith for 1 week are itemized in Figure 33. The expenses amounted to $2.78. The customer's sales volume during the week was $34.37, the goods cost $31.40, and the difference, $2.97, was the gross profit on the transaction. Customer Smith was a profitable customer because, after paying the direct cost of serving him during the week, we had $0.19 left for defraying fixed expenses and for net profits.

Variable Expense	Basis of Allocation	Average Cost per Unit (Col. 1)	Number of Units (Col. 2)	Allocated Expense 1 × 2 (Col. 3)
Delivery	{Number of deliveries	$0.17	6	$1.02
	{Weight	.09	2.9	.26
Salesmen's salaries and travel	Number of interviews	.36	2	.72
Salesmen's telephone calls	Number of phone calls	.07	3	.21
Inside salesmen's salaries	Number of interviews	.19	0	.00
Inside salesmen's telephone calls	Number of phone calls	.10	1	.10
Invoice distribution	Number of invoice lines	.01	20	.20
Order taking	Number of orders	.03	2	.06
Accounts receivable	Number of credit tickets	.01	8	.08
Telephone expense	Number of phone calls	.01	1	.01
Office sales expenses	Volume	.02	0	.00
Auto depreciation	do.	.03	3	.09
Claims	do.	.01	3	.03
Total expense (A)				2.78
Gross profit (B)				2.97
Net profit (B − A)				.19

FIGURE 33. Variable Marketing Expenses, Bases of Allocation, Unit Costs, and Costs of Serving One Customer for One Week (Sevin, *op. cit.*, p. 24)

. . . By classifying all customers according to amounts purchased, significant tendencies may be discerned. Thus, in Figure 34, it may be observed that customers in one area who buy . . . less than 150 units weekly are generally

[1] As reported by Charles H. Sevin in *How Manufacturers Reduce Their Distribution Costs,* Economic Series No. 72, U. S. Department of Commerce (Washington, D. C.: Government Printing Office, 1948), pp. 22–28.

unprofitable. In this particular week, the unprofitable customers . . . were 35 per cent of the total number successfully solicited, yet they contributed only 5 per cent of the volume.

Customer-Volume Group, Number of Units Purchased During Week	Customers, Per Cent of Total	Volume, Per Cent of Total	Gross Profit per 100 Units (Dollars)	Variable Expenses, per 100 Units (Dollars)	Net Profit [1] per 100 Units (Dollars)
Customers unsuccessfully solicited	17.1	.....	.....	.....	.....
1–25	7.6	0.2	$1.66	$4.01	[2]–$2.35
26–50	8.3	.7	1.38	2.55	[2]– 1.17
51–100	12.0	1.9	1.25	1.78	[2]– .53
101–150	9.3	2.4	1.26	1.32	[2]– .06
151–200	7.8	2.9	1.14	1.13	.01
201–250	6.4	3.0	1.12	.95	.17
251–500	17.1	13.2	1.06	.75	.31
501–1,000	12.7	18.6	1.02	.49	.53
1,001–10,000	1.7	57.1	.81	.24	.57
Total	100.0	100.0	.....	.....	.....

[1] Gross profit less variable expenses only.
[2] Loss.

FIGURE 34. Customers, Volume, Gross Profits, Variable Marketing Expenses and Net Profit or Loss, by Customer-Volume Groups (Sevin, *op. cit.*, p. 25)

. . . It is easy to see why these smaller customers are unprofitable. Losses are suffered because the expenses incurred for selling, deliveries, bookkeeping, and other services are greater than the higher gross margins obtained from them. Figure 35 shows the disparity between the volume obtained from large and small buyers and various kinds of effort expended. Buyers of less than 100 units weekly account for only 2.8 per cent of the total volume, yet they were given 24 per cent of the salesmen's interviews, 26.4 per cent of the salesmen's telephone calls, and 16.2 per cent of the number of deliveries.

Volume and Kind of Service		Customer-Volume Groups; Amount of Purchases During Week	
		Less Than 100 Units	More Than 100 Units
Sales volume	Per cent of total	2.8	97.2
Salesmen's interviews	do.	24.0	76.0
Salesmen's telephone calls	do.	26.4	73.6
Deliveries	do.	16.2	83.8

FIGURE 35. Amount of Weekly Services Rendered Customers, by Customer-Volume Groups (Sevin, *op. cit.*, p. 25)

In the two methods of customer analysis illustrated above, it may be noted that two different bases have been employed in the classification of customers. In the first case the grouping was on the basis of separation of distribution effort (and nature of customer operations) ; in the latter the basis is that of volume of purchases for a specified period. Still other bases may be employed, but the foregoing procedure is illustrative of the methods to be employed.

Bases of Allocation.—Comparatively few distribution cost items can be charged directly to customers; most items must be distributed by means of certain bases of allocation. No particular claim is made for the accuracy of the bases suggested in the foregoing illustrations. While suitable for some concerns they would not serve in others. No general statements can be made as to the proper bases to be used; however, by intensive study of a particular case suitable methods can be found for a major part of the distribution cost.

The direct costs of salesmen, including salaries, commissions, traveling expense, payroll taxes, and insurance, may be distributed on the basis of calls made, time actually spent with customers, or some combination of these factors. Where time spent is used, the indirect or traveling and waiting time may be apportioned in accordance with direct time; or the entire cost may be apportioned on the basis of time actually spent with customers. Where such factors as time spent or calls are used, detailed salesmen's daily or weekly reports must be used to supply the data. Figure 36 illustrates such a report.

Delivery costs are frequently merged with direct selling costs as, for example, where the salesman is also the delivery man. Here the bases are similar to those noted above. Where the delivery is distinct from selling, standard delivery costs should be developed as discussed in Chapter 15. A record of deliveries to each customer will then supply the basis for distribution.

The clerical costs of order handling, credit extension, bookkeeping, and collection should be resolved to individual functional costs and bases established for each function. The procedure is as follows:

1. Determine the clerical functions which can be related to customers (e.g., invoice writing).

2. Ascertain the total cost of each clerical function.

3. Select units of measurement of functional service (e.g., one invoice).

4. Determine the unit functional cost for each clerical function. This is the quotient of the total functional cost divided by the total functional units.

5. Ascertain the number of units of functional service required by an individual customer or a customer group.

6. Determine the customer cost, which is the product of 4 and 5 above.

Salesman's Daily Time Report

SALESMAN _____ DATE _____ 19____ DISTRICT.

CODE: T—Time in transit. W—Waiting. L—Lunch. R—Regular call. N—New account.

FROM	TO	CODE	DETAIL OF WORK
9:00	9:45	R	Allison & Brown. OK.
9:45	10:30	T	Whiting & Brooks. Saw L. C. Lyman, buyer of Fittings. They are still placing all orders with C and W. C gets 80%. Lyman promises consideration on Oct. trip. This means nothing. We will have to get to Wallace. Full detail when I come in.
10:30	11:30	N	
11:30	12:00	T	Lunch with Tom Sexton of Gen'l Supply Co. They have the new..............gov. clearance contract. Tom promises full order. This will run about $8,000. Check up on last two returns, only 86% test, also something wrong in machining. Write Tom in full.
12:00	2:00	L R	
2:00	2:30	T	Anderson Supply Co. Same old story here. Only cats and dogs. Erie still in. Crawford claims that his hands are tied. Bell is out of town. Will see him next time for showdown.
2:30	3:30	R	
3:30	4:00	T	Manning & Co. All OK.
4:00	4:30	W	
4:30	5:00	R	

Calls Made
Calls—old accounts......4
Calls—new accounts......1
Total calls.............5

FIGURE 36. Salesman's Daily Time Report

The following clerical functions are illustrative:

Clerical Function	Possible Unit of Measurement	Basis of Distribution to Customers or Customer Groups
Order writing	Individual order Order line [2]	Number of orders Number of lines
Checking items and entering prices	Individual order Order line	Number of orders Number of lines
Billing	Individual invoice Billing line	Number of invoices Number of lines
Accounts receivable, entries and statements	Individual invoice Individual account	Number of invoices Number of accounts

In most instances it is desirable to establish standard costs for such clerical functions.

Where the clerical cost is small, it may be fairly distributed to customers on some general basis, such as the average cost per order.

The cost of the physical handling of orders can sometimes be fairly distributed to customers by some direct method, such as the average cost per order. In other instances, such a method would be grossly inaccurate. Here it is necessary to follow a plan similar to that suggested above for clerical costs, wherein the cost of individual functions is determined and such costs distributed on the basis of the number of functional units of service required. Functional units which may be used are:

Individual packages	Individual items
Units of weight	Individual orders

Here, again, it is frequently desirable to establish standard unit handling costs.

Sales administration and supervision and financial and general costs of distribution can seldom be directly related to customers, but they can, as a rule, be reasonably apportioned. Administration and supervision usually bear a fairly direct relationship to the direct customer costs and can be apportioned accordingly. In some instances a flat charge may be made per customer plus a percentage of direct costs. This allows for the situation in which a certain amount of supervision is directed to each customer, regardless of other customer costs. Likewise, the financial and general costs may be apportioned by a percentage of direct costs plus a percentage of money volume or average receivables. Such methods of apportionment are only illustrative and not to

[2] By order line is meant one written line on an order form; e.g., 10 units of Product A at $1.00 = $10.00.

be accepted as of general applicability. It is generally possible, however, to find a satisfactory plan in a particular case.

There is frequently a remaining group of cost items, including, particularly, advertising and certain fixed charges which bear little or no ascertainable relationship to individual customers or customer groups. Here the apportionment must be arbitrary. It may be made on the basis of such factors as sales volume, cost of goods sold, gross profit, physical volume, or by executive estimate. The method used should be entirely clear to all executives who use the results of the analysis and should be given due consideration in the interpretation of the data. Usually the profit or loss of customers before the deductions of such costs will be the guiding consideration in determining customer policy.

Extent to Which the Analysis Should Be Carried.—The extent to which the analysis of distribution cost items by customers should be carried depends upon the purposes for which the analysis is to be chiefly used. If, for example, the analysis is made chiefly to determine the price differentials admissible under regulatory statutes, it may be necessary to allocate all distribution cost in the fairest manner possible and to extend the analysis to the individual customers in question. If the chief purpose is to determine the lowest prices which can be set temporarily for particular customer groups without suffering out-of-pocket losses, the fixed elements of the cost items may be eliminated from consideration. This sometimes applies in bidding for special work. If the chief purpose is the selection of profitable classes of customers or the detection of weakness in distribution methods, major emphasis may be placed upon those cost items which can be closely related to particular customers or customer groups.

Subanalyses of Customer Costs.—The analysis of distribution costs by customers or customer groups may not be sufficient in itself. It may be necessary to extend the analysis to the determination of customer costs for different commodities, within different territories or for different sized orders, before management is supplied with the requisite information for purposes of sales direction and control. Particularly is this true in relation to unfair trade practice legislation. Here it may be necessary to establish the cost of selling a particular product to an individual customer or customer group in order to justify price differentials. Once the cost of customers is secured, it can be further analyzed by commodities, territories, etc., in accordance with the methods suggested in the chapters dealing with such analyses.

Uses of the Analysis.—The uses of the customer analysis of distribution costs are obvious from a review of the purposes stated on page

129. Such an analysis does not lead to a direct answer to many of the questions which arise relative to customer sales policy, but it does provide an essential part of the information which is necessary for intelligent consideration of the questions. Other factors must also be considered. The cost analysis may reveal that a customer group is definitely unprofitable—possibly it should be dropped; but the question must also be raised as to the future potentialities of the group, the effect of a smaller volume on production costs, the effect of shifting some fixed costs to other groups, and the prestige of the concern within the industry. Even if present accounts are not dropped, the effect may be to direct future effort to the more profitable customers.

When distribution costs are analyzed, many other sales factors must be examined and these in themselves often provide valuable signals for the sales management. Illustrative of such factors are:

The number of customer accounts falling within volume brackets
Frequency of purchases of customer groups
Average value of orders of various groups
Percentage of volume supplied by customer groups representing annual volume brackets

Numerous methods may be used to raise customer accounts from an unprofitable to a profitable level; for example:

1. Place the facts before the customer and solicit his cooperation with a view to securing fewer and larger orders and greater annual volume. This may require education of salesmen as well as customers.
2. Sell the customers more of the high-margin goods.
3. Impose stricter credit terms or sell C. O. D.
4. Increase prices to particular customers or impose a service charge for small orders.
5. Call on customers less frequently.

CHAPTER 8

ANALYSIS BY SIZE OF ORDERS

The Problem of Small Orders.—Many concerns are confronted with the problem of handling a large number of orders which are too small to be profitable. The problem is particularly acute in manufacturing and wholesaling, where there is a relatively large fixed expense connected with each order. In retailing, the presence of small orders cannot be viewed as a "problem" in the usual sense of the word. Small orders or transactions are the essence of retailing since goods must be sold in amounts usable by the ultimate consumer. Retail operations are therefore geared to this small-order type business. Nevertheless, most retailers continually strive to increase the size of the average sales transaction as one means of offsetting rising costs of operations. A problem thus arises when average transaction size lags behind average transaction cost. Small orders pose a problem of serious proportions, furthermore, in those types of retailing in which goods must be taken from warehouse stock and delivered.

Numerous studies have been made in various industries for the purpose of ascertaining the extent to which concerns handle small orders at a loss. Typical of such studies is that made by one of the authors for an office supply company. This study consisted of an analysis of the retail orders of the company for a typical month.

During the month, 5,082 orders were handled. Of this number, 1,612 were for less than $5.00. The average rate of gross profit on the 1,612 orders was 37.6%.

The minimum direct cost of securing, handling, and delivering an order was found to be $1.82. This included no fixed or overhead costs but only the direct out-of-pocket costs for securing and filling the orders. It was then apparent that an order must amount to $4.84 ($1.82 ÷ 37.6%) in order to provide a gross profit adequate to cover the direct order cost. Since the $1.82 was considered as an absolute minimum, and included no general costs whatever, it could be assumed that all orders under $5.00 were unprofitable.

The 1,612 unprofitable orders were then further analyzed by customers. It was found that the orders were received from 418 different customers. Next the annual volume (for the previous calendar year) of these 418 customers was determined and it was found that only 122 of them had provided an annual volume in excess of $50. The 296 customers whose annual volume was $50 or less had provided 1,011 orders out of a total for the month of 5,082.

In brief, approximately one-fifth of the total number of orders were too small to cover even the direct order costs and came from customers whose annual volume could not possibly compensate for the loss incurred on orders of less than the minimum value.

The study was made to test the recommendation of the sales manager that two additional salesmen be added to cultivate small accounts. The sales manager reasoned that small accounts grow into large ones; hence, a strong effort should be made to secure them. To test this theory further, lists of the 296 customers were prepared and given to the salesmen with the request that they estimate the annual volume which could be secured from the individual customers. Of the total of 296, only 48 were estimated at a potential volume above $50 and, of the 48, only 16 were placed above $100. Not only were the 296 customers highly unprofitable, but most of them could never be made profitable. Obviously, such results did not augur strongly for the development of small accounts.

Many similar illustrations could be supplied relative to the problem of small orders and accounts.

It should be noted at this point that there is nothing objectionable in handling small orders, provided the prices are adjusted to produce a gross profit adequate to cover the cost of handling the orders and to leave a profit. The difficulty arises when the cost of the orders exceeds the gross profit.

Relation of Order-Size Analysis to Customers and Commodities. —Since an order is for specific goods and for a particular customer, the problem of profitability of orders is closely related to the profitability of customers and commodities. To illustrate, let us assume that the direct cost of taking and handling an order is $2 and that the average rate of gross profit is 30%. If then we secure 10 orders from customer Smith which average $5 each, our gross profit will be $15, our direct order cost will be $20, and our direct loss will be $5, not to mention a share of other costs which must be absorbed by orders as a whole. If this is typical of Smith's business, and apparently will be in the future, then the problem may be one of customer selection. Again, if the orders we receive for Product X are invariably small orders, averaging about $5, and if Product X carries a gross profit of 30%, then we stand to lose on each order of Product X and the problem may be one of commodity selection.

Such cases as these would appear to present a comparatively simple problem, but, practically, the problem is more complex. Customer Smith may give us some small orders which are not profitable, and other larger ones which are profitable; Product X may sometimes be ordered in small amounts, and in other instances, in large amounts. Moreover, the gross profit of commodities may vary. Product X may carry a gross of 30%; Y, a gross of 10%; and Z, a gross of 50%. Smith may give us an order for $5 worth of Z which carries a gross of $2.50—more than enough to cover the direct order cost of $2. Customer Jones may give us an order for $15 worth of Product Y which carries a gross of $1.50—not enough to cover the direct order cost of $2. Or, to further complicate the problem, the orders from Smith and Jones may include all the products within the same order.

The point to be noted is that any analysis of orders must give consideration to both customers and commodities.

Problem Concerns Orders of All Sizes.—The problem is to ascertain not only the profitability of small orders, but also the relative profitability of larger orders. Price differentials are frequently made for different sizes of orders of individual commodities or for different annual volumes of all commodities. Are the price differences comparable to the differences in costs? To some extent the answer must be supplied by an analysis of the cost of orders of varying size.

Purpose and Use of Order-Size Analysis.—As implied in the previous topics, the purpose of an analysis of the cost of orders of varying size is to assist management in the selection of customers and commodities and in arriving at fair price differentials. Care must be used in the application of the findings, and common sense must govern the extent to which the analysis is carried. The problem is of far greater importance in some concerns than in others. The value lies chiefly in policy determination.

When orders are demonstrated to be unprofitable and to offer no promise of future profit, the loss must be weighed against all counteracting factors, such as advertising value of wide distribution, effect on production cost of any volume changes, and service to customers.

Remedies for unprofitable orders often lie in the direction of education of salesmen and customers. Where these are ineffective or inadequate, resort must be had to price or discount adjustments, imposition of service charges, minimum limits on order size and deliveries, and, finally, to elimination of customers and commodities which give rise to the unprofitable business.

The collective experience of numerous concerns over the years clearly suggests that adoption of firm measures to reduce the number of unprofitable orders has generally resulted in stronger and more efficient marketing organizations. At the same time distribution costs usually have been substantially reduced and profits have tended to increase.

Method of Cost Analysis by Size of Orders.—It is impossible to suggest any uniform or set procedure for the analysis of distribution costs by size of orders, which would be applicable to all concerns. At best, only general suggestions can be made as to the method to be followed. Moreover, it must be admitted that it is difficult in some concerns to determine with a high degree of accuracy the cost of orders of various sizes, at least within the limits of reasonable cost of the analysis. In most concerns, however, this cost can be approximated to a degree of accuracy which will serve successfully to guide the management policy.

The cost of securing, handling, and delivering an order, and of collecting the money, depends upon such factors as:

The dollar size
The physical quantity
The nature of the commodities included
The location of the customer
The financial strength of the customer
The method of securing the order
The credit terms
The method of delivery
The number of items included

If all such factors entered into the cost differential of all orders which vary in size, the problem might be too complicated to be solved at a reasonable cost of analysis. In a particular case, however, many of the factors can be eliminated, either because they do not apply or because their influence on cost is negligible. For example, in some wholesale concerns, only the dollar size and the physical quantity of orders are factors of consequence. The nature of commodities may be sufficiently similar as to have little bearing; the analysis may be restricted to certain territorial limits, thereby eliminating the location factor; sales may be made only to customers possessing a certain standard of financial strength; a uniform method of securing orders may be employed; credit terms may be uniform; and the method of delivery may be the same for all orders.

In such a case the cost items may be separated into three groups:

1. Those which are the same for orders of all sizes; e.g., the cost of mailing the invoice

2. Those which vary with money volume; e.g., credit losses
3. Those which vary with physical volume; e.g., physical handling

While money and physical volume are the variables suggested in this case, other variable factors will apply in other cases.

As a general outline of procedure, these steps are suggested:

1. Determine the size of the order groups to be studied; e.g., below $25, $25 to $50, etc.
2. Classify the costs according to: (1) those which vary with the size of the order, e.g., packing; (2) those which are uniform for orders of all sizes, e.g., accounts receivable bookkeeping; and (3) those which must be considered as general overhead with no direct relation to orders, e.g., certain advertising and supervision costs.
3. Identify the factors which appear to govern the amount of the variable expense (that expense which varies with the size of the order) applicable to orders of different sizes; for example, dollar value, weight, handling time, etc.
4. Apply the factors of variability to the variable expenses and add the uniform costs thereby arriving at a direct cost of order sizes.
5. Apply the overhead costs by some suitable factor such as hundredweight, dollar value, etc., to arrive at the total order cost.

In some instances the last step may be omitted as only the direct cost may be useful in judging the relative desirability of orders of varying sizes.

Where sales are made to different classes of customers or by different methods of sale, a separate analysis of order size may be necessary for each customer or method classification.

Relation of Particular Cost Items to Order Size.—In so far as it is possible to generalize, the distribution cost items may be considered to bear the following relationship to order size:

VARIABLE COSTS

(Those varying with order size)

Distribution Cost Item	Factor of Variability *
Salesmen's commissions	Dollar value
Spoiled work chargeable to salesmen	Dollar value
Out-freight	Weight
Delivery (when physical volume is an important factor)	Weight or bulk
Physical work and supplies related to order filling, handling, and shipping	Number of items Weight

* These factors relate to the average of orders falling within various dollar size classifications.

Distribution Cost Item	*Factor of Variability*
Bad debt losses	Dollar value
Cash discount	Dollar value
Interest and financial expense	Dollar value

UNIFORM COSTS

(Those which tend to be uniform for orders of all sizes)

Salesmen's salaries and expense
Payroll taxes and insurance
Communication
Transportation administration and overhead
Delivery (when physical volume is an unimportant factor)
Clerical work of order writing, filling, handling, and shipping
Credit approval
Accounts receivable bookkeeping

OVERHEAD COSTS

(Those which bear no direct relationship to order size)

Sales administration and supervision
Education and training
Sales occupancy
Advertising
Warehousing and handling administration
Warehouse occupancy
Credit administration
General distribution expense

Illustrative Analysis by Size of Orders.—An illustration of order-size cost analysis is provided by a manufacturer of consumer goods.[1] During the period of the second World War the company made a pilot study of order costs for one month in two of its branches. The methods used in making the study are shown in Figure 37, and the results are shown in Figure 38. From the latter table it may be seen that the total marketing costs for orders of less than $3.75 were 21.52% of sales, whereas the corresponding cost figure for the largest orders was only 4.24%. Orders in the smallest size classes were obviously handled at a loss.

The pilot study was so revealing that the company:

. . . decided to carry out a similar study on a more extended basis in the postwar period when there would be a more normal situation. The techniques that were used in making the preliminary study were revised, and detailed plans for carrying out this revised study were formulated and written up. These tentative plans included detailed instructions to branch managers and other

[1] As reported by Charles H. Sevin in *How Manufacturers Reduce Their Distribution Costs*, Economic Series No. 72, U. S. Department of Commerce (Washington, D. C.: Government Printing Office, 1948), pp. 61–67.

personnel in the various departments of the company who would be making the studies, forms for collecting the data, the final reports for presenting the data, and a time-schedule coordinating the different steps involved.[2]

Functional Costs	*Bases of Allocation to Order-Size Groups* *
1. Selling expense—direct: costs of time spent calling on customers—except sales promotion calls	Time study by salesmen (for test period, salesmen record time of entering and leaving each store called on)
2. Selling expense—indirect: travel time, time spent on nonproductive calls, miscellaneous working time, and travel expenses	Number of calls
3. Routing orders	Time study (number of orders routed and routing time)
4. Assembling orders and loading trucks	Time study (each order is assembled separately)
5. Packing: container forming, packing, container sealing, weighing, preparing bill of lading, stocking containers	Time study (packing one order is completed—by one packer—before next order is started)
6. Truck delivery—direct: cost of time spent in customers' stores	Time study (time clock on truck records time stopped at store and time deliveryman returns to truck)
7. Truck delivery—indirect: travel time (total time worked less direct time)	Number of deliveries
8. Freight delivery	Direct (freight charged direct to order)
9. Billing (cutting orders, pricing, extending and comparing orders and invoices)	Time study
10. Accounts receivable	Time study
11. Other office costs	Number of orders
12. Branch rent	Dollar sales
13. Branch supervision	Total direct time of above functions

* Cross-classified by kind of store.

FIGURE 37. Functional Classification of Expenses and Bases of Allocation to Order-Size Groups (Sevin, *op. cit.*, p. 62)

(Percentages of Sales)

Order-Size Groups, All Customer-Classifications Combined	Warehouse Assembling, Packing, and Routing	Office Billing, Accounts Receivable	Delivery Expenses	Selling Expenses	Other Branch Expense	Total Marketing Costs
$0.01–$3.75	3.11	2.72	5.33	9.40	0.96	21.52
$3.76–$6.25	2.10	1.64	3.28	5.62	.96	13.60
$6.26–$8.75	1.56	1.15	2.44	3.89	.96	10.00
$8.76–$11.25	1.25	.90	1.96	3.05	.96	8.12
$11.26–$13.75	1.06	.75	1.65	2.76	.96	7.18
$13.76–$16.25	.90	.64	1.40	2.29	.96	6.19
$16.26–$23.75	.80	.51	1.25	1.96	.97	5.49
$23.76–$31.25	.64	.40	1.00	1.73	.98	4.75
$31.26–$38.75	.56	.33	.87	1.90	.99	4.65
$38.76–$61.25	.51	.25	.79	2.43	.99	4.97
$61.26–$88.75	.41	.17	.65	1.86	.99	4.08
$88.76–$121.25 ...	.38	.13	.59	2.17	1.00	4.27
$121.26–$168.75 ..	.35	.10	.54	2.06	1.00	4.05
$168.76–$231.25 ..	.36	.08	.57	2.29	.99	4.29
$231.26 and over .	.34	.06	.57	2.27	1.00	4.24

FIGURE 38. Marketing Costs by Order-Size Groups (Sevin, *op. cit.*, p. 62)

[2] *Ibid.*, pp. 61–62.

CHAPTER 9

ANALYSIS BY ORGANIZATION AND OPERATING DIVISIONS

Definition and Purpose.—In some concerns a primary analysis of distribution costs is made by organization or operating divisions. For example, a manufacturing concern may first analyze its costs by branches; a wholesale house or department store, by departments; and a chain retail concern, by stores. Such analyses are similar to those discussed in previous chapters for territories and commodities; however, the problem is approached somewhat differently and, therefore, deserves special comment.

The purpose of such analyses is to center attention directly upon operating divisions and to measure the performance of divisional executives.

Manufacturers' Sales Branches

General Method.—A great many manufacturing concerns maintain sales branches through which they direct their distribution activities. Here the accounts are set up to record the direct costs of all branches separately, as shown on pages 34 to 39, a separate set of general or subsidiary accounts being used for each branch. Home office costs are then allocated to the branches in a manner similar to that explained in Chapter 4 for territories.

While the same analysis procedure will serve for both branches and territories, the two are not always identical. The sales of some products may be directed and controlled by the home office while others are handled through branches. Here the distribution cost directed to a particular territory will differ from that of the branch organization operating within the territory.

Wholesaling

Departmental Analysis.—In wholesale concerns it is customary to make a departmental analysis of distribution costs. The departmentalization is usually based on similarity of commodities; hence, a departmental analysis is similar to that of commodities, discussed in Chapter 5. It frequently happens, however, that quite dissimilar commodities are included in the same department and that similar commodities are found in different departments, because they have been purchased by different buyers or department heads. Thus, a departmental analysis in a wholesale concern may be as much a matter of measuring the performance of the department executives as of determining the results obtained from particular types of commodities.

Classification of Income and Expense Accounts.—The procedure for departmental analysis in wholesale concerns can best be shown by presenting the income and expense section of the classification of accounts for a typical wholesale house.

CLASSIFICATIONS OF ACCOUNTS
INCOME AND EXPENSE
Sales and Cost of Goods Sold Accounts

Control Accounts	*Subsidiary Analysis by Departments*	
100 Sales	100–1	Department 1
	100–2	Department 2
	100–3	Department 3
	Etc.	
111 Sales Returned	111–1	Department 1
	111–2	Department 2
	111–3	Department 3
	Etc.	
112 Sales Allowances	112–1	Department 1
	112–2	Department 2
	112–3	Department 3
	Etc.	
113 Freight-Out	113–1	Department 1
	113–2	Department 2
	113–3	Department 3
	Etc.	
114 Sales Discount Offered	114–1	Department 1
	114–2	Department 2
	114–3	Department 3
	Etc.	
115 Cost of Goods Sold	115–1	Department 1
	115–2	Department 2
	115–3	Department 3
	Etc.	
116 Cost of Sales Returned	116–1	Department 1
	116–2	Department 2
	116–3	Department 3
	Etc.	

Control *Accounts*	*Subsidiary Analysis* *by Departments*
117 Freight-In	117–1 Department 1 117–2 Department 2 117–3 Department 3 Etc.
118 Purchase Discount Offered	118–1 Department 1 118–2 Department 2 118–3 Department 3 Etc.
119 Loss and Gain on Physical Inventory Adjustments	119–1 Department 1 119–2 Department 2 119–3 Department 3 Etc.

Expenses Which Can Be Charged Directly to Departments

200 Buyers' and Department Heads' Salaries	200–1 Department 1 200–2 Department 2 200–3 Department 3 Etc.
201 Buyers' and Department Heads' Expense	201–1 Department 1 201–2 Department 2 201–3 Department 3 Etc.
202 Departmental Salesmen's Salaries	202–1 Department 1 202–2 Department 2 202–3 Department 3 Etc.
203 Departmental Salesmen's Commissions	203–1 Department 1 203–2 Department 2 203–3 Department 3 Etc.
204 Departmental Salesmen's Traveling Expense	204–1 Department 1 204–2 Department 2 204–3 Department 3 Etc.
205 Departmental Salesmen's Direct Expense	205–1 Department 1 205–2 Department 2 205–3 Department 3 Etc.
206 Licenses	206–1 Department 1 206–2 Department 2 206–3 Department 3 Etc.

Control *Accounts*	*Subsidiary Analysis* *by Departments*
207 Sales and Excise Taxes	207–1 Department 1 207–2 Department 2 207–3 Department 3 Etc.
208 Special Departmental Selling Expense	208–1 Department 1 208–2 Department 2 208–3 Department 3 Etc.
209 Special Departmental Advertising	209–1 Department 1 209–2 Department 2 209–3 Department 3 Etc.
210 Special Departmental Warehouse Expense	210–1 Department 1 210–2 Department 2 210–3 Department 3 Etc.
211 Loss on Inventory Price Adjustments	211–1 Department 1 211–2 Department 2 211–3 Department 3 Etc.
299 Other Direct Departmental Expense	299–1 Department 1 299–2 Department 2 299–3 Department 3 Etc.

Functional Expenses

300 DIRECT SELLING EXPENSE
    301 Sales Executives' Salaries
    302 Sales Executives' Expense
    303 Sales Office Salaries
    304 Sales Office Expense
    305 Salesmen's Salaries
    306 Salesmen's Commissions
    307 Salesmen's Automobile Expense (Control)
    308 Salesmen's Traveling Expense
    309 Salesmen's Direct Expense
    310 Commissions—Agents
    399 Miscellaneous Selling Expense

        Detail of 307, Salesmen's Automobile Expense—Subsidiary
      analysis is by units of equipment as follows:
           Depreciation
           Taxes and Licenses

Insurance
Repairs, Washing, and Lubricating
Gasoline
Oil

400   ADVERTISING AND SALES PROMOTION
401   Advertising Salaries
402   Space—General Publications
403   Space—Trade Journals
404   Radio Time
405   Direct Mail Advertising
406   Catalogs
407   Dealer Helps and Displays
408   Demonstration Expense
409   Advertising Agency Commission
410   Advertising Copy and Artwork
411   Advertising Supplies
412   Convention Expense
413   Contest Expense
414   Entertainment
415   Contributions
499   Miscellaneous Advertising

500   WAREHOUSE, HANDLING, AND SHIPPING EXPENSE (Other than occupancy)
501   Warehouse Executives' Salaries
502   Warehouse and Shipping Salaries
503   Shipping Supplies
504   Depreciation—Warehouse Equipment
599   Miscellaneous Shipping Expense

600   TRUCK AND DELIVERY EXPENSE
601   Truck and Delivery Salaries
602   Truck Operating Expense (Control—See Account 307)
603   Purchased Trucking
604   Truck Rental
699   Miscellaneous Truck and Delivery Expense

700   OCCUPANCY EXPENSE
701   Janitor, Watchmen, and Maintenance Salaries
702   Rent
703   Light
704   Heat
705   Depreciation—Buildings
706   Taxes—Buildings and Land
707   Insurance—Buildings, Boiler, Plate Glass, Public Liability, Casualty, Elevator, Etc.
708   Building Maintenance and Repair
709   Elevator Expense
799   Miscellaneous Occupancy Expense

800 CREDIT AND COLLECTION EXPENSE
    801 Credit and Collection Salaries
    802 Credit Services
    803 Legal Expense
    804 Collection Expense
    805 Loss from Bad Debts
    899 Miscellaneous Credit and Collection Expense

900 OFFICE AND ACCOUNTING EXPENSE
    901 Salaries—Office
    902 Office Supplies
    903 Telephone
    904 Telegraph
    905 Postage
    906 Depreciation—Office Equipment
    999 Miscellaneous Office Expense

1000 FINANCIAL EXPENSE
    1001 Interest Expense
    1002 Taxes on Merchandise and Receivables
    1003 Insurance on Merchandise
    1099 Miscellaneous Financial Expense

1100 GENERAL EXPENSE
    1101 General Executives' Salaries
    1102 General Executives' Expense
    1103 General Buying Expense
    1104 General Traveling Expense
    1105 Dues and Subscriptions
    1106 Legal Expense
    1107 Business and Trade Services
    1108 Professional Expense
    1109 Life Insurance on Officers
    1110 Taxes—Corporation, Franchise, Capital Stock, State Income, Excise, Etc.
    1111 Insurance—Use and Occupancy, Fidelity, Burglary, Robbery, Payroll, Etc.
    1112 Freight-Out and -In—Miscellaneous
    1199 Miscellaneous General Expense

1200 INTERDEPARTMENTAL AND FUNCTIONAL EXPENSES
    1201 Insurance on Warehouse and Office Equipment
    1202 Life Insurance on Employees
    1203 Workmen's Compensation Insurance
    1204 Old Age Benefit Taxes
    1205 Federal Unemployment Compensation Taxes
    1206 State Unemployment Compensation Taxes
    1207 Depreciation on Sales and General Office Equipment

1500   OTHER INCOME
     1501   Interest Income
     1502   Sales Discount Not Taken
     1503   Nonoperating Income
     1599   Miscellaneous Income

1600   OTHER EXPENSE
     1601   Purchase Discount Lost
     1602   Cost of Unused Capacity
     1603   Nonoperating Expense

Explanation of Accounts.—The accounts numbered 100 to 119 are directly analyzed by departments through the use of subsidiary analysis records or accounts.

Freight-out is considered as a sales deduction, since it is primarily a matter of price adjustment.

Sales and purchase discounts are given effect in determining gross margins and are recorded as offered rather than as taken. While this is contrary to usual accounting practice, it is often desirable in wholesaling, since such discounts are relatively more important here than in other lines of business. This method eliminates the accidental effect, on departmental profit, of discounts not taken and identifies the loss and gain from discounts, a function which rests with credit and financial executives rather than with department heads. Moreover, sales discounts, while nominally cash discounts, are frequently almost indistinguishable from trade discounts. Adjustment can always be made at the close of the fiscal year for any element of unrealized profit reflected in the accounts for purchase discount not taken.

Departmental freight-in accounts are kept for freight charges which cannot be conveniently added directly to the inventories. Monthly adjustment entries are made transferring a portion of this cost to the cost of goods sold accounts. The adjustment is based on the average relationship of freight-in to cost of goods sold. Balances remaining in the freight-in accounts are included with inventories.

Expenses which can be charged directly to individual departments are recorded in accounts 200 to 299.

Expenses which cannot be charged directly to departments, on account of either the joint nature of the expense or the clerical impracticability, are classified functionally in accounts 300 to 1199. For purposes of departmental analysis, appropriate bases of allocation must be provided for these expenses.

Accounts in the 1,200 group contain certain expenses which must be distributed ultimately to both the departmental and functional groups but which, for convenience in accounting, are charged first to individual accounts. For example, the social security taxes imposed on payroll belong partly to direct departmental expenses and partly to the various functional groups which include payroll expense. In making a departmental analysis, these expenses are so distributed. The share assigned to functions must be determined and added to the functional groups before the latter are allocated to departments.

Other income and expense items, shown in the 1,500 and 1,600 groups of accounts, are not included in a departmental analysis.

Methods of Allocation.—Methods which may be used in allocating functional expenses to departments are as follows:

Functional Costs	*Methods and Bases of Allocation*
Salesmen's commissions, expense of commission salesmen, agents' commissions	Commission sales
Other direct selling expense	Budgeted sales Executive estimate Gross profit Net sales
Advertising and sales promotion related directly to commodities	These costs should be first resolved into media costs such as: general publications, trade journals, radio, direct mail, catalogs, dealer helps, displays, demonstrations, etc., as explained on pages 49 to 52. Individual media costs should then be distributed to departments on such bases as indicated on pages 51 and 52.
General and institutional advertising	Executive estimate Gross profit
Warehouse, handling, and shipping expense	Standard charge per invoice line. A different standard charge should be established for each department.
Truck and delivery expense	Standard charge per invoice line or per delivery
Occupancy expense	Average space occupied (No weighting for space value)
Credit and collection expense	Net sales
Office and accounting expense	Number of invoice lines
Financial expense	Average inventory
General expense	Total of all above expense Executive estimate of individual items composing the group

Department Stores

Development of Uniform Accounting Procedure.—During the second decade of this century consideration of the problems of uniform accounting for department stores was undertaken by the National Retail Dry Goods Association (N.R.D.G.A.) and the Retail Research Association (R.R.A.). Uniformity of accounting procedure was needed in order that member stores might find it possible to exchange operating data. Before 1920 the work of both of these organizations had resulted in accounting manuals which varied in some respects but followed the same general pattern.

The uniform system of the N.R.D.G.A. (the R.R.A. has always had a limited membership) met with such widespread acceptance that in 1920 the Bureau of Business Research of Harvard University issued a bulletin entitled "Operating Results of Department and Specialty Stores," which was based upon reports from several hundred stores. These publications have continued annually, and in 1950 covered reports from about 350 department store firms and 90 specialty store firms.[1] In the main the Harvard bulletins are limited to the presentation of store-wide figures. Since 1925 the Controllers' Congress of the N.R.D.G.A. also has published annually its "Departmental Merchandising and Operating Results." The 1950 edition was based on reports from a total of 385 department stores and specialty stores which furnished data on the performance of more than 100 departments and subdepartments.[2]

Bases of Expense Classification.—The manual of accounting as originally prepared by the N.R.D.G.A. has had some revisions but the principles of expense classification have remained unchanged.[3] The bases of expense classification upon which the accounting plan is developed are as follows:

A. Natural Divisions of Expense
 1. Payroll
 2. Rentals
 3. Advertising
 4. Taxes
 5. Interest
 6. Supplies
 7. Service Purchased

[1] Malcolm P. McNair, *Operating Results of Department and Specialty Stores in 1950,* Bureau of Business Research, Bulletin No. 134 (Boston: Harvard University, 1951).
[2] Raymond F. Copes, *1950 Departmental Merchandising and Operating Results of Department Stores and Specialty Stores* (New York: Controllers' Congress, N.R.D.G.A., 1951).
[3] See *Standard Expense Accounting Manual for Department Stores and Specialty Stores* (New York: Controllers' Congress, N.R.D.G.A., 1948).

    8. Unclassified
    9. Traveling
   10. Communication
   11. Repairs
   12. Insurance
   13. Depreciation
   14. Professional Services

B. FUNCTIONS
    1. Administrative
    2. Occupancy
    3. Publicity
    4. Buying
    5. Selling

C. SUBFUNCTIONS

Large Stores	Stores of Medium Size
1. Administrative—	1. Administrative—
Executive Office	Administrative
Accounting Office	
Accounts Receivable and	
Credit	
Superintendency	
General Store	
2. Occupancy—	2. Occupancy—
Operating and Housekeeping	Operating and Housekeeping
Fixed Plant and Equipment	Fixed Plant and Equipment
Costs	Costs
Light, Heat, and Power	Light, Heat, and Power
3. Publicity—	3. Publicity
Sales Promotion Office	Advertising
Newspaper and General Advertising	Display
Direct Mail	
Display	
4. Buying—	4. Buying—
Merchandise Management and	Merchandise Management
Buying	and Buying and Outside
Domestic and Foreign Buying	Buying Offices
Offices	Receiving and Marking
Receiving and Marking	
5. Selling—	5. Selling—
Compensation of Salespersons	Compensation of Salespersons
General Selling	General Selling
Delivery	Delivery

Department Store Organization.—The functional divisions of the expense accounting plan correspond in part with the organization plan of a great many department stores of medium and large size. This plan consists of four divisions of responsibility, headed by functional executives of equal rank. These are:

Merchandise Manager—in charge of all buying activities

Publicity Director—in charge of all publicity

Controller—in charge of accounting, credit, and finance

Superintendent—in charge of occupancy; selling; after-selling service activities, such as wrapping, delivery, and adjustments; and all personnel activities

While there are many department stores with organizations which differ from this plan, it is the accepted pattern in a sufficient number to make it representative of the trade.[4]

Departmental Analysis.—A department store is what its name signifies, a store of many departments. This departmentalization was developed first for the purpose of directing sales activity and watching sales by lines of merchandise. With the adoption of the retail inventory method of accounting (explained in Chapter 10) it was possible also to exercise control over gross margins and inventories by departments. This method of inventory and merchandising control became increasingly popular after August, 1920, when the Department of Internal Revenue amended existing tax regulations to permit income tax returns on the basis of the retail method.

By means of the retail inventory method, stores were able to construct monthly operating reports, by departments, showing sales, cost of sales, and gross margin. It followed quite naturally, therefore, that many stores would attempt to extend this departmental analysis to the point of net profit by means of a departmental distribution of operating expenses.

Direct Expense Distribution.—Certain expenses can be readily distributed on a departmental basis; these include salespeoples' wages and commissions, newspaper advertising, buyers' and assistant buyers' salaries, traveling expense of buyers, and payroll for stock and clerical help when assigned to certain departments. These expenses are treated as direct charges to departments in the majority of the stores. Many stores also distribute the store rental cost to departments on the basis of square footage used by the departments, after the entire rental has been

---

[4] Deviation from the traditional four-division organization plan has proceeded in two directions. A number of stores have simplified their organization structures by reducing the number of functional divisions to three or even two. On the other hand, certain stores have tended in the opposite direction by establishing more than four divisions. In the latter instances, the personnel function has most often been raised to divisional status.

zoned by floors or sections of floors. Some stores also set a rental value on their display windows and charge the departments which make use of them, on a daily rental basis. Weighting schedules have been developed for delivery cost whereby this is charged to departments on the basis of the number of deliveries multiplied by the weight assigned to each department's merchandise.

Treatment of Indirect Expense.—In the typical store the foregoing direct expenses account for approximately 60% of the total operating expense; the remaining 40% is generally regarded as indirect. The proper treatment departmentally of such indirect expense has proved to be a controversial issue. At least four methods, singly or in combination, are in use at the present time. The methods are:

1. Distribution to departments solely on the basis of sales
2. Distribution to departments on a number of bases
3. The contribution plan (no distribution to departments)
4. Distribution of service division costs to departments by means of standard unit costs

These methods are examined briefly in succeeding sections.

Distribution of Indirect Expense on Basis of Sales.—First in point of history and in widespread usage currently is the distribution of indirect expense to departments on the basis of the money volume of sales. This proration is made on a cumulative basis in order to overcome seasonal inequities which may occur, as the seasonal variations in individual departments differ in many cases from that of the store as a whole. Thus the share of expense prorated to Department A for the first six months of the fiscal year is determined by the ratio of A's sales to total sales for the six months. The amount prorated to Department A for the sixth month is obtained by subtracting its share for five months from its share for six months.

Advantages of Prorating Indirect Expense on Basis of Sales.— The distribution of indirect expense on the basis of sales has certain advantages. The plan is extremely simple and easily understood by all concerned. Some smaller stores make the analysis only quarterly or semiannually. Because of the simplicity of the plan, stores have rapidly accepted the standard uniform practice and have been able, therefore, to prepare complete departmental operating statements and to submit them to trade associations for comparative purposes on a fairly uniform basis.

Disadvantages of Prorating Indirect Expense on Basis of Sales.— While the distribution of a large share of the operating expense to departments on the basis of sales has the advantage of simplicity, it has the obvious disadvantage of not reflecting the true departmental operating cost and net profit. On the basis of such figures management has no dependable guide as to the type of merchandise which should be continued in the store or whether or not a particular line should be actively promoted. Moreover, from the standpoint of control of costs, difficulties arise when a large part of the expense is distributed on a sales basis. When management approaches a buyer concerning an unfavorable profit result for a department, the buyer usually points to the indirect expense item as the cause. He disclaims any responsibility for the indirect cost and sees no reason why it should go up with his increase in volume. There may or may not be merit to his contention but he cannot be proved to be wrong.

Overemphasis on Percentage of Sales Concept.—Influenced by the retail inventory method, the percentage of sales concept has been widely accepted as a measurement of operating results. Markups are universally thought of in terms of percentages of original retail price and practically all other items in total store and departmental operating reports are expressed in terms of percentages of net sales. In this manner the costs of operating a particular department, which usually covers a limited line of merchandise, are thought of in terms of percentages of net sales of that department.

The result of this method of prorating expenses is that all departments are asked to show more or less the same margin of gross profit regardless of whether or not such a margin is necessary to cover the actual operating expense of the department. A buyer, for example, will not take on a certain line if he cannot secure a gross margin which will measure up to that for which his department is being held. Many lines are thereby excluded from the department store stocks and it is in these lines of merchandise that many of the chain and specialty houses have found their field for encroachment on department store volume. A concrete illustration is supplied by a line of nationally advertised rugs which can be sold from samples, since stocks are carried at local manufacturers' warehouses, and on which the margin is about 30%. If the floor coverings department sells a quantity of such rugs, its expense, prorated largely on a sales basis, will increase with the added volume. This expense will approximate 40% of sales. With only a 30% margin, the department will show a loss. The buyer, knowing these results will appear in his report, will not take on the line or, if he does, will not push it. It is entirely possible, however, that, owing to the low actual cost of handling this item, a very satisfactory profit could be made. At the same time the buyer may take on other lines on which a 45% gross margin is available but which would actually reveal a loss were all the costs of handling properly reported.

There appears to be no reason why many low-margin lines cannot be handled at as low or a lower cost under a department store organization than in competing types of stores. It becomes imperative, therefore, that either the distribution of expenses to departments be done in such a way that it will actually reflect the true costs or that this distribution be entirely abandoned as recommended under the contribution plan.

The reliance upon percentages of net sales as a basic guide in measuring operations is unsatisfactory not only in decisions as to the type of merchandise to be handled but also in the control of expense. Net sales for the store as a whole and for individual departments are influenced greatly by variations in market prices. This was particularly apparent during the depression years of 1931–33 when the price level of merchandise declined precipitously. Dollar sales figures dropped month by month but many stores continued to do practically the same volume in terms of transactions. The base against which operations were being measured was fluctuating and consequently was not a satisfactory guide.

Moreover, difficulties arise in the interrelation of operations of selling and service divisions. The general concept in the majority of stores is that the service divisions are responsible for maintaining the cost of their operations at certain levels in relation to sales. Fixed dollar budgets by months and by seasons are established for these service divisions in such a way that the net cost will not be a higher per cent of net sales than in the previous period. Whenever severe price fluctuations occur, these dollar budgets and the expense percentage goals both become useless.

A further difficulty arises from the fact that service divisions have no control over the volume of their operations. The load of work which comes to a service division, such as the receiving and marking division or the delivery department, is entirely dependent upon the activities of the selling departments. With a budget based upon the previous year's operations, and reflecting labor costs of the current period, any service division may find it necessary to overspend its budget early in the period if it is given an excessive volume of work. Moreover, this additional work may not be immediately reflected in sales volume. For example, an expected rise in prices may induce the selling divisions to purchase quantities far in excess of the normal purchasing for that period of the year and thus place upon the receiving division a much greater load of work than could have been foreseen at the time the budgets were prepared. To handle this load of work adequately, the service division must overspend its budget both in dollars and in percentage of net sales. With no other measures except the dollar budget and the percentage of net sales, management is prone to look upon the operations of the service divisions as being unsatisfactory. The result may easily be that the service divisions, in an attempt to hold to their budgets, will force poor service on the selling divisions.

The same situation results when a selling division operates in such a way as to require a variation from normal service, by the promotion of different types of merchandise or merchandise which is especially costly to handle. The service divisions are placed in a position where they must either overspend their budgets and incur the wrath of management, or keep to their original plans and provide an inadequate type of service to the selling division. This may in the long run prove detrimental to the store as a whole.

The conflict between selling and service divisions may be illustrated by the sale of $2 lamps. Assume that the lamp department puts on a special sale of such lamps and sells 1,000 in a few days. The department's sales are increased by $2,000 and its operating expense (that part prorated on a sales basis) will be somewhat higher for the month but not out of proportion to sales. The packing department, however, will be swamped with lamps to be packed and delivered quickly. The cost of packing alone may easily run to 40 cents each. At the end of the month the head of the lamp department will make a good showing and the head of the packing department a poor one, if operating expenses are measured in terms of net sales. The actual facts of performance may be just the opposite. This is by no means an uncommon situation in department stores, when the costs of central service units, such as receiving and packing, are considered in the indirect expense group and prorated to departments on the basis of dollar value of sales.

Distribution of Indirect Expense on a Number of Bases.—In view of the difficulties mentioned above, the more aggressive stores have directed their attention to the analysis and control of the remaining 40% of operating costs.

It should be remembered that department stores experienced a rapid growth between 1914 and 1929. Their increase in volume obliterated somewhat the problem of expense control, but brought with it problems of organization. Many stores grew from relatively small volume and small staffs to large volume and large staffs in a comparatively short period of time. From a small organization in which the owner knew all members and the details of their daily activities, the business grew until it demanded a large staff and the attendant assignment of responsibility for the various activities.

One of the developments during this period of growth was the centralization of functions on a total store basis and a lessening of departmental control over nonselling operations. In the small stores departments had been responsible for receiving, marking, and stocking their own merchandise; but, as store volume expanded, these departmental activities were supplanted by centralized service units performing the work for the entire store.

The accounting committees of the department store organizations were not idle during this time. The original accounting committee and a later committee on standardization acted as clearing houses for questions which arose by stores adopting the uniform method and gave continuous study to the problems of accounting for the trade. In 1928 an Expense Manual Committee was appointed. This committee prepared a manual which defined and indexed all expenses and provided for their proper allocation. This revised plan provided methods for charging directly to departments a larger share of the expense and also limited the number of bases to be used in allocating centrally controlled expenses. The plan provided for the direct distribution or special proration to departments of approximately 86% of the expense; leaving only 14% for distribution on the basis of sales. For example, the expenses of the selling function are distributed on the bases shown below.[5]

Selling	*Basis of Distribution*
Compensation of salespersons	Direct
General Selling	
Floor managers and assistants	Average weekly number of employees on a clerk-day basis
Stock and clericals	Direct
Wrapping and packing (including supplies)	Per package cost
Salespersons' supplies	Direct
Miscellaneous selling expense	Sales
Mail and telephone shoppers	Number of orders
Delivery	Weighted schedule

This later recommendation did not receive as widespread adoption as the earlier efforts. The original work of the committees had reached the stores at a time when growth and change made an improvement in their accounting practices imperative. By the time the revision was recommended, the weight of custom, whereby the expense distribution had been made according to a simple pattern, rendered difficult the

[5] *Standard Expense Accounting Manual, op. cit.,* p. 120.

change to a more intricate method. In general, it may be said that the revised plan has not been widely adopted.

The Contribution Plan.—Soon after the issuance of this revised expense distribution manual, its adequacy and need were both sharply challenged on the grounds that the distribution of expenses of centrally controlled functions to selling departments is arbitrary, and that for a large part of the operating expenses there is no logical basis for departmental distribution. Therefore, it was recommended that any effort to arrive at net profits by departments be abandoned in favor of a new theory called "The Contribution Plan." [6] Briefly stated, this is a method of charging to a department only such expenses as are directly incurred by the department and which would disappear if the department were discontinued; all other expenses are placed in a general bracket with no attempt at departmental distribution.

In connection with the contribution idea the terms *escapable* and *inescapable* are applied to expenses. From the point of view of the store as a whole, or of management, an expense is escapable if it would not be incurred save for the express purpose of operating a department, and conversely an expense is inescapable if it has no direct relation to the operation of any one department and if it would still continue were the department eliminated.

Under this definition the allocation of store rental disappears along with certain other costs which were distributed under the original plan. The items considered as *escapable* expense are selling costs, delivery costs, and direct newspaper and direct mail advertising expenditures. These expenses when deducted from a department's gross margin leave a resultant figure termed as the department's *contribution.*

The argument for adoption of the contribution plan rests on the assumption that a reasonably accurate allocation of most indirect expense to departments cannot be made. If this were a valid assumption, the plan might well be preferable to the alternative of using dollar sales as the sole basis for indirect expense distribution. But dependable bases of allocation are available for the bulk of indirect expense under the revised N.R.D.G.A. procedure and, to an even greater extent, under the standard unit cost plan now being pioneered by a few stores. To accept the contribution plan as a *regular* procedure of expense analysis and control is to deny the fruits of years of progress toward more exact and meaningful procedures.

[6] So termed by its leading proponent, the late Carlos B. Clark. It will be recalled that the contribution plan, as a general approach to distribution cost analysis, was introduced in Chapter 3. Although the plan has received perhaps greatest attention among department store accountants, it also has been rather widely adopted in other areas of business. Consequently, a searching examination of its characteristics and practical applications is made in Chapter 12.

The criticisms here made of the contribution plan are not intended as a total indictment. The contribution idea has a place in retail expense accounting, namely, in certain special analyses. The particular applications can be summarized as follows:

1. To serve as a preliminary guide to management thinking relative to decisions concerning the continuation or discontinuation of a department, or the addition of a new department
2. To measure the effectiveness of the department managers' efforts in isolation from cost factors over which they have little or no control

The kinds of information thus obtained can, however, be the products of regular analysis under the expense distribution plans. All that is required is the determination of profit after direct departmental expense—or after escapable expense if a precise distinction should be maintained. This procedure is, of course, the one recommended in this text for all analyses by manner of application of marketing effort.

Present-Day Problems of Department Stores.—In spite of the development in standardization of accounting and the availability of data concerning the operations of stores as a whole and of individual departments, department stores have not achieved a high degree of perfection in the control of operations and operating costs.

A glance at practically any of the published reports on department store operations will reveal that considerable sections of these reports are devoted to an analysis of the total expenses; moreover, that these expenses, in relation to sales volume, increased continuously for a number of years prior to the World War II period. The war years witnessed a rather sharp decline in the total expense ratio attributable to expanded sales volumes and curtailed services. For five consecutive years, 1945–49, the expense ratio, however, moved upward to a level in 1949 somewhat under that of immediate prewar years. If wartime experience is discounted, there is little question that the long-term trend of total expenses in relation to sales has been generally upward. The increase in the size of stores and the change to centralized operations and centralized control of expense, which should have brought economies, have failed to show this in the total expense ratio. Of course, this problem is not singular to department stores and much of the increase in expense has been due to factors which affect other industries and trades as well; namely, increases in the general wage level, a shortening of the working day, and an increase in the tax load. However, department stores as a whole have had difficulty in maintaining their competitive position. The variety chains have increased in relative importance and have expanded their lines; and specialty chains have become increasingly important. In many lines of merchandise these specialty stores appear to be able to serve the market at a lower cost than that maintained by the average department store.

A further development and refinement of the accounting control procedure in department stores has much to offer in the solution of these problems.

Actual Departmental Costs Needed.—Management should have at hand an adequate measure of the profit or loss realized on each line of merchandise. In determining and using these profit results due consideration should be given to the *escapable* and *inescapable* expenses of the *contribution plan,* but expense distribution should be carried much further than the easily measured direct expenses. Sales of lines such as furniture may yield a handsome contribution measured in per cent to net sales and in dollars, after deduction of direct selling, advertising, buying, and investment carrying costs. These, however, are largely offset by the high payroll and occupancy costs related to the merchandise. On the other hand, the large unit of sale produces a low cost of office activities. Again, the large amount of instalment business may produce additional financial revenue over and above the costs of bookkeeping, financing, and bad debts. Management should have at hand reliable reports reflecting these data, for guidance in decisions regarding the lines of merchandise to be expanded or contracted.

The actual cost of handling each line of merchandise can and should be determined but this can never be done by a method which relies upon the proration of a large part of the store expenses on a sales basis. The costs must be determined by developing unit costs of each one of the operations which must be performed in the entire process from purchase and receipt of the merchandise until final delivery at the customer's home. The service divisions of any store have grown to their present size and have developed their present routines in response to the growth of the selling divisions and the demands of enlarged and varied selling activities. The cost of these service operations can, for the most part, be measured in terms of work units and these costs charged to departments in accordance with the actual work units required and used by the various types of merchandise of the individual departments.

Standard Unit Operation Costs of Service Divisions.—What is really needed in the department store is standard work unit costs. Such costs facilitate the work of planning and free the management from the curse of the "per cent to net sales" method of control which has such damaging results during periods of rising and falling price levels.

When prices are moving upward, a control of expense which is based on past performance in terms of percentages of net sales automatically increases the budgets for the service divisions of the store although the load of work as measured by the number and type of transactions handled may not increase. When the price level drops, the reverse is true. Service divisions are forced to reduce personnel, although the load of work may not change materially, with resulting poor service to customers and increased adjustment expense for the store.

In a somewhat more limited way, this same problem results from the extreme seasonal fluctuations of the department store. This seasonal problem has also been inadequately met due to the failure to use a standard cost approach. Many service departments are overstaffed during the dull months and understaffed in the busy months. This seasonal problem has been recognized on the selling floor where the sales transaction measure has been applied, but in the service divisions, data pertaining to transactions, unit costs, and standard costs have been used to a very limited extent in the planning and control of operations.

The use of standard costs for service divisions also accomplishes much toward the elimination of organization difficulties and internal warfare. With service divisions attempting to operate on fixed dollar budgets, based upon estimated sales, there is continual friction between selling and service departments. If a selling division places an abnormal load on a service division, the service department head knows that he will receive no extra credit for the work or no addition to his budget. As a result the merchandise may be slowly or carelessly moved.

With adequate standard costs and flexible budgets such situations are largely avoided. True results are reflected in the reports of both service and selling divisions. For example, in the illustration of the lamps mentioned earlier, the service division would be judged on the load of work actually handled and its ability to do this work on the basis of standard unit costs. The selling department would be charged for the work actually done for it, would see at once through its operating statement that it had created a costly operation, and could judge the desirability of future operations accordingly. Other departments, meanwhile, would not be required to share in the high expense of the lamp department nor to suffer from the poor service which frequently arises.

Standard unit operation costs can be applied in the typical department store to approximately 35% of the total operating expense. Illustrative of the service operations to which standard costs can be applied are the following:

Service Divisions	Bases of Cost Measurement
Auditing department	Transactions
	Cash registers
	Salesbooks
Accounts payable:	
Order section	Orders placed
Record section	Invoices and debits
Payment section	Checks issued
Statistical—Department ledgers	Departments
Payroll	Number of employees
Cash office—Department cash division	Number of banks used
C. O. D. department	C. O. D. transactions
Accounts receivable	Number of postings
Advertising artists	Drawings produced
Copywriting	Lines of advertising space
Sign shop	Number of signs by size
Display expense	Number of windows used
Receiving expense	Number of pieces marked
Returns to vendors	Number of shipments
Buying office	Number of orders placed
Wrapping and packing	Number of *send* and *take-with* transactions
Returns from customers	Number of return transactions
Mail and telephone division	Number of transactions—mail and telephone
Delivery	Number of delivered transactions
Handling costs:	
Storerooms	Pieces received
Workrooms	Units of work produced

Standard unit costs of the various service divisions listed above are usually established as the result of sample studies. In one large Midwestern department store [7] unit costs are studied and standards revised as needed every six months. It is recognized that seasonality of sales is an important factor affecting the validity of standard unit costs. Variations in costs arise from the influence of seasonal volume shifts on the absorption of fixed costs per unit.

Direct and General Costs.—Operating costs which can be charged directly to departments include salespeoples' salaries, advertising space, radio time, occupancy space, occupancy costs, buying salaries, traveling expense, fixtures and repair, window space occupied, and interest on average stock investment. These items usually represent about 60%

[7] The F. & R. Lazarus & Co., Columbus, Ohio. Lazarus' accounting and research personnel, under the able leadership of Miss Josephine A. Lowrie, have pioneered in the use of unit costing procedures in department stores.

of the total cost and include some of the items for which standard unit costs are suggested in the preceding topic. In addition to the costs charged direct to departments now, and the costs which should be charged on the basis of standard unit operating costs, there are other expenses which can be prorated to departments on bases which reflect department operations but cannot be measured in work units. These include such items as the Credit and Collection Division, Employment, Training and Welfare, Floor Managers, and Interior Display.

There will then remain certain general store expenses (not more than 15% of the total) including the salaries of management, controller, and superintendent; donations; pensions; institutional publicity; etc., for which there is no reasonable basis for charging to departments. These should be budgeted in total and assigned to departments in advance on a fixed basis. Thus, Department A may be budgeted with $1,000 for these general expenses and will be charged with this amount regardless of volume. The determination of the amount to be so distributed to the individual departments may be on the basis of budgeted sales, ability to contribute, or arbitrary allocation by management.

By this method selling department managers can know in advance their overhead load. The fluctuating expenses which appear on their reports reflect only the direct costs, largely under their control, and standard charges per unit for the services actually used by their departments. In this manner, responsibility for unfavorable profit trends can be definitely placed and intelligent action taken for correction.

Chain Stores

General Method.—Most concerns which operate a chain of stores reduce their analysis to the point of individual stores. All direct store expenses are charged to individual store accounts which provide an analysis of store expenses by nature of cost items. The practice varies with regard to the distribution of central and district overhead. Some concerns make no such distribution, simply arriving at a store profit or loss after direct store charges, others apportion the overhead on such bases as sales volume, direct expenses, number of employees, or equally. One large concern with national coverage charges a standard cost per dollar of sales. General and district executives are then required to hold the overhead costs within these limits. Another concern sets a flat standard charge for stores falling within various size classes, the size classification is based on number of employees. Thus a store employing 10 persons may have a standard monthly charge of $100; one with 15 employees, of $125 per month; and so on. The standards are revised yearly. In still another concern, an amount is added to the actual cost of the goods billed to a store to cover all central and district office and warehouse expense.

Illustrative Case.—Figure 39 illustrates the periodic operating statement prepared for each store of a concern operating some eighty retail shoe stores directed from one central home office. A period consists of four weeks. The gross earning of a store is determined by allowing

STORE No. AND CITY						OPERATING STATEMENT		STORE No. AND CITY					
PERIOD No		ENDED						YEAR TO DATE					
BUDGET		ACTUAL		LOSS* OR GAIN	A/C NO.			BUDGET		ACTUAL		LOSS* OR GAIN	
% SALES	AMOUNT	% SALES	AMOUNT					% SALES	AMOUNT	% SALES	AMOUNT		
						Shoe Sales—Pairs							
						Average Selling Price							
					9001	Sales—Shoes							
					9011	Hosiery							
					9012	Findings							
					9013	Rubbers							
					9014	Slippers							
					9015	Bags							
						TOTAL SALES							
					101	Commission—Shoes							
					111	Hosiery							
					112	Findings							
					113	Rubbers							
					114	Slippers							
					115	Bags							
						TOTAL INCOME							
					216	Managers' Salaries							
					218	Non-Prod. Salaries							
					219	Salesmen's Salaries							
					221	P.M.'s							
					222	Cashiers & Hosiery Stylists							
					223	Comm. on Findings							
					225	Janitor Services							
					231	Wrapping Supplies							
					232	Printing & Stat'y							
					233	Postage							
					236	Freight & Drayage							
					240	Light & Heat							
					244	Store & Window Cleaning							
					259	Gratis Mdse.							
					261	Travel Expense							
					264	Mdse. Repairs							
					265	Allow. on Mdse.							
					268	Uncollectable Checks							
					269	Telephone & Telegraph							
					270	Donations							
					271	Dues & Subscriptions							
					280	General Expense							
						SUB-TOTAL EXPENSE							
					342	Repairs to Buildings							
					343	Maint. of Store Equip.							
					345	Comp. Insurance							
					348	Misc. Insurance							
					355	Display Advertising							
					356	Newspaper Advertising							
					358	Direct Mail Advert.							
					377	Unemp. Comp. Taxes							
					378	Fed. Old Age Taxes							
					386	Rent							
					388	Fire—U. & O. Insur.							
					389	Local Taxes							
						TOTAL EXPENSE							
						Loss* or Gain							
						Res. for Amort. & Depr.							
					151	Res. for Shoe write down							
						TOTAL RESERVED							
						Net Loss* or Gain							

FIGURE 39. Store Operating Statement (Chain Retail Shoe Store)

Form 856-5

INDIVIDUAL STORE OPERATING STATEMENT

Rent Per Month $ ___
Option to Renew ___ At $ ___ Total
Date ___ 19 ___ Amount Spent $ ___
Remodeled ___

Lease Expires ___
Per Month ___
Type of Store ___
Miles from Warehouse ___
Trans. Code or Factor ___

Produce Sales Based on ___
Cash Reg. ___
Deliveries ___

District No. ___
Street Address ___
City or Town ___
Store No. ___

PERIODS		8		9		10		11		12		13	
YEAR 19	BASIS OF %	AMOUNT	% OF SALES	AMOUNT	% OF SALES	AMOUNT	% OF SALES	AMOUNT	% OF SALES	AMOUNT	% OF SALES	AMOUNT	% OF SALES
1 SALES Grocery	T												
2 Produce	T												
3 Total Grocery and Produce	T												
4 Meat	T												
5 TOTAL SALES	T		100|0		100|0		100|0		100|0		100|0		100|0
6 Grocery Mark-up Profit	G												
7 Grocery Shrinkage and Spoilage	G												
8 [Inv Adj (Retail Bal) included with above]	G												
9 GROCERY GROSS PROFIT	G												
10 Produce Mark-up Profit	P												
11 Produce Shrinkage and Spoilage	P												
12 PRODUCE GROSS PROFIT	P												
13 TOTAL GROC and PROD GROSS PROFIT	GP												
14 MEAT GROSS PROFIT	M												
15 TOTAL GROSS PROFIT	T												

No.		Code	
	STORE EXPENSE—VARIABLE		
16	Store Manager's Wages	20-01	T
17	Grocery Clerks' Wages	20-02	GP
18	Head Meat Cutter's Wages	20-05	M
19	Meat Clerks' Wages	20-06	M
20	Vacation Wages	20-07	T
21	TOTAL WAGES		
22	Wrapping Supplies	20-12	T
22a	Store Supplies	20-13	T
23	Cash Over and Short	20-29	T
24	Store Repairs and Maintenance	20-35	T
25	Laundry and Towel Service	20-54	T
26	Heat, Light, Power, Water and Ice	20-62	T
27	Hired Service and Sundry	20-67	T
28	TOTAL VARIABLE EXPENSE INCL. WAGES		T
	STORE EXPENSE—FIXED		
29	Rent	20-81	T
30	License Fees	20-83	T
31	Amortization Leasehold Improvements	20-87	T
32	Depreciation Store Equip	20-88	T
33	TOTAL FIXED EXPENSE		T
34	TOTAL STORE OPERATING EXPENSE		T
35	STORE OPERATING GAIN		GP
36	Transportation and Warehousing		T
37	Newspaper and Handbill Expense		T
38	All Other Overhead		T
39	TOTAL		T
40	NET PROFIT		T
41			

FIGURE 40. Store Operating Statement (Chain Retail Food Store)

the store a commission on goods sold, the rate varying on different classes of commodities. This commission approximates the gross profit earned by the store. Operating expenses are divided into three groups: those over which the store manager has complete control; those over which he has a limited control, or no control; and provisions for depreciation, amortization, and inventory adjustment. The total of these expenses deducted from the total commission earned gives the net gain or loss. No attempt is made to allocate the central office expense to stores. Figures are provided for both the period and the year to date and for both the budgeted and actual results.

A Second Case.—One of the nation's largest food chains uses the form shown in Figure 40 to determine monthly operating results of each store. The retail inventory method is used in figuring monthly closing inventory, cost of sales, and gross profit for the entire grocery stock of each store. Actual physical inventories are used in determining costs and inventories for meats and produce. Transportation cost to the various warehouses is included in cost of sales; however, deliveries from warehouses to stores are treated as expense items and the cost is not included in the value of merchandise charged to stores. The delivery cost is ordinarily expensed to individual stores only two or three times a year. As in the case of the shoe store chain, store expenses are classified in several ways. Variable expenses, as well as fixed store expenses, are taken into account in arriving at store operating gain. Each store's share of such cost items as transportation, warehousing and newspaper and handbill expense is considered separately from store operating expense in calculating final store profit or loss.

Store costs are controlled primarily by rigid budgetary control of costs as percentages of sales. No analysis or control of expenses by commodity groups is practiced. Thus, in adding or dropping stock items the main thing considered is their gross margins. Each level of operation—store, district, branch, and home office—is treated separately, no attempts being made to apportion higher level costs to lower level operating units.

CHAPTER 10

THE GROSS PROFIT AND RETAIL INVENTORY METHODS

In order to determine the profitability of territories, departments, and commodity groups, it is necessary first to determine the sales, cost of goods sold, and resulting gross profit of each group or segment of operations. Where a perpetual inventory plan can be maintained, or where it is feasible to take monthly physical inventories, there is no problem in determining gross profit. In many companies neither of these plans can be used and resort must be made to the gross profit method or to the retail inventory method of determining periodic inventories and resulting gross profit.

Since in many companies, particularly in retailing and wholesaling, the gross profit analysis is closely related to the distribution cost analysis, it is thought desirable to review at this point the use of the gross profit and retail inventory methods.

The Gross Profit Method.—The gross profit method affords a very simple means of estimating the gross profit (margin) for a given period and the cost value of the inventory at the end of such period. The basis of the method is the application of the average rate of gross profit, as determined from operating data of recent periods, to the net sales of a given period in order to arrive at a reasonably accurate estimate of cost of sales. Once the latter figure has been obtained, it is an easy matter to calculate the estimated cost value of the ending inventory. The example which follows provides an illustration of the essential steps in the use of the method for arriving at estimates applicable to operations of a marketing concern during June, 1952.

Net sales	$100,000
Less: Estimated gross profit (25%)*	25,000
Estimated cost of goods sold	$ 75,000
Inventory, June 1, 1952	$ 35,000
Net purchases	85,000
Total goods handled	$120,000
Less: Estimated cost of goods sold	75,000
Estimated inventory (cost value), June 30, 1952	$ 45,000

* The average rate maintained, for sake of illustration, for the previous three years.

183

In order that the reader may readily observe the close similarity between the gross profit method and the retail inventory method, as explained below, an alternate procedure for computing the cost value of the ending inventory is presented as follows: [1]

Inventory, June 1, 1952	$ 35,000
Net purchases	85,000
Total cost of goods handled	$120,000
Sales value of goods handled	$160,000*
Deduct: Net sales	100,000
Sales value of inventory, June 30, 1952	$ 60,000
Deduct: Gross profit element (25% of $60,000)	15,000
Estimated inventory (cost value), June 30, 1952	$ 45,000

* Since the average rate of gross profit is 25%, then $120,000 must equal 75% of the sales value of the goods handled. Hence, to find the dollar amount of the sales value of goods handled, merely divide $120,000 by 0.75. The quotient is $160,000, or 100%.

Utmost care must be exercised in using the gross profit method to insure that the gross profit percentage is based on adequate and representative data. Continued use of the method demands frequent testing of the percentage in the light of recent events and observable trends. For example, if depressed business has forced a decline in gross profit rates in very recent periods, it would not be wise to include data for earlier years in the calculations of the average rate.

The gross profit method can be advantageously used by many types of businesses, whether in manufacturing, wholesaling, or retailing. The method is particularly useful for retail stores handling a wide variety of low unit value items.[2] Departmentalization of operations materially enhances the utility of the gross profit method.

The Retail Inventory Method.—The retail inventory method of accounting, although cut from the same basic pattern as the gross profit method, is a much more elaborate and managerially useful plan. The retail inventory method is so called because all records required for the maintenance of a book inventory are shown at retail prices (in a retailing concern) and physical inventories are usually taken on the basis of retail prices. In effect, the method makes possible a type of perpetual stock control in terms of selling prices instead of cost prices. In practical use, however, the method is more than just a stock control system. It provides for effective control over all merchandising activities of a firm.

[1] The steps in this procedure are those set forth in J. B. Taylor and H. C. Miller, *Intermediate Accounting* (2d ed.; New York: McGraw-Hill Book Co., Inc., 1938), p. 112.
[2] For a discussion of the application of the gross profit method to the needs of retail drug stores, see J. B. Heckert and W. E. Dickerson, *Drug Store Accounting* (New York: McGraw-Hill Book Co., Inc., 1943), pp. 260–61.

Best results are obtained under the retail method — as well as under the gross profit method — when merchandise is segregated into classes, each class consisting of goods bearing similar rates of markup. Since merchandise classification is most easily accomplished on a departmental basis, department stores and departmentized specialty stores have been the principal users of the method. However, many types of stores having sufficient sales volume (perhaps a minimum of $100,000 annually) to justify its establishment are obtaining excellent results with the method. Use of the method, moreover, is not confined to retailing. For example, a large manufacturer of pharmaceuticals has employed the method for over a decade in evaluating inventories and costing shipments. A modification of the retail method has been successfully applied to replacement parts costing by a leading industrial equipment company.

Advantages of Method.—Numerous advantages can be cited for use of the retail method. Among these, the following are considered to be especially noteworthy:

1. Inventory pricing is greatly simplified, with attendant gains in accuracy and lowered expense. Departmental inventories can be taken on a staggered basis and adjusted to the concern's over-all fiscal closing.
2. The profit or loss in each department or class of merchandise can be determined periodically without the necessity of taking a physical inventory.
3. Stock shortages (and overages) are readily located by merchandise classes.
4. A factual basis is provided for insurance coverage and adjustment of claims.
5. Finally, and most important to marketing management, the wealth of statistical data accumulated periodically through operation of the method facilitates effective planning and controlling of sales, purchases, and inventories on a dollar basis.

Steps in Operation of Method.—Under the retail method cost of goods sold, gross profit, and cost of inventory are direct derivatives of the actual selling prices of merchandise. Operation of the method typically comprises the following fundamental steps:

1. Establishment (as indicated previously) of commodity classes or departments characterized by merchandise bearing similar markup rates. Stock records must be kept on a departmental basis.
2. Cumulation of purchases at retail price, as well as at cost.

3. Maintenance of complete records at retail of all other additions to, or deductions from, stock whether arising from movements of goods or from changes in price.

4. Determination of the amount and percentage of markup of all merchandise handled during the accounting period.

5. Calculation from the records of the retail value of inventory. The formula for this calculation can be expressed as follows: (Beginning inventory at retail + Purchases at retail + Upward price adjustments) — (Sales + Markdowns) = Ending book inventory at retail.

6. Derivation of the cost value of inventory by applying the cost complement of the markup percentage (of Step 4) to the retail inventory.

7. Calculation, by conventional procedure, of cost of goods sold and gross profit.

8. Verification of the book inventory through occasional physical inventories at retail, usually taken no more frequently than once or twice a year.

A Simple Illustration.—In order that the computations necessary for carrying out the simple mechanics of the retail method may be seen clearly, the following illustration is presented without complicating factors such as markdowns and interdepartmental transfers. The same figures employed in the earlier gross profit method illustrations are again used here.

	Cost	Retail	Per Cent of Markup (Based on Retail)
1. Beginning inventory	$ 35,000	$ 45,000	22.22
2. Net purchases	85,000	115,000	26.09
3. Total goods handled	$120,000	$160,000	25.00
4. Net sales		100,000	
5. Ending inventory (at retail)		$ 60,000	

6. Calculation of cost percentage:
  a) Total % 100
  b) Markup % (Line 3) 25
  c) Cost complement % 75			

7. Inventory at cost ($60,000 × 75%)	45,000		
8. Cost of goods sold (Line 3 less Line 7)	$ 75,000		
9. Gross profit (Line 4 less Line 8) ..		$ 25,000	

Note the exact similarity of the foregoing procedure to the alternate procedure for computing the ending inventory by the gross profit method. In the operation of each method deduction of sales from the retail value of goods handled produces the retail value of the ending inventory. In turn, removal of the gross profit element or markup from this inventory figure leaves as a remainder the cost value of the inventory.

An Expanded Illustration.—A more detailed illustration of the mechanics of the retail method is presented in Figure 41 in order that attention may be given to the techniques of handling several items which

	Cost	Retail	Markup	Per Cent of Markup
1. Beginning inventory	$35,000	$50,000	$15,000	30.00
2. Net purchases	5,000	7,000	2,000	28.57
3. Freight, express, and cartage inward	125		(125)	
4. Additional markups, less additional markup cancellations ..		425	425	
5. Interdepartmental transfers (credit)	(70)	(100)	(30)	30.00
6. Total of inventory and net additions	$40,055	$57,325	$17,270	30.13
7. Net sales		$ 6,000		
8. Markdowns, less markdown cancellations		325		
9. Inventory shortage		125		
10. Total retail deductions		$ 6,450		
11. Inventory at retail (Line 6 less Line 10)		$50,875		
12. Calculation of cost percentage: *a*) Total % .... 100.00 *b*) Markup % (Line 6) 30.13 *c*) Cost complement % 69.87				
13. Inventory at cost ($50,875 × 69.87%)	35,546.36			
14. Cost of goods sold (Line 6 less Line 13)	$ 4,508.64			
15. Gross profit (Line 7 less Line 14)		$ 1,491.36		

FIGURE 41. Detailed Mechanics of the Retail Inventory Method

affect the accuracy of valuations arrived at under the method. The comments which follow will serve to clarify the meaning and order of the items and computations shown.

Line 1. The beginning inventory figures at cost and at retail are the starting point for mechanical operation of the method.

Line 2. Purchases are net of any returns to vendors. Each invoice, when received, is retailed, i.e., the unit selling price is placed on each item and extended at retail. The cost value of purchases is further adjusted for any allowances by vendors. Any retail price reductions made in response to such allowances are correspondingly treated as deductions from the accumulated retail purchases. discounts are regarded as deductions from purchases, net amounts after discount deductions are shown for purchases in the cumulative Cash discounts on purchases are handled in either of two ways. If

markon and inventory calculations. However, if cash discounts are considered as financial income, they are not included in these calculations. The latter treatment is recommended by the Controllers' Congress of the N.R.D.G.A.

Line 3. Transportation charges are recorded only at cost.

Line 4. Additional markups are increases in selling prices above the original figures placed on merchandise. Additional markup cancellations are subsequent reductions which do not go below the original prices. Any reductions below the latter should be treated as markdowns. Note, particularly, that additional markups are not offset against markdowns.

Line 5. Interdepartmental transfers include the value of goods transferred from, or to, other departments. In Figure 41 a balance in favor of outward transfers is recorded. Goods taken from stock and used as expense items may be accounted for at this point.

Line 6. The total shown is the value, at cost and at retail, of all merchandise handled during the particular period. The markup of $17,270, or 30.13% of retail, is often termed the initial markup or cumulative markon. In practice the markon is usually accumulated over a period of six months, or even a year.

Line 7. Net sales are gross sales less customer returns.

Line 8. Markdowns are reductions in the original selling prices, usually taken in order to move merchandise more rapidly. Markdown cancellations restore marked down prices to higher (but not necessarily to the original) prices. Unsold items of merchandise previously marked down for a special sale are frequently so repriced. Customer allowances and discounts given to customers and employees are treated in the same manner as markdowns.

Line 9. Inventory shortages represent the discrepancy between the value of stock revealed by a physical inventory and the greater value shown by the book figures. Pilferage, unauthorized markdowns, errors in pricing, and errors in writing sales slips help to account for shortages. Inventory overages are seldom likely to occur. An operating statement should recognize shortages at a normal rate even though no physical inventory has been taken during the period.

Lines 10–15. The sum (Line 10) of the several retail deductions is subtracted from the retail total of Line 6 to obtain the retail value of the ending inventory (Line 11). The remaining steps, Lines 12 through 15, are self-explanatory. It should be noted, however, that the designation of Line 15 as gross profit is correct (a) if the department has not earned any cash discounts, or, if earned, such discounts are classified as financial income; and (b) if the department has not incurred any workroom costs. If this is not the case, then Line 15 should be retitled "maintained markup." Addition of earned discounts to maintained markup and deduction of net workroom costs (net of any workroom sales) accordingly would result in the figure for gross profit.

Principle Governing Order of Computations.—Understanding of the mechanics of the retail method is greatly furthered by keeping in mind that determination of inventory cost under the method is in harmony with the basic principle—cost or market, whichever is lower. Observe that the markup percentage (Line 6) is computed after the adjustment for additional markups, but before the provision for markdowns. This order is necessary to insure that losses, but not profits, will be anticipated in the current period. Adding of additional markups to the retail accumulations increases the markup percentage and thereby properly effects a decrease in inventory values and gross profit.

Correct treatment of markdowns conservatively assumes that the entire markdown loss is taken in the current period. If markdowns were to be deducted prior to calculation of the markup percentage, the loss would be spread over the total value of goods handled, instead of over the goods actually sold during the period. Hence, inventory at cost and gross profit would be overstated, the inventory being valued at approximately original cost. The correct handling of markdowns achieves the desired result of reducing inventory values to a practical cost or market basis.

Sources of Error in the Retail and Gross Profit Methods.—Both the retail inventory method and the gross profit method are averaging methods; as such they are subject to two principal sources of error. These have been suggested in the discussion to this point; however, they require explicit statement. In brief, the sources of error are:

1. Dependence on past experience
2. Lateral volume shifts during the current period

In the case of the gross profit method the first source of error is particularly serious. It has already been emphasized (on page 184) that care must be exercised in the proper choice of a period for determination of the average rate of gross profit to be used in current applications. Error from this source is less serious in the operation of the retail method because fairly recent experience is utilized in the determination of cumulative markon.

The second source of error is really a corollary of the first. It tends to explain why the average markup on the ending inventory of goods is likely to differ from the average initial markup whether the latter figure is taken from the experience of prior periods (as in the gross profit method) or from opening inventory plus purchases of the current year or part of a year (as in the retail method). These average markups will not be identical when goods bearing different markups are sold in proportions which vary from the proportions obtaining initially. If it is assumed that low markup goods have a faster rate of turnover than high markup goods, then, at any given instant, the former type will have a lesser degree of representation in inventory than it had in purchases.

Therefore, use of the initial markup percentage to reduce the selling price inventory to cost will result in some overvaluation of cost. This is particularly apt to occur in departments which carry goods bearing widely different markup rates, or which run many special sales events. The comparative turnover assumption is probably not wholly valid, however, in the case of departments or stores where long-margin, private brand merchandise is featured and promoted to the detriment of short-margin, manufacturers' brands.

CHAPTER 11

OTHER ANALYSES OF DISTRIBUTION COSTS

Analyses for Particular Cases.—In addition to the analyses of distribution costs discussed in Chapters 4 to 9, various other analyses are useful in particular instances and in special types of concerns. Some of these are noted below.

Analysis by Salesmen.—In those concerns in which the sales effort is built largely around individual salesmen, and where the direct expense of salesmen constitutes the major part of the cost of the sales effort, it is frequently desirable to analyze the sales, costs, and results by individual salesmen or groups of salesmen.[1]

In such concerns the salesmen are frequently given considerable latitude in their activities. They may be allowed to select their customers and push such commodities as they think desirable. Moreover, they may be allowed a certain degree of freedom in setting prices and granting credit. While their actions are usually subject to review by the home office and some restrictions are imposed, yet they may exercise considerable freedom of judgment and action. Their duties may consist of cultivating new customers, advising and counseling customers, securing orders, assisting in collections, surveying market possibilities, counseling production executives on the nature of products to be made, etc.

In such cases the analysis usually extends to sales, cost of goods sold, sales returned, cost of goods returned, allowances and special sales deductions, gross profit, distribution cost, and net profit. The primary analysis is usually by salesmen with subanalyses by commodities and customers. Sales returned, allowances, and deductions are usually further analyzed by causes.

The purpose of such analysis is to guide the salesmen in their activities and finally to measure their performance in terms of profit. More specifically, such an analysis will reveal:

Customers and commodities which are neglected or under-emphasized
Unsatisfactory gross margins

[1] For concerns wherein a salesman's route or area of coverage is established as a sales territory, there is little, if any, difference between analysis of costs by salesmen and analysis by territories.

Selling costs which are above acceptable standards
Unsatisfactory cost-result relationships

The analysis of sales, returns and allowances, cost of goods sold, and gross profit by salesmen offers no special difficulties. In analyzing the distribution costs, the procedure is to divide the costs as follows:

1. Direct—those which can be directly allocated to individual salesmen
2. Semidirect—those which can be allocated to the sales of individual salesmen through some reasonable basis of allocation
3. Indirect—those which cannot be allocated to the sales of individual salesmen except by some arbitrary method of allocation

Direct salesmen's costs consist of such items as:

Salesmen's salaries
Commissions
Traveling expense
Entertainment
Payroll insurance and taxes
Such advertising as dealer helps, direct advertising allowances, and demonstrations
Transportation
Bad debts
Sales discounts

Semidirect salesmen's costs and suggested bases of allocation to the sales of individual salesmen are:

Cost Item	Suggested Bases of Allocation
Sales administration and supervision salaries	Salesmen's direct costs Equal distribution Number of customers
Sales clerical, accounting, and communication	Number of orders
Warehousing, storing, and handling	Standard unit charges based on shipments
Education and training	Salesmen's compensation
Financial expense	Dollar sales or cost of sales (adjusted where necessary for important differences in credit terms and commodities sold)
Credit and collection expense other than bad debts	Dollar sales (adjusted where necessary for important differences in classes of customers and size of orders)

Indirect salesmen's costs include such items as:

Sales administration occupancy and general expense
General advertising
General distribution expense

Such indirect costs as the above may be allocated to the sales of individual salesmen on such bases as:

Total of direct and semidirect costs
Direct costs
Cost of goods sold
Gross profit
Budgeted sales

In some instances no allocation is necessary as the profit remaining after deducting direct and semidirect costs supplies a better index as to the profitability of individual salesmen.

Once the analysis is made by salesmen, the sales, cost, and profit of individual salesmen or groups of salesmen can be compared with each other and with predetermined sales programs to reveal individual weaknesses.

An Illustrative Analysis.—Charles H. Sevin presents the case of a manufacturer of industrial goods that made a fairly complete analysis of "sales in relation to potential, and of margins, direct and indirect marketing costs, and net profits for each salesman." [2] The results, for eight of the company's fifteen salesmen, are summarized in Figure 42. The conclusion is clear that salesmen's volume is far from a good indicator of net profit. Some specific comments from the case are of particular interest.[3] For example:

Salesman F is our number one volume man. He sold [125] percent of his quota; he wasn't overpaid in salary and commissions. However, he is a pretty free spender so his expenses were high. We had trouble with his orders. He thinks so much of his customers that he is always willing to take anything back, make allowances, and generally prove that he and the house are good fellows, so we had to charge him extra on cost of handling. Being a volume man, he quoted the limit to get business. This hurts his profits, so we found despite that big volume, he was only putting $2,300 into the net-profit column, making 4.3 percent net on his sales. (By way of contrast, salesman C with a lower volume gave us a bigger net profit.)

Salesman G had a volume less than half that of salesman F. He is a careful spender and kept his expenses down. His orders were clean, his credits were

[2] *How Manufacturers Reduce Their Distribution Costs,* Economic Series No. 72, U. S. Department of Commerce, Office of Domestic Commerce (Washington, D. C.: Government Printing Office), p. 106.
[3] *Ibid.,* p. 107.

Salesmen (Col. 1)	Ship-ments (Col. 2)	Per Cent of Quota (Col. 3)	Salary and Commis-sion (Col. 4)	Travel Expenses (Col. 5)	Cost of Handling (Col. 6)	Total Cost (4+5+6) (Col. 7)	Gross Profits (Col. 8)	Net Profit (8−7) (Col. 9)	Net Profit, Per Cent of Sales (9÷2) (Col. 10)	Ship-ments, Per Cent of Total (Col. 11)	Poten-tial, Per Cent of Total (Col. 12)
A	$26,000	80	$2,000	$3,000	$2,340	$7,340	$7,540	$200	0.8	6.7	9.0
B	26,000	122	1,900	1,800	2,340	6,040	7,800	1,760	6.8	6.7	5.5
C	39,000	100	2,800	2,100	3,500	8,400	11,700	3,300	8.5	10.1	10.5
D	22,000	108	1,800	2,000	1,980	5,780	7,050	1,270	5.8	5.8	5.5
E	21,000	110	1,700	1,700	1,890	5,290	6,720	1,430	6.8	5.4	5.0
F	54,000	125	3,500	3,100	5,700	12,300	14,600	2,300	4.3	14.0	10.0
G	21,000	98	1,600	1,200	1,700	4,500	6,720	2,220	10.6	5.5	5.5
H	46,000	101	3,400	1,000	4,100	8,500	13,800	5,300	11.5	12.0	12.0

FIGURE 42. Sales, Costs, and Profits by Individual Salesmen (From Sevin, *op. cit.*, p. 106)

good, and he had few returns, which made his cost of handling somewhat under the average. He earned $2,200 in net profits, making 10.6 percent on each dollar of sales. Salesman G, with less than half the volume, earned practically the same amount of net-profit dollars as salesman F.

And thus:

A whole book could be written on the steps that were taken for the correction of the faults disclosed by this first cost and profit analysis. Even with a sales force as small as ours—15 men—we were kept pretty busy during 12 months, working with salesmen to increase their volume, diplomatically to accomplish reduced traveling expenses, to train men to sell cleanly, refuse unauthorized and unjustified allowances and requests for returns, and to insist upon adequate profit margins. Volume alone without the other factors doesn't help much of anything except the factory overhead account. Volume and the other factors together helped to cut our selling costs and increase our profits.

Some few concerns have used the plan of grouping salesmen. This plan has certain psychological advantages, especially where the compensation is based directly on performance. It is sometimes more effective to have one salesman prod another than to have the "boss" do it. In such cases, the entire analysis is made by small groups rather than by individual salesmen.

An entirely different approach to the problem of analyzing distribution costs by salesmen is that of establishing standard or average distribution costs for products and applying this cost to the products sold by the salesman. While this method can serve only as a very general index of the profit performance of a salesman, it is useful in some few cases where the distribution costs vary widely as between products and where salesmen's direct costs are relatively unimportant.

Analysis by Method of Delivery.—Different methods of delivery are often used for different classes of customers. Where such delivery costs are relatively important, and where such cost differentials are not revealed by customer cost analysis, some special analysis of the delivery cost should be made as a guide to price differentials. Again, different methods of delivery may be used for different commodities. Here, likewise, special attention should be given to the cost differential unless it is supplied through a commodity cost analysis. The differences in delivery cost may result from either different methods of delivery or the frequency of deliveries. In the latter case effect may be given to the cost differential through an analysis by size of orders. Delivery cost is usually an important item for those concerns which make deliveries direct to consumers, and many deliveries of small orders are made at a loss. Unless this cost is properly controlled through the various analyses discussed in previous chapters, it should be subjected to a special analysis. The problem of control of delivery costs is considered at length in Chapter 15.

Analysis by Size or Number of Physical Units.—In manufacturing and wholesaling concerns, the question frequently arises as to whether or not goods should be sold in full or broken cases; in gross, dozens, or half dozens; in full sets or by individual pieces; etc. The answer lies chiefly in cost analysis. The additional cost of handling broken packages is considerable. Extra space is required, more clerical work is entailed, additional handling and packing are necessary, and frequently more breakage and deterioration result. Small units likewise entail additional cost.

The following methods may be suggested for reducing broken-package or small-unit business:

1. Higher prices may be set.
2. Smaller rates of commission (or no commission) may be allowed to salesmen.
3. Active solicitation of orders from customers who frequently purchase in broken lots or small units may be discontinued.
4. Orders may be refused.
5. Sizes of cases or cartons may be reduced.

Analysis by Terms of Sale.—Goods may be sold for cash or credit. If the latter, either open book or instalment credit may be granted. Terms may vary from a few days, in the case of open book credit, to many months on instalment sales. Obviously, the cost will vary considerably with such terms. A service charge is generally made when instalment credit is utilized by the customer, hence the seller's cost of granting such credit is likely to be either wholly or partially recouped. In contrast no charge is ordinarily made for the privilege of buying goods on open book or (in retail parlance) charge account credit. Its value as a "volume builder" is regarded as more than sufficient justification for any costs engendered by its use. That there are costs attached to this type of credit, as well as to instalment credit, is very evident. The following items of cost merit careful analysis:

1. Direct selling time cost of handling credit details
2. Credit office expense
3. Collection expense
4. Bad debt losses
5. Financial expense

CHAPTER 12

CONTRIBUTION MARGIN APPROACH TO DISTRIBUTION COST ANALYSIS

Purpose of the Chapter.—In Chapter 3, and again in Chapter 9, brief consideration was given to the contribution margin approach to distribution cost analysis by segments of the business. In each instance discussion of the approach was purposely abbreviated in order that the principal thread of the chapter content might be maintained with a minimum of tangential exposition. In view of the philosophical as well as the practical importance attached to the plan, it now seems essential to devote an entire chapter to examination of the nature and applications of the marginal approach.[1] Prior to such examination there is need for reiteration of the position taken earlier that both the net profit and marginal approaches have areas of usefulness peculiarly their own. In the opinion of the authors, however, the greater utility of the former plan in historical analysis and long-range planning has warranted predominant consideration.

Meaning of Contribution Margin.—The contribution margin of a given segment of sales is the figure obtained by deducting from gross profit only those distribution costs which are specific to the segment. These specific costs may be conveniently regarded as those which would not need to be incurred if the segment were discontinued or which would be incurred if a new segment were added or substituted. In the literature of cost analysis these costs are clothed in a variety of titles. Some of the more common terms include direct, variable, separable, savable, differential, marginal, and escapable. This plethora of designations has been responsible for no little confusion in proper understanding of contribution margins.

Perhaps the word "escapable" is the best choice from a descriptive point of view; whereas "direct" and "variable" are the least happy choices. It is true that escapable costs are almost always direct costs, but they may also include some items ordinarily treated as semidirect or indirect in practice. For example, the cost of bags used in shipping pipe fittings is generally allocated as a semidirect cost in segment analy-

---

[1] The contribution margin approach is variously referred to throughout the chapter as the contribution plan and the marginal approach.

ses of pipe fitting manufacturing concerns' distribution costs. Theoretically, this cost is a direct cost that could be so delineated if clerical expense were no barrier. As a semidirect item, however, and one of substantial amount, it must be included in the escapable category. Similarly, escapable costs are usually variable; nevertheless, they may include some fixed items in cases where volume is not an important factor in the decision in question. Decisions of this nature "usually involve a proposed change in methods, of which a study to determine whether to use owned or rented warehouse space may be cited as an example." [2]

Costs not deducted from gross profit in determining contribution margins are those "which are not changed in total amount by the decision in question. The contribution margin is therefore the income balance contributed by the segment toward the unallocated costs and profit combined." [3]

The thesis of the contribution margin approach is that individual segments are viewed as component parts of an organization. This is in contrast to the thesis of the net profit approach that each segment should be viewed as a separate business. In consequence, staunch supporters of the marginal approach hold that costs incurred for the business as a whole have no measurable relation to any one segment, but instead that all segments share in the benefits accruing from such costs.

Applications of Contribution Margin Data.—The principal use of the contribution plan is in problems of limited scope involving alternative courses of action as far as a given segment of the business is concerned. The basic assumption is that nonescapable costs will not be changed in total by a proposed decision and hence allocation of such costs is unnecessary and even undesirable. As a corollary, managerial action is facilitated by concentrating attention on only the escapable costs, even though these costs are likely to be in the minority in the case of a small segment. Such limitation carries with it two concurrent benefits. First, an indication is given of the comparative performance of the segment and, second, information is at hand as to the effect of proposed changes on over-all company profits. With respect to the latter benefit the N.A.C.A. Committee on Research states: [4]

Where management is considering alternatives that will change relative volumes of the various segments, the net profit approach is roundabout because it is necessary to take into account the effect which a redistribution of indirect

[2] N.A.C.A. Research Series No. 19, "Assignment of Nonmanufacturing Costs for Managerial Decisions," *N.A.C.A. Bulletin,* May, 1951, p. 1163.
[3] *Ibid.*   [4] *Ibid.,* p. 1166.

costs will have upon costs of other segments. When a product, territory, or other unit shows a net loss after being charged with a full share of all costs, dropping the unit does not increase over-all profit by the amount of the loss. The reason is that fixed costs formerly allocated to the unit are not saved but instead are charged to other units or against profits as unabsorbed overhead. Similarly, the benefit from increased volume in one segment is not accurately measured by the increased net profit from that segment alone. Instead, the benefit is diffused over all segments by averaging fixed costs over a larger number of units. On the other hand the change in contribution margin measures directly the change in over-all net profit which results from a change affecting one segment by itself and it is unnecessary to consider repercussions on costs allocated to other segments.

Perhaps the key message of this statement is that by use of the marginal approach a company is not apt to commit the error of immediately eliminating a segment whose sales income exceeds its marginal costs. An illustration of just such a possibility is furnished by a hypothetical case concerning the operating results of one particular department in a department store. Analysis of operations for a representative year revealed that the department was definitely unprofitable on the basis of a full allocation of costs. Although departmental sales volume of $225,000 produced a gross margin of $75,000, the total of direct and allocated costs amounted to $85,800. A net loss of $10,800 was thus experienced for the year. Continued operation of losing departments was contrary to the policy of the store; however, time was needed for thorough study of all factors involved in elimination of the department and substitution of another class of merchandise. Contribution margin information consequently was required which would give management an initial appraisal of the probable effect on costs and profits of elimination of the department.

In Figure 43 the total costs of the department are separated into their escapable (Col. 2) and nonescapable (Col. 3) elements. For example, most of the compensation of salespersons is escapable, but a small amount is regarded as nonescapable because of the assumed circumstance that one or two clerks divide their time between two or more departments. If the department in question were discontinued, in all probability the apportioned compensation of these clerks would continue as an item of cost to the store. The services of the clerks would merely be transferred to other departments. On the other hand, occupancy costs, as well as administrative and general costs, are assumed to be nonescapable in their entirety.

It is very evident that the separation of escapable from nonescapable costs is not always easy to accomplish. In the case of a given item of cost proper classification "depends on the relative amount and perma-

Functional Cost Category	(Col. 1) Direct and Allocated Costs	(Col. 2) Escapable Costs	(Col. 3) Nonescapable Costs
SELLING AND DELIVERY			
Payroll of salespeople	$16,050	$14,100	$ 1,950
Other selling expense	8,250	2,050	6,200
Delivery expense (store has its own facilities)	3,450	1,150	2,300
BUYING AND MERCHANDISING			
Merchandise management and buying	9,600	5,500	4,100
Receiving and marking	1,500	500	1,000
PUBLICITY			
Sales promotion and general advertising	8,400	6,000	2,400
Display	1,350	300	1,050
OCCUPANCY			
Operating and housekeeping	4,950		4,950
Fixed plant and equipment costs	10,650		10,650
Heat, light, and power	1,350		1,350
ADMINISTRATIVE AND GENERAL			
Accounting office, accounts receivable, and credit	5,100		5,100
Executive and other administrative and general	15,150		15,150
Total costs	$85,800	$29,600	$56,200
Gross margin		75,000	
Contribution (gross margin less escapable costs)		$45,400	

FIGURE 43. Determination of Contribution Margin of a Department

nency of the anticipated change in sales volume, as well as on the circumstances in the particular business, such as the contractual arrangements." [5]

The contribution of the department to nonescapable costs is shown as the last item in Figure 43. Escapable costs totaling $29,600 are subtracted from the gross margin of $75,000 to give a contribution margin of $45,400. The analysis thus clearly indicates that it would not be profitable immediately to discontinue the department. The gross margin which would be given up is sufficient to absorb $45,400 of nonescapable costs. If, however, the original departmental analysis had revealed that certain groups of merchandise now carried within the department were more unprofitable than others, the store management might well consider the feasibility of eliminating some of them at once. A limitation to this step is the ever-present possibility that, regardless of their poor profit showing, some items of merchandise must be stocked if the store is to continue to serve its customers properly.

In deciding whether to substitute a new department (i.e., a different class of merchandise) for one currently in operation, management must determine whether sales of the new merchandise will afford suffi-

[5] Charles H. Sevin, *Distribution Cost Analysis,* Economic Series No. 50, U. S. Department of Commerce, Bureau of Foreign and Domestic Commerce (Washington, D. C.: Government Printing Office, 1946), p. 26.

cient gross margin and whether over-all costs of operation will be changed in amount. A series of analyses such as that illustrated in Figure 43 will be desirable in this connection. Estimates of what escapable costs and gross margins will be on the basis of previously determined nonescapable costs can be made for various alternative classes of merchandise.

A second illustration of the use of contribution margins in problems of alternative courses of action concerns the desirability of ware-housing in branch establishments as opposed to shipping direct from factories to customer locations. I. Wayne Keller, of the Armstrong Cork Company, has outlined the procedure for obtaining comparable margin data for each distribution method:[6]

Profits are first determined by deducting from the actual gross profit of shipments from a branch warehouse the costs of operating the warehouse and the freight charges on shipments to it. As an independent operation, the quantities shipped from the warehouse are priced at the manufacturer's lowest wholesale price, delivered, in that city and the standard cost of sales deducted from that figure. If the resultant profit is less than the actual branch warehouse profit, the operation of the warehouse is justified from the profit standpoint.

A number of companies determine contribution margin data periodically as a part of their regular analysis procedure. From such information management can readily ascertain which segments require remedial attention or which should be exploited to a greater degree. In addition, marginal data make possible current evaluation of the efficiency of segment operating personnel.

An example of the use of a periodic contribution margin report—in this instance, by territories—is cited below:[7]

This report shows, for each salesman, figures for sales, gross profit, direct expenses (salesman's salary and commissions, traveling expenses, freight outward, etc.) of the territory, and contribution to company profit. In addition, a sales budget is prepared which provides in advance the sales and the profit contribution expected from each territory. The budgeted contribution for all territories is the amount necessary to cover the general expenses plus the budgeted profit. This total is then broken down to provide a similar budgeted contribution figure for each territory.

Monthly territorial profit contribution reports show: (1) what contribution each territory has made toward general expenses and profit and (2) how this contribution compares with the contribution required by the budget. When a

[6] "Relative Profit Margin Approach to Distribution Costing," *N.A.C.A. Bulletin*, March 1, 1949, pp. 764–65.

[7] "Assignment of Nonmanufacturing Costs for Managerial Decisions," p. 1164. The illustration is based upon Granville F. Atkinson, "Profit Control by Territories and Products in the Food Processing Industry," *N.A.C.A. Bulletin*, March, 1950.

territory shows an unsatisfactory result, sales management can analyze the situation and plan such action as it considers desirable. Exclusion of costs not specifically incurred in the territory makes it easy to see what effect any out-of-line expenses have had on territorial operating results. When a territory fails to show a positive contribution to general selling and administrative expenses, the company often finds it desirable to determine how much fixed factory overhead has been absorbed. This information is also available and from it management can ascertain whether or not the territory is contributing anything toward any of the company's fixed expenses.

Operational Advantages of the Contribution Plan.—The simplicity of the contribution margin approach is a decided advantage in the eyes of many executives and analysts. Marginal figures can frequently be assembled with less clerical work than is necessary to obtain net profit data. This advantage is particularly important to companies whose executives must make quick decisions as to the acceptance or rejection of special order business. Then, too, the approach is readily understandable by executives who may have difficulty in following—or may even refuse to follow—the intricacies of allocation techniques. Finally, use of contribution margins avoids much of the argument that frequently develops over selection of proper allocation bases.

Precautions in Use of Contribution Margins.—It should constantly be kept in mind that the validity of contribution margins as a tool of management rests upon the premise that volume or method changes relative to a given segment will not appreciably affect the total of nonescapable costs. If, however, some of the fixed items in the total are incurred in capacity use of personnel and equipment, even a slight increase in volume may necessitate acquisition of additional personnel and/or facilities. Thus, whereas a contemplated volume increase might seem to carry with it a positive contribution to profits, actually it may lead to a decrease in profits. For example, if warehousing space is being fully utilized at present, the decision of a wholesaler to add a new line of products will necessitate contracting for additional space— assuming that there is no intention to drop any of the lines currently handled. Failure to recognize this probable effect on space costs will lead to serious inaccuracies in contribution margin figures.

As explained previously, contribution margins are extremely useful to management for making immediate decisions in numerous situations of a temporary character that arise in day-to-day operations. Shall a lower price be granted to capture a large, special order? Shall Department No. 25 be kept in operation for another month? Was Salesman Smith's contribution to company profits last month in line with budgetary requirements?

When, however, long-run considerations govern, the utility of the contribution margin approach as a foundation for policy decisions is severely lessened and dependence upon marginal data may even lead to unfortunate consequences. This is particularly true when the contribution plan is adopted as the sole procedure for distribution cost analysis. The reason lies in the absence of a base or standard for the measurement of the adequacy or inadequacy of the contribution. To clarify this point, the discussion is confined to one kind of business so that concreteness will lend emphasis to the remarks. Since the contribution plan was considered in connection with department store retailing in Chapter 9, and again in the present chapter on pages 199 to 201, this same kind of business is selected here for illustration.

One of the prime responsibilities of retailing management is the selection of the optimum combination of merchandise departments. In order to make the proper selection, management must have data which will show the relative profitableness of each department currently operated. Information should also be available for the determination of estimated profitableness of alternative uses of given store areas. Allied to the problem of departmental selection is the responsibility of insuring that departmental gross margin rates are "right" competitively. The detailed cost information necessary to proper fulfilment of these long-range responsibilities cannot be furnished under the contribution plan.

It is apparent that the contribution made by a particular department may frequently be insufficient to cover all expenses properly assignable to the department. But there also exists the danger that the contribution may be too much instead of too little. As was emphasized earlier, adherence to gross margin rates which are excessive competitively can have unfortunate consequences. Out-of-lineness of margins is, however, likely to be concealed rather than pointed up by the operation of the contribution plan. In support of this statement two illustrations are presented of departmental results under both the contribution plan and the net profit plan.

Illustration 1.—Department X: Insufficient Contribution

CONTRIBUTION PLAN		% of Sales	NET PROFIT PLAN		% of Sales
Gross margin	$40,000	40	Gross margin	$40,000	40
Escapable expense	20,000	20	Direct expense	25,000	25
Contribution	$20,000	20	Profit after direct expense	$15,000	15
			Semidirect and indirect expense	20,000	20
			Net loss	($ 5,000)	(5)

Illustration 2.—Department Y: Excessive Contribution

CONTRIBUTION PLAN		% of Sales	NET PROFIT PLAN		% of Sales
Gross margin	$20,000	40	Gross margin	$20,000	40
Escapable expense	6,000	12	Direct expense	8,000	16
Contribution	$14,000	28	Profit after direct expense	$12,000	24
			Semidirect and indirect expense	4,500	9
			Net profit	$ 7,500	15

In the first illustration Department X, after distribution of all expenses, shows a net loss of $5,000; nevertheless, under the contribution plan there is a contribution of $20,000. This amount is $6,000 more than the contribution made by Department Y in the second illustration. Yet when all expenses are considered, Department Y shows a net profit of $7,500, or 15% of sales, a figure assumed here to be excessive in terms of competitive reaction. That is, selling prices that are at a level sufficient to provide a 40% gross margin and a 15% net profit on sales are likely to be undercut by competing types of retailers. These firms, by employing the net profit approach to cost analysis, may well recognize the attractive profit potential still available with reduced prices. There is thus a grave danger that valuable business will be lost on certain goods sold in Department Y, as well as in other departments where a similar situation may exist.

Whether or not the store management wishes to initiate price changes in order to stave off a possible siphoning away of sales is a discretionary matter. The point is, however, that the showing in each department after allocation of total expense must be known to management if intelligent decisions are to be made. A comparison merely of the dollar contributions of each department cannot provide the needed information.

PART II

CONTROL AND PLANNING OF DISTRIBUTION COSTS

CHAPTER 13

DISTRIBUTION COST STANDARDS AND CONTROL

Analysis of Past Performance Not Enough.—In the preceding chapters, methods have been suggested for analyzing distribution costs with a view to ascertaining in detail the direction which has been given to the distribution effort and the cost of so directing it. If such analysis is correlated with a similar study of sales potentialities and actual sales results it is possible to see where the sales effort has been misdirected and where the results have not been commensurate with the costs. This is highly important; in fact, it is the foundation of successful control of distribution costs but it is not enough in itself. Assuming that the distribution effort has been properly coordinated with sales possibilities, there is still the question as to whether or not the various distribution activities have been performed efficiently and whether or not the results are what they should have been. Even the profit or loss revealed by the analysis is not a safe test of efficiency of performance. It is possible to conduct a business with 100% efficiency and yet for a time it may be unprofitable; and, conversely, by some gratuitous circumstance the business may be highly profitable for a time even though operated inefficiently.

A complete analysis of past operations must be taken as a starting point. By this we may determine that 1,000 calls have been made by salesmen in a given territory, at a cost of $5 per call, and with certain sales results. But the questions are left unanswered as to how many calls should have been made by the salesmen, and what the cost per call should have been. These must also be ascertained if effective control of sales effort is to be exercised. We may know that 1,000 orders have been handled at a clerical cost of 50 cents per order; but we need to know also what the cost would have been if the clerical work had been efficiently directed. In brief, we need standards by which to judge the distribution performance and signal its weaknesses. Knowing in detail what it has been, we need also to know in detail what it should be in the immediate future.

Management determines in advance what something ought to be under certain circumstances, and "what ought to be" is called a standard. Any difference of actual from standard automatically signals that some investigation is necessary.

The investigation may be brief and informal (being done solely in a person's mind) or it may constitute a long and systematic check by many people using highly developed statistical and other scientific techniques. The purpose is to track down the reason for the variation and then to decide whether any change either in the standard or in management is required in the future.[1]

While standards have come to be accepted as essential to the efficient control of production costs, it is only comparatively recently that much consideration has been given to their application to distribution costs.

Can Standards Be Established for Distribution Activity?—It would be foolish to contend that all distribution activity can be highly standardized. In fact, it is never possible completely to standardize production activities. Just exactly what results should be obtained from a dollar expended for advertising or direct sales effort when developing a new territory or a new product; or just what costs will be necessary to accomplish certain definite ends pertaining to customer goodwill is frequently problematical. But it would be equally foolish, and a fatal management error, to evade the fact that standards can be successfully applied to a vast amount of the distribution activity. If no one is competent to judge what distribution effort is necessary to secure certain results and what it will cost to do it, then management must indeed be in a helpless position.

While a new venture may be undertaken here and there on something of an experimental basis, the entire distribution effort will scarcely be directed along such lines continuously. It is hardly to be expected that an intelligent executive will direct a million dollars into distribution effort in the vain hope that profit will result at the end of the year. Rather, he may be expected to provide for the continuous measurement of individual and group performance as expressed in costs and results. He will want to know when billing clerks are wasting time, when automotive equipment is too costly, when direct mail pieces fail to "pull," when bad debt losses are excessive, when warehouse labor hours are too high, when long distance telephone costs are exorbitant, and when salesmen produce insufficient orders. If these cost and performance factors are not under constant control, his hope of profit is almost certain to be unfulfilled. But such control implies standards and depends entirely upon the establishment and use of standards. Warehouse labor hours never appear too high in the absolute. They become too high only when measured against what they should be under the circumstances— only when a standard is applied.

---

[1] James W. Culliton, *The Management of Marketing Costs* (Boston: Graduate School of Business Administration, Harvard University, 1948), pp. 84–85.

While it must be admitted that it is difficult to establish standards for some distribution activities; that psychological factors are relatively more, and physical and mechanical factors relatively less, influential than in production; that relatively more depends upon the judgment of executives and relatively less upon objective measurements; and that a somewhat greater tolerance must be allowed in the consideration of variances; yet it should be understood that this applies only to a part of the distribution activity. Much of the distribution activity is fully as measurable as production. There is no important difference, for example, between the method of establishing standards for order handling, warehousing, shipping, delivery, and clerical work and the methods employed in production. Even those distribution activities which are largely affected with psychological factors, such as advertising and personal selling, are usually capable of reasonably accurate measurement when the activities are continuous or repetitive.

Characteristics of Distribution Standards.—Standards, as used here, may be defined as criteria of satisfactory performance under existing conditions and circumstances. They are not to represent an ideal which can seldom be attained nor should they be considered as marks to shoot at; but, rather, as fair measures of immediately attainable performance and results under existing conditions. If an individual reaches the standard which has been set he should know that management will look upon the work as satisfactory. If he falls below, he should know that his performance will be looked upon as unsatisfactory.

Just as production standards must apply to both cost and quality of output, so must the distribution standards apply to both cost and results. Not only must the various distribution functions be performed at satisfactory costs but also the effort must be productive of sufficient sales volume to justify the cost. While this book is directed primarily to the analysis and control of costs, some consideration will be given to measurements of results and the relationship of costs and results.

To be effective for cost control purposes, the standards must be reduced to the measurement of individual activity or performance. It is not sufficient to know that traveling expenses on the whole are in excess of standard; it must be known which particular men are exceeding the standard. In some instances the measurement may apply to small groups where close personal supervision can be exercised over the group. Thus, a unit billing cost may be applied to the billing clerks as a whole as a measure of the success of the supervisor. It is then up to him or her to detect the individuals who are responsible for lowering the average performance. As a general principle, however, the standards should be directed to the point of individual responsibility.

Since standards are to be used as measures of individual perform-ance, they should be so designed as to measure only those factors over which the individual responsible has control. A warehouse manager, for example, may have control over the labor hours used in his division but his rent and occupancy costs may be fixed by the general manage-ment. Such cost standards as are used to measure his performance should exclude the noncontrollable costs.

How to Set the Distribution Cost Standards.—The *first* step in setting the distribution cost standards is to classify the costs according to functions and activities expressive of individual responsibility. How far such classification can and should be carried depends of course on the nature of the business, its size, methods of operation, and internal organization. The cost of such major functions as direct selling, ad-vertising, transportation, warehousing, credit and collection, and financ-ing can be separated in most businesses and subjected to individual study and control. Even such a general classification as this is not universal. For example, in a baking concern doing a house-to-house business, the functions of direct selling and credit and collection are merged, since the work is done by the same men under the same super-vision.

The costs of the major functions should be further classified by individual activities which make up the functional service. For ex-ample, the credit and collection costs may be separated into credit ap-provals, posting charges, posting credits, preparing customers' monthly statements, writing collection letters, etc.

The *second* step is to select units or bases of measurement through which the standards can be expressed. Such units or bases will vary with the type of measurement which is to be applied; thus the measure-ment may apply to effort used, to cost, to results achieved, or to the relationship of these factors. To illustrate, a salesman may be expected to make a given number of calls per day. This constitutes a measure of effort used and the unit of measure is the call. The cost of writing orders in the order department may be measured in terms of number of orders or order lines [2] written. This is a measure of cost and the unit of measurement is the order or order line. The salesman may be expected to produce a certain number of orders or to secure a certain number of new accounts. These are measures of results and the units of measurement are orders and new accounts. Finally, a salesman may be required to hold his direct costs within 10% of his sales volume. Here the measurement is in terms of relationship of particular costs

[2] By *order line* here is meant the writing of one line on a sales order; e.g., "200 ½" Malleable Iron Nipples No. 682 at $8.00 = $16.00."

to results in sales volume and the basis of measurement is the ratio of one to the other.

While such specific units of measurement are not available for all distribution activities, some basis must be selected before the standards can be applied. Where specific units are not available, more inclusive or composite bases must be used. For example, the entire credit and collection cost may be measured by the number of accounts carried; or the entire advertising cost may be measured by its ratio to dollar sales volume.

The *third* step is thoroughly to analyze past experience relative to the cost of the functions and specific activities involved with a view to selecting the best experience and indications as to the best procedure. Ideally this should involve intensive study of individual methods of procedure and operation similar to that employed in the development of production standards. If such study is not feasible or if the particular activity defies analytical measurement (with existing techniques), less scientific means of judging satisfactory performance must be used.

It is important that persons entrusted with the responsibility of setting cost standards refrain from the tendency to think in terms of functional unit costs prior to completion of Step 3. The difficulties inherent in such premature thinking are pointedly illustrated in the following excerpt from a case cited by James W. Culliton.[3]

First, it was found that some people working on cost studies seem instinctively to set as their goal the development of unit cost figures. Thus, early in the committee's work (after the decision had been made to start with a study of order-processing costs) the assumption crept in that the cost of processing an order was what the committee was seeking. This, of course, involved making decisions as to what costs should be included as order-processing costs, and as to what unit of orders should be used. Both decisions were time-consuming, troublesome, and, in the last analysis somewhat unsatisfactory. The temptation always was present to divide the costs (determined as the committee decided they should be) by the units (also as defined by the committee) in order to get a unit order-processing cost which would then be used by management.

The committee found, however, that much could be learned by examining the historical data relating to costs and units separately before expressing them as ratios. It found, for instance, that when the cost figures and the unit figures were examined separately, cost variations which were not due to unit volume variations were revealed. In some instances, the effect of such variations upon the data could be eliminated statistically to make the data more useful. In others, their cause could be removed and their effect upon future data eliminated actually. In any event, premature expression of the data in terms of unit costs had the dual danger of being statistically meaningless and of burying very pertinent information in a net figure.

[3] Culliton, *op. cit.*, p. 159.

The *fourth* step is to consider the effect on costs of expected changes in external conditions and of the sales program as planned. If increased sales resistance is expected, an estimate must be made as to its effect on such costs as advertising and direct selling. If the program calls for a lengthening of the instalment credit period, the effect on the financing cost must be estimated.

The *final* step is to summarize the judgment of those executives, division heads, department heads, and the salesmen whose experience and training qualify them to judge the measures of satisfactory performance. The standards set must be the final expression of such judgment, based upon an intelligent study of past experience and future outlook.

Standards as finally set will result in much overlapping. Thus a standard cost may be applied to the warehousing function as a whole. Within this general function many individual cost standards may be applied which relate to specific activities such as clerical costs of order handling and physical assembling.

Finally, different standards must frequently be set for different territories, products, channels of distribution, classes of customers, departments, etc., wherein different conditions prevail.

Flexibility of Standards.—As stated previously, the distribution standards may serve as measures of both costs and results. Where the standards are used to measure costs, consideration must be given to the effect on the costs of variations in the amount of distribution services rendered. Where there are elements of fixed cost, the cost per unit of service will vary with the volume of service provided. For example, the transportation department may have a large investment in trucks with heavy fixed costs such as depreciation, insurance, taxes, licenses, permits, etc. If the tonnage which is being handled is suddenly reduced, the total cost per ton will obviously rise. In such cases different unit cost standards may be set for different volume levels or the standards may be applied only to the variable costs. Not infrequently, both plans can be used.

General and Divisional Standards.—Some very general standards can be applied to the distribution cost as a whole. For example, the following may be used:

1. Cost per dollar of net sales
2. Cost per dollar of gross profit
3. Cost per unit sold

4. Cost per sales transaction
5. Cost per order received
6. Cost per account sold

While such over-all standards are of no value in signaling specific points of weakness they are indicative of trends and are useful as general measures of the success of the entire distribution program. Moreover, where the costs are properly analyzed, such standards can be applied not only to the business as a whole but also to individual territories, products, channels of distribution, classes of customers, branches, departments, and stores.

Who Should Set the Standards?—The standards for distribution activities should be set by those executives who are best qualified by training and experience to judge what constitutes good performance. This is usually the joint responsibility of sales, sales research, and accounting executives. The sales and sales research executives must supply the information pertaining to market potentialities and sales methods while the accounting executives must provide the analyses of past performance, trends, and relationships. Jointly they must interpret these data in the light of future possibilities.

Moreover, the functional distribution executives, salesmen, and others whose performance is to be measured should be consulted and their counsel carefully cultivated. Men on the "firing line" frequently have an insight into the immediate problems faced which does not reach to general executives. The setting of standards of performance and the infusion into an organization of a will to meet them are by no means a statistical problem alone; the problem is largely psychological and should be so approached. Men will respond to a task when persuaded, by the logical presentation of factual data which they understand and believe to be true, that the task is fair and reasonably attainable. But no amount of enthusiasm can long be sustained in the face of uncertain facts or false logic. Distribution activities are performed largely with people rather than machines; counsel must be had with those whose performance is to be measured and the standards, when finally determined, must be accepted by them as fair and reasonable.

Revision of Standards.—Many external influences affect distribution costs and results and the distribution procedure is characterized by flexibility; hence any measure of cost and results must be subject to constant review and revision. To some executives this difficulty looms so large as to nullify any attempt at setting standards. The authors do not share this view. There is no escape from the fact that considerable revision is required in most concerns, if standards are to be fully effective, but the difficulty can be easily exaggerated. Much of the work of distribution offers no greater problem in this respect than production, where it is now accepted as a matter of course. If an orderly program is developed for continuous review and revision, reasonably accurate standards can be maintained for by far the larger part of the distribution cost. The authors would be inclined to venture the estimate that from 80% to 90% of the distribution cost can be so measured.

Use of Standards.—Standards are primarily a tool of control by which performance is held to what it should be. If we know what effort should be applied and what is actually used, what the costs should be and what they are, what results should be secured and what are actually being secured, and if we can definitely place the responsibility for unsatisfactory performance, we are in a position to control operations. This can be effected by the prompt reporting of adverse variances with full investigation of cause and responsibility. Standards are also essential to a satisfactory budget procedure. The development of the future program must be predicated upon a knowledge of what can be done and what it will cost to do it. This is discussed in Chapters 18 and 19.

In the following chapters suggestions are made as to cost standards which are applicable to the various distribution functions. It is not intended to suggest that all such standards will be useful in every concern, but rather that from many such possible measurements certain ones can be selected which will serve in the control of the costs.

Additional Information Needed.—To establish and use distribution cost standards successfully, a concern must accumulate and have available a considerable amount of information relative to distribution activities and the cost factors pertaining to such activities. This includes a considerable body of information not available in the regular accounting records. Permanent records must be designed for regularly recording and accumulating this data in readily usable form. Just as it is now the custom to regularly record such production factors as labor hours, chargeable hours, idle hours, machine hours, power loads, and number of operations, so, likewise, records must be made of the distribution factors.

Illustrative of such distribution data are the following factors:

1. Analyses of sales in physical units
2. Number of sales transactions classified as to size, hour of day, etc.
3. Number of quotations made
4. Number of orders classified as to size, period in which received, etc.
5. Number of order lines written
6. Average number of salesmen
7. Number of salesmen—days
8. Number of calls on old and new customers
9. Number of days of salesmen's travel

10. Number of miles of salesmen's travel
11. Average number of customers classified as to location, annual volume, etc.
12. Number of labor hours of: salespeople, advertising and display people, warehouse workers, truck drivers, deliverymen, maintenance workers, clerical workers, etc.
13. Number of returns and allowances classified as to cause
14. Number of units of advertising space or time used in the various advertising media
15. Number of advertising pieces mailed: letters, circulars, folders, calendars, etc.
16. Number of pieces of advertising material distributed: window cards, store displays, inserts, etc.
17. Number of samples distributed
18. Number of demonstrations made
19. Number of inquiries received
20. Number of new customers secured
21. Number of shipments
22. Analyses of shipments in physical units
23. Dollar value of shipments
24. Number of ton-mile units of shipping
25. Number of deliveries
26. Number of parcels delivered
27. Number of miles of truck operation
28. Number of shipping claims handled
29. Physical volume of goods handled in warehouses
30. Average size of physical inventory carried
31. Rates of turnover in dollars and physical units
32. Average number of accounts carried
33. Number of invoices
34. Number of invoice lines
35. Number of remittances received
36. Number of credit letters sent
37. Average number of days accounts are outstanding
38. Average amount of receivables carried
39. Number of mail pieces handled
40. Number of postings
41. Number of letters written—distribution sections
42. Number of units filed
43. Number of tabulating cards punched

Many of the above items must be further classified by territories, commodities, departments, etc., to supply the full information needed.

Such information will be found useful for many purposes in the direction of distribution activity but is essential to a program of standards. Many concerns have in the past neglected to accumulate and use such information. It is not uncommon to find a concern which has the most exacting records of a production machine—the date of its purchase, full detail as to its cost, working hours, number and cause of idle hours, cost of maintenance, etc.—almost to the point of a complete diary of the machine's daily routine over a long period of years. During the same time, the concern may have been employing a salesman whose total cost through the years has greatly exceeded the cost and maintenance of the machine, but little detailed record of his activities has been kept. How he has spent his time, the number of calls made, the number of prospects interviewed, orders received, gross profit, and even the type of goods sold have not always been recorded.

With many concerns the distribution information is entirely too meagre. More information must be collected if the distribution program is to be wisely directed.

Standards and Compensation Plans.—The subject of standards is directly related to problems of wage incentives and compensation plans. The final test of any compensation plan, whether applied to salesmen, clerical workers, or warehousemen, is: *Does it reward merit with certainty and fairness?* When employees know that performance will be fairly and accurately measured and promptly reflected in their wages, they will bring to their tasks intelligence, energy, and enthusiasm. There is no substitute for this incentive. Nothing is so destructive of interest and effort in an organization as a prevailing uncertainty as to whether or not effort will be rewarded. While this is particularly true of employees in the higher brackets it may be accepted as a general principle for all workers. The principle has particular force in much of the distribution activity due to the fact that some of the employees cannot be under immediate personal supervision. The foreman of the forge department may cast a watchful eye over the thirty men at the hammers but even here experience demonstrates that the quantity and quality of the output of each worker must be carefully measured as a basis for his pay. But the district sales manager cannot peal his eye on the salesman who is cultivating a territory one hundred miles away. What should the salesman do, what results should be achieved under existing circumstances? If there are no standards by which to judge, fairness of reward is impossible.

With the clerical and mechanical types of distribution activity, the methods of establishing wage incentive plans are the same as those employed in the usual production operations and these methods are too widely used to require comment here. In brief they consist of payments based upon quantity of standard operations or measurable units of service performed with accompanying tests of quality. In distribution, such methods apply to much of the work of packing, delivery, shipping, handling, and maintenance; to routine clerical work; and even to some order taking and direct selling of a routine nature.

It is beyond the scope of this book to discuss compensation plans for salesmen. There is a vast amount of literature on this subject. It is desired only to drive home the point that any plan, to be successful, must be predicated upon dependable standards of performance.

CHAPTER 14

CONTROL OF SELLING EXPENSE

Direct Selling Expense

Extent to Which Cost Standards Can Be Applied.—The direct selling expense, as the name implies, includes those items of distribution costs which pertain directly to securing orders, as contrasted with the work of handling, filling, and delivering the orders after they are secured. It does not include advertising and sales promotional expense, although the two are sometimes indistinguishable. The latter is discussed in the next section of this chapter. The nature of direct selling expense varies from the wages of the salesgirl in the five-and-ten-cent store to the salary of the engineer-salesman who consults with the prospective customer. In more general terms it may be said that expense is incurred for either of two broad types of direct selling, namely, *repetitive* and *nonrepetitive.*

Repetitive selling, by far the more common type, is found at all levels of business but is particularly characteristic of retailing and merchant wholesaling. Thus, as noted above, the work of the retail salesgirl is largely repetitive in nature and can be currently measured by the cost per sales transaction. In like manner, the work of wholesale grocers' salesmen can be evaluated on the basis of the cost per call.

Nonrepetitive selling, on the other hand, is not well adapted to the establishment of cost standards for control purposes. No one would question that the performance of the engineer-salesman referred to earlier is extremely difficult—perhaps impossible—to measure on the basis of meaningful and workable standards. Unfortunately, a number of writers of highest competence have tended to confuse nonrepetitive selling with *all* selling and in consequence have concluded that there is little merit in attempting to control direct selling costs by reference to functional cost standards. Further advances in distribution cost analysis and control can only be slowed by failure to appreciate the preponderance of repetitive tasks susceptible to cost measurement.

All-Inclusive Cost Standards.—While cost standards for direct selling expenses taken as a whole will not serve to measure the individual performance of those engaged in the direct selling activity, they will,

218

over a period of time, serve to indicate adverse market trends or changing sales resistance not readily apparent from the monthly comparisons
of individual activities. General standards which can be applied to the
total cost of nonrepetitive as well as repetitive selling activities are:

> Cost per dollar of net sales
> Cost per dollar of gross profit
> Cost per unit of product sold
> Cost per sales transaction
> Cost per sales order
> Cost per customer served

Cost Standards for Controllable Expense Only.—Where the standards are needed particularly to measure the performance of the executives in charge of the direct selling activity, it is usually desirable to
eliminate from consideration those costs, falling within the direct selling group, over which the executives have no immediate control. These
include such items as:

> Rent
> Amortization of leaseholds
> Fixed property depreciation
> Fixed property taxes
> Fixed property insurance

The remaining cost can then be measured by the same type of standards as have already been mentioned for all direct selling expense.

**Standards Applicable to Functional and Individual Expense
Items.**—The extent to which the standards should be refined depends
upon the importance of individual cost items and the manner in which
the selling activity is organized and directed. The standard cost measurements listed below are illustrative of those applicable to functional
and group activity and to individual cost items. A given concern would
make use of only one or a very few of the measurements shown for
each item of expense. Hence, the listed measurements afford a fairly
complete range of possibilities for many types of concerns.

Direct Selling Expense	*Cost Measurements*
Total sales administration and supervision, including salaries of sales executives and all general sales office salaries and expense	Cost per salesman Cost per salesman's hour Cost per dollar of salesman's compensation Cost per sales transaction Cost per dollar of other selling expense Cost per sales order

Direct Selling Expense	*Cost Measurements*
Sales administration and supervision salaries	Cost per salesman Cost per salesman's hour Cost per dollar of salesman's compensation Cost per sales transaction Cost per dollar of other selling expense
Sales office expense, including all clerical salaries and expense of general sales office	Cost per salesman Cost per sales transaction Cost per sales order Cost per customer account
Sales correspondence	Cost per letter
Total salesmen's expense, including compensation and traveling expense	Cost per dollar of net sales Cost per dollar of gross profit Cost per call Cost per customer account Cost per sales order Cost per unit of product sold Cost per salesman's hour
Salesmen's compensation	Cost per dollar of net sales Cost per dollar of gross profit Cost per call Cost per sales order Cost per sales transaction Cost per unit of product sold Cost per salesman's hour
Salesmen's traveling expense, including transportation, automobile expense, lodging, meals, and miscellaneous	Cost per day Cost per call Cost per mile of travel Cost per dollar of net sales Cost per customer Cost per sales order Cost per salesman's hour
Salesmen's traveling expense, other than transportation	Cost per day Cost per call Cost per salesman's hour
Salesmen's automobile expense	Cost per mile of travel Cost per day Cost per month
Commission to agents and brokers	Cost per dollar of net commission sales Cost per unit of product sold by agents and brokers
Entertainment	Cost per customer Cost per dollar of net sales

Direct Selling Expense	*Cost Measurements*
Education and training, including sales conventions	Cost per salesmen Cost per dollar of salesman's compensation
Communication; including stenographic expense, telephone, telegraph, and postage related to direct selling activities	Cost per order received Cost per sales transaction Cost per shipment Cost per customer account
Order taking (handling phone calls and house visits)	Cost per customer handled Cost per sales order Cost per dollar of gross sales
Order writing	Cost per order written Cost per order line
Making quotations	Cost per quotation made
Payroll taxes and insurance and supplemental labor costs	Cost per dollar of payroll
Handling returns and adjustments	Cost per return and adjustment handled

Divisional Standards Necessary.—With regard to all standards and cost measurements mentioned in this chapter, it should be understood that different standards must usually be established for different divisions such as:

Territories
Commodity classes
Classes of customers
Channels of distribution
Branches
Departments

An Illustrative Control Program.—A program leading to effective control of the direct selling costs of manufacturers having extensive territorial distribution of sales might well include the following steps:

1. By means of a market analysis based on internal records and pertinent external data, determine the sales potential for each region and market area segment.

2. By means of time and duty analysis, establish job standards for direct selling effort in each market or geographic area. Among the standards so established might be a standard time per customer call and a standard frequency per call (per customer class).

3. On the basis of potentials and job standards, lay out proper territories for salesmen. A valuable illustration of the details of this step is furnished by William E. Perry, Controller, Scranton Lace Co.[1]

[1] *N.A.C.A. Bulletin*, February 15, 1947, p. 735.

If there is nationwide distribution the planning generally begins at one coastline and territories are progressively worked out across the country. If the sales season is a six-month period and a salesman is scheduled for a five-day week he has 1,040 working hours available. A standard miles per hour travel speed is set and an estimate of travel time hours is deducted from the total working hours, leaving the remaining hours for actual selling contacts. The standard time per call divided into this figure gives the number of calls the salesman can make. Now the preplanning of the salesman's territory and travel schedule really begins. The planner carves out of the market survey a group of towns which will add up the total calls that this salesman can make. Then with a good map showing mileage, a series of colored pins to represent difference frequencies, and some string to show line of travel, he goes to work. I shall not attempt to describe the detailed technique; however, the final result would be . . . a series of planned trips through the territory, each trip list showing the towns to be covered in proper sequence, the number of calls in each town, and the mileage between each town. A summary of the territory shows the number of calls to be made in the season and the mileage to be covered.

4. Finally, set standards for the expenditures required to obtain planned sales volume through planned territorial coverage. The principal cost items for which standards are needed are salesmen's compensation and travel expense.

Advertising and Sales Promotional Expense

General Problem of Advertising Cost Standards.—Advertising and sales promotional activity is the most difficult of all elements of distribution effort to measure in terms of cost standards. For some advertising and sales promotional activities accurate and immediate cost standards can be applied; but for others the cost measurement must be very general in nature and applied to periods of considerable length of time. A manufacturer selling neckties exclusively by direct mail will be able currently to measure its advertising performance with reasonable accuracy by applying a standard cost per unit of product sold, particularly if different standards are established for different territories and seasons. But even here a varying cost per unit sold will reflect changes in general market conditions as well as the factor of advertising performance. When it comes to the establishment and maintenance of trade names, brand consciousness, dealer and customer goodwill, only general long-run cost measurements can be used. Since the advertising and sales promotional expense of most concerns is relatively large, every possible cost standard which will serve to guide management in the intelligent direction of the effort and measurement of performance must be applied, whether of an immediate or long-run nature.

Classification of Advertising Costs.—For measurement, the advertising and sales promotional costs should be classified:

Advertising administration and overhead
Preparation of advertising copy
Physical production of advertising material
Direct media costs
Miscellaneous

Cost Standards for Advertising Overhead.—Administration and overhead cost as a whole may be measured by such standards as:

Cost per dollar of all direct advertising and sales promotional cost
Cost per unit of principal medium used; e.g., direct mail piece, newspaper inch (where advertising is restricted chiefly to one medium)

The standards may pertain to the advertising administration and overhead as a whole or to those parts of the overhead which pertain to copy preparation, physical production, direct media, or miscellaneous advertising activity.   Thus different cost measurements may be applied as follows:

Administration and Overhead Costs	*Cost Measurements*
Preparation of advertising copy	Cost per copy unit prepared
	Cost per labor hour
	Cost per dollar expended for copy preparation
Physical production of advertising material	Cost per direct labor hour
	Cost per physical unit
Direct media supervision	Cost per medium unit
	Cost per direct medium dollar
Miscellaneous	Cost per dollar expended for miscellaneous advertising and sales promotion

Cost Standards for Copy Preparation.—The preparation of advertising copy, including the overhead pertaining thereto, may be measured by such standards as the cost per copy unit, for example, catalog page and newspaper inch.   Such standards are obviously quantity measurements only and give no effect to quality of output.   This must be subjected to the judgment of executives and its effectiveness measured in the long run by sales results.

Cost Standards for Physical Production of Advertising Material.—The physical production of advertising material, such as printing, and the construction of signs, dealer helps, etc., present no particular difficulties.   These costs can be measured by standard unit production operations the same as all production costs.

Cost Standards for Advertising Media.—Ultimately all of the advertising costs, except certain miscellaneous items, should be resolved into individual advertising and sales promotional medium costs. Each medium cost should consist of its advertising copy, its physical production, its direct cost, and its share of the overhead, in so far as these are applicable. Cost standards should then be selected for each medium.

The ideal procedure is to apply both cost and result standards. Thus in direct mail advertising the standard cost of preparing and mailing a certain type of circular may be $100 per 1,000 pieces; the standard measurement of results expected may be 50 units sold per 1,000 circulars mailed, or $1,000 of sales per 1,000 circulars mailed. Such definite standards can usually be applied currently to individual media costs but seldom to the results. Both types of standards should be applied, however, in so far as practicable. Result standards must frequently apply to longer periods of time.

Advertising and sales promotional media and standards applicable in certain instances are as follows:

Media	*Standards*
Publications of general and national circulation	Total cost per unit of space Cost per inquiry received (e.g., when identification coupons are used) Cost per unit of product sold or per dollar of sales when identifiable
Special publications directed to particular groups, such as business, trade, farm, industrial, technical, professional, religious, or class	Total cost per unit of space Cost per inquiry received Cost per unit of product sold or per dollar of sales to corresponding groups
Miscellaneous publications, including directories, theater programs, and house organs	Total cost per unit of space Cost per inquiry received
Newspapers	Total cost per unit of space Cost per sales transaction (particularly in department and local retail stores) Cost per dollar of net or gross sales (where this is the chief medium used)
Direct mail, including circulars, booklets, folders, letters, calendars	Total cost per unit mailed for each type of direct mail piece used Cost per dollar of gross or net direct mail sales Cost per inquiry received

Media	*Standards*
Catalogs	Total cost per page or standard space unit
	Cost per dollar of gross or net catalog sales when identifiable
Outdoor advertising, including billboards, signs, street cards, railroad cards, advertising on trucks	Total cost per outdoor unit for each type used
Radio and television	Total cost per unit of time factored by reported or tested coverage
	Cost per dollar of net sales of featured items
Store and window displays	Total cost per unit distributed of store and window cards and displays
	Total cost per day of window trimming and display
Dealer helps, including dealer advertising, sales assistance, and management aid	Total cost per account sold
Sample distribution	Total cost per sample distributed
Demonstrations	Total cost per demonstration
Advertising allowance to dealers	Cost per dollar of net sales
	Cost per unit of product sold (such as a case)
Missionary selling [2] (if classified as sales promotion)	Cost per account sold
	Cost per man-day

Miscellaneous Advertising and Sales Promotional Costs.—Most concerns have certain advertising and sales promotional expenditures of a miscellaneous nature which cannot be classified with the regular media costs and for which cost standards are not available. The cost control here must be left to the direct supervision of executives. Illustrative of such miscellaneous items are:

Special exhibits
Contests
Public service of employees
Motion pictures of an educational nature
Stockholders' letters and dividend inserts

[2] In brief, the principal duty of missionary salesmen, as employees of consumer-goods manufacturers who sell mainly to wholesalers, is to build retailer demand for their companies' products. Any orders obtained during the course of retail calls are usually turned over to wholesalers who handle the products. These orders are tangible evidence to the wholesalers of trade demand. Since solicitation of orders is subordinate to promotional effort, missionary selling is frequently classified as sales promotion rather than direct selling.

Contributions
Community welfare
Pure research sponsored as a public service

Cost Standards for Total Advertising and Sales Promotional Effort.—The advertising and sales promotional effort as a whole may be measured by such result standards as:

Cost per dollar of net sales
Cost per unit of product sold
Cost per prospect secured
Cost per sales transaction

Such standards are very general measures of the results secured from the general advertising and sales promotional cost. Over long-run periods they are valuable and, in some instances, the only measurements possible.

CHAPTER 15

CONTROL OF PHYSICAL DISTRIBUTION EXPENSE

Transportation Expense

General Problem of Transportation Cost Control.—Transportation expense as considered here starts at the point where goods are packed ready for shipment or delivery and consists of the shipping or delivery cost incurred in getting the goods into the hands of customers. In some instances, where goods are shipped by freight and the freight is borne in total or in part by the selling concern, the consideration is simply one of price adjustment and should be recorded as a sales deduction. In many instances, however, it is the custom of the industry or trade to ship or deliver the goods to the customer and the expense incurred must be considered as a cost of distribution.

In some instances, the transportation function is merged with those of selling and collecting as in the case of house-to-house selling of baked goods, milk, groceries, etc. Here the combined effort and performance must be measured by the total cost of selling and delivering.

In general, the transportation services consist of:

1. Traffic planning
2. Preparation of shipping and delivery papers
3. Shipment or delivery of goods sold to customers and transportation of goods returned by customers
4. Handling traffic claims

In performing these services the following costs are incurred:

1. Administration and general overhead
2. Clerical work
3. Purchases of transportation services, such as freight, express, trucking, and postage
4. Maintenance and operation of delivery equipment
5. Miscellaneous costs, such as containers and freight auditing.

The transportation operations are largely of a physical or mechanical nature; hence, they lend themselves to much the same type of standardization and control as that commonly applied in production operations. However, with concerns which maintain their own trucking and delivery facilities, there is one important variable factor related to unit shipment and delivery costs. This is the volume of sales. At any one time it is necessary to maintain adequate facilities to supply the normal requirements. If sales fall materially below this figure it may be impossible immediately to adjust the equipment and labor costs to the lower level. Such circumstances give rise to higher unit costs.

The control of the transportation costs requires the standardization and measurement of individual transportation operations and consideration of the success of the executives in coordinating transportation facilities to volume requirements.

Transportation Cost Standards, All-Inclusive.—Some general cost measurements of the entire transportation outlay are frequently useful in judging the efficiency of the transportation functions as a whole. For example, such over-all standards as the following may be applied:

1. Cost per dollar of shipments or deliveries
2. Cost per unit of product shipped or delivered
3. Cost per weighted unit of product (see page 55) or cost per unit of various classes of product

Other over-all standards, applicable to particular situations, are as follows:

Where shipments or long distance truck deliveries are made	Cost per weight-mile unit (e.g., ton-mile) shipped
	Cost per mile of truck travel
Deliveries made where distance is not an important factor	Cost per dollar of gross or net sales
	Cost per unit of product delivered
	Cost per weighted unit of product delivered
	Cost per delivery
	Cost per sales transaction
House-to-house deliveries as, for example, bakery and milk products	Cost per dollar of sales
	Cost per customer

Obviously, such cost measurements can serve only as general tests of efficiency. They do not reveal the effect of volume changes on unit costs nor do they point to the specific operations which are giving rise to excessive costs. While they are useful as signals and guides to further investigation, a satisfactory control of the costs usually requires much more detailed measurements.

Transportation Administration and Overhead.—Transportation administration and overhead consists of salaries of executives, general clerical and office expense, office occupancy, etc. General cost standards which may be applied as a test of the reasonableness of this overhead are:

1. Cost per dollar of direct transportation expense
2. Cost per direct transportation labor hour
3. Cost per unit shipped
4. Cost per ton-mile
5. Cost per driver-salesman
6. Cost per route
7. Cost per customer served

Transportation Clerical Work.—In concerns where there is a very large number of shipments, the clerical work is of sufficient importance to require measurement by cost standards. Illustrative of such standards are:

Entries in shipping records	Cost per shipment or delivery
Preparing shipping documents	Cost per shipment
Auditing freight bills	Cost per unit audited
	Cost per shipment
Handling traffic claims	Cost per claim handled
	Cost per shipment

Purchased Transportation Services.—Purchased transportation services consist of railway, motor, water and air freight, express, and postage. Rates are fixed but vary with weight, distance, and class of goods shipped. The chief method of cost control here consists of auditing classifications and tariffs; however, standard costs per weight-mile unit for each class of goods shipped may be used to measure the efficiency of the traffic department in the selection of routing, transportation agencies, and methods of combining and packing the goods for rate classification purposes.

Operation and Maintenance of Delivery and Trucking Equipment.—With the tremendous increase in motor truck delivery, this cost is, with many concerns, an item of major importance; and one which must be closely controlled.

The most effective method of exercising control over these costs is through the establishment of standard costs and rates, for the services performed, which correspond to the charges which would be made by outside transportation agencies, were the services to be purchased.

To establish such standards it is necessary first to make a thorough study of the quantity and nature of the services required, the type of equipment needed, and the most effective distribution and routing of such equipment.

Since the problems vary somewhat as between concerns doing long-distance trucking and those making only local deliveries or doing house-to-house selling, these situations will be discussed separately.

Long-Distance Trucking.—Many concerns have the problem of trucking their goods a considerable distance to customers or from their own warehouses to branch stores and distributing points. Here the costs are affected chiefly by the tonnage hauled, the miles traveled, and the regularity of volume. To establish standard costs in such cases, careful studies must be made to provide the following information:

1. Estimated tonnage of various classes of goods to be handled
2. Time when goods are to be delivered (i.e., hours, days of week, season)
3. Number of road hours which can be secured per year from truck units
4. Type of equipment required (e.g., refrigeration, tanks, special bodies)
5. Routing and miles to be traveled

With such information at hand, the costs should next be classified according to the following groups:

1. Loading and unloading labor
2. Time costs—those trucking costs related to the time factor regardless of mileage or tonnage
3. Mileage costs—those trucking costs affected by the miles of truck travel
4. Overhead—those general trucking costs which cannot be directly related to individual units of equipment

LOADING AND UNLOADING LABOR. Where the loading and unloading are done by men other than the drivers, the labor cost should be separated from that of driving and standard rates per ton established. These rates should include payroll insurance and taxes pertaining to the loaders and other direct costs which are related to the loading and unloading operations.

TIME COSTS.

1. Depreciation of equipment[1]
2. Insurance—fire, theft, collision, public liability, property damage
3. Taxes—registration, license, property tax, permits
4. Garage rent
5. Drivers' wages
6. Payroll insurance and taxes on drivers' wages
7. Interest on investment

These costs should be estimated for each type of equipment used and standard road-hour rates established. The proper procedure is to

---

[1] Also chargeable on a mileage basis. In most cases either method will give satisfactory results.

estimate the costs for a year and divide the total for a particular type of equipment by the number of road hours estimated for the year. In estimating drivers' wages, due allowance should be made for union wage scales pertaining to different types of equipment and overtime. By road hours here is meant the time during which drivers are on duty with trucks.

It is recognized that there is a valid theoretical objection to placing drivers' wages, as well as payroll insurance and taxes on such wages, among time costs. A prominent trucking company executive voices this objection in the following words: [2]

Drivers' wages are not included with vehicle fixed or time expenses because wages are different in nature from the items of depreciation, insurance, taxes, and general overhead. The latter items of expense are related to time and increase or decrease per hour according to the number of vehicle hours of operation; that is, the greater the number of hours of operation in a given period, the less will be the cost per hour. If drivers are paid on an hourly basis, the wages paid, although a set amount per hour, vary directly with the number of driver-hours worked.

Wages, therefore, are segregated from fixed time costs and are grouped with compensation insurance and social security taxes. Compensation insurance and social security taxes vary directly with the wages and are parts of the variable hourly costs of operating vehicles. These wages include only those paid the drivers; the remuneration of service and shop personnel is a part of the mileage expenses and is treated as being variable with the miles operated by each truck. Social security taxes and compensation insurance likewise should be recorded separately for the different classes of labor, and only that part of each which is applicable to the drivers should be included in the variable vehicle hourly expense.

The soundness of this argument is fully appreciated, particularly as it applies to companies operating trucks for hire. The separation of drivers' costs from other time costs, however, scarcely seems necessary for the general case of concerns that are engaged in trucking only as an auxiliary to industrial or commercial operations.

MILEAGE COSTS.

1. Cost of gasoline and oil
2. Cost of tires
3. Repairs [3]

These costs should be resolved into a cost per mile for each type of equipment. Here again the best procedure is to make the estimates on a yearly basis.

[2] J. Frank Dickson, Jr., Vice-President, H. B. Church Truck Service Co., *N.A.C.A. Bulletin*, April 15, 1947, pp. 1023–34.
[3] Some concerns find it desirable, after accumulating experience, to classify *Repairs* as a time cost.

Overhead Costs.

1. Supervision
2. Office salaries
3. General office expense
4. Wages of general labor, such as washers, greasers, and watchmen
5. Small tool expense
6. Depreciation of shop equipment
7. Shop occupancy
8. Service car expense
9. Miscellaneous insurance and taxes
10. General shop expense

The overhead costs should be carefully estimated for the year and the total divided by the total number of expected road hours to arrive at standard road-hour burden rates.

Standard Cost Rates. With the foregoing costs established for each type of equipment used, the next step is to develop standard cost rates for the year or period under consideration. To illustrate this procedure, assume that a concern utilizes two types of trucking equipment designated as Class 1 and Class 2, and that its products are classified for delivery purposes into three groups, designated as X, Y, and Z. Standard trucking rates may then be developed as follows:

Assumed Factors

	Products		
	X	Y	Z
Labor cost per ton for loading and unloading	$1.20	$1.00	$0.90

	Class 1 Equipment	Class 2 Equipment
a) Tons to be handled		
Product X	10,000	
Product Y	20,000	
Product Z		30,000
b) Road hours required	90,000	48,000
c) Total time cost	$45,000	$38,400
d) Number of miles required (including empty miles)	2,400,000	1,500,000
e) Total mileage cost	$86,400	$97,500
f) Total overhead cost	$7,200	$4,320
g) Total cost exclusive of loading and unloading (c + e + f)	$138,600	$140,220
h) Average number of miles goods are handled (assumed)	66⅔	80
i) Total number of ton-miles (a × h)	2,000,000	2,400,000

Standard Costs

	Class 1	Class 2
j) Time cost per road-hour (c ÷ b)	$0.50	$0.80
k) Mileage cost per mile (e ÷ d)	.036	.065
l) Overhead cost per road-hour (f ÷ b)	.08	.09
m) Ton-mile cost (g ÷ .i)	.0693	.05842

Since Products X and Y are trucked only in Class 1 equipment, the ton-mile cost of these products is $0.0693. The total standard cost of a shipment of Product X would be determined by multiplying $0.0693 by the number of ton-miles represented by the shipment and adding a loading and unloading cost of $1.20 per ton. Thus a ton of Product X to be taken 60 miles would have a cost of $5.36 [(60 × $0.0693) + $1.20]. The cost for a ton of Product Y would be $5.16 [(60 × $0.0693) + $1.00]. Where the same product is carried in more than one class of equipment, the ton-mile cost must be secured by weighting the ton-mile cost of each equipment class by the proportion of the product carried.

COST VARIANCES AND CONTROL. By such detailed analysis of trucking costs, the establishment of standard rates, and the analysis of variances, it is possible to exercise a close control over the costs and to definitely place responsibility for excessive costs.

Loading and unloading costs can be tested currently by applying the standard tonnage rates to the tonnage hauled. Variances are caused by the speed of workers, wage rates, and irregularities in scheduling which result in idle time or require overtime wage rates.

Standard time costs are based on estimated road hours, that is, the time during which drivers are on duty. Reasonable allowance must be made for idle time due to irregularities of volume. Variances from standard costs may result from excessive idle time, drivers' wage rate changes, and excessive overtime hours.

Mileage costs can be tested currently by applying the standard mileage rates for each class of equipment to the miles run. Variances may result from changes in gasoline and tire prices, excessive repairs, low gasoline mileage, excessive use of oil, and theft of gasoline from trucks.

The variance in overhead cost rates will result chiefly from volume fluctuation. If road-hours drop below expectation, the actual rates will increase.

Summary costs such as cost per road-hour, cost per mile, and cost per ton-mile, as applied to different classes of equipment and different products, will vary with changes in any of the foregoing cost factors. Moreover, these summary costs will be affected by shifting products from one class of equipment to another, distance which goods are hauled, average size of load, etc. When important changes occur in the general transportation program, new rates must be calculated as a matter of course.

While the foregoing method of establishing standard trucking rates is only illustrative and must be modified to suit individual needs, the basic plan is widely applicable and essential to satisfactory control of trucking costs.

DELIVERIES FROM BREAK-BULK POINTS. Producing concerns that provide delivery service to customers frequently find it necessary to set up intermediate dispersion points to which goods can be shipped in carload or truckload quantities, and from which local area deliveries can be made. The procedure followed by a meat-packing firm is illustrative of this arrangement. In the operations of this company, transportation cost on shipments from plant to break-bulk points is included in cost of sales. This treatment of plant freight-out prevents distortion of local route costs due to varying distances of break-bulk points from the plant. Delivery expense—the cost of movement from break-bulk points to customers—is controlled by means of a standard cost per cwt. for each route. Once a year the company's traffic department establishes these standard costs on the basis of a combination of four factors. These are:

1. Tonnage forecasted for each route
2. Extent of area to be covered from break-bulk points
3. Number of deliveries anticipated, in relation to
   a) Weight per order
   b) Time required for delivery of various product groups
4. Type of transportation to be utilized—owned, contract, or common carrier trucks

From an accounting standpoint each route is charged its standard rate per cwt. on the tonnage delivered each week, the credit being made to the garage account. The credits are in turn offset by actual expenses incurred. A review of the performance and cost of the delivery function is made quarterly to see if any adjustments in standard costs are required.

Local Deliveries.—Concerns such as department stores and other retail stores which deliver to local customers have a somewhat different problem. Here the delivery cost is determined by the number of parcels and deliveries and, to some extent, by the size of the parcels. Weight and distance are usually not important factors.

To establish standard rates, the delivery costs are classified as to:

Fixed costs—those which do not vary greatly on account of the physical characteristics of the packages—e.g., supervision, occupancy, clerks, cashiers

Variable costs—those which are influenced by the physical factors of packages—e.g., truck operation and maintenance, drivers' wages

The total fixed costs are divided by the estimated number of packages to arrive at a uniform fixed cost per package for the goods of all departments.

Total variable costs are estimated and divided by the number of weighted package units. To arrive at these units, the goods may be classified as follows:

Class A—small packages which carry a minimum charge
Class B—larger packages, within certain size measurements
Class C—all packages larger than Class B but not including certain goods of large bulk, such as furniture and refrigerators
Class D—items of large bulk, such as furniture and refrigerators

For purposes of weighting, Class B goods may be considered as 1¼ times Class A; Class C may be considered as 1½ times Class A. Class D goods usually require special equipment and their variable costs can be separated from those of the other goods. In this manner standard variable, fixed, and total costs per package can be developed for each class of goods.

In making the distribution of the delivery costs to departments, each department is usually placed into one of the four classes and all of the packages of that department are charged one standard rate. Some stores use more than four classes, adding additional ones for goods of especially high value or those requiring delicate handling. Many large department stores do not establish classes but simply apply a separate weight factor to the packages of each department.

For purposes of estimating and controlling the detailed cost items, the costs should be classified by time and mileage factors in much the same manner as that described for long-distance trucking. To do this, data must be collected and estimates made as to:

1. Number of parcels of each class which will be delivered
2. Number of deliveries which will be made
3. Number of deliveries per truck per hour
4. Equipment which will be required
5. Number of miles which will be run

With such information at hand, various other standards can be developed for control purposes, such as:

1. Cost per mile of truck operation and maintenance
2. Cost per hour of truck operation
3. Labor cost per delivery
4. Overhead cost per labor-hour
5. Total cost per delivery
6. Total cost per sales transaction

House-to-House Deliveries.—Many concerns such as baking, milk, and laundry companies make regular daily or weekly house-to-house deliveries. Here the cost of transportation is merged with that of selling and collections. The cost is determined by the number of customers served and the mileage necessary to reach them. The relation of cost to sales varies considerably with different circumstances. With a baking company, for example, a route operating in a wealthy suburban district will have a high cost. Houses are far apart and unit sales are small, because of small families and the fact that some families employ cooks. In congested sections of industrial workers, the costs will run much lower.

Where standards are set for individual routes, a considerable element of judgment is necessary; however, various over-all standards are useful as general tests of the costs; for example:

1. Total delivery cost per dollar of sales
2. Total delivery cost per customer served
3. Total truck operating costs per week
4. Time-factor truck operating costs per week
5. Mileage-factor truck operating costs per mile
6. Container costs per dollar of sales

One of the best methods of controlling house-to-house operations is that of providing profit and loss records for each route. Figure 44 illustrates such a record used by a large baking company. A separate record is kept for each of some 200 routes. The company operates on a five-week period and the record covers one period.

Collecting Cost Data.—Where truck operating costs are to be closely controlled, accurate data relative to hours, miles, load, costs, etc., must be collected. Procedure for the collection of data must vary with the circumstances. Figure 45 illustrates a truck ledger sheet kept by a house-to-house concern operating a large number of trucks. Here depreciation is entered monthly for each unit. Figure 46 illustrates an in-and-out time and mileage record. A time stamp is used to record the time. Mileage readings are entered daily by inspectors and summarized at the end of the week. Figure 47 illustrates a monthly cost record sheet for one truck. Actual costs accumulated for the month are transferred to other records for comparison with standards. Figure 48 illustrates a daily truck record showing trips, time, miles, weight, and cost. Such a record serves also as a check on wasted time by drivers.

Illustrations of Analysis of Comparative Shipping Advantage.— The importance of control of transportation costs to operational plan-

BRANCH _____ PERIOD _____

ROUTE NO. _____ SALESMAN _____

GASOLINE			OIL			TRUCK COST AND EXPENSE	
Date	Gals.	Cost	Date	Qts.	Cost	Description	Cost
						Total gasoline	
						Total oil	
						Depreciation	
						Insurance	
						License	
						Other costs such as repairs, etc. Describe below:	
					TOTAL		
				(a) Total truck cost			

OTHER EXPENSE

Cost of goods sold including wrapping materials

Salesman's commission_____ per cent of sales

Bridge tolls

Supervisor

Total truck cost and expense

SPEEDOMETER READING	Sales
End of period _____	Cost and expense
Beginning of period_____	Profit (b)
Miles run _____	Loss (c)

Totals

	This period	To date this year
Miles run		
Gallons of gas used		
Truck cost (a)		
Profit (b)		
Loss (c)		

TO DATE THIS YEAR

Miles per gallon of gas _____

Truck cost per mile_____ ¢

FIGURE 44. Profit and Loss Record for House-to-House Bakery Routes—
Five Weeks' Period

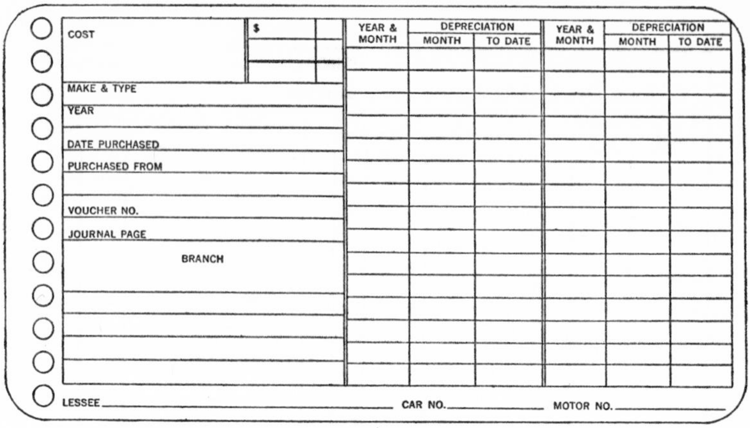

COST $

MAKE & TYPE

YEAR

DATE PURCHASED

PURCHASED FROM

VOUCHER NO.

JOURNAL PAGE

BRANCH

YEAR & MONTH	DEPRECIATION MONTH	DEPRECIATION TO DATE	YEAR & MONTH	DEPRECIATION MONTH	DEPRECIATION TO DATE

LESSEE ______ CAR NO. ______ MOTOR NO. ______

(*face*)

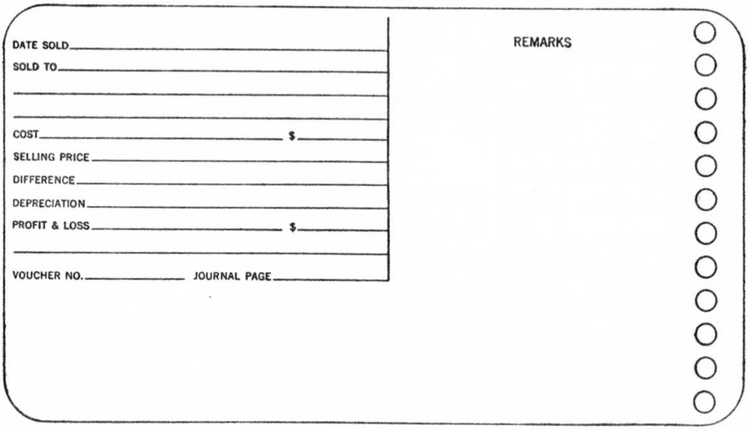

DATE SOLD ______

SOLD TO ______

COST ______ $ ______

SELLING PRICE ______

DIFFERENCE ______

DEPRECIATION ______

PROFIT & LOSS ______ $ ______

VOUCHER NO. ______ JOURNAL PAGE ______

REMARKS

(*reverse*)

FIGURE 45. Truck Ledger Sheet

ning is recognized by the managements of most companies. Few, however, have studied the problem as deeply or as minutely as the two manufacturing concerns referred to below. The problems presented and the methods of solution devised are of utmost interest and significance.

1. A GLASS CONTAINER MANUFACTURER. Products of this company are shipped from 10 factories to some 2,000 destinations throughout the United States. Since many products can be made in any of

several of the plants, the essential problem was to determine the comparative advantage or disadvantage of each factory in shipping to particular destinations. About 600 destinations, accounting for better than 90% of the total shipping tonnage, were selected for study. From information contained in daily freight reports of each plant, freight

Weekly Truck Record

Driver_____

Truck No._____ Week Ending_____ 19___

DAY		SPEEDOMETER READING	MILES	TIME
SUN.	IN			
	OUT			
MON.	IN			
	OUT			
TUES.	IN			
	OUT			
WED.	IN			
	OUT			
THU.	IN			
	OUT			
FRI.	IN			
	OUT			
SAT.	IN			
	OUT			

FIGURE 46.   Weekly Truck Time and Mileage Record

rate differentials were first calculated for each factory-destination case. These differentials had to be viewed, however, in the light of the location features of each plant, as reflected in cost of materials, packaging, and power. A "location penalty" factor accordingly was calculated for each factory in relation to the most advantageously situated plant. The sum of the freight differential factor and the location penalty factor for each factory-destination case thus was the total differential sought for an indication of comparative shipping advantage. The manner in which these final differentials were set forth is shown in the

TRUCK COST RECORD

Month.. 19......   Branch..

Make of Car..   Car No................   Driver....................................

Date	GASOLINE		OIL		PARTS		OTHER COSTS	
	Gals.	Cost	Qts.	Cost	Description	Cost	Labor for Repairs; Washing; Greasing; etc.	Cost
1								
2								
3								
4								
5								
6								
7								
8								
9								
10								
11								
12								
13								
14								
15								
16								
17								
18								
19								
20								
21								
22								
23								
24								
25								
26							Total Labor	
27							Interest on Investment	
28							Garage Rent	
29							License	
30							Insurance	
31							Depreciation	
							Total Fixed Cost	
		Month	To Date				Month	To Date
Total Cost					Miles			

FIGURE 47.   Monthly Truck Cost Record

following tabular excerpt. Thus, for shipments to Destination x, Factory No. 7 was most advantageously located, whereas Factory No. 5

Destination	Factory Number and Differential in Cents per Cwt.			
x	No. 7—0	No. 2—0.002	No. 6—0.009...etc....	No. 5—2.103
y	No. 3—0	No. 6— .008	No. 4— .102...etc....	No. 9—2.670

was the least desirable choice. With regard to Destination y, however, a different ranking of plants prevailed. Factory No. 3 enjoyed the zero differential (best advantage) and Factory No. 9 suffered the maximum differential.

Tabulations were made of the shifting of shipments that would occur if each factory shipped only to those destinations for which it had the zero differential. The results indicated substantial losses in volume for certain factories and gains for others; little change was foreseen for one or two plants. Obviously this analysis did not adjust for the ability of a given factory to produce a certain type of product, neither did it consider the physical limitations to taking on additional volume or the repercussions of loss of volume. These qualifying con-

Daily Truck Record

Date........................ Truck No.................................. Driver..............................

Trip No.	Trip Time		Pick-ups	Load Weight	
	Leave	Return		Out	In

Speedometer Reading
Final ____________
Begin ____________
Miles for Day ____________

Gas Used ____________
Oil Used ____________
Expenses ____________

FIGURE 48. Daily Truck Record

siderations were taken into account, nevertheless, in the establishment of policies concerning the direction of production and shipments. For example, if Factory No. 7 could fill an order calling for delivery to Destination x, it would be so directed because of its comparative advantage. If, however, circumstances prevented Factory No. 7 from taking on the order, the next best choice (Factory No. 2) would be made, and so on. This common-sense control of order scheduling resulted in such tangible savings in delivery costs that the study was put on a continuing basis. The scope of analysis was subsequently extended to include annual tabulations of shipments by product lines and color of glass. This refinement permitted allowances to be made for the capabilities of factories in regard to variety of glass-making facilities.

2. A FOOD PRODUCTS MANUFACTURER. As one means of giving better service at lower cost, this company inaugurated significant changes in delivery and warehousing operations. A leading processor of a broad line of packaged food products, the company operates a

number of specialized plants in various sections of the country. Customers—chiefly grocery wholesalers and chain warehouses—had been receiving shipments from individual plants in straight carloads, in pool cars,[4] or to a minor degree, in less-than-carload quantities. Since relatively few customers were sufficiently large to order in full carloads, the greater portion of the products of each plant was shipped in pool cars. These cars were typically consigned first to pool car distributors (mostly public warehouses) in break-bulk cities. Customers in or near these cities would pick up merchandise at their own expense; whereas those at a distance would receive their orders by truck.

Neither straight carload nor pool car shipping was considered satisfactory, however. From the standpoints of desired stock-turn rates and low inventory investment, an entire carload of one product was excessive even for large customers. Small customers found pool cars difficult to arrange and supervise, and they could not get the full advantage of carload discounts. For either method of shipment, delivery dates were uncertain and clerical details troublesome. The company's traffic department realized that a new plan must be evolved, not only to gain customer benefits but to achieve better control over the cost of deliveries. The entire problem was studied intensively for several years, during which time a plan was developed for the establishment of several strategically located "transit" warehouses from which mixed carloads and mixed pool cars [5] would be the principal methods of shipment. Basic data were collected on each customer's purchases of the products of each plant for a representative year in order to determine the warehouse locations of greatest comparative advantage. Railroads had to be convinced of the advantages of the plan to them because its success depended on the company's receiving the "through" rate [6] on products moving from plants to warehouses to customers. After all hurdles had been cleared, the first warehouse was established in Toledo, Ohio, for the servicing of an extensive geographical area (see Figure 49). To this warehouse, each plant sent straight carloads of product for transshipment to customers in mixed cars.

To customers the new plan meant ease of ordering, quick delivery, a single invoice per order, and money saved because of smaller stocks and larger discounts. To the sales division of the company the plan offered the opportunity of expanded volume through enhanced customer satisfaction, a lessening of salesmen's problems in meeting customers' questions concerning delivery, lightened clerical work, and greater con-

---

[4] Carload quantities of a single product shipped from one plant, but instead of being the order of only one customer they are the pooled orders of several customers in a given area.

[5] Mixed cars are "mixed" in the sense that they contain assorted products—typically, products of more than one plant.

[6] The freight rate for a carload of one commodity shipped from origin to destination without stopping off points.

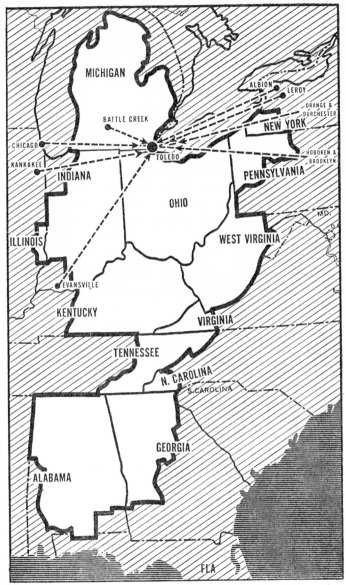

FIGURE 49. Area Served by Toledo Warehouse. (Heavy black lines enclose area; arrows indicate movement of products from plants to warehouse. Map courtesy of General Foods Corporation.)

trol of transportation and storage costs. Finally, to the producing plants, the plan meant that much of their output would move directly from production lines to freight cars ready for immediate shipment to the warehouse. The burden of performance of the finished goods storage function could thus be largely removed from the plants. Additional warehouses were later established at carefully chosen points in line with the company's long-run program of handling all distribution according to the described plan.

Warehousing and Handling Expense

Cost Items Included.—The warehousing and handling of goods in manufacturing concerns includes the costs incurred from the time finished goods are received from the factory until they are prepared ready for shipment or delivery. In trading concerns, the cost of the receiving department is usually included with this same general functional group.

The individual cost items included in this group are:

1. Administration and supervision, including administrative salaries, general office and clerical expense, communication, and related payroll insurance and taxes
2. Clerical, including salaries, office supplies, and related payroll insurance and taxes
3. Direct labor, including wages of handling, packing, and shipping (and in some instances receiving) workers, and related payroll insurance and taxes
4. Packing and shipping supplies
5. Labels and tickets
6. Spoilage and breakage
7. Building occupancy, including rent, taxes, insurance, repairs and maintenance, depreciation, storage charges, heat, light, power, elevator expense, janitor supplies, and janitors' and watchmen's wages
8. Insurance and taxes on all finished goods and merchandise carried in inventory
9. Equipment costs, including taxes, insurance, maintenance, and depreciation

Warehousing and Handling Functional Operations.—While the warehousing and handling activities vary widely with different types of concerns, the following are illustrative of the nature of such functional operations:

1. Receiving—As noted above, in wholesaling and retailing concerns, receiving is frequently merged with the work of handling and storing

2. Storing
3. Assembling
4. Packing and wrapping for shipment or delivery
5. Order filling—clerical
6. Pricing, tagging, and marking
7. Keeping stock records
8. Taking physical inventory
9. Handling returns

Variable Cost Factors.—As in the case of transportation, the work done here is largely of a routine or mechanical nature and lends itself to standardization and cost control in a manner similar to that of production operations. In the control of the individual items of cost and the functional activities to which they are related, consideration must be given to the effect of such variable factors as the following:

1. Physical volume of goods handled
2. Nature of goods handled
3. Number of orders received and shipments made
4. Size of physical inventory carried
5. Regularity of the volume of sales, orders, and shipments of goods

Moreover, consideration must be given to those costs which are directly controllable by the executives in charge, such as labor; and those not directly or immediately controllable, such as warehouse rent and occupancy expense.

With these factors in mind, standard cost measurements should be established for the individual cost items and for functional warehousing and handling operations, the actual results measured by such standards, and management signaled as to any adverse variances.

Cost Standards Applicable to Warehousing and Handling.—In those large concerns having a tremendous number of orders to handle or carrying thousands of items in inventory, it is possible to separate the individual warehousing and handling operations required into minute operations, study these operations intensively by means of time studies, and establish detailed standard operation time and costs. Such methods have been applied, for example, by the Dennison Manufacturing Company, the General Electric Company, and a few mail order concerns and department stores. In most concerns, however, a more inclusive type of cost standard is desirable.

ALL-INCLUSIVE COST STANDARDS. The following cost standards are illustrative of those commonly used to measure the work of warehousing and handling in its entirety. They serve as general tests in addition to such detailed standards as may be provided. In some small concerns, only such measurements are practicable. Even in larger companies such over-all tests are useful. In any event, the choice of particular standards will be governed by the type of concern and the nature of the goods handled.

1. Cost per physical unit of goods handled (here the unit must be based on products, weight, or various weighted factors). For method of weighting refer to page 248.
2. Cost per shipment
3. Cost per order filled
4. Cost per order line
5. Cost per item handled
6. Cost per sales transaction
7. Cost per dollar of gross sales
8. Cost per dollar of goods sold at cost
9. Cost per dollar of average inventory

The above cost standards apply to all costs—both controllable and noncontrollable. The same standards may be applied, however, to only the controllable costs, thereby centering responsibility more definitely and immediately on the warehouse executives and their assistants.

STANDARDS FOR INDIVIDUAL COST ITEMS. A number of cost standards can be used in the control of individual cost items. Illustrative of these are the following:

Cost Item	*Standard Measurement*
Administration and supervision	Cost per direct labor hour
	Cost per dollar of direct labor
	Cost per shipment
	Cost per order filled
Direct labor—all-inclusive	Cost per physical unit of goods handled
	Cost per shipment
	Cost per order filled
	Cost per order line
	Cost per item handled
	Cost per sales transaction
	Cost per dollar of average inventory
Packing and shipping supplies	Cost per physical unit shipped
	Cost per shipment
	Cost per order filled
	Cost per sales transaction
Spoilage and breakage	Cost per shipment
	Cost per order filled
	Cost per sales transaction
	Cost per dollar of net sales
	Cost per dollar of average inventory

Cost Item	*Standard Measurement*
Insurance and taxes on finished goods and merchandise inventories	Cost per dollar of average inventories
Fixed costs; including building occupancy and equipment costs	Cost per physical unit of goods handled Cost per shipment Cost per sales transaction Cost per dollar of sales Cost per dollar of average inventory

COST STANDARDS FOR FUNCTIONAL OPERATIONS. Where the volume of business is sufficient to justify a more intensive control over the warehousing and handling activities, the costs should be resolved into functional activities. Units of functional service should be selected for each functional activity, and standard unit costs established. In this manner it is possible to ascertain the amount of the functional costs justifiable by the volume of service performed. Fixed costs should be eliminated from the standard functional unit costs.

The following are illustrative of functional unit standards:

Functional Operation	*Unit Cost Standard*
Receiving—when included as a distribution function	Cost per physical unit received Cost per purchase invoice line Cost per dollar of goods purchased
Storing	Cost per physical unit of goods stored Cost per dollar of average inventory Cost per item handled
Assembling	Cost per order line Cost per order Cost per item Cost per shipment Cost per sales transaction
Packing and wrapping	Cost per physical unit shipped Cost per shipment Cost per order Cost per order line Cost per item Cost per sales transaction
Order filling—clerical	Cost per order line Cost per order Cost per item Cost per shipment Cost per sales transaction
Pricing, tagging, and marking	Cost per item
Handling returns	Cost per return

Securing the Data.—Costs can be measured in terms of physical volume of goods handled when the product is expressed in uniform physical units such as pieces, tons, barrels, dozens, etc. Where the goods are of mixed units, the various types can sometimes be weighted to provide a common unit of physical volume. Assume, for example, that Product A is measured in pieces and Product B in tons. It may be determined that, for storing purposes, 1 ton of Product B is equivalent to 5 pieces of Product A. Product A would then be given a weighting of 1; and Product B, of 5. The units of physical volume would then be calculated as follows:

Product		Weight Factor	Common Physical Units
A	3,000 pieces	× 1	3,000
B	1,000 tons	× 5	5,000
Total weighted units			8,000

Such factors as number of shipments, orders filled, order lines, items handled, sales transactions, dollar sales, dollar cost of sales, average dollar inventory, direct labor hours, direct labor dollars, invoice lines, dollar purchases, and number of returns can be readily secured from the shipping, sales, purchasing, payroll, and accounting records.

An Illustration of Control of Space and Handling Costs.—The descriptive material which follows furnishes a concrete example of the application of sound procedure to the cost control problems of a manufacturing concern operating several warehousing locations.

The statement exemplified in Figure 50 compares the space and handling costs for four company-operated locations. It is for the use of the operating or sales service responsibility. It is true that space costs must be controlled at the time premises commitments are made. They then become fixed for the period of the commitment. Comparisons of prospective cost per square foot with standards and with actuals for other locations, are made at time of acquisition.

However, an operating manager can be held responsible currently for space utilization. This is the reason comparison of space costs on the basis of weight of goods received is featured in the report. The relative space cost per hundredweight indicates space utilization. It may be stated (although it is not shown) that the cost per square foot of floor area for Location D is comparable with Location C. Since it is important only at the time the premises are acquired, the cost per square foot of floor area is not a part of this operating report. The hundredweight cost for space of $.07, indicated for Location D, illustrates good space utilization.

The handling costs, as distinguished from space costs, shown in the second section of Figure 50, can be measured against standards which have been set by operating management. The type of handling equipment used in each instance must be considered in establishing the standard. It may be noted that Warehouse

Monthly Average, Third Quarter, 19—

	Location A	Location B	Location C	Location D
Space Costs (Warehouse only)				
Refrigeration Supplies	$ 50.25	$ 280.64	$ 39.19	$ 20.23
Utilities	126.28	323.79	101.56	176.57
Repairs & Maintenance	52.46	351.75	92.02	5.13
Outside Services – Other	7.77	523.33	42.18	8.20
Depreciation	58.97	578.39	–	51.05
Amortization Leasehold Impr.	49.59	–	–	–
Rent	446.40	–	745.73	625.00
Taxes & Licenses (Real Estate Taxes only)	–	415.35	–	–
Total Average Monthly Space Cost	$ 791.72	$ 2,473.25	$ 1,020.68	$ 886.18
Average Monthly cwt. Received	6,309	17,000	7,413	12,352
Space Cost Per cwt.	.13	.15	.14	.07
Handling Costs				
Total Payroll	$ 1,157.82	$ 3,095.29	$ 725.04	$ 1,656.95
Overtime Premium	4.28	61.69	26.07	12.16
Payroll Overhead	53.46	222.08	28.12	115.17
Supplies – All other	18.70	100.10	67.71	26.35
Outside Services – Other	–	–	–	–
Charges on Shipments In & Out	.48	64.08	–	7.93
Expenses Not Otherwise Specified	–	–	–	–
Depreciation (Handling Equip.)	28.69	39.72	58.32	5.61
Total Average Monthly Handling Cost	$ 1,263.43	$ 3,582.96	$ 905.26	$ 1,824.17
Average Monthly cwt. Received	6,309	17,000	7,413	12,352
Handling Cost Per cwt.	.20	.21	.12	.15
Total Warehousing Cost Per cwt.	.33	.36	.26	.22
Total Average Monthly Warehouse Costs	$ 2,055.15	$ 6,056.21	$ 1,925.94	$ 2,710.35
Comparable Public Warehouse Costs	$ 2,008.15	$ 7,140.00	$ 4,442.81	$ 3,555.08
Inventory Adjustments	$ 14.53	$ 563.93	$ 78.62	($ 23.57)

FIGURE 50. Comparative Space and Handling Costs of Four Warehouses. (Kelley, op. cit., p. 917)

C has a lower hundredweight handling cost than any of the others. In fact, it is lower than for the warehouses with greater volume. In spite of this the cost may show up unfavorably when compared with a statistical standard for a warehouse of this size with this type of handling equipment.

The total warehouse costs for Location B indicate poor space utilization and high cost handling. In spite of this, the location is operating at a cost less than public warehousing. On the other hand, public warehouse costs for Location A would be less than the company-operated warehouse costs. All of these matters receive the scrutiny of operating sales management and are followed for corrective action.[7]

[7] E. W. Kelley, "Distribution Cost Control—And Beyond," *N.A.C.A. Bulletin*, April, 1951, pp. 917–19.

CHAPTER 16

CONTROL OF CREDIT AND COLLECTION EXPENSE

Measurements of Credit Performance.—It is the general function of the credit and collection department to extend credit and subsequently collect the money. The following four tests must be applied fully to measure the success of this department:

1. Are bad debt losses normal?
2. Does the average length of time, during which accounts are outstanding, represent a period considered satisfactory by the management?
3. Is the credit policy such as to give the sales department an even chance with representative competitors?
4. Is the cost of performing the credit and collection function satisfactory?

Bad Debt Losses.—Most credit departments would have no difficulty in holding bad debt losses to a satisfactory figure by rejecting all those customers whose credit strength is open to question, but this would immediately react on the third test of the department's success. Bad debt losses may be very low, but if the business is shifting to competitors who are able to successfully take the risks the work of the credit department cannot be considered as satisfactory.

However, two different concerns, both assuming approximately the same degree of risk, can experience considerable difference in bad debt losses, because of the alertness and diligence of their credit departments.

Assuming that the credit department has struck that point of risk which experience has demonstrated as desirable and which approximates that of representative competitors, the bad debt losses over a period of time should bear some standard relationship to credit sales volume. The specific tests applied may be as follows:

1. Percentage of total net sales where practically all sales are on a credit basis
2. Percentage of total net credit sales
3. Different percentages for sales made on various credit terms; e.g., short term, instalment, etc.

4. Different percentages for different classes of customers; e.g., industrial consumers, dealers, etc.

5. Different percentages for different territories

Length of Credit Period.—The average length of time receivables are outstanding also represents a factor of cost to be measured. If net credit sales are $1,000,000 a year, and if the average credit term is 30 days, the annual investment cost alone (assuming an interest rate of 6%) is $5,000, or ½% of sales. If the average term is six months, this cost increases to $30,000, or 3% of sales. Moreover, the longer term increases other costs, such as bookkeeping, and may affect the rate of bad debt losses. In this connection it should be noted that the actual average credit term, not the nominal term, is the governing factor. Nominal terms of 30 days, for example, frequently result in an actual average credit period of 40 to 60 days.

A shortening of the credit term will reduce the investment cost but may result in increased sales discount, a lower rate of gross profit, or increased sales resistance.

Assuming that management has established a policy as to the proper length of the credit period, the success of the credit department in following this policy can be readily measured by reporting regularly the average number of days receivables are outstanding. This is determined by the following formula:

$$\frac{\text{Average receivables}}{\text{Annual net credit sales}} \times 365 = \begin{array}{c}\text{Average number of days accounts}\\\text{are outstanding}\end{array}$$

Another approximate test which can be applied is that of the ratio of actual cash collections on receivables to the amount which should be collected in accordance with established credit terms. To illustrate, assume the following figures for a retail instalment furniture store:

Annual instalment sales	$480,000
Average credit period expected to be enforced by credit department ...	6 months
Instalment accounts on May 1	$260,000
Cash collections on instalment accounts in May	$38,640
Average rate of bad debt losses	1% of sales

It is now desired to determine the amount of cash which should have been collected in May:

⅙ of $260,000 of May 1st receivables. (Since $260,000 represents 6 months' sales, one-sixth should be collected.)*	$43,333
Deduct average monthly losses from bad debts	400
Cash which should be collected in May	$42,933
Actual collections	$38,640
Percentage collection	90%

* Note that the amount of $260,000 represents receivables incurred for the six-month period prior to May 1; that is, from November 1 of the preceding year to May 1 of the current year.

Effect of Credit Period on Cost of Carrying Accounts Receivable.

—It is never possible to determine exactly the effect of the length of the credit period on the cost of carrying receivables because of the uncertainty of the relation of the time factor to bad debt losses; however, the facts can usually be closely approximated and such analysis is useful in deciding what credit and discount terms are most profitable. The procedure can be presented best by illustration.

A certain company had under consideration the matter of changing its cash discount policy. In an attempt to throw some light on its cost of carrying accounts receivable, the following study was made. Certain general facts of the business, related to this problem, may be stated as follows: [1]

Annual sales	$960,000.00
Terms offered: Net 30 days (no cash discount was offered but terms of 2%, 10 days were taken by certain customers)	
Amount of sales on which the terms 2%, 10 days were taken	$160,000.00
Average amount of accounts receivable outstanding	$146,000.00
Average number of days discounted accounts were outstanding	15
Average number of days nondiscounted accounts were outstanding	64
Average number of days all accounts were outstanding	56
Number of active accounts	4,000
Average amount of account	$38.50
Net worth of company	$240,000.00
Net profit on sales	3%

Based upon the foregoing facts and other information available, the cost of carrying accounts receivable for various periods was determined in the manner indicated by Figure 51. The individual items of cost are discussed below.

	Nominal Terms 10 Days but Actual 15 Days *	Nominal Terms 30 Days but Actual 40 Days *	Actual 60 Days	Actual 90 Days	Actual 120 Days
Interest, 6%	0.25	0.666	1.000	1.50	2.00
Bad debts	.52	.587	.640	.72	.80
Bookkeeping	.51	.700	.900	1.10	1.30
Credit department and collection expense	.39	.450	.494	.58	.64
Total	1.67	2.403	3.034	3.90	4.74

* It was considered that nominal terms of 10 days, if enforced, would actually result in terms of approximately 15 days, and nominal terms of 30 days in actual terms of not to exceed 40 days.

FIGURE 51. Cost, in Percentage of Net Sales, of Carrying Accounts Receivable

INTEREST. Since bad debt losses are calculated separately, a rate of interest should be used which could be secured with comparative safety.

[1] Figures are approximate.

In this case, 6% was used. The calculations are simple, being merely the interest for the term indicated.

BAD DEBT LOSSES. The total bad debt losses for one year were $7,680, or approximately 0.8% of the sales. Each one of the losses was examined in cooperation with the credit manager, in an effort to determine whether the loss was due to the financial condition of the customer at the time the credit was granted or to something that happened between that time and the time the account was determined to be bad. It was found that in 60.1% of the cases the accounts were bad at the time the sale was made, and hence the losses would have occurred had the terms been 10 days. In the other 39.9% of the cases the cause of loss occurred between the date of sale and the time the account was found to be bad. These facts could not, of course, be determined with complete accuracy, as it was in some instances difficult to determine the position of the customer, but these figures are believed to be substantially correct in this case.

As all losses were determined to be bad by the end of the 120-day period, it was considered that this period should stand the maximum loss of 0.8%.

The loss for the other periods was then determined by taking the base loss of 60.1% and by giving effect to the time element in determining what the additional loss would be. To illustrate, the calculations are shown in Figure 52.

	10 Days, Actual 15 Days	30 Days, Actual 40 Days	Actual 60 Days	Actual 90 Days	Actual 120 Days
Losses which would have occurred regardless of the length of the credit period (60.1% of $7,680)	$4,616	$4,616	$4,616	$4,616	$4,616
Losses which occurred in 120 days due to time element					3,064
Proportional loss for each credit period due to time element	(15/120 of $3,064) 383	(40/120 of $3,064) 1,021	1,532	2,298	
Total	$4,999	$5,637	$6,148	$6,914	$7,680
Percentage of sales	0.52	0.587	0.64	0.72	0.8

FIGURE 52. Calculation of Rate of Bad Debt Losses

There seems to be considerable difference of opinion among credit men as to the relation of the length of the credit period to the bad debt losses. The authors are inclined to the opinion that the degree to which losses are related to the length of the credit period is considerably exaggerated. It is true, of course, that firms who are in doubt as to their ability to pay, direct their business away from vendors who have a short credit term and a rigid policy of collection; but here the smaller losses are due more to the collection policy than to the length of term of credit. It is also true that firms which intend to pay but which are having a hard time to make ends meet will prefer creditors having a short term and a strict policy, and delay payment to firms who do not push them; but here again the smaller losses are more a matter of collection policy than credit term.

It is believed that the amounts shown in Figure 52 represent a reasonable approximation of what the credit losses would have been in this case had all of the business been done on the terms indicated in the respective brackets.

BOOKKEEPING. The bookkeeping expense can be quite accurately determined. It consists of the expense of hiring, training, and maintaining bookkeepers and providing the mechanical equipment needed. Duplicate invoices and statements, and regular monthly statements, are often included in the work of the bookkeeping department and were included in this calculation. The increasing cost for the longer term is caused by the additional work of sending periodic statements, looking up inquiries, making duplicates and handling more open accounts. This additional cost is greater than generally supposed.

CREDIT DEPARTMENT AND COLLECTION EXPENSE. This expense, consisting of salaries and maintenance of the credit department, legal services, etc., was found upon investigation to adjust itself in practically the same manner as the bad debt losses. Certain fixed expenses of the credit department, such as salaries and credit services, remain practically fixed regardless of the credit period. Special collection expenses bear a close relationship to the bad debt losses. The longer credit term slightly increases the clerical cost in the credit department. The calculations in Figure 51 give effect to this increase as well as the bad debt relationship.

Three proposals had been made by the credit manager, as follows:

1. That all customers be offered 2%, 10 days, for the purpose of reducing bad debt losses and collection expense.
2. That all customers be offered 1%, 30 days, and that these terms be rigidly enforced for the purpose of reducing the length of time that accounts remain outstanding.
3. That both terms be offered.

Figure 53 shows the result in net profit of the suggested proposals and of other longer credit periods. The net profit is expressed in percentage of net sales and, in order to make the figures comparable, interest on the net assets is included as a part of the cost of doing business.

	Nominal 10 Days, Actual 15 Days	Nominal 30 Days, Actual 40 Days	Actual 60 Days	Actual 90 Days	Actual 120 Days
Sales	100.00	100.00	100.00	100.00	100.00
Cost of goods sold	55.69	55.69	55.69	55.69	55.69
Gross profit	44.31	44.31	44.31	44.31	44.31
Cost of doing business, exclusive of the cost of carrying accounts receivable	39.32	39.32	39.32	39.32	39.32
Interest at 6% on net assets less accounts receivable	.58	.58	.58	.58	.58
Cost of carrying accounts receivable, including interest (Figure 51)	1.67	2.40	3.03	3.90	4.74
Cash discount proposed	2.00	1.00			
Total	43.57	43.30	42.93	43.80	44.64
Net profit after deducting interest at 6% for comparison	.74	1.01	1.38	.51	.33*
Add back the interest included above to secure net profit	.84	1.25	1.58	2.08	2.58
Net profit	1.58	2.26	2.96	2.59	2.25

* Loss.

FIGURE 53. Effect of Credit Terms on Net Profit, Expressed in Percentage of Net Sales

This interest is included in two parts: first, interest on net assets exclusive of accounts receivable; and, second, interest on accounts receivable, which is included as a part of the cost of carrying accounts receivable. This shows that with terms of 2%, 10 days, the company would show a profit of 0.74% of net sales, over and above 6% return on its net assets; with terms of 1%, 30 days, this would be 1.01%; with terms of 60 days net, 1.38%; with terms of 90 days net, 0.51%; and with terms of 120 days net, the result (over and above 6% on net assets) would be a loss of 0.33% of net sales. The most profitable terms obviously would be 60 days net. Since the company was actually granting 64 days, on the average, on terms of 30 days net, it would seem that its most profitable policy would be to retain its present terms of 30 days net and make a greater effort to enforce these terms so as to bring the actual period nearer to the nominal terms. If it could succeed in bringing the average time to 40 days it would show a profit of 2.01% of net sales (1.01% as shown in Figure 53 with 1% cash discount added back) over and above 6% on net assets. The comparison of profit under the proposed and present terms is shown in Figure 54.

Figure 53 shows further, in the last line, what the net profit would be, in percentage of net sales, exclusive of the interest consideration. To determine the relative desirability of terms, however, it is necessary

		Net Profit
Terms		
2%, 10 days—proposed:		
6% of net assets	$14,400	
0.74% of net sales	7,104	$21,504
1%, 30 days—proposed:		
6% of net assets	$14,400	
1.01% of net sales	9,696	24,096
Net 30 days, average 64 days—present terms:		
6% of net assets	$14,400	
1.38% of net sales (60-day figure is used)	13,248	27,648
Present terms of 30 days net, with average brought to 40 days:		
6% of net assets	$14,400	
2.01% of net sales (1.01% plus 1% discount)	19,296	33,696

FIGURE 54.   Comparison of Profit under Different Credit Terms

to make the comparison with interest considered as a cost of doing business.

It will be noted that the net profit, exclusive of interest consideration, is shown as 2.96% of net sales for terms of 60 days net. This closely approximates the actual experience of the company in making 3% on net sales with mixed terms of 2%, 15 days (taken by some customers), and an average of 64 days net on the major part of the accounts.

The figures in this case are in no sense offered as standards or as absolutely accurate for the firm in question, but rather as an illustration of the possibility of such analyses and the value they may hold. The figures in this case were gathered with extreme care and with the full cooperation of the credit manager and, it is believed, fairly represented the situation. They were a decided factor in the determination of the future credit policy.

Speaking generally, such an analysis suggests three important points. First, it indicates that the cost of carrying accounts receivable is a more important cost than frequently supposed. Second, it raises the question as to the relation of the length of the credit period to the bad debt losses and collection expense. There seems to be little information on this point. Third, it emphasizes the important relation of the credit policy to net profits. Incidentally, it calls attention to the fact that no satisfactory comparisons can be made without the inclusion of interest. The final net profit figures in Figure 53, after interest has been added back, naturally show an entirely different relationship than the net profit with interest deducted.

Effect of Credit Policy on Sales.—The effect of the credit policy on sales does not lend itself to accurate statistical measurement. The performance of the credit department in this respect must be judged chiefly by direct observation of sales executives and the contact of sales executives and salesmen with customers. If any sudden change is made in the credit period or discount terms, other circumstances remaining the same, the immediate effect may, of course, be reflected in sales volume. Usually, however, so many factors affect sales volume that it is difficult to isolate the effect of changes in credit policy and measure them in definite statistical terms. Moreover, the contact of the credit department with customers is a factor of importance. In many concerns, the salespeople and collectors afford the only direct contact which customers have with the business. If the work of collection is done tactfully and efficiently, goodwill results; if it is done poorly, customers are lost. The authors think of one large instalment house which attempts never to let its customers get out of debt. One of the factors used to measure the performance of its collectors is the number of accounts lost. A number higher than the established normal is thus indicative of unsatisfactory performance.

Cost of Performing the Credit and Collection Functions.—The fourth test of the performance of the credit and collection department is the cost of operating the department. It must be apparent from the foregoing discussion that this is by no means the most important test. The cost of operating the department may be very low but if credit investigation and the work of collection are done carelessly or by unqualified personnel, the ultimate cost as represented by bad debt losses, investment in receivables, and loss of goodwill may be very high.

Assuming a satisfactory degree of efficiency, however, the cost of operating the department should be held to reasonable limits.

Credit and Collection Cost Standards.—In large concerns having a sufficient volume of credit activity to justify it, the work may be divided into individual functions, functional units of activity selected, and standard unit costs established. While the nature of the functions and the functional units applicable vary considerably with different types of concerns, the following are illustrative:

Functional Activity	Unit Cost Standard
Credit investigation and approval	Cost per sales order
	Cost per account sold
	Cost per credit sales transaction
Credit correspondence records, and files	Cost per sales order
	Cost per letter
	Cost per account sold
Preparing invoices	Cost per invoice line
	Cost per item
	Cost per invoice
	Cost per order line
	Cost per order

Functional Activity	*Unit Cost Standard*
Entire accounts receivable records, including posting of charges and credits and preparation of customers' statements	Cost per account Cost per sales order Cost per sales transaction
Posting charges	Cost per invoice Cost per shipment
Preparing customers' statements	Cost per statement Cost per account sold
Posting credits	Cost per remittance Cost per account sold
Calculating commissions on cash collected	Cost per remittance
Making street collections	Cost per customer Cost per dollar collected
Window collections	Cost per collection

It will be noted that some of the credit activities listed above are normally placed in the accounting department; however, they are a part of the general credit function and should be so classified for cost control purposes.

In smaller concerns and those in which the credit activity does not justify the use of detailed functional standards, overall measurements of the cost of the credit and collection function may be used. The following general measurements are illustrative:

1. Cost per dollar of net credit sales
2. Cost per account sold
3. Cost per credit sales transaction
4. Cost per sales order

Such measurements should be applied to all credit and collection costs other than loss from bad debts.

Records of Charged-Off Accounts.—Most concerns keep inadequate records of charged-off accounts. The usual accounting records are not sufficient. Each account as charged off should be carefully analyzed as to cause, responsibility, territory, commodities, and class of customers represented. The full detail with all circumstances pertaining to the case should be recorded in a special record designed for that purpose. Such procedure greatly facilitates the control of bad debt losses.

CHAPTER 17

CONTROL OF FINANCIAL AND GENERAL
DISTRIBUTION EXPENSE

Financial Expense

Financial Requirements of Distribution Activity.—The financial cost of a business as considered here includes those costs incurred in securing its capital and administering its financial program. It includes interest paid on funds borrowed and some fixed rate of return on funds provided by owners. While interest on owners' investment should not be included as a cost for external accounting purposes, it must be included for internal analysis purposes if cost and result relationships are to be fully developed for different territories, commodities, customers, etc.

In trading concerns, the entire financial expense is either distribution or nonoperating cost. In manufacturing concerns, the cost must be separated as between production, distribution, and nonoperating activities. The method of making this division is explained in pages 62 to 64. As stated there, the financial cost of distribution activity is governed by the following factors:

1. Physical facilities used in distribution
2. Amount of finished goods or merchandise carried in inventories
3. Amount of receivables carried
4. Amount of working funds, other than the above, used for distribution purposes

If the investment represented by such factors is higher than necessary, financial cost will be excessive. On the other hand, if the investment is inadequate, the business will be hampered by its inability to provide satisfactory service to customers and to operate efficiently. An intelligent and informed management will attempt to strike a proper balance by the use of financial standards.

Physical Facilities Used.—The physical facilities used in distribution consist of buildings used for storerooms, sales offices, warehouses, etc.; equipment used for sales, office, storing, handling, and delivery; and miscellaneous items. Some of these facilities, such as buildings, may be either leased or owned. If leased, the cost may be included in some of the general functional costs previously discussed. For example, the rent paid for a warehouse may be included as a part of the warehousing cost and controlled through warehousing cost standards. If the facilities are owned, the investment cost may or may not be so included. It is frequently necessary to so include it as a means of judging the relative profitability of different divisions. In any event, the total investment represented by facilities used should bear some normal relationship to the physical volume of business done.

While it is true that the investment in physical equipment cannot always be quickly adjusted to decreases in volume, there is frequently some opportunity for adjustment through sale or subleasing. Even though the costs may be fixed it is desirable that management should know the amount of cost which is resulting from excessive investment in physical facilities. Moreover, in making new investments in fixed facilities, the question must certainly be raised as to whether or not the expected volume justifies the larger investment as tested by the standard relationships set.

The standard to be used is a relationship between dollar investment in physical facilities and physical or money volume of sales. If sales cannot be expressed in units of physical volume, then the changes in physical volume must be ascertained by adjusting money volume for price changes; or the relationship must be directly to money volume.

Inventories Carried.—It is not within the province of this book to consider methods of inventory control. The problems vary widely as between chain stores, department stores, mail order houses, wholesalers, manufacturers and other distribution agencies; and include such matters as purchasing methods and procedure, stock records, and internal organization. There is much useful literature on these subjects. It should be emphasized here, however, that the ability to maintain a satisfactory rate of turnover of finished goods or merchandise is an important factor in the control of financial costs. Standards should be expressed in terms of dollar rate of turnover for the finished goods and merchandise as a whole and for important divisions of these inventories.

Receivables Carried.—The importance and methods of controlling the amount of investment in receivables were considered in connection with the control of credit and collection costs in Chapter 16. Here standards can best be expressed in terms of number of days receivables are outstanding.

Working Funds Used.—A certain amount of working funds, in addition to the investment in inventories and receivables, is necessary for carrying on the distribution function of the business. This consists of requirements for payroll, operating expenses, and necessary cash reserves. Here too some measure should be established of a satisfactory relationship between volume of business done and average investment required. This may be expressed in terms of a percentage of working funds to sales volume or to direct distribution expenditures, such as payroll, advertising, and any other direct services.

All-Inclusive Financial Standards.—In addition to the divisional financial standards mentioned above, certain over-all standards may be applied as general tests of the adequacy of the investment and the reasonableness of the financial costs. The following are illustrative:

> Percentage of total distribution financial costs to sales volume
> Rate of turnover of total distribution investment (net sales divided by average distribution investment)

In trading concerns where the entire operating profit results from distribution activity, the relationship of net operating profit to total operating investment may also be used as a test.

General Distribution Expense

Method of Cost Control Depends on Importance of Cost Items.— In addition to the functional distribution costs considered in this and previous chapters, there are certain general costs relating to distribution activity which vary considerably in importance in different concerns. In some instances they are of sufficient importance to justify intensive study and the establishment of detailed cost standards for purposes of control; in others, their importance does not justify this method and cost control must be exercised by close personal supervision of the activities or by the use of general standards of cost measurement. Consideration will be given next to certain of these general distribution cost items.

Accounting and Office Costs.—In relatively recent years the accounting, office, and clerical work of business has increased tremendously. This has been caused by the expanding number of governmental regulatory and tax measures, such as social security taxes, sales and excise taxes, wage and hour laws, price regulatory measures, and their attendant records and reporting, and by the necessity of providing management with more and better statistical data relative to operations. This increased accounting load has been offset to some extent by more efficient direction and control of accounting activity, a better-trained accounting personnel, and greater mechanical efficiency. Continuous progress is being made in this direction. In many concerns, however, the accounting and office procedure entails a cost of sufficient importance to justify detailed operation standards as a basis for cost control.

Accounting and office costs result from both production and distribution activity and the methods of controlling the cost are common to both. Distribution activities give rise to such operations as:

Mail handling	Sales analysis
Order handling	Distribution cost analysis
Pricing orders	Stenographic
Order writing	Filing
Billing	Sales auditing
Posting	Punching cards
Customers' statements	Tabulating
Vouchering	Cashiering
Payroll	

It will be noted that some of these clerical operations have been considered in connection with other functional costs to which they particularly relate.

In the standardization and measurement of these tasks certain principles should be observed:

1. All clerical tasks can be standardized and measured; but standards should be applied only in those cases where the cost savings justify the effort.
2. The purpose of such standards is to measure the performance of individual employees or groups.
3. The human element in most clerical tasks is greater than in the typical production task; hence, a slightly greater tolerance must be allowed.

The method of procedure for measuring clerical tasks, where there is a large volume of such work, is well outlined by F. D. Lehn, Export Manager, Underwood Elliot Fisher Company, as follows:[1]

ANALYZE THE ACTIVITY.—First, it is necessary to analyze the activity under consideration through the medium of a survey conducted with due regard for local conditions. An attempt should be made to strike a happy medium between essential and nonessential factors. This analysis should disclose any inherent weaknesses of the existing routine, with the result that attention can be directed to the design of improved methods to remedy the situation. The analysis, if faithfully performed, likewise puts us in a position to apply the next principle of measurement which we shall describe as the determination of a proper unit of work.

[1] N.A.C.A. Bulletin, May 15, 1939, pp. 1170–73.

DETERMINE THE UNIT OF WORK.—By a unit of work we mean some *repetitive* task that is simple and invariable, in terms of which the results of an office activity can be measured. For example, the results of typewriting effort can be expressed in terms of the number of standard lines of typewritten matter produced. The decision regarding the determination of a proper unit of work for measurement depends largely on the number of employees engaged in the activity under consideration and the amount of specialization in their work. If there is a considerable amount of specialization, different units may be required for each specialized task in the group. For example, in a shipping department, the bill to the customer would probably represent the unit. However, in a large organization, it might be well to assign different units to freight, express and parcel post shipments. In any event, it should be an easy matter to show the results produced by each employee in terms of the unit of work decided upon.

The analysis already referred to, if scientifically made, should likewise place in our possession, facts that will assist in setting a reasonable standard of performance for each activity under consideration, which we shall refer to as our third principle.

SET STANDARDS.—Measurement reports in themselves tell what has been done. The answer to the even more important question "What should be done?" can only be given after proper standards of performance have been determined.

It might be well to state that standards predicated on time and motion studies are far more effective than standards which merely represent average performances. When no goal has been set, the slowest worker sets the pace and average production is likely to be low. On the other hand, when standards are set scientifically through the medium of time and motion studies, allowances for fatigue and personal needs should always be taken into consideration. Office work requires a high degree of concentration. Not even so-called high powered executives can keep going at high speed all day long and they are deluding themselves if they really think they can do so. The truth of the matter is that the mind wanders off by itself if pressed too hard and too steadily. Accordingly, standards should allow for occasional "time out" periods and should merely represent what can be done under normal existing conditions by an employee of ordinary accomplishments. It is also important that standards should be flexible rather than fixed. At reasonable intervals the standards set should be reviewed to determine whether changed conditions warrant revisions being made. Of course, the setting of proper standards represents an important technical subject in itself to which we can only give honorable mention in passing to our fourth principle—

MAKE REPORTS SIMPLE AND EASY TO PREPARE.—The methods of recording production should be easy to apply and should involve but a small expenditure of time and effort on the part of the employee. Both excessive details and valueless simplicity should be avoided. However, it is far better to err on the side of simplicity; otherwise a complex system of recording, laboriously constructed, will fall before the first onslaught of rush work. Getting the real work done will and should take precedence over the preparation of voluminous detailed measurement reports.

MEASURE THE INDIVIDUAL.—Our fifth principle is self-explanatory: Measurement and recording work should be done by individuals wherever possible so that the proficiency of individuals may be compared. Obviously, group efficiency of a number of employees performing similar duties is readily determined by the application of simple mathematics. However, when employees report their own output, it is well to realize that errors are likely to occur, chiefly on the side of increased production. Therefore, an effort should be made to incorporate a simple correlative system of checks and balances in all measurement plans.

SECURE EMPLOYEE SUPPORT.—Our sixth, last, and perhaps most important principle is that measurement plans, in order to function effectively, must be designed to win wholehearted employee support. This phase of the subject is largely philosophic in character, dealing as it does with the vagaries of human nature. However, the human factor does not necessarily make the application of the principle more difficult. Although, admittedly, there is a considerable amount of plain ordinary cussedness bound up in human nature, there is a much larger amount of charitable good will.

There are several practical means of winning employee cooperation and support.

First, induce employees to participate actively in carrying forth your plans from the time the analysis is undertaken until the measurement routine is established and functioning. Tell them frankly that the goal of measurement is to get more and better work done with less effort.

Second, fair play for the accurate worker demands that some penalty, either in time or in production, be exacted for errors.

Third, *unassigned time* should not be charged to the employee when determining the results of productive effort.

Fourth, in so far as it is possible to do so, the results reported by each individual should be made available for inspection by all employees in the same group.

Ordinarily, measurement appeals to ambitious employees who take pride in their work and the cooperation and support of these employees can be won with little effort. The attitude of the other kind of employees to measurement is immaterial because ordinarily they do not stay around very long anyway.

Mr. Lehn illustrates the method of applying such standards to the machine posting operation as follows:[2]

Figure 55 illustrates a "Ledger Posting Control Sheet." As its name implies, this record is kept by the control clerk. Each batch of unit posting media is accompanied by an adding machine list showing a predetermined total of the items to be posted. The use of a ruler similar to the one illustrated in part, makes it an easy matter for the control clerk to determine the number of items to be posted. When the work is given to an operator the type of posting is indicated, together with the starting time. The number of tickets and the predetermined amount thereof are also entered in the columns provided, debits and credits being shown separately.

[2] *Ibid.*, pp. 1183–88.

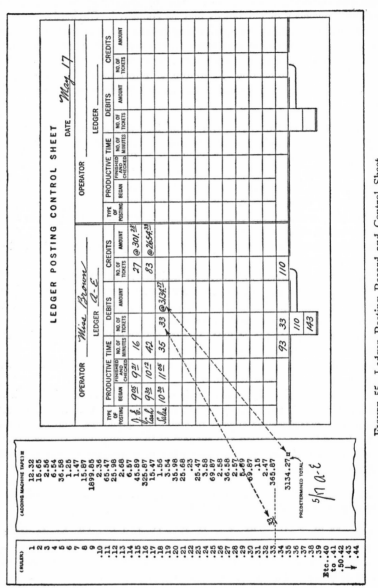

FIGURE 55. Ledger Posting Record and Control Sheet

When the posting run is completed, the control clerk compares the machine total which appears on the operator's proof sheet with the predetermined total entered on the control sheet. If the amounts agree, the finish time is recorded and the number of minutes of productive time extended. In this manner, time spent in correcting errors is charged to productive effort and has the effect of reducing the average number of tickets posted per minute.

The column captioned "No. of Min." and the two columns headed "No. of Tickets" are added daily and the totals carried to a form illustrated by Figure 56 which is a "Monthly Summary of Operator Production Results," reflected both in minutes and in number of postings. The number of minutes represents the time spent in actual posting plus time spent in correcting errors. In other words, the operator is not penalized because of unassigned time.

The source of the information necessary to prepare this form is the ledger posting control sheet just described. At the end of the month the columns are totaled and the total number of postings divided by the total number of minutes in order to determine the average number of postings per minute for each oper-

MONTHLY SUMMARY OF OPERATOR PRODUCTION RESULTS

DATE May	Miss A Ledger A-E		Miss B Ledger F-K		Miss C Relief-Extra		Miss D		Miss E		Miss F etc.	
	Minutes	No. Postings	Minutes	No. Postings	Minutes	No. Postings	Minutes	No. Postings	Minutes	No. Postings	Minutes	No. Postings
1												
2												
3												
4												
5												
6												
7												
8												
9												
10												
11												
12												
13												
14												
15												
16												
17	170	362										
18	365	840										
19												
20												
21												
22												
23												
24												
25												
26												
27												
28												
29												
30												
31												
TOTALS	535	1202										
Average No. Of Postings Per Minute	$2\frac{24}{}$											

FIGURE 56. Monthly Summary of Posting Machine Operator Production. Minutes represent time spent in actual posting plus time spent in correcting errors.

ator. These averages may be compared with properly set standards of production as a means of judging operator efficiency.

Accounting and clerical operations which lend themselves particularly to such standardization, and units of measurement which can be applied, are:

Operations	Terms of Standard Measurement
1. Mail handling	Number of pieces in and out
2. Order handling	Number of orders handled
3. Pricing orders	Number of order lines
4. Order writing	Number of order lines
5. Billing	Number of invoice lines
6. Posting	Number of postings
7. Customers' statement	Number of accounts
8. Vouchering	Number of vouchers
9. Payroll (Distribution)	Number of employees
10. Sales analysis	Number of invoice lines
11. Stenographic	Number of lines written
Dictation	Number of pages of notes or number of lines of transcription
Transcription	Number of lines written
12. Filing	Number of units filed
13. Sales auditing	Number of sales slips
14. Punching cards	Number of cards
15. Tabulating	Number of cards run
16. Cashiering	Number of transactions

The problem of control of costs in small offices is constructively considered by Francis L. Haskell, Chief Accountant and Office Manager, Associated Spring Corporation. With special reference to office costs in small manufacturing concerns, Mr. Haskell writes:[3]

This paper offers three principal suggestions, with some elaboration of each, which direct attention to ways of office cost control which are not too expensive and might be used to good effect in a small office. They are:

1. Know the standards for each office operation.
2. Constantly check all methods of communication within the office.
3. Establish a yardstick in each office department to measure production.

Availability of Standard Data for Mechanical Operations

Standard data for office processes is rather readily obtainable from a variety of sources and may be checked with actual production, and the company's own standards may be set on the basis of this information and good judgment. It is necessary to know what is reasonable to expect of individuals before it is pos-

[3] "Three Approaches to Management of Costs in the Small Office," *N.A.C.A. Bulletin*, May, 1950, pp. 1091–96.

sible to fairly criticize or commend them. A few hints on how to obtain standard data from outside sources follow:

Typing—From good schools and other firms

Stenography—From good schools and other firms

Transcribing—From the manufacturers of cylinder, disc, and wire recorders, as well as from schools and other companies

Calculating—From manufacturers of key drive and rotary calculators and from schools

Bookkeeping machines—From the manufacturers, their salesmen, and other companies

P-B-X boards—From the telephone company

In addition, of course, there are outside consultants who have these factors as parts of their working knowledge and will evaluate office work without the use of stop watches. The company's own staff can take over from there.

Communication Economy Analysis

A key point in efficient operation may be found in the channels of communication employed in the office and between the office and the world of company business contacts. It is there that much time may be lost or gained and company outlays either extravagantly or effectively made use of. Accountants should know many appropriate questions to ask about methods of communications. Possibly a few suggestions with respect to ten of these will be in order:

1. Telephones
   a) Analyze the needs represented by the toll calls placed during a period.
   b) Instruct new employees in phone etiquette and use.
   c) Have the telephone company survey the equipment and make recommendations.
2. Letters
   a) Investigate the possibility of a centralized stenographic department.
   b) Check whether or not dictating and transcribing equipment is up to date.
   c) Do not use a horse-and-buggy letterhead.
3. Inter-com System
   a) Look into the uses of such a system to save time, money, and nerves.
   b) Investigate a public address system.
4. Forms
   a) Try to reduce the number of forms used.
   b) Keep new forms simple, standard size, and make them pay their way.
   c) Do not let forms "break" the company.
5. Duplicating systems—Remember there is a place for:
   a) Typewriters.
   b) Liquid and stencil duplicators.
   c) Cameras.
   d) One-time carbons, etc.

6. Incoming mail
   a) Check on proper sorting.
   b) Make use of a practical tickler system designed to see that mail is answered promptly.
7. Outgoing mail
   a) Watch the use of postage stamps and meters.
   b) Make sure that someone in the company really knows the postal regulations.
8. Factory mail
   a) Arrange delivery and collection on a time schedule.
   b) See that every department uses this service.
9. Messenger service
   a) Determine whether this is an expensive luxury or necessity.
   b) Eliminate it where possible by merger with the factory mail job.
10. Letters and reports to employees
   a) Inquire into the necessity of letter communication with employees.
   b) Substitute bulletin boards and personal contact where practicable.

Productivity Measurement in Principal Office Departments

If, as has been suggested, it has been possible to obtain and use standard data for mechanical operations in the office and if the methods of communication (which represent a large portion of office time outlay between such operations) are under scrutiny, we are in a position to make effective use of yardsticks of departmental activity. If it is remembered that methods of control involving extensive research or voluminous detail have been rejected, partly because of the size of the office and partly because of cost, the practical method of looking for a measuring device or yardstick or unit of production already available in the departments, will be adopted. It is quite possible that it will be found that the head of each department is currently keeping statistics reflecting activity, possibly as a basis of requests for additional help.

These figures can be used to control and lower the cost of running the particular department. For example, to arrive at unit data to effectively control the cost of the work done in an order writing department, it seems basically sound to divide the cost of operating the department for a period by the number of orders entered during the period. Some of the over-all yardsticks which, despite defects, might prove serviceable for other departments are as follows:

Department	*Basis*
Accounting	Invoices mailed to customers
Purchasing	Purchase orders entered
Cost	Orders costed
Payroll	Employees paid
Posting	Postings made
Transcribing	Letters written
Personnel	Active and retired employees
Sales	Percentage of net sales

The yardsticks mentioned above are readily available in most cases and will provide usable information at practically no additional cost. For example, in the transcribing department, it is not ordinarily necessary to count the letters to get the production for activity determination. The progressive small firm that has a postage meter can get the figure from a reading before and after running the transcribing department's letters. The counting of labor tickets, job tickets, requisitions, etc., can possibly be saved by constructing a calibrated rule that will measure from one hundred to a thousand slips in a stack.

Charting Departmental Activity

The next step is to chart activity and resulting unit cost data so that the trend of performance will be apparent. There are certain rules for making charts. For the type of chart appropriate here, a few suggestions may be given which will markedly enhance the value of the charts. They are:

1. In order that the chart will reflect trends immediately, it can be constructed to show the activity and cost performance of prior months and years.
2. It helps to use the same chart paper for each department in the office, making it easier for more people to interpret results.
3. Many questions will be automatically answered by the charts if the same period of time serves as the basis for the preparation of all of them.
4. It is vitally important to the person interpreting any chart that the peaks and valleys be labeled clearly.
5. Showing names and dates of layoffs and new hirings saves much questioning.
6. Explanatory legend should be simple and clear.

It is the "end use" of any chart that determines its importance. It will thus be apparent that all steps taken to find bases for and to construct such charts, as well as to discern ways of measuring performance of functions in the office, are without merit unless actually applied to the problem of control.

Conclusion

The three approaches to which this article has been directed, will lead to better handling of operating costs of the small office and should provide real savings. It is clear, also, that they may be developed to any desired degree. Standard time data on office equipment performance, reduction of communicative processes to their essential operations, and the establishment of yardsticks to measure productivity in office departments are sound elements of office cost control. They may be applied with any degree of thoroughness and integration warranted by the situation.

Purchasing.—Although purchasing costs are, strictly speaking, a part of the cost of the goods sold rather than of the cost of distribution, they are, in many smaller manufacturing concerns, frequently included in general distribution or administrative expense. In trading concerns purchasing costs are almost universally considered as a part of operating expense and hence are not included in the cost value of merchandise inventory. In the latter type of concern purchasing costs are commonly treated as items of general distribution expense; however in large organizations, such as department stores, a separate functional category is customarily established for these costs. Within this category are generally found many items of receiving cost which, in most trading concerns, are classified as storage and handling costs.

Broadly conceived, then, purchasing activity includes certain routine clerical and mechanical tasks for which standards can be set, such as purchase order writing, checking invoices, and stock counting. It may also include receiving tasks, such as recording and checking incoming goods, and marking goods. The method of establishing standards for these tasks is the same as that suggested for other clerical and handling operations.

The work of purchasing as a whole may also be measured by such cost standards as the cost per physical unit or cost per dollar of purchases or net sales. The more significant tests of the performance of the various buyers or department heads are their respective rates of turnover and gross profit percentages.

Special Distribution Functions.—There are a number of special activities which either form a part of the distribution function or are closely related thereto and for which a procedure of cost control must be established. This is particularly true in retailing. These consist of:

1. Handling mail orders
2. Approving and handling returns
3. Making adjustments
4. Making exchanges
5. Alterations
6. Repairs to goods sold
7. Installations
8. Operation of restaurants, garages, etc.

Such activities are largely in the nature of routine operations to which standard unit operating costs can be applied. For example, in the store restaurant, the labor cost can be measured in terms of number of meals served and the food cost as a percentage of sales; alterations can be classified as to nature of work required, and standard unit or operation costs set.

CHAPTER 18

THE DISTRIBUTION COST BUDGET

Purposes of Budgeting Distribution Activities.—The efficient direction and control of distribution effort require not only a thorough analysis of past operations and the establishment and use of standards of performance, but also an intelligent plan of action for the future. Such a plan can be supplied by the procedure of budgeting.[1]

It is no longer necessary to present arguments in favor of budgeting. No business can expect to reach its full measure of success without a well-advised and intelligently conceived program; and in no phase of business are the reasons for such a program stronger than in distribution. In general, it is the purpose of distribution cost budgeting to determine how much it is necessary to spend, what type of expenditures to make, and when and where to make them in order to produce certain sales results; to see that such expenditures are made as planned; and, finally, to see that such expenditures secure the results intended.

More specifically, the purposes of budgeting the distribution effort may be outlined as follows:

1. To base action on thorough study, investigation, and research
2. To enlist the assistance of the entire organization
3. To serve as a declaration of policies
4. To define objectives
5. To coordinate the sales effort with the sales, production, and financial program
6. To select the most profitable combination of distribution factors
7. To direct sales effort into the most profitable channels
8. To control the distribution costs

Basing Action on Thorough Study.—If a concern has a systematic program of budgeting whereby it proceeds, in ample time, to develop its distribution plans for coming periods, it is far more likely to base its action on careful study and considered judgment than if it proceeds to make its decisions from day to day as emergencies demand. In the

---

[1] For a fuller treatment of budgeting than that provided in this and the following chapter, see J. B. Heckert, *Business Budgeting and Control* (New York: The Ronald Press Co., 1946).

latter case, the decisions are frequently based upon inadequate facts. Moreover, if executives and assistants know that their plans are to be formally expressed and that they will be held responsible for their execution, they can be brought to an earlier and more intensive study of their problems. Budgeting requires the executives to think and makes them think before, rather than after, the money is spent.

Enlisting the Assistance of the Entire Organization.—Salesmen who are on the firing line, in close touch with customers and competitors; district executives who are close to the conditions in their respective territories; department managers familiar with commodity problems; credit men in daily touch with collection problems; warehouse superintendents; and all minor executives have certain information and knowledge bearing upon the company's problems which, if intelligently cultivated, can be used to advantage in formulating the future plans. If the work of planning is undertaken in ample time and on a regular schedule this assistance can be enlisted. The final program should be the summation of the best judgment of the entire organization.

Furthermore, there is a strong psychological factor involved here. Men do not like to be told what to do, they resent arbitrary orders. Particularly is this true of department heads and minor executives who feel that they must possess some ability and judgment or else they would not have been selected for their positions. Moreover, they usually feel that they know more about their respective divisions than anyone else and if any plans are to be made for such divisions they should have a part in making them. It is true, of course, as anyone knows who has tried it, that it is not always easy to stimulate interest on the part of some minor executives in plans for the future. There is often a notable lethargy on the part of such executives, but this is a dangerous sign. It usually implies a disregard for the judgment of such executives in the past and a failure on the part of management to cultivate their interest.

Moreover, men will try harder to carry out plans which they have helped to make. This principle holds true from the head janitor who has estimated his requirements for janitor supplies to the manager of a district sales force. While those who are responsible for executing the plans should have a part in making them, this does not mean that the responsibility should rest entirely with subordinates. The entire organization should share in the plans, contributing one to another pertinent information relating thereto. Before a subordinate is asked to make suggestions relative to the plans, he should be supplied with information concerning conditions beyond his control, actual past performance, new developments, and all facts which will assist him in making an intelligent decision.

The Budget as a Declaration of Policies.—What are to be the company's policies in regard to price, service, credit, quality of product, style changes, customer selection, order size, etc.? These should be given definite expression in the budget. Nothing so restrains the energy and enthusiasm of an organization as uncertainty in regard to basic policies. Basic policies, not temporary expediency, should be the guiding factors in the development of a distribution program.

Defining Objectives.—Distribution activity is particularly the work of men rather than machines. Men must be directed toward definite objectives. Such objectives should be clearly expressed and, to a degree, may stand as goals of accomplishment. Objectives, however, must not be the product of hope but rather the logical consequence of carefully laid plans. The sales executive who can clearly define his objectives, and delineate a program which can logically be expected to reach such objectives, can command the cooperation and loyalty of his organization. To do this, he himself must first know the program.

The budget deals with the future. It concerns itself with things yet to take place while there is time to prevent errors or misdirection of effort. It should constitute a clear expression of objectives.

Coordinating the Distribution Cost and Sales Programs.—The ultimate purpose of the business is profit and the task of budgeting is to secure that combination of factors which will, in the long run, produce the most profit. Almost any sales volume can be secured if enough selling effort is used, but such effort is governed by the law of diminishing returns and eventually reaches a point where the additional sales produced do not compensate for the additional effort. Conversely, the selling cost can be reduced to almost any minimum desired but with the ultimate effect that sales volume will be reduced to a point where no profit will result.

Somewhere between such extremes must be found the proper amount of sales effort to be used. This principle applies not only to sales volume as a whole, but also to individual classes of products, individual territories, and individual customer groups.

Neither the distribution cost nor the sales program can be developed independently of the other. A coordination must be effected with the production and finance programs. The selling effort must be of a type designed to sell products which can be profitably produced, particularly those products in which the concern holds a competitive equality or advantage. Moreover, the program of selling effort must not exceed that which can be safely financed.

Interdependence of Sales and Distribution Cost Factors Illustrated.—To illustrate the interdependence of sales and distribution cost factors, let us assume that a certain company manufactures revolving head roof ventilators for installation on farm buildings and sells them direct to dealers throughout the United States. Sales are made by traveling salesmen who call on the dealers and the salaries and the traveling expense of the salesmen constitute the major element of the distribution cost. Figures for the past year are given as follows:

Sales		$400,000
Costs:		
Direct field costs	$150,000	
Factory variable costs (30% of sales)	120,000	
Fixed distribution and production costs	130,000	
Total costs		400,000
Net profit		None
Other data:		
Number of salesmen		16
Number of calls made		30,000

For purposes of sales direction and control, the country is divided into six territorial districts. Figure 57 shows the sales, number of salesmen's calls made, and the sales potential (as a percentage of the total of all districts) for each district. Sales and call figures are for the past year. Sales potential figures have been statistically determined from selected indexes for a representative period of time.

Figure 58 shows for each district the number of calls made and the sales per 1% of potential. The superimposed graph shows the relationship of calls to sales. Thus it is revealed that, in the North Atlantic district, salesmen average 23 calls per 1% of potential with resulting sales of $2,014 per percentage point; whereas, in the West North Central district, 471 calls produce sales of $4,799 per 1% of potential.

This indicates a wide variance in sales effort and results. Twenty times ($471 \div 23$) as many calls per unit of potential are made in the North Atlantic district as in the West North Central district; but sales per unit do not increase proportionately. Sales in the latter district, per 1% of potential, are only 2.4 times ($4,799 \div $2,014) sales in the former.

Two facts are apparent from this analysis: first, the sales effort varies widely in relation to sales possibilities, being 20 times greater in one district than another; and secondly, sales do not increase in proportion to effort. With 20 times' greater effort, sales increase only 2.4 times.

The question is first raised as to the profit results which would be secured were the sales effort (in this case, salesmen's calls) to be dis-

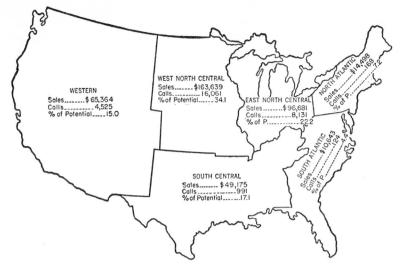

FIGURE 57. Sales Districts of Manufacturing Concern

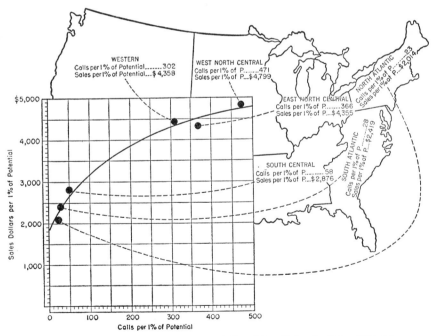

FIGURE 58. Chart of Calls Made and Resulting Sales in Sales Districts

tributed in accordance with sales potentialities. Such results may be estimated as follows:

BASIS FOR DATA

Number of calls per 1% of potential if evenly distributed (30,000 ÷ 100) ... 300
Sales which would be obtained per 1% of potential if effort were evenly
distributed .... $ 4,330
(This may be seen by reference to the curve plotted on Figure 58. It is
the point on the vertical scale opposite the point on the curve established
by 300 on the horizontal scale. It approximates the situation in the West-
ern district where 302 calls produce $4,358 of sales per 1% of potential.)
Total sales which would be secured by distributing the calls in proportion
to potential (100 × $4,330) $433,000
Increase in sales ($433,000 − $400,000) .... $ 33,000

It is apparent from these figures that sales can be substantially increased by redirecting the sales effort. If calls are directed in accordance with sales potentialities, the following profit results may be expected:

Sales $433,000
Costs:
  Direct field costs (same as before) $150,000
  Factory variable costs (30% of sales) 129,900
  Fixed distribution and production costs (same as before) 130,000
    Total costs 409,900
Net profit .... $ 23,100

The question is next raised as to whether or not 30,000 calls represents the most profitable amount of sales effort to be expended. Figure 59 charts the relationship between varying amounts of sales effort, as expressed in number of salesmen's calls, and resulting profit. If 30,000 calls are made under the new distribution, sales volume will be increased to $433,000 and net profit to $23,100. This is revealed both by the figures above and by Figure 59. If, however, the number of calls is reduced to 15,000, the resulting relationship will be as follows:

Sales $363,000
(15,000 calls will represent an average of 150 calls per 1% of potential.
By referring to the curve on Figure 58, it will be seen that this relation-
ship of calls to potential produces sales of $3,630 per 1% of potential.
Sales would then be obtained by multiplying 100 by $3,630.)
Direct field cost (one-half of former figure, since calls are re-
duced from 30,000 to 15,000 .... $ 75,000
Factory variable cost (30% of $363,000) 108,900
Fixed costs (same as before) 130,000
  Total costs 313,900
Net profit .... $ 49,100

Here it is apparent that the company has not only misdirected its sales effort but also, in its quest for more volume, has exceeded the amount of sales effort justified by its potential market. The 16 men now making 30,000 calls should be reduced to 8 men making 15,000 calls and the calls made should be correlated with the market.

For the sake of simplicity, various factors have been omitted. For example, no consideration is given to the difference in cost per call in different territories, the possibilities of higher prices with lower vol-

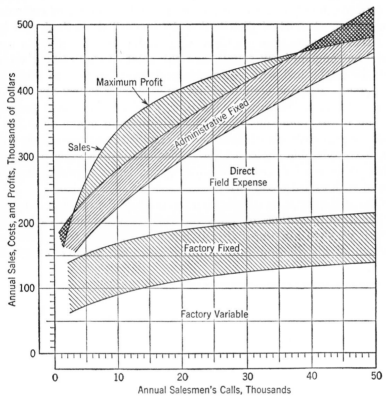

FIGURE 59. Graphic Presentation of Profit Possibilities by Varying the Sales Effort

ume, the possibility of selecting more profitable classes of customers, etc. But such considerations do not change the basic method of such analysis.

The foregoing illustration merely hints at the problem of developing a sales program. Literally hundreds of methods may be used in gathering and interpreting data pertaining to sales possibilities, in determining the sales avenues which show promise of leading to profitable results, in balancing sales with cost factors, and, finally, in extending the detailed sales plans to territories, commodities, channels of distribution, and classes of customers. This involves the entire subject of sales budgeting which cannot be discussed here. It should be understood, however, that a vast amount of study and analysis of distribution costs must accompany the work of sales budgeting and that the two can never be entirely separated.

Selecting a Combination of Distribution Cost Factors.—Were a concern to sell only one product, at one price, to one class of customers, through one channel of distribution, by one selling method, and in a restricted territory, the problem of planning the distribution costs would be comparatively simple, and the point of diminishing returns could be established with reasonable certainty; but few, if any, such cases exist. Perhaps certain public utilities most nearly approximate such a situation. In general, however, there are numerous products, varying prices, numerous classes of customers to whom sales can be made, several channels of distribution employed, various selling methods, a considerable choice of territories, and many other variations. What program of distribution effort would be most profitable in the face of such varied possibilities?

One of the purposes of planning the costs of distribution is to compel the sales executives to study the various possibilities early, while there is yet time for proper investigation, and thereby to find the combination of distribution factors which offer the promise of greatest profit.

Directing Sales Effort Into the Most Profitable Channels.—In general, the distribution effort should be directed in accordance with market possibilities. The attainment of this objective is one of the most important purposes of careful planning. Many concerns, upon analyzing the potentialities of the market and the manner in which the distribution effort has been related, have found astonishing misalignment. By intelligent redistribution, the returns from the selling effort have been greatly increased.

For example, if there are 1,000 potential buyers in Territory A and 2,000 in Territory B, it would seem quite logical, other conditions being the same, to direct twice as much effort to Territory B as to Territory A. It is the effort, not the cost, which should be apportioned. It is quite possible that the amount of effort per dollar of cost may vary in the two territories, because of such factors as density of population or the intensity of competition. The point to be emphasized is that the more intelligently the effort is directed, the more profitable will be the results.

Controlling the Costs.—While the budgeting of distribution activities is first of all a matter of establishing policies, determining the direction which effort should take, and coordinating the program in actual operation, it does afford a definite means of control over certain distribution operations and costs.

Assuming that sufficient study has been made to know what can and should be done and that the program has been developed accordingly, any failure to follow the program will constitute a signal of unsatisfactory performance. This will be true, of course, only if the budget is frequently revised to meet changing conditions. If action is taken quickly to correct unsatisfactory performance before it has disrupted the entire program, the operations can be held under control.

Some distribution expenditures, such as advertising and sales promotional effort, can be held rigidly to the budget; others, such as handling and delivery, must be held to the proper relationship with volume. This requires a certain degree of flexibility in the budget figures.

While the budget constitutes a tool of control over the distribution operations as a whole, it does not take the place of individual standards of performance as discussed in the preceding chapters. The latter are necessary as measures of individual performance. The one supplements the other. An intelligent program of operations as a whole can be developed only when it is known what individual performance can be reasonably expected. On the other hand, failure to carry out the program as developed will provide signals of individual weakness, the responsibility for which can be quickly traced and the faults corrected.

Budget Should Be Based on Actual Expectations.—The question frequently arises in budgeting distribution activities as to whether the budget should constitute a mark to shoot at or a program based upon actual expectation, accepting as inevitable the fact that entirely satisfactory performance in every quarter is seldom accomplished. For example, it may be assumed that 1,000 units can be sold at a price of $2 each and at a distribution cost of $0.60 each, if everybody engaged in distribution effort turns in entirely satisfactory performance. Assuming a production cost of $1.20 per unit, the budget might then be expressed in financial terms as follows:

Sales of 1,000 units at $2.00	$2,000
Cost of goods sold	1,200
Gross profit	$ 800
Distribution cost	600
Net profit	$ 200

On this theory a concern would then proceed to plan for the production of 1,000 units and the financing of a volume of $2,000. Such a budgeting procedure would be ideal but can seldom be reached in actual practice. Let us assume further that the sales operations in Territory A, in which 300 of the 1,000 units should be sold, have not been running smoothly. Performance is down and the general sales executives are hard at work on this territory in an effort to strengthen the personnel and correct the weakness. But this will require time. Standard sales performance in this territory is definitely 300 units; but during the period under consideration, it is more likely to be 200 units. Again, let us assume that Territory D, while expected to give satisfactory performance of 200 units in sales, is running a distribution cost of $0.70 per unit, because of an excessive number of small orders. The correction of this weakness will also require time. In the period immediately ahead it can hardly be brought to less than $0.65 per unit. Actual expectations may then be expressed as follows:

Sales of 900 units at $2.00		$1,800
Cost of goods sold, 900 units at $1.20		1,080
Gross profit		$ 720
Distribution cost:		
700 units at $0.60	$420	
200 units at $0.65	130	550
Net profit		$ 170

The budget should be based upon the latter figures or actual expectation. Plans should be made for the production of 900 units and the financing of a volume of $1,800 with a distribution cost of $550. Unless the budget is so constructed, it will not serve the important purpose of coordination.

At the same time, detailed standards of sales results and distribution costs must be applied for the measurement of individual performance. If Territory A produces a sales volume of 200 units, performance, while up to expectations, will still be rated as unsatisfactory. If distribution cost in Territory D is $0.65 per unit, it too will reflect unsatisfactory performance.

While the illustration somewhat exaggerates and oversimplifies the problem, it should serve to emphasize the fact that, over an organization at large, the budget does not simply represent the sum total of individual standards of performance. Both individual standards and the coordinated program are essential tools to efficient control and direction of operations.

Length of the Budget Period.—The question arises as to how far ahead the plans should be made. The sales program and its related plan of sales effort must be predicated upon expected business and market conditions. These can never be known with certainty; they must be estimated. The plans then can be extended into the future only so far as it is possible to make reasonably intelligent estimates of conditions affecting sales and distribution costs. The period usually ranges from a quarter to a year, although investments or commitments in fixed sales facilities, such as buildings, leases, display fixtures, and delivery equipment, must frequently be planned some years ahead. Tentative programs may be made for a year or more in advance with final plans determined each quarter or half-year.

There can be no general rule regarding the length of time. Such factors as the sensitiveness of sales volume to external conditions, seasons, frequency of style changes, turnover periods, and length of production period must be considered. The budget period may vary in length of time for different distribution functions within the same concern. Moreover, the periods may be shorter in times of marked uncertainty than under more stabilized conditions.

There is much to be said in favor of a continuous, as opposed to a periodic, program of planning. If definite plans can be made one quarter in advance, they may be revised monthly, progressively dropping and adding a month thereby always keeping a three-month program ahead. For example, assume that in late December a plan is made for the first quarter (January, February, and March) of the calendar year. When actual results for January become known, the progressive quarterly estimate is revised to include April. As April is added, January is automatically dropped from the program period.

If a tentative program can be made for one year, this may also be revised quarterly or monthly by the same progressive procedure. This is particularly advantageous in a seasonal business. As one month ends, plans can be laid for the corresponding month one year hence while seasonal conditions are fresh in the minds of the executives and subordinates. A further advantage of continuous planning is that it keeps the problems constantly before the organization with a continuous process of examination and revision. Moreover, plans which are continuously revised are more useful as tools of control.

Who Should Make the Budget.—The ultimate responsibility for all budgeting is with the chief executive; in fact, there can be no effective budgeting without the full strength of executive force behind it. Other executives, major and minor, must know that the chief executive insists upon the investigation; and, conversely, that the chief executive will himself come forward at the proper time with the necessary decisions as to basic policies.

The work of preparing the budget of distribution activities is a joint task of distribution executives and the controller or chief accounting officer. The controller accumulates, analyzes, and assists in the interpretation of records and statistical data bearing upon past performance and market potentialities. The distribution executives, such as the sales manager, advertising manager, traffic manager, credit manager, warehouse manager, and sales research manager, supply the technical knowledge relative to their particular divisions. Together they must develop a program which offers the most promise of profitable results.

Steps in the Development of the Distribution Cost Budget.— Assuming that a detailed sales program has been formulated, certain basic steps may be suggested for the development of the distribution cost budget.

The *first* step is to determine the major classifications and subclassifications through which the distribution costs are to be expressed. For example, the budget may be set up by territories, commodities, channels, or some other major divisions. If the basic division of costs is by territories, the costs for each territory may be further subdivided by commodities. The classification employed usually follows closely that of the sales budget though it is frequently not carried to the same degree of refinement.

The *second* step is to classify the individual cost items in accordance with the directness of their relationship to each of the classifications and subclassifications decided upon in Step 1. Whereas, for purposes of cost analysis, it is desirable to distinguish among direct, semidirect, and indirect costs (see Chapter 3), for budgeting it is sufficient to consider only two classes of costs—direct and indirect. Such a classification is necessary for control purposes. The executives in charge of a particular product group, territory, channel of distribution, or class of customers can be held directly responsible for only those cost items over which they have actual control. Then, too, only the direct costs can be immediately related to individual performance.

The *third* step is to classify the individual cost items as to whether they are variable, semivariable, or fixed. Generally speaking, variable costs are those which vary in approximately direct ratio to money or physical volume of sales; semivariable costs are those which vary with volume of sales but not in direct ratio; whereas fixed costs are those which remain approximately the same throughout the budget period without regard to money or physical volume of sales.[2] The necessity of this third step is very apparent when it is realized that no matter

---

[2] These definitions are admittedly oversimplified in order that the steps in the development of the cost budget may be explained succinctly. More precise treatment of the three classes of costs is given in Chapter 3. It should be appreciated that proper classification of cost items requires a thorough knowledge of the business and of cost behavior. Because many ledger accounts are a mixture of variable and fixed elements, it is not always easy to tell the nature of a cost item from its account title.

how carefully the sales may be budgeted, the actual sales volume is likely to vary somewhat from the estimates. As the volume varies, the variable and semivariable costs will likewise vary, whereas the fixed costs will remain essentially unchanged in total.

For control purposes, it is necessary to know what the costs should be at the various actual sales levels. This analysis should be extended to the ultimate cost classification mentioned in the first step.

The *fourth* step is to estimate the individual cost items in accordance with the classifications indicated in the previous steps. These estimates must express the best judgment of sales executives based upon adequate analysis of past experience, external data, and distribution cost and performance standards. The assistance and judgment of subordinates and field men should be enlisted relative to local conditions.

The *fifth* step is to break down the estimates by months or quarters. This is done for the purpose of gaining closer control over operations and to assist in predetermining financial requirements.

Finally, the cost budget figures must be reported to those responsible for the execution of the sales program; variances between the budgeted and actual cost must be promptly analyzed as to cause, and corrective measures applied; and where unexpected circumstances arise, the budget must be revised.

CHAPTER 19

THE DISTRIBUTION COST BUDGET
(CONTINUED)

Classification of Distribution Costs for Budgeting Purposes.—
As stated on page 284, one of the essential steps in the preparation of
the distribution cost budget is to classify the costs in accordance with
their relation to changes in sales volume. Such a classification may be
illustrated as follows:

DIRECT SELLING EXPENSE
    Variable
        Commissions to salesmen, agents, and brokers
        Order handling expense—clerical
        Communication
        Spoiled work chargeable to salesmen
        Adjustments
    Semivariable
        Sales clerical and office expense
        Salesmen's salaries and traveling expenses
        Insurance and taxes relating to payroll of sales office and salespeople
    Fixed
        Sales administration and supervision salaries and expense
        Entertainment
        Education and training
        Insurance and taxes relating to payroll of sales administration
        Insurance, taxes, depreciation, and maintenance of sales facilities
        Rent and occupancy expense of sales facilities
ADVERTISING AND SALES PROMOTIONAL EXPENSE
    Fixed
        All costs fixed by appropriation
TRANSPORTATION EXPENSE
    Variable
        Purchased transportation services
        Truck drivers' salaries
        Truck operation and maintenance
        Transportation supplies
        Insurance and taxes relating to transportation labor
    Semivariable
        Transportation clerical and office expense with related payroll insurance and
            taxes

Fixed
> Administration and supervision salaries and expense with related payroll insurance and taxes
> Insurance, taxes, licenses, and depreciation of transportation facilities
> Occupancy and maintenance expense of transportation facilities

Warehousing and Handling Expense

Variable
> Warehouse labor with related payroll insurance and taxes
> Shipping and warehouse supplies
> Storage charges
> Breakage and damage

Semivariable
> Warehousing clerical and office expense with related payroll insurance and taxes

Fixed
> Administration and supervision salaries and expense with related payroll insurance and taxes
> Insurance, taxes, and depreciation of warehouse facilities
> Occupancy and maintenance expense of warehouse facilities

Credit and Collection Expense

Variable
> Bad debt losses
> Legal expense
> Traveling expense
> Taxes on receivables
> Communication

Semivariable
> Clerical and office expense with related payroll insurance and taxes

Fixed
> Administration salaries and expense with related payroll insurance and taxes
> Credit services
> Occupancy expense of credit department

Financial Expense

Variable
> Cash discount on sales
> Interest on temporary funds

Fixed
> Administration salaries and expense with related payroll insurance and taxes
> Financial clerical and office expense with related payroll insurance and taxes
> Interest on permanent funds
> Fees of fiscal agents, accountants, and attorneys

General Distribution Expense

Variable
> Distribution accounting
> Personnel expense

Fixed
  Market and sales research
  Pensions
  Dues and subscriptions
  Franchise and general corporation taxes
  Use and occupancy insurance
  Public relations expense

It must be understood, of course, that such a classification is only illustrative and would not apply universally. Cost items which are fixed in some concerns may be variable in others. The point is that such a classification must be made as one step in the development of the budget.

Method of Estimating Costs.—In so far as possible the distribution cost budget should be based on the number of units of functional service required to execute the sales program. Unit costs should be taken at standard. For example, if it is estimated that 50,000 salesmen's calls will be necessary to secure the sales volume planned and the standard cost per call is $5, then $250,000 will be budgeted for this particular functional operation; if it is estimated that 30,000 orders will be secured and the standard clerical cost of handling orders is $0.28 each, then $8,400 will be budgeted; and so on throughout all distribution activity which can be resolved into such measurable operations.

When this method is used, the budget becomes a valuable tool in the control of operations. If the actual cost differs from the budget, it may be determined by analysis whether the variance is due to: (a) differences in the number of units of service required, (b) differences in the unit costs from standard, or (c) a combination of the two factors. For example, it may be assumed that actual results for those budgeted items are:

51,000 calls at a total cost of $252,450
28,000 orders handled at a total cost of .... $ 8,400

Here the actual cost is above the budget in the first item but the analysis reveals that the cost per call was only $4.95 ($252,450 ÷ 51,000), or better than standard. The second item is exactly as budgeted but the actual cost per order was $0.30, or above the standard. This method of analysis is more fully illustrated on pages 22 to 23 in Chapter 3.

Numerous distribution operations which can be budgeted in this manner, and the units of measurement applicable, are discussed in Chapters 14 to 17 in connection with standards. In fact, the use of costs in this manner emphasizes again the value of establishing distribution cost standards.

Where this method is applied the classification of costs as shown in the preceding topic must be extended to the point of individual functional operations as, for example, the cost of handling orders.

Two difficulties will be met in applying the above method of budgeting the distribution costs. First, not all of the distribution operations can be subjected to definite measurement in terms of units of functional service. This can seldom be done, for example, with national advertising. Second, where the functional operations contain an important element of fixed or semivariable cost, the functional unit costs will vary with volume. These difficulties can be easily exaggerated and they are not sufficient to nullify the value of the method. Cost items which cannot be subjected to such measurement must be estimated separately; thus, advertising cost may be fixed by appropriation. Likewise, the fixed and semivariable elements of the cost may be eliminated in establishing standard unit costs of functional service, and estimated separately. Or different unit costs may be set for different volume levels.

While the method cannot as a rule be applied to all distribution costs, it should be used to the fullest extent practicable.

Direct Selling Expense.—On pages 219 to 221 there are listed the functional operations and individual cost items related to direct selling effort. With these are shown illustrative measurements of the cost in terms of the amount of service performed or effort expended. If the sales program is then fully analyzed as to its requirements in terms of functional service and effort, much of the direct selling cost can be readily estimated. This plan can be applied particularly to the variable costs.

The semivariable and fixed costs cannot always be estimated in this manner. The budget for these items must often be developed from executive estimates based on past experience, expected conditions, and company policy. Certain of these costs will be considered separately.

Sales Clerical and Office Expense. Sales clerical and office expense should bear a close relationship to volume; hence, to the extent that such relationship can be maintained, this item assumes the nature of a variable cost. In fact, one of the purposes of budgeting is to raise the question of such relationships before the money is spent, rather than to detect maladjustment after it is too late to correct it. There are times, however, when it is not profitable to enforce a rigid relationship. It may be necessary to maintain an efficient working force in the central office or in a particular district regardless of immediate volume expectations. In such instances this item becomes semivariable in nature and the budget must be based on executive estimate of requirements.

SALESMEN'S COMPENSATION. Salesmen's compensation, including salaries, commissions, and bonuses, frequently constitutes the largest single item of distribution cost. Aside from the development of new territories, introduction of new products, and various kinds of promotional work to be done by salesmen, the compensation of salesmen should bear some standard relationship to volume. It may be that compensation cannot profitably exceed 12% of net sales or 5% of gross profit. Such general standards are useful as a starting point. Beyond this, local conditions must largely govern. Salesmen's compensation cannot be subjected to the same degree of flexibility as that applied to direct factory labor. It is often necessary to maintain a trained sales organization and keep it "at the front," even though it is known that general or local business conditions are such that standard cost relationships cannot be maintained. One of the important advantages of budgeting is the consideration of such special conditions in advance when there is time to weigh the advantages of alternative proposals. In the long run, the standard relationship must be maintained or the company will fail, but it is usually possible to maintain such general standards only by making intelligent exceptions to meet exceptional circumstances.

If salesmen are paid a straight commission on sales, the budget is merely a translation of the sales budget into its commission equivalent. Since the commission rates frequently vary for different classes of commodities, types of customers, etc., it is necessary to examine the sales budget in full detail. Where the salesmen are paid straight salaries, the salary schedules must be determined by the sales executives and the aggregate tested by general standards of cost relationship. Where both salaries and commissions are used, the two must be combined to form the budget. Under the commission plan the costs will vary directly, or nearly so, with volume; under the salary plan, costs are largely fixed, flexibility arising only through the adjustment of salaries and number of salesmen; under the combined plan, costs are semivariable. Under either plan it is possible to develop the budget for each period with considerable accuracy, if the sales budget is developed in full detail.

Special consideration must be given by sales executives in making estimates for new ventures, special promotions, etc.

Once the budget of sales compensation is completed and properly adjusted to conform to standard relationship of cost to expected results, it should serve as a valuable tool of control by sales executives. Variances, if promptly reported, will signal the need of special investigation and corrective action. While variance from standard is often temporarily justifiable, it should be stressed that such variances *must be* justified. It should be clear that adverse variances, no matter how justifiable they may appear, will wreck the concern if continued. Sales executives not infrequently direct more attention to the justification of such situations than to their correction. Broadly speaking, salesmen's compensation is a controllable cost. Plans must be made by which it will conform to the sales results obtained, and ultimate responsibility for such conformance must be centered directly on general and divisional sales executives. The procedure of budgeting should aid materially in establishing such control.

SALESMEN'S TRAVELING EXPENSES. In many concerns the traveling expenses of salesmen are an item of considerable importance, running in some cases as high as 3% or 4% of net sales. These expenses in many instances are poorly planned and improperly controlled. In fact, there is a feeling on the part of some sales executives that strict control of salesmen's expenses is subversive of the most enthusiastic effort. The authors do not share this view. In a fairly wide acquaintance with actual situations they have found many instances where the best salesmen were the least expensive. An experienced, intelligent, and capable salesman knows what expenses are necessary to do his work efficiently; and he has no hesitation in reporting to his firm the detail as to when and how the expenditures were made. He expects to be rewarded on the basis of his sales performance and is not interested in a form of petty larceny by which he extracts a few dollars from his expense account. With less experienced men there is need for guidance which may well be imposed through standards and strict accounting. Dissatisfaction, misunderstandings, and internal dissension arise more frequently with loose, than with strict, control of salesmen's expense items.

This does not imply that it is good sales management to be niggardly with salesmen's expenses but rather that each salesman should be given the *proper* expense allowance and that the treatment of all should be equitable.

One of the chief weaknesses in planning these expenses is the failure thoroughly to investigate the actual expense requirements of traveling in different territories. These requirements vary considerably and they must be known before an intelligent budget can be made. This information can be secured by an intensive study of territories, routes, classes of customers, and existing prices. Strange as it may seem, such information is very frequently lacking. Either no scientific study has been made or, if once made, it has not been continuously revised to make it currently applicable. Comparisons with past performance are not enough, they tend to perpetuate weakness. A proper allotment for salesmen's expenses requires a scientific analysis of the local situation plus intelligent consideration by sales executives. Salesmen should be given a chance to review the facts as determined and to present modifying factors; but once the expense budgets are set, they should be strictly enforced.

With the sales program fully developed, and with adequate information at hand as to what the salesmen's expenses should be, the salesmen's expense budget can be developed to a point where it will serve both as an expression of actual expectation and as a basis for expense control. For purposes of such control, expenses must be promptly reported by the salesman and a summary of such expenses, with variances from the budget, must be reported back to the salesmen and to sales executives.

In some instances the expense budget can be linked with bonus plans. For example, one concern which pays the salesmen a bonus of 10% of the gross profit, above a stated amount, deducts from this bonus any excess of expense over the budget. Another concern adds to the bonus of district managers 25% of all savings on salesmen's expenses from the budget.

SALES ADMINISTRATION AND SUPERVISION SALARIES AND EXPENSE. Sales administration and supervision salaries and expense are not always adjusted immediately to volume changes. This may be done to some extent in field organizations, but many of the salaries are temporarily fixed and vary only as salary scales are changed. Here the general and sales executives must be called upon to estimate the number of administrative personnel and the salary scales to be effective during the budget period under consideration.

ENTERTAINMENT. Entertainment expense is frequently budgeted together with salesmen's expenses. Some concerns, however, appropriate a fixed amount for this purpose based upon executives' estimates of requirements. This cost item is usually of a semivariable or fixed nature.

EDUCATION AND TRAINING. When regular training and instruction are carried on, some definite standard should be established in relation to number of salesmen or amount of salesmen's compensation. In any one budget period, however, a fixed appropriation is likely to be made for this activity. The amount to be expended for conferences and conventions should also be decided upon by the executives and definite appropriations made. Once made, such appropriations should be enforced. The value of conventions is always open to question. Some are highly instructive and contribute largely to sales effectiveness, others are merely entertainment for the sales force which contribute nothing to the sales strength of the organization. Before the money is appropriated, sales executives should clearly justify the need and value of such conventions.

FIXED COSTS. There are numerous costs pertaining to the direct selling activity which are practically fixed for any one budget period. These include the maintenance of sales facilities such as storerooms, display fixtures, and sales offices. Individual expense items include property insurance and taxes, rent, heat, light, power, elevator, depreciation, and maintenance. No particular problem arises in budgeting these items as the amounts are usually known.

Advertising and Sales Promotional Expense.—It is a singular fact that, while it is more difficult intelligently to budget advertising cost than perhaps any other important element of distribution cost, yet the budget method was applied to advertising earlier than to other costs. This anomalous situation arose from the fact that early advertising budgets were frequently merely "lump-sum" appropriations which served as maximum limits of expenditure. Little intensive study was directed to the problem as to just how much advertising should be done —when, where, and how—in order to realize the greatest benefit. The answer to these questions can never be secured with absolute certainty. Too much depends upon such factors as future business conditions, competition, new developments in markets and products, and finally the effectiveness of the advertising itself, to permit of exact answers. A large element of judgment will always be necessary. Yet, much analysis of value can be made. While some of these factors are obviously uncontrollable, their past movements can be studied, their relationships and effects noted, and their importance weighed to a degree that will provide at least some basis for intelligent decisions as to advertising expenditures.

There is probably no one single item of business cost in which there is greater waste than in advertising. This does not signify that too much is spent for advertising, but rather that the amounts spent are subjected to less rigid tests of probable relation of cost and result than are most cost items.

The authors are personally familiar with executive conferences in which lengthy and heated discussions waged over the desirability of adding a few salesmen at a cost of $15,000 or $20,000 a year. Paradoxically, in these same conferences advertising appropriations of many times the maximum amount of the proposed increase in direct selling costs were approved by merely noting that a given appropriation represented some *reasonable* increase over the expenditure of the previous year. No justification for the increase was presented or called for. The impression seemed to exist that the advertising expenditure represented some imponderable element entirely beyond the pale of analytical test. While such an attitude is no longer general among executives it is still true that advertising expenditures are subjected to less critical tests than most cost items.

It is extremely difficult to generalize upon the methods which should be employed in the budgeting of advertising costs due to the wide variety of circumstances existing in different concerns; for example:

> In a relatively few concerns advertising is the sole form of selling effort as, for example, in strictly mail order companies. Most concerns, however, use both advertising and personal selling.

> Some concerns do not have an advertising department within their own organization, but place all responsibility for advertising with a professional agency. Some concerns depend entirely upon their own advertising departments. Still other concerns maintain their own departments which function in cooperation with an advertising agency.

> In some concerns the advertising manager reports to the sales manager, whereby sales and advertising programs are closely correlated; in others, the advertising manager is independent and coordination is effected by conferences or through the chief executive.

> In some concerns the advertising is largely of an institutional nature; in others it is directed mainly to immediate sales projects.

> In some concerns advertising is chiefly local, as with the typical department store; in others, it is national in scope, as with the manufacturers of automobiles.

> In some manufacturing concerns expenditures are made directly by the manufacturer; in others, the manufacturer contributes to the advertising of jobbers and dealers.

> In some instances it is comparatively easy to identify the advertising costs with individual products and territories; in others no such definite identification is possible.

> Finally, many different media and combinations of media are employed as, for example, newspapers, periodicals, direct mail, outdoor advertising, radio, and television.

STEPS IN DEVELOPMENT OF ADVERTISING PROGRAM. There are, however, some basic steps in the planning and control of advertising costs which are applicable to all concerns. Among these should be noted particularly the following:

1. The purpose or objectives of the advertising program should be clearly defined. This should extend to both immediate and ultimate objectives.
2. An intensive study should be made of the probable cost and appropriations necessary to accomplish objectives.
3. A detailed program should be constructed showing when, where, how, and for what the advertising expenditures are to be made. "Lump-sum" appropriations should be avoided except as a summarization of properly classified items.
4. The advertising costs should be closely coordinated with other selling costs and with the sales, production, and financial program generally.
5. Costs should be classified as to direct—those chargeable directly to individual projects, such as trade paper advertising of Product A; and indirect—those not chargeable directly to specific projects, such as the salary of the advertising manager.
6. Direct costs should be classified according to media used.
7. Where possible, the direct costs should be analyzed by products or groups of products and by territories.
8. In so far as possible, standards of relationship between cost and sales and profit results should be developed and used in the direction and control of advertising effort.

PURPOSE OF ADVERTISING. In general, advertising is a form of selling effort, the ultimate purpose of which is to assist in selling goods; but the nature of the advertising effort and the direction which it may take in the accomplishment of this ultimate purpose vary considerably with the circumstances. Directly, the objectives may be such as the following:

1. To increase immediate sales
2. To maintain prices
3. To reduce the cost of other selling effort
4. To educate consumers in the use of products or services or in particular policies
5. To establish and maintain trade marks and brands
6. To establish new products in the market
7. To develop new markets
8. To meet competition
9. To establish in the minds of consumers a favorable attitude toward, and confidence in, the concern and its products and policies
10. To create favorable public opinion and prevent hostile legislation

It is obvious that there is a certain overlapping in these objectives; however, they assume individuality when applied to concrete cases.

The more definitely a concern can define the objectives of its advertising effort, the more intelligently can its advertising program be formulated, its effort controlled, and its results measured.

As with all selling effort, the ultimate end is increased profit. This can be secured only if there is ultimately a favorable effect upon physical volume, price, or costs.

METHOD OF DETERMINING THE NECESSARY APPROPRIATION. Once the objectives of the advertising program are clearly defined and their relative importance weighed by the executive group, estimates must be made as to the amounts necessary for their accomplishment.

There are two general methods in use in determining the amount of the advertising budget. The *first* plan is to make a "lump-sum" appropriation based upon some such factor as a percentage of previous or budgeted sales. The total appropriation is then split up by the advertising department, or outside agency, and applied to individual projects. The *second* plan is to examine carefully the objectives of the advertising program, the probable cost of reaching the objectives; and, from this detailed analysis, to arrive at a total amount required.

To the extent that the advertising is done for immediate results, the sales budget must serve as the basis. The advertising executives, with such outside counsel as may be employed, must estimate the cost of the advertising necessary to produce the sales budgeted. It is never possible, even under the most favorable circumstances, to tell exactly the amount of advertising necessary to produce a given sales volume; but, with adequate records of past experience properly analyzed as to cost and results, reasonably close estimates can be made. Department stores and mail order houses are illustrative of the types of concerns in which much of the advertising expenditure is directed to immediate results.

To the extent that the advertising is directed to less immediate results, such as the creation of goodwill, establishment of brands, and development of new markets, the amounts to be appropriated must be tested by such factors as:

1. The amount of funds that can be released in any one year. No matter how attractive an advertising program may appear, it must first be tested by its effect upon the financial position of the company.

2. Amount necessary to make the program effective. Small expenditures are sometimes sheer waste, whereas larger expenditures may accomplish desired results.

3. The general program of future expansion. Where advertising is largely of an institutional nature, the amount to be expended depends upon the rate of expansion contemplated.

Lump-Sum Appropriations. Under the first plan mentioned in the preceding topic, that is, of making lump-sum appropriations, the total advertising budget may be determined as follows:

1. A percentage of the previous year's sales or an average of several years' sales
2. A percentage of budgeted sales
3. A fixed amount per unit of product
4. An amount comparable to or determined by the appropriation of competitors
5. An arbitrary increase or decrease in the past year's expenditure
6. A percentage of the net profit of the previous year

Where the advertising appropriation is based upon a percentage of sales, it is quite generally agreed that budgeted sales should be used in preference to sales of the previous year. This at least gives some consideration to changes in sales policies and the expected trend in general business conditions. The exact percentage used is frequently based on the average of the industry. There are certain advantages to the plan of basing the advertising appropriation on a percentage of budgeted sales. The plan is simple and easily understood by the executive group generally. It automatically controls the advertising expenditure in relation to dollar volume. Where a great variety of goods is sold, and where much of the advertising represents joint cost, it is difficult to make appropriations for individual products. With well-established lines, reasonably stable conditions, and considerable past experience as a guide, the results are likely to be similar to that secured by more intensive analysis. On the other hand, the plan is basically weak in that it does not require a critical analysis of definite objectives and the probable cost to attain them. In most concerns the sales program is constantly shifting; new ventures, new projects, new products must be considered; shifts are being made in the emphasis on various types of sales effort. Simply to perpetuate a plan of allotting a percentage of budgeted sales to advertising may result in disproportionate and misdirected sales effort. Such a plan tends to set a *maximum* rather than a *proper* allowance for advertising.

A modification of this plan is to use a different percentage for the budgeted sales of each class of goods. This method is used to a considerable extent by department and other retail stores. For example, a large furniture store uses a much higher percentage for living-room suites than for kitchen specialties.

Some concerns manufacturing or selling a uniform product or only a few products appropriate a given amount of advertising per unit.

The plan is used particularly by the manufacturers of specialty goods, such as electric sweepers, washing machines, automobiles and the like. A certain brewery, for example, uses $0.40 per barrel. Exceptions are made when new territory is being developed. Where this plan is used the appropriation should be based on budgeted unit sales.

This plan lends itself particularly to vertical cooperative advertising. Thus, the manufacturer may appropriate a dollar in advertising for each dollar required of the distributor. The plan, being based on budgeted units, is simple and easily applied. Moreover, it is expressive of at least some relationship between the advertising appropriation and the specific task to be performed. Where there is sufficient past experience to base intelligent judgment on the expenditure necessary to sell the product, this is usually the most satisfactory method for concerns of the type mentioned.

One of the most difficult factors to contend with in setting the advertising appropriation is action of competitors. Some smaller concerns use the plan of following the leader, on the theory that they may benefit by the more extensive research and study of the larger competitor. Concerns of comparable strength may attempt to match the appropriations of their leading rivals or even to out-advertise them on the theory that they cannot afford to do otherwise. When this becomes the governing factor in determining appropriations, it is obviously poor marketing strategy. Somewhere the increased advertising meets the law of diminishing returns. Moreover, there are other types of selling effort which must be considered. Company X may increase its advertising appropriations from $1,000,000 to $1,500,000, but its rival, Company Y, may show greater earnings by appropriating an extra $500,000 for other types of selling effort or product research; or even by limiting its total sales effort to previous amounts.

There is no denying the fact that advertising appropriations must give some effect to the actions of competitors, but such influence should not be the governing factor. An intensive study of advertising objectives, their relative importance, and their cost-result relationship should ultimately govern the appropriation.

The plans of making an arbitrary increase or decrease in the appropriation over the previous year or of appropriating a percentage of the previous year's profit have little to commend them. They are based upon the assumption that there is no intelligent basis for determining what amount of advertising effort will contribute most to the long-run profit and consequently the matter should be determined by such considerations as expected trends in general business, financial position, dividend policy, and tax savings. This policy is more often used in concerns where there is little direct or immediate effect of advertising upon sales volume. While this policy is still followed by some large and successful concerns, its adherents are becoming fewer.

Appropriation Based upon Detailed Study. The second general plan of developing an advertising program is to examine carefully the objectives, the detailed methods by which such objectives can be accomplished, and the costs which will be involved. These individual costs are then combined into a total appropriation. This plan involves such detailed considerations as the following:

1. Necessary marketing and advertising research
2. Selection of individual advertising projects relative to products and territories
3. Selection of detailed advertising methods and media
4. Detailed estimates of direct and indirect costs
5. Detailed analysis of time when expenditures will be made, that is, in what month or quarter
6. Research as to effectiveness of methods

It is beyond the scope of this book to consider these detailed steps; this is a specialized task for those trained and experienced in the field of advertising. It must be performed by either the company's own advertising staff, by outside advertising agencies, or both. It should be made clear, however, that the advertising department should not be given a carte blanche appropriation to do with as it pleases and without reckoning. The department should be required to justify its program before the money is appropriated and spent. This can be done by requiring it to clearly define objectives, to outline the exact methods by which it plans to attain them, and to estimate the cost of each element of the program. In brief, the advertising department should be compelled to justify its program before, rather than after, the money is spent, with an understanding that it will be held accountable for the results as planned.

SETTING FORTH THE DETAILED PROGRAM. Once the detailed program is developed, it should be given definite form in writing. This has the following advantages:

1. The advertising department (or agency) is placed on record as to what it proposes to accomplish and at what cost.
2. The expenditures are timed and can thus be provided for in the financial budget.
3. The detailed program, once approved, will serve as a basis for definite control over expenditures.

4. Various department heads will know in advance the nature and extent of the advertising assistance they are to receive and when it will be given.

The timing of the advertising expenditures is especially significant. In some instances, as in the promotion of new products or the development of new markets or territories, the plans may extend, at least tentatively, for several years in advance. In well-established markets the program is usually for the fiscal year with a breakdown by months or quarters.

COORDINATION OF THE ADVERTISING PROGRAM. Advertising is only one of numerous types of selling effort. It should be timed and coordinated with other sales effort to form the most effective results. The entire program of sales effort should then in turn be coordinated with the sales, production, and finance programs generally. Elementary as this statement may appear, the lack of such coordination is one of the chief sources of waste in advertising expenditures.

It is frequently desirable to hold a part of the advertising appropriation in reserve to meet unexpected circumstances. This permits the use of special effort where the regular program has failed in its effectiveness or where a sudden change in conditions has altered the sales program. Many such situations arise as a result of unexpected moves on the part of competitors, introduction of new products, or quick changes in general business conditions.

Transportation Expense.—No particular problems arise in budgeting the transportation costs. If standard costs have been established as suggested in Chapter 15, it is necessary only to translate the sales budget into its transportation requirements and apply the standards. If this method cannot be applied to transportation costs as a whole it may be applied to individual transportation functions or operations. Thus, if 500,000 miles of motor truck operation will be required, and the standard cost rate is $0.092 per mile, this item would be budgeted at $46,000. Likewise, if 20,000 driver hours will be required and the standard rate is $1.40 per hour, the budget would be set at $28,000.

This method is particularly suitable for transportation costs since the major part of such costs is of a variable nature. There are, however, some fixed elements of the cost to be considered. If the volume expected is below normal, and if standard rates are being used, the budget should contain an item for the estimated unabsorbed cost.

Where no standard costs are available, each individual cost item must be estimated by transportation executives on the basis of past experience.

Warehousing and Handling Expense.—The method of budgeting warehousing and handling costs is the same as that of transportation mentioned above. Warehousing functions and related cost standards are suggested in Chapter 15. The cost standards here are usually applied only to the variable elements of the cost, leaving the semivariable and fixed costs to be estimated on the basis of past experience and future commitments. The occupancy expense of warehouse buildings, for example, represents a fixed item of cost and can be accurately estimated. In preparing the warehousing budget, use must be made of not only the sales but also the purchase and inventory budgets.

Credit and Collection Expense.—Where credit and collection costs are a factor of importance, functional standard costs, such as those suggested in Chapter 16, should be set and the costs budgeted accordingly. Such standards can be applied to the major part of the variable costs. Semivariable and fixed costs can be estimated with little difficulty once the sales and financial budgets are known and the credit policy established.

Financial Expense.—The financial costs can be estimated with little difficulty as the greater part of this cost is fixed. The variable costs consist of interest on temporary borrowings and sales discount. Interest cost can be secured from the finance budget which will be prepared for the business as a whole. The method of separating the distribution and production shares of this cost is explained on pages 62 to 64. Assuming no major change in credit terms or in their enforcement, and assuming that general business conditions will remain approximately the same, it is possible, from past experience, to estimate closely the amount of sales discount which will be taken by customers. The accounting department can supply the information as to the average rates of discount which have been taken by various classes of customers or on various products and these rates applied to the budgeted sales will supply the estimate. When credit terms are to be changed, dependence must be placed upon the judgment of salesmen and sales and credit executives as to what the effect of the changes will be. In fact, expression of such judgment must be had before the desirability of such changes can be ascertained. When any important change is expected in general business conditions, the effect of the change on sales discount must be estimated by the credit department.

General Distribution Expense.—Some general distribution costs are fixed in nature as, for example, franchise taxes and pensions. Such items can be closely approximated in advance. Other items, such as dues, subscriptions, and market research cost, should be fixed by definite appropriations. Such items as accounting, office, and personnel costs must be estimated on the basis of standard rates, applied to expected sales operations, or estimated by the functional executives in charge. No special problems will arise in budgeting these general distribution costs.

Making the Budget Effective.—Once the distribution cost budget is completed, it should be reported in full detail to all major and minor executives responsible for its execution. No uncertainty should exist relative to the tasks to be performed and the anticipated cost of such performance. As the work progresses, regular reports should be prepared and issued on schedule showing actual performance and cost. Variances from the budget should be thoroughly analyzed to the point where the cause and responsibility are known. This may be done by resolving the variances, so far as possible, into their volume, price, and efficiency factors.

To illustrate such analysis, assume that the tonnage to be hauled in company trucks was estimated to require 20,000 truck-driver hours at a wage rate of $1.40 per hour. A cost of $28,000 was therefore budgeted. Assume next that the actual tonnage hauled during the period proved to be 10% more than expected and should have called for an equal percentage increase in the number of driver hours. This would not necessarily follow but may be assumed here for the sake of simplicity. Assume further that an unexpected increase of 10% in hourly rates was necessary after the budget was made, and that the actual operations resulted in 22,500 hours at a total cost of $34,650. The total variance from the budget of $6,650 can be resolved as follows:

Volume factor
   2,000 additional hours at $1.40 per hour $2,800
Price factor
   22,500 hours at a wage increase of $0.14 per hour 3,150
Efficiency factor
   500 hours in excess of standard at a cost of $1.40 per hour 700
      Total variance $6,650

While the cost was far in excess of the budget, only $700 of the increase can be placed to the responsibility of transportation executives.

For cost items which are fixed by definite appropriations, the budget reports should show amounts actually expended, commitments, and available balances. Figure 60 illustrates such a report for the advertising appropriation.

Revision of Budget.—The distribution cost budget must be promptly revised to accord with any change in sales policy or changes in local conditions which vitiate the cost standards. The sales organization

To _August 31, 19___

Media	Appropriated		Expended		Committed and Planned			Balance Not Planned
	Total for Year	To Date	To Date	Unexpended Balance	Non cancel·able	Balance avail·able	Planned but Cancelable	
Trade Papers	84,000	56,000	60,000	(4,000)	4,000	20,000	10,000	10,000
Dealer Signs								
Direct Mail								
Etc								
Total								

FIGURE 60. Report of Advertising Appropriation

must be measured against its opportunity; as this changes, the measurements must be changed. One of the dangers in the use of distribution cost standards is that appropriate revision will not be made promptly.

Limitations of Standards and Budgets.—In this and the six preceding chapters considerable emphasis has been placed on the value of standards and budgets as tools in the direction of distribution effort and the control of its costs. This emphasis is fully deserved; the use of such tools is essential to good management. But executives should not be deceived. They are only tools. They are by no means a substitute for executive vision and leadership. Budgetary plans will not execute themselves and standards are not self-enforcing. Moreover, much hard work, time, and patience are necessary to develop these tools to a point of usefulness. Those who expect quick and easy results should be discouraged from the attempt.

CHAPTER 20

ACCOUNTING FOR DISTRIBUTION COSTS

Chart of Accounts and Organization Factors.—In this chapter brief consideration will be given to the two basic methods of accounting for distribution costs, namely, the actual cost method and the standard cost method. Prior to a discussion of the distinguishing characteristics of each method, recognition should be given to the vital importance of a good chart of accounts to an effective distribution cost accounting plan. Illustrations of such charts are found in Chapters 3 and 9. Perhaps the most important single criterion of proper charting is that the system of accounts be tailored to the organization structure of the particular company. This point is emphasized by Warren G. Bailey, partner of A. T. Kearney & Company, as follows:[1]

It is commonly stated—and I think well stated—that distribution or other cost accounts must parallel organization responsibility. This means that they must conform to the grouping of personnel for supervisory purposes; that closely related activities must be grouped as to responsibility of certain executives and supervisors; that physical location of offices, branches, and warehouses must be given careful attention. This means that the summaries of cost and expenses shall be prepared in accordance with this departmentalization of the organization.

Departmentalization for both supervisory and accounting purposes should also parallel the classes of products, as well as the channels of trade.

So often the whole distribution cost accounting and cost operation plan is complicated because of the failure to recognize these organization factors.

So many times the whole distribution cost accounting problem is involved also because of the failure to develop carefully and properly the *chart of accounts*. Developing a chart of accounts is really a job that requires the skill of an architect, the thought of a scientist, and the perspective of an artist. There are so many factors and so many problems which need special attention.

Actual Cost Method.—It is the usual practice in accounting to include all the distribution expenditures of an accounting period as expense of that period, even though some of the distribution effort represented by the expenditures may have been directed toward sales to be secured in subsequent periods. There are, of course, some exceptions to

[1] "The Importance of Developing Distribution Costs," *The Controller*, November, 1949, pp. 512 and 540.

this practice. Specific items of distribution cost which can be definitely related to subsequent periods are sometimes deferred. Thus, if $10,000 is expended for sales catalogs in one fiscal period but the catalogs are to be used in a subsequent period, the cost would normally be deferred. Barring such exceptions, however, the practice usually prevails. For purposes of identification this method of accounting for distribution costs will be referred to here as the *actual* cost method.

ADVANTAGES AND DISADVANTAGES OF THE ACTUAL COST METHOD. The chief argument advanced in support of the actual cost method is that the values accruing from the distribution expenditures are of an intangible nature, difficult of measurement, and of uncertain duration; and, therefore, conservative practice demands that they be charged against current revenue. It is reasoned that, if executives and accountants were given freedom to eliminate from current operating expense considerable portions of the distribution costs assumed to be applicable to subsequent periods, the integrity of financial and operating statements might be imperiled. Owing to the great variety of circumstances, it is argued that no dependable rules of valuation could be established and enforced, that any measure of value would be a matter of personal judgment, and that, consequently, operating statements would be largely an expression of the degree of executive optimism currently prevailing.

There is merit to this argument. The practice is, in final analysis, based upon conservatism. No experienced executive or accountant will deny that much of the value of sales promotional work carries forward to subsequent periods; that an inventory of widely advertised and branded merchandise may have a value far in excess of unknown goods. But they know also that business stability demands a reasonably conservative expression of financial position and operating results, with safeguards against the fallibility of individual judgment and honesty.

On the other hand, the actual cost method has serious disadvantages, particularly when applied to short periods such as the month or quarter. In seasonal businesses, selling expense may be very high in periods when sales are very low, with the result that statements are meaningless. Moreover, statements which reveal only the actual costs are of little value to distribution executives in the control of operations. They supply no signals as to excessive costs or unsatisfactory cost and result relationships. Again where operations are analyzed by territories, products, etc., and where each period is required to absorb its actual cost, irrespective of related sales, volume declines in one territory or product penalize other territories and products, and thereby tend to nullify the value of the divisional analyses.

These disadvantages are of sufficient weight in some types of business, that a standard cost plan serves as a more effective method of accounting for distribution costs.

Standard Cost Method.—The standard cost method of accounting for distribution costs is developed on the assumption that at least the major part of the distribution operations can be standardized, and that the cost of performing these operations can be subjected to some standard relationship to sales results or to some specific measurement in terms of service performed. Thus it may be determined that the standard cost of advertising is 2% of net sales, that salesmen's compensation and expense should be 10% of net sales, that the clerical cost of handling orders should be $0.30 each, that the physical cost of handling orders should be $2 each, and so on for the various functional operations performed. After a concern has had sufficient experience to prove the dependability of the standards, they may be reflected in the accounts and operating statements.

By this method the total expenditures are resolved into the following elements:

1. Those chargeable to current operations at standard
2. Those which represent variances from standard performance
3. Those which can reasonably be deferred to subsequent periods

The variances from standard are further analyzed as to cause and responsibility and thereby serve to guide management in the control of operations. Different standards are established for different divisions, such as territories and commodities, thereby directing the analysis of variances to specific points of responsibility.

This method of accounting has been rather widely extended to production costs and to a considerable extent can be applied to distribution costs.

It should be noted that the development and use of the budget are essential to the standard cost plan.

ADVANTAGES AND DISADVANTAGES OF THE STANDARD COST METHOD. The advantages of the standard cost method may be stated as follows:

1. Through the analysis of variances, it gives management a better understanding of why the costs were not what they should have been and who is responsible for the result.
2. By means of frequent variance reports, it sets forth the nature and extent of inefficient performance as a basis for corrective action.

3. It has a stimulating effect on performance and results. If employees know that costs are under continuous measurement, they become cost conscious.
4. It automatically assigns to each period, such as the month or quarter, the distribution costs which relate to the sales of that period, thereby providing more accurate and intelligent statements of operation.

Objections to the standard cost plan, with comment as to their validity, may be noted as follows:

1. It involves additional records and more work. The additional clerical work required in operating the standard plan is negligible. The real increase in work comes with the setting of the standards. If this is done intelligently, a considerable amount of information must be continuously gathered as a basis for decisions. The additional work, however, is of small consequence if distribution costs are actually brought under control.
2. Standard costs tend to become merely averages of past costs and therefore unsatisfactory measures of performance. There is a real danger here, and unless it is prevented the method is of little value. Any plan which depends entirely upon past performance as a measure of efficiency simply perpetuates weakness.
3. In some types of business, the operating results as reported monthly under the standard plan are practically the same as under the actual cost method. It is true that in some types of business, particularly retailing, the total operating results are much the same under both methods. That is, the amount of cost absorbed monthly under a standard plan will approximate the actual cost. These are cases in which the deferred element of cost is of minor significance. The standard method will, however, reveal individual, divisional, and departmental variances.
4. It is impossible to determine the actual causes of variances. This is tantamount to saying that when an item of cost is higher than it should be, no one in the organization is qualified to say why or who is to blame. While admitting that a greater degree of tolerance is necessary than in some production costs, management can scarcely afford to abandon all hope of cost control. For some distribution activities, the causes of and the responsibility for cost variances can be ascertained with certainty, and within reasonable limits, all are subject to control.
5. It is impossible to establish standards for much of the distribution activity. The extent to which such standards can be established was discussed in Chapters 13 to 17.

Actual and Standard Methods Used Jointly.—Some concerns have found it desirable to apply the standard cost method to only a part of the distribution costs, the actual cost method being used for all others. Thus a concern may reflect in the accounts the standard cost of order handling, warehouse operations, and transportation or delivery, these being the operations which, in its particular case, are adaptable to the standard method. No difficulties are encountered in the use of a joint method. It is particularly desirable to employ this plan when the standard method is being introduced.

Choice of Method Not Fundamental.—It is the opinion of the authors that the choice of accounting method is of no great consequence so long as the costs are actually subjected to proper measurement and control. The establishment and use of cost standards are essential to cost control; but whether the standards are actually reflected in the accounts, given effect through auxiliary statistical procedure, or partially reflected in the accounts and partially by separate procedure, is not fundamental.

The use of the standard cost method of accounting is obviously dependent upon the establishment of cost standards; but the purpose and value of cost standards are by no means limited to their use in connection with a standard cost method of accounting. Even though a concern continues with a plan of so-called actual costs, much the same results may be obtained by separate statistical analysis.

The standard cost accounting method does provide an orderly and more or less compulsory plan of cost analysis and, in some concerns, has much to commend it. In other concerns, separate statistical procedure is preferable.

Regardless of the accounting method applied and the nature of periodic statements prepared for internal managerial use, the final external statements should conform to accepted accounting practice.

Illustration of Standard Cost Method.—No one plan of standard distribution cost accounting can be illustrated which is widely applicable in its detailed procedure. Individual circumstances surrounding the nature, organization, and direction of distribution activities are too varied to permit a high degree of uniformity of procedure. Moreover, a detailed illustration of any one plan is impossible in the space available here. The basic method is, however, much the same for all concerns. This is illustrated in Figures 61 to 70.

In this illustration the following assumptions are made:

1. The company is a manufacturing concern.
2. The business can be separated into two major divisions: that pertaining to goods manufactured to special order, designated as *Spe-*

cial; and that pertaining to goods manufactured for stock and sold from inventories carried, designated as *Stock.*

3. The distribution activities are largely organized around these two divisions and costs can be reasonably separated as between the two.
4. Sales administration and effort of the two divisions are largely distinct.
5. The sales volume is somewhat seasonal in nature.
6. Approximately the same amount of direct selling effort is employed each month; however, monthly advertising appropriations are not uniform.
7. Special orders are delivered, upon completion, direct from the factory itself—consequently, with no warehousing and handling costs.
8. Standard costs have been developed for all distribution functions except credit and collection, financial, and general distribution activities. For these, actual costs are to be used.
9. Distribution activities are fully budgeted.

Figure 61 illustrates the distribution cost standards which have been established for both divisions. Some of the standards are based on the relationship of cost to sales results; for example, in the *Special* division, Salesmen's Compensation is expressed as 12% of budgeted sales. Others are expressed as a definite cost per unit of service; thus, Salesmen's Automobile Expense is given a standard of $0.045 per mile. No standards have been set for cost Items 10, 11, and 12. Here the costs will be estimated for budgeting purposes and the actual costs charged as expense.

Figure 62 presents the sales and operation factors upon which a budget for the month of January is prepared. Owing to the seasonal factor, sales for January are expected to be only 78.3% of average monthly sales.

Figures 63 and 64 present the January budgets for the *Special* and *Stock* divisions respectively. These budgets show the expected actual expenditures, the standard amounts chargeable as January expense, and the estimated amounts to be deferred.

Since Sales Administration (Item 1) is contingent on the three cost items immediately following in the budget, it should not be calculated until those items have been estimated. Referring to Figure 63, Salesmen's Compensation expenditure is shown as $16,000, or 12% of average monthly sales. It is assumed that the sales effort will be practically uniform throughout the year; hence, this average expenditure may be expected. The amount to be charged as expense is shown as $12,000, or 75% of the expenditure. This is based on the theory that only 75% of the results of the year's effort can normally be ex-

STANDARDS

Distribution Costs	Special	Stock
1. All sales administration and sales office salaries and expense except order handling	15% of salesmen's compensation and expense (Total of Items 2, 3, and 4)	10% of salesmen's compensation and expense (Total of Items 2, 3, and 4)
2. Salesmen's compensation (Salaries and bonuses)	Total should not exceed 12% of average monthly budgeted sales.	Total should not exceed 8% of average monthly budgeted sales.
3. Salesmen's traveling expense and all other salesmen's expense except automobile expense	$8 per day of travel	$7 per day of travel
4. Salesmen's automobile expense	$0.045 per mile	$0.045 per mile
5. Order handling—clerical	$3 per order	$0.40 per order
6. All advertising	2% of budgeted sales	4% of budgeted sales
7. Transportation (Trucking)	$0.05 per ton-mile	$0.04 per ton-mile
8. Variable warehousing and handling expense	None	$2 per order
9. Fixed warehousing and handling expense	None	Fixed monthly cost of $1,000 or 0.4% of average monthly budgeted sales
10. Credit and collection expense	Actual costs used	Actual costs used
11. Financial expense	Actual costs used	Actual costs used
12. General distribution expense	Actual costs used	Actual costs used

FIGURE 61. Chart of Distribution Cost Standards

SALES AND OPERATING FACTORS ON WHICH DISTRIBUTION COST BUDGET IS BASED

Month of January

	Special	Stock	Total
Average monthly budgeted sales for year	$133,333	$250,000	$383,333
Sales budgeted for January	$100,000	$200,000	$300,000
Percentage of January sales to average	75	80	78.3
Number of salesmen-days of travel	480	1,000	1,480
Number of miles of automobile travel	10,000	50,000	60,000
Number of sales orders	200	2,000	2,200
Advertising appropriation for January	$3,000	$5,000	$8,000
Number of ton-miles of trucking	150,000	300,000	450,000

FIGURE 62. Sales and Operating Factors Used for Distribution Cost Budget

pected in January. The balance of the expenditure, or $4,000, should therefore be deferred. This plan is applied to cost Items 1, 2, 3, and 4. With Items 5, 7, and 8, the full expenditure should be considered as cost of the month. With Item 6, Advertising, it is assumed that monthly appropriations have been made which, for the year, are equal to 2% of the budgeted sales. The amount appropriated for January is $3,000, but of this amount only $2,000 should be expensed for January, the balance being deferred. Cost items 10, 11, and 12 are estimated, as no standards have been set; total expenditures of the month are to be charged as expense. Item 9, which appears only on Figure 64, illustrates a fixed cost. This is expected to be approximately $1,000 per month, regardless of volume; however, it is expected to average 0.4% of *Stock* budgeted sales. It should, therefore, be currently expensed at that rate. Should the budgeted volume of operations fall substantially below normal, a part of such fixed costs should be assigned to an account for Unused Capacity and thereby eliminated from consideration as an operating cost.

Figure 65 shows the actual sales and operations for the month of January. Figures here are assumed. It will be noted that *Special* sales are 105% of budgeted sales, whereas *Stock* sales are only 90% of budgeted sales.

Figures 66 and 67 illustrate the method of separating the actual expenditures according to their elements of cost variance, chargeable expense, and deferred expense.

Referring to Figure 66, the cost items are first shown at the actual expenditures expected on the basis of a budgeted volume of $100,000. Next, these are revised to show what would have been estimated for a volume of $105,000—the actual volume realized. Cost Items 1, 2, 3, and 4 are the same, as it is assumed that a uniform monthly sales effort is used. Items 5 and 7 are increased in proportion to volume as they represent services whose cost varies directly with volume. Item 6

BUDGET OF SPECIAL ORDER OPERATIONS FOR MONTH OF JANUARY

	Estimated Operations on Basis of Actual Expenditures		Estimated Operations on Basis of Standard Chargeable Expense		Estimated Deferred Expense
Sales.............................	From Figure 62	$100,000	From Figure 62	$100,000	
Gross Profit......................	35% assumed	35,000	35% assumed	35,000	
Distribution Costs:					
1. Sales administration, etc......	15% of items 2, 3, and 4 below or $20,290	3,044	15% of items 2, 3, and 4 below or $15,217	2,283	$ 761
2. Salesmen's compensation........	12% of $133,333	16,000	75% of $16,000	12,000	4,000
3. Salesmen's traveling expense, etc....	480 days at $8	3,840	75% of $3,840	2,880	960
4. Salesmen's automobile expense.....	10,000 miles at $0.045	450	75% of $450	337	113
5. Order handling—clerical...........	200 orders at $3	600	200 orders at $3	600	None
6. Advertising.......................	Appropriation	3,000	2% of $100,000	2,000	1,000
7. Trucking..........................	150,000 ton-miles at $0.05	7,500	150,000 ton-miles at $0.05	7,500	None
8. Variable warehousing, etc.........		None		None	None
9. Fixed warehousing, etc............		None		None	None
10. Credit and collections...........	Estimated expenditure	300	Estimated actual	300	None
11. Financial........................	Estimated expenditure	400	Estimated actual	400	None
12. General..........................	Estimated expenditure	500	Estimated actual	500	None
Total Distribution Cost...........		$ 35,634		$ 28,800	$6,834
Net Operating Profit or Loss.....		($ 634)		$ 6,200	

FIGURE 63. Budget of *Special Order* Operations

BUDGET OF STOCK OPERATIONS FOR MONTH OF JANUARY

	Estimated Operations on Basis of Actual Expenditures		Estimated Operations on Basis of Standard Chargeable Expense		Estimated Deferred Expense
	From Figure 62 40% assumed		From Figure 62 40% assumed		
Sales...............................	$200,000		$200,000		
Gross Profit.......................	80,000		80,000		
Distribution Costs:					
1. Sales administration, etc...........	10% of items 2, 3, and 4 below or $29,250	2,925	10% of items 2, 3, and 4 below or $23,400	2,340	$ 585
2. Salesmen's compensation............	8% of $250,000	20,000	80% of $20,000	16,000	4,000
3. Salesmen's traveling expense, etc....	1,000 days at $7	7,000	80% of $7,000	5,600	1,400
4. Salesmen's automobile expense......	50,000 miles at $0.045	2,250	80% of $2,250	1,800	450
5. Order handling—clerical............	2,000 orders at $0.40	800	2,000 orders at $0.40	800	None
6. Advertising.......................	Appropriation	5,000	4% of $200,000	8,000	(3,000)
7. Trucking..........................	300,000 ton-miles at $0.04	12,000	300,000 ton-miles at $0.04	12,000	None
8. Variable warehousing, etc...........	2,000 orders at $2	4,000	2,000 orders at $2	4,000	None
9. Fixed warehousing, etc.............	Fixed costs	1,000	0.4% of $200,000	800	200
10. Credit and collection..............	Estimated expenditure	700	Estimated actual	700	None
11. Financial.........................	Estimated expenditure	1,000	Estimated actual	1,000	None
12. General...........................	Estimated expenditure	700	Estimated actual	700	None
Total Distribution Cost...........		$ 57,375		$ 53,740	$3,635
Net Operating Profit.............		$ 22,625		$ 26,260	

FIGURE 64. Budget of *Stock* Operations

ACTUAL OPERATIONS AND EXPENDITURES FOR MONTH OF JANUARY

	Special		Stock
Sales..	$105,000		$180,000
Gross Profit......................................	36,750	35% / 40%	72,000
Distribution Expenditures:			
1. Sales administration, etc...............	3,000		2,900
2. Salesmen's compensation..............	17,000		20,000
3. Salesmen's traveling expense........	3,900	500 days at $7.80 / 980 days at $7	6,860
4. Salesmen's automobile expense.....	494	10,500 miles at $0.047 / 45,000 miles at $0.044	1,980
5. Order handling—clerical.............	615	205 orders at $3 / 1,700 orders at $0.40	680
6. Advertising...............................	3,000		4,000
7. Trucking..................................	8,190	157,500 ton-miles at $0.052 / 240,000 ton-miles at $0.054	12,960
8. Variable warehousing, etc............	None	1,700 orders at $2.10	3,570
9. Fixed warehousing, etc...............	None	Fixed costs	1,100
10. Credit and collection.................	400		700
11. Financial.................................	420		900
12. General..................................	300		800
Total Distribution Expenditures..	$ 37,319		$ 56,450
Net Operating Profit on Basis of Actual Expenditures...........	($ 569)		$ 15,550

FIGURE 65. Actual Operations and Expenditures

DETERMINATION OF COST VARIANCES, CHARGEABLE EXPENSE, AND DEFERRED EXPENSE—SPECIAL ORDERS

Month of January

	Estimated Expenditure at Volume of $100,000 from Figure 63	Estimated Expenditure at Volume of $105,000	Actual Expenditure from Figure 65	Variance from Standard Favorable	Variance from Standard Unfavorable	Amount to be Charged as Expense	Amount to be Deferred
1. Sales administration, etc.	$ 3,044	Same $ 3,044	$ 3,000	$44		78.75% of $3,044 $ 2,397	$ 647
2. Salesmen's compensation	16,000	Same 16,000	17,000		$1,000	78.75% of $16,000 12,600	3,400
3. Salesmen's traveling expense, etc.	3,840	Same 3,840	3,900		60	78.75% of $3,840 3,004	836
4. Salesmen's automobile expense	450	Same 450	494		44	78.75% of $450 354	96
5. Order handling—clerical	600	105% of $600 630	615	15		100% of $630 630	None
6. Advertising	3,000	Same 3,000	3,000		None	2% of $105,000 2,100	900
7. Trucking	7,500	105% of $7,500 7,875	8,190		315	100% of $7,875 7,875	None
		(a)34,839	(b)36,199	(c)59	(d)1,419		
10. Credit and collection	300	Estimated 300	400			400	None
11. Financial	400	Estimated 410	420	Expensed at actual; no variances or deferred elements considered.		420	
12. General	500	Estimated 520	300			300	
Totals	$35,634	$36,069	$37,319 (e)	$59 (f)	$1,419 (g)	$30,080 (h)	$5,879 (i)

NOTE: (a) = (b) + (c) − (d)
  (e) = (g) + (h) + (i) − (f)

FIGURE 66. Determination of Cost Variances, Chargeable Expense, and Deferred Expense—*Special Orders*

remains the same as it is fixed by appropriation. Items 10, 11, and 12 are changed slightly by direct estimate.

Actual expenditures for the month are recorded next. The differences between the revised estimates (that is, the amounts which should have been spent with a volume of $105,000) and the actual expenditures are then recorded as variances from standard.

The next step is to resolve the standard expenditures (those based on a volume of $105,000) into their chargeable expense and deferred elements. Since $105,000 represents 78.75% of the average monthly budgeted volume, this percentage of cost Items 1, 2, 3, and 4 is taken as chargeable expense, the balance being deferred. This is based on the theory that sales for the year will still average $133,333 per month; hence, this percentage must be used ultimately to absorb the expense. Items 5 and 7 are charged entirely to expense. Item 6 is expensed on the standard basis. With Items 10, 11, and 12, no attempt is made to separate expense and deferred elements, the entire amounts being expensed.

Referring now to Figure 67, the actual sales are $180,000, or 90% of the budget; hence, this figure is used in revising the estimated expenditures and ascertaining the variances. A special case arises with Advertising. The original appropriation for January was $5,000 (see Figure 64). For some reason, however, only $4,000 was actually spent. If the same advertising projects were carried out as originally planned but at $1,000 less cost, the $1,000 would be recorded as a favorable cost variance. This is, of course, unlikely. The reasonable supposition is that the advertising department delayed their January expenditures with the intention of increasing those of subsequent months. This difference is therefore passed to the deferred expense column. Likewise, the Fixed Warehousing expenditures exceeded the estimated figure by $100. This may be recorded as an unfavorable cost variance on the assumption that costs were excessive; or it may be assumed that these costs will average $1,000 per month for the year and, therefore, the excess expenditure should be deferred. The latter assumption is made here. In actual procedure, such cases must be subjected to further analysis.

Actual *Special* sales are 78.75% of the average monthly budget sales; hence this percentage is used in Figure 66 in determining the amount of chargeable expense, as related to selling effort costs. *Stock* sales are 72% of the average monthly budgeted sales; hence, by the same analogy, this percentage should be used in Figure 67. If it were certain that the loss in sales in January (January sales were $20,000 below the budget) would be made up in subsequent months, this method would be satisfactory; but since this is always doubtful, there is danger

DETERMINATION OF COST VARIANCES, CHARGEABLE EXPENSE, AND DEFERRED EXPENSE—STOCK

Month of January

	Estimated Expenditure at Volume of $200,000 from Figure 64	Estimated Expenditure at Volume of $180,000		Actual Expenditure from Figure 65	Variance from Standard Favorable	Variance from Standard Unfavorable	Amount to be Charged as Expense		Amount to be Deferred
1. Sales administration, etc.....	$2,925	Same	$2,925	$2,900	$25		80% of $2,925	$2,340	$585
2. Salesmen's compensation.....	20,000	Same	20,000	20,000		None	80% of $20,000	16,000	4,000
3. Salesmen's traveling expense, etc.....	7,000	Same	7,000	6,860	140		80% of $7,000	5,600	1,400
4. Salesmen's automobile expense	2,250	Same	2,250	1,980	270		80% of $2,250	1,800	450
5. Order handling—clerical.....	800	90% of $800	720	680	40		100% of $720	720	None
6. Advertising.....	5,000	Same	5,000	4,000 (a)1,000	(a)1,000		4% of $200,000	8,000	(4,000)
7. Trucking.....	12,000	90% of $12,000	10,800	12,960		$2,160	100% of $10,800	10,800	None
8. Variable warehousing, etc.....	4,000	90% of $4,000	3,600	3,570	30		100% of $3,600	3,600	None
9. Fixed warehousing, etc.....	1,000	Same	1,000	1,100		(b)100	0.4% of $200,000	800	300
			(c)53,295	(d)54,050	(e)505	(f)2,160			
10. Credit and collection.....	700		780	700			Expensed at actual; no variances or deferred elements considered.	700	None
11. Financial.....	1,000		950	900				900	
12. General.....	700		750	800				800	
Totals.....	$57,375		$55,775	$56,450 (g)	$505 (h)	$2,160 (i)		$52,060 (j)	$2,735 (k)

NOTE: (c) = (d) + (e) − (f) [plus or minus net (a) and (b) adjustments]
(a) and (b) are deferred variances
(g) = (i) + (j) + (k) − (h)

FIGURE 67. Determination of Cost Variances, Chargeable Expense, and Deferred Expense—*Stock*

in applying this percentage to the cost items representing sales effort. The preferable plan is to require January to absorb as expense its full budgeted share (80%) of the expenditure. A safe rule to follow is that the percentage of sales effort costs, to be absorbed as expense, shall be the percentage of the month's actual sales to the average monthly budgeted sales, or the percentage of the month's budgeted sales to average monthly budgeted sales, whichever is higher. This rule should also be applied to the to-date figures throughout the year.

Figures 68 and 69 illustrate the accounts in which the cost items are recorded. It is assumed that the cost items have been previously recorded in primary accounts and adjustments made for obvious deferred elements such as inventories of supplies, etc. Moreover, that proper separation has been made as between the two product divisions. Accounts numbered 1 to 12, inclusive, in Figures 68 and 69, thus illustrate the accounts for the adjusted costs of the *Special* and *Stock* divisions, respectively. Accounts 1 to 12 are closed monthly or periodically on the basis of the analysis shown in Figures 66 and 67. The Standard Distribution Cost accounts are debited with the chargeable expense for the month, Variance accounts are debited or credited with the unfavorable and favorable variances, and Deferred Distribution Cost accounts are debited or credited with the deferred elements of the costs. The last three groups of accounts are closed either monthly or yearly to Profit and Loss. The identity of the three groups should be maintained for statement purposes.

Figure 70 illustrates a monthly summary operating statement. It is apparent from this statement that operating results on the basis of an actual cost method would by no means reflect the true situation. *Special* orders, for example, result in a net loss of $569, whereas a proper accounting reveals a profit of $5,310. Likewise, the total profit by the two methods varies from $14,981 to $23,595 or from 5.3% of sales to 8.3%.

Figure 70 reveals that the *Special* order costs were $1,360 in excess of standard; and *Stock* costs, $1,655 in excess. These variances should be analyzed in detail to ascertain the cause and responsibility. The method of analysis may be suggested by taking certain individual variances of the *Special* order costs as shown on Figure 66.

Sales administration was $44 less than the allowance of 15% of salesmen's compensation and expense. Since this is a favorable variance no further analysis is required.

Salesmen's compensation was $1,000 in excess of the average monthly expenditure of $16,000, which is assumed to be necessary to provide the annual sales volume budgeted. Since the volume secured in January was 5% in excess of the budget, sales executives may claim

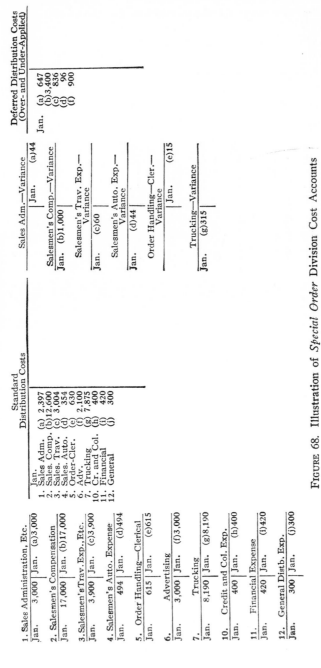

SPECIAL ORDER ACCOUNTS

FIGURE 68. Illustration of *Special Order* Division Cost Accounts

STOCK ACCOUNTS

1. Sales Administration, Etc.

| Jan. | 2,900 | Jan. | (a)2,900 |

2. Salesmen's Compensation

| Jan. | 20,000 | Jan. | (b)20,000 |

3. Salesmen's Trav. Exp., Etc.

| Jan. | 6,860 | Jan. | (c)6,860 |

4. Salesmen's Auto. Expense

| Jan. | 1,980 | Jan. | (d)1,980 |

5. Order Handling—Clerical

| Jan. | 680 | Jan. | (e)680 |

6. Advertising

| Jan. | 4,000 | Jan. | (f)4,000 |

7. Trucking

| Jan. | 12,960 | Jan. | (g)12,960 |

8. Variable Warehousing, Etc.

| Jan. | 3,570 | Jan. | (h)3,570 |

9. Fixed Warehousing, Etc.

| Jan. | 1,100 | Jan. | (i)1,100 |

10. Credit and Col. Exp.

| Jan. | 700 | Jan. | (j)700 |

11. Financial Exp.

| Jan. | 900 | Jan. | (k)900 |

12. General Distb. Exp.

| Jan. | 800 | Jan. | (l)800 |

Standard Distribution Costs

Jan.		
1. Sales Adm.	(a)	2,340
2. Sales. Comp.	(b)	16,000
3. Sales. Trav.	(c)	5,600
4. Sales. Auto.	(d)	1,800
5. Order-Cler.	(e)	720
6. Advertising	(f)	8,000
7. Trucking	(g)	10,800
8. Var. Whse.	(h)	3,600
9. Fixed Whse.	(i)	800
10. Cr. and Col.	(j)	700
11. Financial	(k)	900
12. General	(l)	800

Sales Adm.—Variance

| Jan. | (a)25 |

Salesmen's Trav. Exp.—Variance

| Jan. | (c)140 |

Salesmen's Auto. Exp.—Variance

| Jan. | (d)270 |

Order Handling—Cler.—Variance

| Jan. | (e)40 |

Trucking—Variance

| Jan.(g)2,160 | |

Variable Warehousing, Etc.—Variance

| Jan. | (h)30 |

Deferred Distribution Costs (Over- and Under-Applied)

Jan.	(a)	585	Jan.	(f)4,000
	(b)	4,000		
	(c)	1,400		
	(d)	450		
	(i)	300		

FIGURE 69. Illustration of *Stock* Division Cost Accounts

OPERATING STATEMENT
Month of January

	Special		Stock		Total	
	Budget	Actual	Budget	Actual	Budget	Actual
Sales.........	$100,000	$105,000	$200,000	$180,000	$300,000	$285,000
Cost of Goods Sold......	65,000	68,250	120,000	108,000	185,000	176,250
Gross Profit........	35,000	36,750	80,000	72,000	115,000	108,750
Distribution Costs at Standard........	28,800	30,080	53,740	52,060	82,540	82,140
Operating Profit on Basis of Standard Distribution Costs...	6,200	6,670	26,260	19,940	32,460	26,610
Excess of Actual Distribution Costs Over Standard.......	None	1,360	None	1,655	None	3,015
Operating Profit before Deducting Deferred Costs........	6,200	5,310	26,260	18,285	32,460	23,595
Deferred Distribution Costs.........	6,834	5,879	3,635	2,735	10,469	8,614
Net Operating Profit.........	($ 634)	($ 569)	$ 22,625	$ 15,550	$ 21,991	$ 14,981

FIGURE 70. Operating Statement for Month

that they should be allowed a 5% increase in salesmen's compensation or an additional $800. This would leave an unfavorable variance of only $200. There is danger here, as an average of only $16,000 per month has been budgeted for the entire year. Since $17,000 has been used in January, some subsequent month must be correspondingly reduced with the possibility of a corresponding decrease in sales; consequently, the full $1,000 should be considered as an unfavorable variance.

Salesmen's traveling expense was $60 in excess of standard.

Actual: 500 days at $7.80 per day	$3,900
Budget: 480 days at $8.00 per day (Standard)	3,840
Variance	$ 60
Cause of variance:	
20 extra days used at $8.00	$ 160
Saving of $0.20 a day on 500 days	100
Net loss	$ 60

Here the responsibility may be placed with the routing and scheduling of the salesmen. The salesmen themselves were within the standard daily expense.

Salesmen's automobile expense was $44 in excess of standard. This can be explained as follows:

Actual: 10,500 miles at $0.047 per mile	$494
Budget: 10,000 miles at $0.045 per mile	450
Variance	$ 44
Cause of variance:	
500 excessive miles at $0.045 per mile	$ 23
10,500 miles at excessive cost of $0.002 per mile	21
Total loss	$ 44

Here there is a dual responsibility. Salesmen were apparently routed over too much mileage and automobile operation is too costly. A further study would be necessary to ascertain the particular car operating costs which are excessive.

Such analysis must be made of all variances and carried to the point of individual responsibility.

This illustration indicates the method by which the standard cost plan may be applied to a part of the costs while other costs are recorded at actual. It shows also that the budget is an essential requirement in the application of the standard cost plan.

In this particular illustration, a considerable portion of the January expenditures is deferred and deducted as the last item on the operating statement. If the January sales were above the average for the year, the reverse situation would exist and the overabsorbed costs would be shown as an addition to profit.

CHAPTER 21

DISTRIBUTION COST REPORTS

Making the Information Effective.—No amount of analysis of distribution costs will result in the successful direction of distribution effort and the control of costs unless the resulting information is presented to executives in such a manner that they can understand it and will act upon it. Much of the reporting done by accountants for internal control purposes is unsatisfactory. Data are frequently gathered relative to operations and passed on to management without proper correlation and interpretation. Reports are frequently more in the nature of raw material than finished product. To use the data, executives must refine it and search out the significant facts and signals which provide a basis for decision and action. Many executives, pressed with administrative duties, do not have the patience—and in some instances lack the ability—to ferret out the significant points; and, therefore, make only limited use of the reported data. Here a double loss results. The cost of gathering the data itself is wasted and operations are directed without the use of adequate information necessary for successful operation.

It is not to be inferred from this that the accountant should make the decisions for management or even that the accountant can fully interpret all of the data. But, with his general purview of the entire operations, their trends and relationships, he can go far toward refining the operating data, selecting from a vast array of statistics the significant facts and presenting them in such a manner that they can be readily used as a basis for managerial decision and action. There is no aspect of accounting which offers a greater opportunity for resourcefulness, ingenuity, and keen analysis than the interpretation and presentation of distribution cost data.

Essential Characteristics of Satisfactory Reports.—The essential features of distribution cost reports are the same as those which apply to managerial reports generally. Briefly they may be reviewed as follows:

1. Reports should be as clear and simple as it is possible to make them. They should be so designed and expressed that the reader will get the essential facts with the least possible effort. Technical

language should be avoided as far as possible; thus, it is usually better to say that, "On the average it is 70 days from the time goods are sold to the time the money is collected"; than to say, "The rate of turnover of receivables is 5.21 times per year."

2. Reports should contain only essential information; all unnecessary data should be eliminated. If, for example, the traveling expense of seven men is satisfactory and three men unsatisfactory, data are necessary for only three.

3. The scope of the reports should be suited to the needs of the particular executives who will use them. A foreman in the warehouse may require a daily report on the performance of his individual workers, but general executives will require general summaries of performance, and these at less frequent intervals. As reports are graduated from lower to higher executives, they should take a wider sweep.

4. Reports should not contain merely recitals of actual costs and operations but rather relationships, trends, and signals as to what should be done or what requires attention. Thus it is one thing to report that warehouse labor cost for the month is $1,000 and quite another to show that the labor cost has steadily increased, in relation to physical volume, during the past six months. In general, the reports should be of a nature to motivate action.

5. In general, reporting should follow the "exception" principle; that is, only "out-of-the-ordinary" operations need be shown. While this is not entirely true with regard to the reports for major executives, even here the main stress should be on such operations.

6. Reports should be prepared and presented with extreme promptness. Regular reports should be presented on a definite schedule.

7. The information contained in the reports should be accurate and dependable.

8. The form of reports should be suited to individual executive preference. Some prefer narrative reports; others, tabular reports; others, graphical charts.

Adapting the Reports to the Executives.—To a considerable extent, reports must be adapted to the executives who will use them—both in content and form. The accountant should attempt to view the problems through the eyes of the executives. It is the executive, not the accountant, who finally uses the information. It is not the information which the accountant would use, were he the marketing executive in question, but that which the executive himself needs that must be supplied.

The general functional executives, such as the sales manager, advertising manager, traffic manager, warehouse superintendent, credit manager, and purchasing agent, should receive general summaries of the operations and performance of their respective divisions, with long-term trends and relationships. Figures 71 and 72 illustrate such reports for the sales manager. Detail of operations is necessary for such executives only as particular problems arise.

SALES REPORT No. 2

MONTHLY SUMMARY OF SALES

MONTH OF February 1953

TOTAL SALES

Comparison of this month with previous years and budget

(Even 100 dollars)

		DEPARTMENTS BELOW BUDGET				
			Budget	Actual	Amount Below	Per Cent
1949	$200,700					
1950	220,400					
1951	180,200	Legal Blanks	$30,100	$29,100	$1,000	97
1952	215,600	Tax Records	20,600	16,100	4,500	78
1953	220,500					
Per Cent Increase or (Decrease) Over Last Year	2.3%					
Five-Year Average	$207,500	TERRITORIES BELOW BUDGET				
Per Cent Increase or (Decrease)	6.2%	E. West Va.	15,600	15,000	600	96
Budget	$223,000	W. West Va.	20,500	19,500	1,000	95
Per Cent of Budget	98.9%	N. E. Ohio	40,200	37,200	3,000	92

This report must be given to Mr. Murphy, Sales Manager, by 10:00 A.M. of the third working day of the following month. Report is filed in Binder No. 2.

FIGURE 71. Monthly Sales Summary Report for Sales Manager

Divisional executives such as district, branch, and store managers and heads of departments require more frequent and more detailed reports. Figure 73 illustrates a weekly report given to the store manager of a retail furniture chain store. This is a condensed operating statement. The Sales, Gross Profit, Commissions, Payroll, and Advertising are actually correct figures for the week. Other Expense includes the remaining costs of doing business which run fairly uniform. This is estimated for the year and the cost for one week is taken as 7/365ths. Other operating items are also included on the report. The manager is also supplied with a daily report of sales and collections and complete

MONTHLY SUMMARY OF SELLING EXPENSE

MONTH OF February 1953

	Amount	Per Cent of Sales	EXPENSE ITEMS SUBSTANTIALLY ABOVE BUDGET			
			Item	Budget	Actual	Amt. Over
1949	$34,120	17.0				
1950	36,370	16.5				
1951	30,630	17.0	(1) Traveling Expense	$10,000	$10,200	$200
1952	34,500	16.0	(2) Conventions	300	400	100
1953	33,900	15.4	(3) Salesmen's Salaries	20,000	20,300	300
Budget	33,450	15.0				
(Increase) or Decrease from Budget	(450)	(.4)				

EXPLANATIONS:

(1) John Whiting $150; Bowman, two extra trips to Charleston $50.

(2) Charleston convention for County Auditors exceeded budget by $90.

(3) John Whiting loaned from Legal Dept. for 3 weeks on new West Virginia tax blanks.

This report must be given to Mr. Murphy, Sales Manager, by 1:00 P.M. of the fourth working day of the following month.
Report is filed in Binder No. 3.

FIGURE 72. Monthly Summary Report to Sales Manager of Selling Expense

WEEKLY STORE REPORT

STORE Columbus

WEEK ENDED October 28, 19___

Sales		$6,400
Less Returns and Allowances		400
Net Sales		6,000
Gross Profit		2,700
Expense:		
Commissions	$300	
Other Payroll	700	
Advertising	600	
Other Expense (Estimated)	900	
Total Expense		2,500
Profit or Loss		$ 200
Advertising Inches used		1,600
Gross Profit Per Cent		45
Number of Customers		126
Collections		$5,040

FIGURE 73. Weekly Store Report for Store Manager of Retail Furniture Chain Store

detailed monthly reports. Figure 74 illustrates an activity report prepared for the territorial sales executive of a hypothetical paper mill.[1] The number of budgeted calls and the number of actual calls, by four-week periods, are shown for cities and salesmen. This type of summary report is posted by periods from salesmen's daily field reports. Although the report does not indicate the degree of thoroughness in calls represented, it does provide the sales executive with a comparative measurement of salesmen's utilization of their time.

Minor executives, such as sales supervisors, warehouse foremen, garage foremen, and clerical supervisors, should receive weekly or even daily reports of the current performance of those employees under their direction. Figure 75 illustrates such a report for the supervisor of the billing department of a medium-sized manufacturing concern in which this operation is on a piece work and bonus basis.

Content of Distribution Cost Reports.—The content of the distribution cost reports must, of course, conform to the needs of the concern in question. The following outline may be useful in suggesting the information to be reported:

1. ACTUAL COSTS
    Analyzed as to:
        Nature of cost items
        Functions and operations
        Manner of application (i.e., to territories, commodities, customers, channels of distribution, etc.)
    Compared with:
        Previous periods
        Standards
        Budget
        Results

    A report showing the actual cost items of a territory for the current month and for the same month last year is illustrative of information within this general group.

2. ACTUAL OPERATIONS
    Pertaining to:
        Functions
        Units of effort used
        Units of service rendered
    Analyzed as to:
        Manner of application
        Actual cost

[1] Irving C. Barnes, "A Paper Mill Accounts for Its Selling Costs," *N.A.C.A. Bulletin,* July, 1950, p. 1394.

RECORD OF CALLS ON CUSTOMERS

Territory _____   Page _____

Periods	1 S	1 A	2 S	2 A	3 S	3 A	4 S	4 A	5 S	5 A	6 S	6 A	7 S	7 A	8 S	8 A	9 S	9 A	10 S	10 A	11 S	11 A	12 S	12 A	13 S	13 A	Total S	Total A
City and Customer																												
Detroit—No. of Days	4	3	4	4	4	5	4	4	—	—	4	3	4	3	—	3	4	2	4	2	4	5	4	4	—	—	40	38
Detroit																												
No. of Merchant Calls	4		6		2		7		4		5		—		3		2		9		5		6		3		56	
No. of Merchant Cust. Calls	7		2		—		4		1		2		4		1		—		4		2		2		—		29	
Customer No. 1	2		1		1		3		1		2		—		1		—		3		2		1		1		18	
Customer No. 2	1		3		1		2		2		2		—		1		—		4		1		4		1		22	
Customer No. 3	1		2		1		2		1		1		—		1		1		2		2		1		1		16	
Salesman A—Territory 1																												
Number of Days	10	9	15	16	15	18	20	18	20	18	20	22	10	12	15	12	18	16	18	17	18	20	18	16	18	20	215	214
Number of Merchant Calls	15		33		44		39		38		37		31		41		37		43		53		47		52		510	
No. of Merchant Cust. Calls	19		67		67		89		94		51		77		51		77		65		64		57		63		841	

EXHIBIT 1

FIGURE 74. Summary Report of Salesmen's Calls on Customers, by Four-Week Periods

DAILY REPORT OF BILLING DEPARTMENT

DATE October 12, 19___

Beatrice Fisher
Supervisor

	Lines Written	*Errors	Net Lines	Hours	Per Cent of Standard	AMOUNT EARNED		
						Piece Rate	Bonus	Total
Madeline Forrest	1,004	2	1,000	7	95	$ 5.00	$0.25	$ 5.25
Elizabeth Maloney	1,212	6	1,200	7	114	6.00	.90	6.90
Fay Morgan	1,010	5	1,000	7	95	5.00	.25	5.25
Marjorie Newhall	808	4	800	5	107	4.00	.40	4.40
Total	4,034	17	4,000	26	103	$20.00	$1.80	$21.80

*Errors are counted double.

FIGURE 75. Daily Report to Supervisor of Billing Department

Compared with:
 Previous periods
 Standards
 Budget
 Results

A report showing the number of salesmen's calls made, the cost of the calls, and the sales results obtained is illustrative of this type of information. Other illustrative operations are: number of sales transactions, number of deliveries, physical volume of shipments, number of returns and adjustments handled, and number of price tags marked.

3. RELATIONSHIP OF COSTS AND RESULTS
 Pertaining to:
 Functions
 Operations
 Manner of application
 Compared with:
 Previous periods
 Standards
 Budget

Figure 76 is illustrative of a report of this type. Here the direct selling function consists primarily in the work of traveling salesmen. This report supplies a weekly approximation of the results of the salesmen's effort in sales and profit. A more complete statement is prepared at the close of the month giving a comparison of results with previous periods and standards.

4. INFORMATION USEFUL IN SETTING AND TESTING COST STANDARDS
 Pertaining to:
 Expected money and physical volume of sales
 Units of functional service applicable
 Quantity of functional service required
 Fixed and variable costs
 Controllable and noncontrollable costs
 The results of special studies made to determine proper costs

Figures 77 and 78 illustrate types of reports which provide signals for the direction which cost investigation should take. Such information is valuable as a basis for starting the work of establishing standards.

5. COMPARISON OF ACTUAL AND STANDARD PERFORMANCE AND COSTS
 Pertaining to:
 Cost of effort used
 Cost of service rendered
 Relationship of cost to effort
 Relationship of cost to service rendered
 Relationship of effort to results
 Relationship of cost to results

WEEKLY REPORT ON SALESMEN

WEEK ENDED WEDNESDAY NIGHT _____ 19___

	Net Sales	Gross Profit		Direct Expense		Balance After Direct Expense	Number of Calls Made	Number of New Customers Secured
		Amount	Per Cent	Amount	Per Cent of Sales			
Diehl	$ 500	$ 210	42	$ 60	30	$ 150	31	3
Zuck	100	45	45	72	72	(27)	22	0
Bell	300	120	40	50	17	70	27	1
Etc.								
Total	$8,000	$3,520	44	$1,500	19	$2,020	600	18

FIGURE 76. District Manager's Weekly Report on Salesmen

	COMPARISON OF TRAVELING EXPENSE OF INDIVIDUAL TERRITORIES WITH AVERAGE YEAR ENDED _____ 19 ___			
Territory	Sq. Miles per Salesman	Average Cost per Salesman	Average Cost per Sq. Mile	Per Cent of Average
A	40,000	$2,400	$0.0600	200%
B	90,000	2,600	.0267	89
C	160,000	3,600	.0225	75
D	40,000	2,000	.0200	67
E	80,000	3,000	.0350	117
Etc.				
Average	90,000	$2,700	$0.0300	100%

FIGURE 77. Comparison of Traveling Expense per Square Mile of Individual Territories with Average

	COMPARISON OF BRANCH OFFICE TELEPHONE AND TELEGRAPH EXPENSE WITH AVERAGE YEAR ENDED _____ 19 ___			
Branch Office	Number of Orders	Telephone and Telegraph	Cost per Order	Per Cent of Average
A	20,000	$2,400	$0.12	120%
B	10,000	1,500	.15	150
C	30,000	2,400	.08	80
D	30,000	3,000	.10	100
E	15,000	2,250	.15	150
Etc.				
Average	20,000	$1,000	$0.10	100%

FIGURE 78. Comparison of Branch Office Telephone and Telegraph Expense with Average

Analyzed as to:
Efficiency variance
Volume variance
Price variance
Responsibility

Figure 79 is illustrative of a report falling in this group. Here the cost of operation of salesmen's automobiles is compared with the standard.

REPORT ON SALESMEN'S AUTOMOBILE COSTS

QUARTER ENDED ———— 19 ——

Include only those automobiles, the cost of which is above standard.

Our Car No.	Description of Car		Salesman	Miles to Date	Miles per Gallon		Total Operating Cost per Mile Excluding Accidents	
	Make	Year Model			Std.	Actual	Std.	Actual
51	* Std. Coupe	19—	Hall	30,016	14	12.4	$0.049	$0.054
76	* Std. Coupe	19—	Willis-Mack	21,402	14	12.6	.049	.053
84	* Std. Coupe	19—	O. Toole	40,670	15	13.1	.049	.061
Etc.								

* Name of automobile manufacturer.

FIGURE 79.   Report on Salesmen's Automobile Costs Which Are Higher than Standard

6. Expression of Budgets
    Pertaining to:
        Effort to be used
        Services to be rendered
        Cost of effort
        Cost of services
        Relationship of effort to results
        Relationship of cost to results
    Analyzed as to:
        Individual cost items
        Functions
        Manner of application

These are the usual reports which give expression to the budget in its various divisions. Figure 80 is a budget summary report.

7. Comparison of Actual and Budgeted Operations and Costs
    Pertaining to:
        Effort used
        Cost of effort
        Relationship of effort to results
        Relationship of cost to results
    Analyzed as to:
        Individual cost items
        Functions
        Operations
        Cause of variances
        Expended amounts and available balances

Figure 81 illustrates a comparison of total budgeted and actual costs for major distribution functions. Figure 60 (Chapter 19) presents an advertising budget report giving the appropriation and unexpended balances for each medium used. Figure 82 illustrates a more detailed comparison of budgeted and actual credit and collection costs.

8. Data Required for Purposes of Price Setting
    Such as:
        Actual costs
        Standard costs
        Out-of-pocket costs
        Fixed and variable costs
        Specific order costs
    Pertaining to:
        Long-term price policies
        Short-term price policies
        Bidding

Figure 83 sets forth the relationship between costs and prices.

REPORT ON DISTRIBUTION COST BUDGET

To ———— 19 ——

Functional Divisions	Appropriations				Expenditures			Balance Available for Use or Transfer
	Original	Additions	Deductions	At Present	Made	Contracted For	Total	

Figure 80. Summary Report of Distribution Cost Budget

COMPARISON OF BUDGETED AND ACTUAL DISTRIBUTION COSTS

MONTH OF August 19____

	Amount			Per Cent of Actual to Budget	Per Cent of Sales	
	Budget	Actual	(Over) Under		Budget	Actual
Net Sales	$200,000	$190,000	($10,000)	95%		
Cost Groups:					24.0	26.3
Selling	$48,000	$50,000	($2,000)	104%	24.0	26.3
Order-Handling	1,000	1,000	None	100	.5	.5
Advertising	10,000	8,000	2,000	80	5.0	4.2
Shipping	6,000	6,500	(500)	108	3.0	3.4
Credit & Collection	4,000	3,600	400	90	2.0	1.9
Financial	6,000	5,400	600	90	3.0	2.9
General	5,000	5,000	None	100	2.5	2.6
Total	$80,000	$79,500	$ 500	99%	40.0	41.8

FIGURE 81. Summary Comparison of Budgeted and Actual Costs

REPORT ON CREDIT AND COLLECTION COSTS
QUARTER ENDED ―――― 19 ――――

	Basis of Cost	Original Budget	Actual No. of Units	Standard Cost per Unit	Corrected Budget	Actual Cost	Change from Corrected Budget — Loss	Change from Corrected Budget — Gain
Controllable Costs:								
Posting and statements	Number of invoices	$ 2,500				$2,650		
Postage		250				250		
		2,750	6,000	$0.40	$2,400	2,900	$500	
Credit services		250				250		
Traveling expense	Average number of accounts	300				400		
Long-distance telephone		200				150		
Telegraph		100				100		
Supplies		300				250		
Stenographic, clerical and filing		2,000				2,100		
Miscellaneous		350				200		
		3,500	9,714	$0.35	3,400	3,450	50	
Payroll ins. and taxes	Payroll	600	12,200	5%	610	610		
Bad debt losses	Net sales	9,200	$3,000,000	.3%	9,000	7,000*		$2,000
Total controllable		16,050			15,410	13,960		
Fixed Costs:								
Adm. salaries	Fixed	8,000			8,000	8,000		
Occupancy and deprec.	Fixed	600			600	600		
Total Fixed		8,600			8,600	8,600		
Total Costs		$24,650			$24,010	$22,560	550	2,000
								550
						Net Gain		$1,450

* Losses actually taken.

FIGURE 82. Quarterly Report Comparing Budgeted and Actual Credit and Collection Costs

HOW SELLING PRICES SHOULD BE RELATED TO COSTS UNDER VARIOUS CONDITIONS

(Shaded portions represent costs to be covered by net collectible selling price)

CLASS OF COST		ORDERS—CUSTOMERS — SHORTER RANGE						PRODUCTS—LONGER RANGE			
		When Factory Capacity exceeds selling Capacity		When Factory & Selling Capacities Balance		When Selling Capacity exceeds Factory Capacity		Big Brother	Self Supporting	Weak Sister	Problem Child
								Very Good	Good	Bad	Very Bad
		Every Order (1)	Average Order (2)	Every Order (3)	Average Order (4)	Every Order (5)	Average Order (6)	(7)	(8)	(9)	(10)
Providing the Capital	Compensation for research, invention, risk assumption &/or marginal efficiency	Get back at least shaded costs and as much more as can				Use Limited Factory Capacity for most Profitable Business		Ponder	o.k.	Study now to limit	Improve profit or slate for elimination
	Recovery in prosperity of Losses in depression									prove profit	
	Compensation for use of tangible capital										
	Financial Management										
Soliciting Sales Contracts (Order Getting)	Selling & Publicity not variable with Customer Calls or Sales					Direct effect in auction Sales					
	Marginal Cost of Salesmen's Calls on Customers — Products Sold in Combination					machine hours effort to					
	Marginal Products					highest bidders accordingly					
	Publicity & Sampling Specialized by Products										
Executing Sales Contracts	Order Filling Cost — Sunk or Lagging										
	Slowly Variable by Reorganization										
	Automatically & Quickly Variable										
	Factory Indirect Cost — Sunk or Lagging										
	Slowly Variable by Reorganization										
	Automatically & Quickly Variable										
	Factory Direct Cost — Direct Labor										
	Direct Material										

FIGURE 83. Chart of Cost-Price Relationship (E. Stewart Freeman, *Year Book* of the National Association of Cost Accountants, 1939, p. 25)

9. OTHER INFORMATION

> Pertaining to:
>> Future distribution policies
>> Distribution program
>> Trends
>> Compensation plans
>> External factors

Reports must be prepared concerning many special matters pertaining to policy and operations. Frequently these are in the nature of the results of special studies. Figure 84 presents the results of a special study concerning the cost of handling orders of different size, under varying conditions.

COST (IN PERCENTAGE OF SALES) OF DISTRIBUTION OF GOODS OF AVERAGE BULK AND VALUE AT RATES OF STOCK TURN FROM 1 TO 10 AND IN VARIOUS–SIZED UNITS OF SALE

BASIS OF BUDGETED VOLUME OF $_____ DATE_____

Stock Turn-over	UNIT OF SALE						
	$ 1	$ 5	$10	$20	$30	$50	$100
1	40	31	23	20	17	14	11
2	40	31	23	20	16	14	11
3	40	31	22	19	16	13	11
4	39	30	20	19	15	12	10
5	38	29	19	18	15	11	9
6	37	29	19	17	14	10	8
7	36	28	18	16	13	9	7
8	35	28	17	15	12	9	6
9	34	27	17	14	11	8	5
10	34	26	16	13	10	7	4

FIGURE 84. Chart of Distribution Cost for Orders of Different Sizes and at Various Rates of Turnover

The foregoing outline of the nature of information to be included in distribution cost reports by no means exhausts the list.

On the other hand, not all such information is necessary in every concern. Ultimately, the only way by which the accountant can learn what to report is to study diligently the distribution problems of his industry and of his own concern in particular.

Form of Reports.—A primary consideration in selecting the form of reports is to adapt them to the preference of the executives who use them. This may require some experimentation on the part of the accountant. Marketing executives are supposed to be somewhat more resistant to elaborate statistical displays than are production executives, although this distinction is gradually disappearing. Care should be taken not to include too much on one report.

Three forms of reports may be used—tabular, graphic, and narrative. Numerous illustrations of tabular reports have already been presented. Figures 85, 86, and 87 are illustrative of graphic reports. Figure 85 shows the trend of the relative importance of major cost elements for a manufacturing concern through a period of six years. Figure 86 presents a comparison of the relationship of distribution costs to sales and the trend of this relationship through a period of five years.

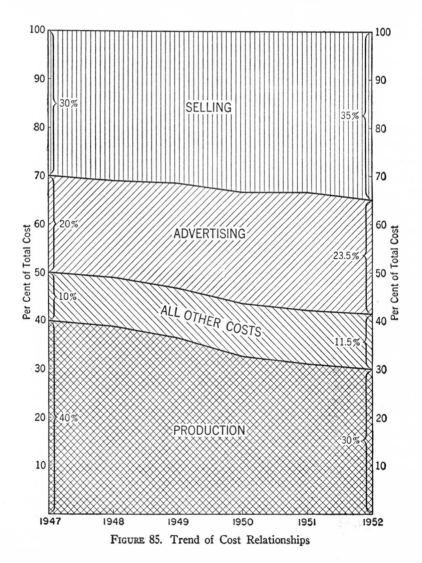

FIGURE 85. Trend of Cost Relationships

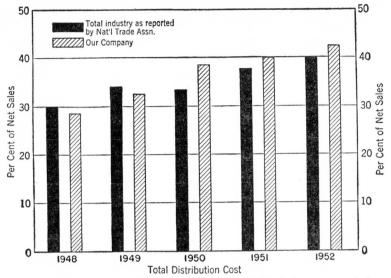

FIGURE 86. Comparison of Distribution Cost of Individual Company to Industry
as a Whole

The comparison is between the industry as a whole and an individual
company. It is apparent here at a glance that: (1) distribution cost has
gradually risen in relation to sales, and (2) that the increase for the individual company has been much greater than for the industry as a
whole. Figure 87 merely presents graphically the important divisions
of the cost of doing business for a chain of retail furniture stores.

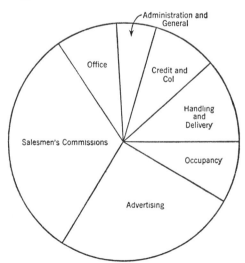

FIGURE 87. Distribution of Cost of Doing Business—
Chain of Retail Furniture Stores

Where tabular and graphic reports are used, they are usually more effective when supported by narrative comment.

Some special emphasis should be placed on the effectiveness of narrative reports. The accountant should be able to present his findings in clear, concise, and convincing language. On the whole, accountants make too little use of this form of reporting. It is one thing to prepare a table of related figures and quite another to state concisely the significant facts revealed by the figures. Particularly in reporting special studies is the narrative form effective.

Frequency of Reports.—The frequency with which the reports should be given to the executives varies with the level of responsibility of the executive. Some minor executives, such as supervisors in a warehouse, may require daily reports on the performance of their individual men. Major executives, on the other hand, require mainly monthly reports with quarterly and yearly summaries. In general, the higher the level of responsibility, the less frequent the reports. For all executives, the reporting should be done more frequently when the operations of their particular departments are running below standard.

CHAPTER 22

GOVERNMENT REGULATION AND DISTRIBUTION COSTS

A. Early Antitrust Legislation

General Statement.—Although both federal and state governments have imposed some regulatory measures on business almost from their inception, there has been a marked increase in such regulation in relatively recent years. One of these measures, the Robinson-Patman Act of 1936, has a particularly important bearing on the subject of distribution cost analysis. As a very general statement, this Act forbids certain price discrimination which cannot be justified by differences in certain costs. Therefore, it becomes necessary to analyze the costs as related to different customers and commodities in order to establish price differentials which fall within the law and to defend the prices as set should legal action be instituted.

This Act is the most recent major enactment in the field of antitrust legislation. The principal previous enactments are the Sherman Act of 1890, the Federal Trade Commission Act of 1914, and the Clayton Act of 1914 (one section of which is amended by the Robinson-Patman Act). A brief discussion of the preceding acts will furnish a better understanding of the objectives and provisions of the Robinson-Patman Act.

The Sherman Act.—The basic federal antitrust law is the Sherman Act of 1890. This Act forbids contracts, combinations, or conspiracies in restraint of trade; and actual monopolies or attempt to monopolize trade or commerce. It was passed as the result of a prevailing fear of the trust movement and of the rapid increase in powerful industrial mergers, consolidations, and combinations. It was the purpose of this Act to preserve the competitive system as an essential characteristic of the American economic order by maintaining the natural flow of trade, and freedom of competition, in interstate commerce. The effectiveness of the Act was almost nullified by early restrictive court decisions. On the one hand, the phrase "in restraint of trade" was interpreted in a very literal manner and with slight regard for the degree of competitive injury resulting from certain contracts or combinations.

On the other hand, the traditional judicial view that manufacturing is not commerce served temporarily to disarm the Act in several important cases involving combinations of producers. In later decisions, however, the Supreme Court widened the scope of the Act's applicability and, in addition, injected the so-called "rule of reason." By this interpretation contracts and combinations were deemed to be unlawful when in unreasonable restraint of trade.

Federal Trade Commission Act.—The Federal Trade Commission Act, passed in 1914, is in reality a reinforcement and extension of the Sherman Act, which was ineffective in curbing monopolistic and immoral practices. The Federal Trade Commission Act contains two major provisions: (1) it created the Federal Trade Commission, a continuous agency of inquiry and warning on the legitimacy of competitive practices; and (2) it provided that "unfair methods of competition are hereby declared unlawful." It was hoped that the Commission could police the field of interstate commerce, seek out, warn against, and stop the newer forms of illegitimate competitive practice as they arose. The power of the Commission has been extended by subsequent legislation until it now has jurisdiction over a wide range of unfair methods and practices. These include not only unfair methods of a monopolistic or trade restraining nature but also such immoral practices as fraud, misrepresentation, and deception, which may injure the public or competitors. While the jurisdiction of the Commission extends only to interstate trade, recent court decisions have construed this jurisdiction very broadly.

The Clayton Act.—The Clayton Act of 1914 followed immediately the Federal Trade Commission Act. It was designed to eliminate certain competitive methods which litigation under the Sherman Act had shown to be the most conspicuous weapons of monopoly. By nipping in the bud certain steps in the growth of a monopoly, Congress attempted to check such a monopoly before it became too strong. Specifically, the practices against which the Clayton Act was directed were price discrimination, tying contracts which force the buyer to purchase supplementary and possibly undesirable lines in order to secure desired goods, acquisition of stock in competing corporations, and interlocking directorates. Another important provision of this Act was that authority to enforce compliance with the law was vested principally in the Federal Trade Commission, subject to final review by the federal courts. This differed from the Sherman Act in which all proceedings were initiated directly in the federal courts.

Of particular interest here is the provision against price discrimination. The practice of price discrimination has been one of the most potent weapons of monopoly. It has by no means been unknown for large corporations to temporarily institute local campaigns of price cutting for the mere purpose of driving small competitors out of business. Accordingly, Section 2 of the Clayton Act forbade discriminations in price not based upon differences in grade, quality, or quantity of the commodity sold, or upon differences in the costs of selling or transportation, where the effect of such discrimination was to substantially lessen competition or to tend to create a monopoly in any line of interstate commerce. It left to the courts the problem of determining when competition was substantially lessened or when monopoly was threatened.

The Clayton Act and its predecessor antitrust enactments were designed primarily to curb monopolistic powers of large industrial concerns; the problems created by the growth of mass distribution had not expanded to a point of sufficient importance to receive public attention.

B. The Robinson-Patman Act

General Purpose of the Act.—The general effect of the Clayton Act, in so far as price discrimination was concerned, was to prohibit discrimination only where it had a serious effect on competition generally. But an individual concern was not so much interested in injury to competition generally as in injury to its own competitive equality. Consequently demands arose for further regulatory legislation. In response to this the Robinson-Patman Act was approved in 1936. This Act may be said to have resulted from two factors:

1. Resentment which arose in some quarters, following the depression years of 1930–35, against big business generally, and particularly against the rapid growth of chain stores
2. A belief on the part of Congress that there was need for still stricter regulation of trade practice generally, especially pertaining to concerns engaging in large scale distribution

While the desirability of imposing regulation on business merely because it is big is open to serious question, the desirability of restraining unfair practice in business, whether big or little, is now generally accepted.

Aside from the general objective of the Robinson-Patman Act, its specific purposes may be outlined as follows:

1. To secure uniform treatment for all customers falling within a certain classification (an equitable basis of customer classification to be provided)

2. To eliminate pseudo-brokerage fees and commissions
3. To secure equitable treatment of customers in respect to advertising allowances and services

While the Act does not compel entirely uniform treatment of customers within the same classification, its purpose is undoubtedly to provide a degree of uniformity which was thought by Congress to be equitable.

General Outline of the Act.—The Robinson-Patman Act consists of four sections. Section 1 amends Section 2 of the Clayton Act; it deals with price discrimination in interstate commerce. Section 2 relates to rights of action and enforcement proceedings pending at the time of the passage of the law; it was merely temporary in its effect and no longer is of significance. Section 3, commonly known as the criminal section, introduces new legislation. This section was originally considered as the Borah-Van Nuys Act but was finally incorporated in the Robinson-Patman Act. To some extent it overlaps the amended Clayton Act. This section designates specifically certain discriminations and price cutting practices which are rendered illegal and provides criminal penalties. Section 4 deals with cooperative associations, and (after amendment in 1938) with purchases by schools, hospitals, and other nonprofit institutions.

Basic Provision Against Price Discrimination.—Subsection (a)[1] of the Act is the basic provision which prohibits discrimination in price between customers of a given seller. This section is, in effect, an attempt to regulate the competitive relations between a given seller and his different customers, and to limit price differentials. Not all price differentials are prohibited as the statute applies only under certain conditions:

1. There must be discrimination between two or more customers of a given seller.
2. The purchases involved must be in interstate commerce.
3. The commodities involved must be sold for *use, consumption, or resale* within the United States, or within its territories, insular possessions, or other place under its jurisdiction; and not for *export*.
4. The discrimination in price must be made with respect to goods of like grade and quality.
5. There must be a sale of goods and not a sale of services.

---

[1] Reference is made here and in subsequent paragraphs to the subsections of Section 1 of the Robinson-Patman Act. Since Section 1 of the Robinson-Patman Act is really an amendment to Section 2 of the Clayton Act, these subsections really relate to Section 2 of the Clayton Act as amended.

6. The discrimination must have certain defined effects on competitive relationships. The discriminations prohibited by the Act are those where the effect may be:

    a) to substantially lessen competition in any line of commerce; or

    b) to tend to create a monopoly in any line of commerce; or

    c) to injure, destroy, or prevent competition:

        (1) with any person who either grants or knowingly receives the benefits of such discrimination; or

        (2) with customers of either of them.

The Act is inoperative if any one of the six above-mentioned conditions is not present.

Cost Proviso.—Even if all of the above conditions are present, a violation of Subsection (a) does not necessarily result from price differentials. A price differential may be permitted for a number of reasons, because the general prohibition is narrowed in scope by certain provisos. The first proviso reads as follows:

Provided, That nothing herein contained shall prevent differentials which make only due allowance for differences in the cost of manufacture, sale, or delivery resulting from the differing methods or quantities in which such commodities are to such purchasers sold or delivered.

Thus, the law expressly permits different prices to different customers where the differential in price makes only due allowance for differences in the cost of manufacture, sale, or delivery of the goods involved in the transactions. However, these differences in cost must result from differing *methods* or *quantities* in which the commodity is sold or delivered to the purchasers. This proviso sets the limits of quantity differentials as well as those due to differing methods of sale or delivery. It marks the zone within which differentials may be granted. It does not require differentials to be granted; and if granted, the differential need not be the arithmetic equivalent of the difference in cost. It is sufficient if it does not exceed that amount. The language used would seem to give the Commission, or the courts, a sound basis for a recognition of the many practical difficulties in the field of distribution cost analysis. These difficulties would tend to make exactitudes and precision impractical, and perhaps defeat the objective of the law itself, were exact costs demanded. Finally, it is to be noted that the cost clause is in the form of a proviso. The effect thereof is to place upon the seller the burden of proof as to the differences in cost which are reflected in price. The accountant, therefore, is vitally concerned with the problem of determining what the differences in cost are, and what price differentials will make only due allowance for them.

Setting of Quantity Limits.—The Act empowers the Federal Trade Commission to establish maximum quantity limits beyond which quantity discounts will not be permitted; and this is true even if the aforementioned differences in cost would otherwise justify such discounts. The Commission is also permitted to revise any or all quantity limits set. However, it is permitted to establish these quantity limits in the first instance *only* when it finds that the purchasers who may take advantage of particular quantity discounts are so few in number that it becomes "unjustly discriminatory" or promotive of monopoly. This is the power solely of the Federal Trade Commission, and is applicable only after due investigation and hearing to all interested parties. Until the Commission fixes the quantity limits, the granting of price differentials remains subject only to the other limitations of the Act. The first and only quantity limit rule (at this writing) issued by the Commission became effective in April, 1952, and applied to manufacturers' sales of replacement tires and tubes made of natural or synthetic rubber. The rule established a limit of 20,000 pounds, ordered at one time for delivery at one time.

Changing Market Conditions.—A second exception, under which a price differential is permitted, even if all the conditions usually prohibitive of such action are present, is the case in which the differential is due merely to a price change made in response to changing conditions affecting the market for, or the marketability of, the goods concerned. This proviso relates to the time interval between sales or the time of fixing two different prices. The Act cites examples indicating some conditions under which differentials might be made as a result of changing market conditions: actual or imminent deterioration of perishable goods, obsolescence of seasonal goods, distress sales under court process, or sales made with the true intent to discontinue the handling of the line of goods concerned.

It is expressly noted in the proviso that these examples are not the only conditions under which price changes may be permitted. In effect, the Act does not force a seller to stay with an established price or discount schedule. Shifts in a discount schedule should, however, preserve the cost-savings relationship among various discount classes. Furthermore, any price changes must be made available to all competing customers at the same time. Observance of the latter point is especially pertinent to sellers who make future delivery contracts or to those who offer price guaranties, i.e., rebates in case of a decline in price.

Selection of Customers.—As a third exception, a seller is not required to sell his product to all who desire to purchase it. Sellers are permitted by the original Clayton Act to select their own customers in bona fide transactions and not in restraint of trade. Therefore, the Robinson-Patman Act, continuing this provision of the old law, does not require that a seller make a sale to any particular customer at a particular price merely because he is selling the same product to another customer at that price. So long as the activities of the seller do not amount to a restraint of trade, as defined by the law, he is free to sell to a single purchaser, to any type of purchaser, or to any selection of purchasers.

Discrimination to Meet Competition.—Finally, as the last exception, a price discrimination *may* be justified, even if all the conditions usually prohibitive of such action are present, when it is shown that the lower price was made in good faith to meet an equally low price of a competitor, or the services or facilities furnished by a competitor. This particular justification is found, not in Subsection (a) with the others, but in Subsection (b), the paragraph (considered further below) which relates to proceedings before the Federal Trade Commission. That this justification constitutes a complete defense against a prima facie case of discrimination was not finally determined until January, 1951. In a decision on an appeal by the Standard Oil Co. (of Indiana) the U. S. Supreme Court [2] reversed and remanded a previous ruling of the Circuit Court of Appeals (Seventh Circuit). The lower court had upheld the Commission's contention that justification under Subsection (b) is merely procedural and is not controlling where injury to competition is proved.[3] The Supreme Court found, however, that the reduction of price in a good-faith attempt to meet competition is a complete defense not to be rebutted by considerations of competitive injury. In certain earlier decisions the Supreme Court had condemned the adoption of a competitor's pricing *system* which itself results in unlawful discriminations, but by inference had seemingly upheld the validity of the Subsection (b) proviso as an affirmative defense in localized instances.[4]

Burden of Proof.—Subsection (b) provides that proof of discrimination in price or services or facilities furnished, which is prohibited by the Act, shall constitute a prima facie case against the person complained of. Upon such person or persons is thrown the burden of showing the justification of his actions; and unless this is shown in a positive manner, the Commission is authorized to issue an order to

---

[2] *Standard Oil Co. v. F.T.C.* (January 8, 1951).
[3] *Standard Oil Co. v. F.T.C.*, C.C.A.-7, 173 Fed. (2d) 210 (1949).
[4] *F.T.C. v. A. E. Staley Mfg. Co.*, 324 U. S. 746 (1945); and *F.T.C. v. The Cement Institute, et al.*, 333 U. S. 683 (1948).
　　Additional clarification of Subsection (b) was made in a lower court decision subsequent to the *Standard Oil* (of Indiana) ruling. In *F.T.C. v. Standard Brands, Inc.* (March 30, 1951) the Circuit Court of Appeals interpreted the wording "equally low price of a competitor" to mean an equally low price for a given *quantity* of goods.

terminate the discriminations. This subsection does not shift the entire burden of proof from the Federal Trade Commission to a respondent. It simply provides that where the Commission has produced substantial evidence to establish an unlawful discrimination, the burden of refuting the prima facie case is shifted to the respondent who must establish the justification.

Unlawful Commission or Brokerage.—Subsection (c) prohibits the payment or acceptance of anything of value as a commission, brokerage, or any allowance or discount in lieu thereof, *except* for *services rendered,* either to the party or to any intermediary acting for, or subject to, the direct or indirect control of any party other than the one paying the commission. This provision is aimed primarily at the discriminations in price made under the pretense of paying a brokerage fee to a "broker," when in fact such "broker" is under the control of the other party to the transaction. There need be no evidence of injury to competition; each such payment is unlawful *per se.*

This subsection of the Act might be summarized as follows:

1. It permits the seller to pay his broker or agent compensation for services actually rendered in behalf of the seller; and it permits the buyer to pay his agent or broker compensation for services actually rendered in behalf of the buyer.

2. It prohibits the payment or allowance by the seller directly to the buyer of any brokerage, or commission, or other compensation, or any allowance or discount in lieu thereof; and it prohibits the payment or allowance by the buyer directly to the seller of brokerage, or commission, or other compensation, or any allowance or discount in lieu thereof.

3. It prohibits the payment or allowance of brokerage, or commission, or other compensation, or any allowance or discount in lieu thereof, by the seller to an agent or intermediary acting in fact for or in behalf of or subject to the direct or indirect control of the buyer; and it prohibits the payment or allowance of brokerage, or commission, or other compensation, or any allowance or discount in lieu thereof, by a buyer to an agent or intermediary acting in fact for or in behalf of or subject to the direct or indirect control of the seller.

A number of cases have been decided under this brokerage section of the Act and in 1938 the United States Circuit Court of Appeals sitting in New York validated the cease-and-desist order of the Federal Trade Commission against the Biddle Purchasing Company by finding that the company had violated this section of the Act. The court in its opinion said: "It is clear that the statute prohibits payment of brokerage by the seller to the buyer or his agent or representative or controlled intermediary except for services rendered. Congress intended to prohibit such payments as an unfair trade practice." The court went further and sustained the constitutionality of this section of the Act, holding that it was not inconsistent with the due process clause of the Fifth Amendment to the Constitution. In sustaining the constitutional validity of the brokerage provision of the Act, the court by implication upheld the constitutionality of the entire Act as this section was the one generally considered as most open to constitutional doubt.

Furnishing Services and Facilities to Customers.—Subsections (d) and (e) prohibit the seller from providing or paying for allowances, services, or facilities for the benefit of the buyer unless such service or facilities are:

available on proportionally equal terms to all other customers competing in the distribution of such products or commodities.

This provision is directed against supplying advertising and other allowances to selected customers whereby such allowances are subterfuges for price concessions. The general intent is that competing customers should be treated equitably in matters of facilities and services furnished or allowances granted. Numerous cease-and-desist orders have been issued by the Commission under this provision of the Act.

Application of Act to Buyer.—Subsection (f) reads as follows:

That it shall be unlawful for any person engaged in commerce, in the course of such commerce, knowingly to induce or receive a discrimination in price which is prohibited by this section.

This subsection is directed against the buyer, and makes him liable if he "knowingly" induces or receives a discrimination in price. His liability, however, appears to be limited to discriminations in *price*, whether direct or indirect; and there may be a question as to whether or not the provision extends to the receiving of advertising allowances, or other allowances or services or facilities, which constitute indirect price discriminations. This subsection provides a strong support to the seller to abide by the purpose of the law. It enables him to resist the demand for unfair price cuts, coming from mass buyers, by informing them that the price differentials demanded are in excess of cost differences. In this manner the seller can charge the buyer with knowledge of unlawful discrimination, should such discrimination result, and make the buyer equally liable. To date, comparatively few cases have been decided under the provisions of this subsection.

Civil Liability Under the Act.—That part (Section 1) of the Robinson-Patman Act which amends Section 2 of the Clayton Act is subject chiefly to cease-and-desist orders by the Federal Trade Commission and creates civil liability. In the fields of transportation, communications, and banking, the Interstate Commerce Commission, the Federal Communications Commission, and the Board of Governors of the Federal Reserve System, respectively, have authority of enforcement of Section 2 of the Clayton Act. Cease-and-desist orders are enforceable by U. S. Circuit Courts of Appeals. Civil action may also be initiated by any one of the following three methods:

1. Injunction suit brought by the Attorney General in a U. S. District Court.
2. Injunction suit brought by a private individual in a U. S. District Court.
3. Suit for treble damages brought by a private individual in a U. S. District Court.

Criminal Provision.—Section 3 of the Robinson-Patman Act is a separate criminal statute, and not an amendment to the Clayton Act. Therefore, it is subject to enforcement, not by the Federal Trade Commission, but by proceedings instituted by the Attorney General of the United States through a federal court. This section prohibits certain conduct, and provides that violations of its prohibitions are punishable by a maximum fine of $5,000 or imprisonment for not more than one year, or both.

By this section it is declared unlawful for any person engaged in commerce, in the course of such commerce:

1. To be a party to, or assist in, any sale, or contract to sell, which discriminates to his knowledge against competitors of the purchaser, in that, any discount, rebate, allowance, or advertising service charge is granted to the purchaser over and above any discount, rebate, allowance, or advertising service charge available to the competitors of the said purchaser. These specific grants mentioned must be available at the time of the transaction, and relate to the sale of goods of like grade, quality, *and quantity.*
2. To sell, or contract to sell, goods in any part of the United States at prices lower than those exacted by the said person elsewhere in the United States, for the purpose of destroying competition, or eliminating a competitor in that part of the United States where the lower prices are charged.
3. To sell, or contract to sell, goods at *unreasonably low prices* for the purpose of destroying competition or eliminating a competitor.

It is evident that Sections 1 and 3 of the Act are much alike. In Section 3, however, greater stress is laid upon price discrimination as a weapon for destroying or eliminating competition. Note, too, that meeting of competition in good faith is not specified as a defense in rebutting proved discrimination. The emphasis accorded the *quantity* of goods sold differs markedly between the two sections. Whereas Section 1 refers only to sales of goods of like grade and quality, and thus imposes restrictions on quantity discounts, Section 3 prohibits only discriminations in sale of goods of like grade, quality, *and quantity*. In this respect, Section 3 reiterates the phrasing of the original Clayton Act.

Cooperative Associations and Nonprofit Institutions.—Section 4 of the Act deals with its application to cooperative associations. This section merely states that nothing in the Act shall be so construed as to prevent a cooperative association from returning "to its members, producers, or consumers the whole, or any part of, the net earnings or surplus resulting from its trading operations, in proportion to their purchases or sales from, to, or through the association." However, where the cooperative, as an individual purchaser, takes title to the goods, the prices and concessions obtained by it are subject to the provisions of the law. The law is thus fully applicable to the operations of cooperatives except that patronage dividends are expressly permitted.

The Act was amended in 1938 to limit its application in relation to institutions not operated for profit. The amendment reads: "That nothing in the Act . . . shall apply to purchases of their supplies for their own use by schools, colleges, universities, public libraries, churches, hospitals, and charitable institutions not operated for profit." The status of purchases by government departments and agencies has not been clearly determined; however, the weight of opinion is that such purchases are exempt from the operation of the Act.

Cost Differences Permitting Price Differentials.—It is obvious from the foregoing review of the provisions of the Robinson-Patman Act that this measure has added new significance to distribution cost analysis. Concerns engaged in interstate commerce must now examine their costs not only for the purpose of efficient control of operations and proper guidance of marketing policy, but also as a safeguard against illegal and criminal practice. The Robinson-Patman Act seeks to prohibit differentials in selling price which are greater than the differences in cost. The yardstick, then, is *differences in cost;* and many factors which are usually considered in the determination of selling prices, but which cannot be reduced to cost figures, such as the value of enhanced prestige in the market, are excluded.

Types of Discounts.—Prior to examining cost concepts and differences in cost as related to the provisions of the Act, it is expedient to survey the typical methods whereby price differentials are established by business concerns. Price differentials between customers or groups of customers are generally effected by the seller's use of one or more of the following types of discounts: (1) quantity discounts, (2) trade (or functional) discounts, (3) cash discounts, and (4) special discounts and allowances, such as payments for advertising or for brokerage. None of these types of discounts (with the exception of pseudo-brokerage payments) is valid or invalid in itself; each must be interpreted in a particular case in the light of the various proscriptions and provisos of the Act. Neither trade discounts (i.e., discounts granted to customers in recognition of functions performed on a given level of distribution) nor cash discounts given for prompt payment are mentioned in the Act. In the absence of specific court decisions bearing upon the validity of these discounts, the seller must make sure that use of such discounts does not result in unjustifiable discrimination.

Cost Justification of Quantity Discounts.—Quantity discounts present a number of problems. In the first place, there are two kinds of quantity discounts in general use: (1) discounts based upon the size of the individual order or shipment, and (2) discounts based upon a customer's total orders, shipments, or even consumption of a commodity, over a specified period of time. Discounts of the latter kind—often termed cumulative quantity discounts or *volume* discounts—are much more difficult to justify on the basis of cost savings, especially if the buyer is not restricted as to the size or delivery method of individual shipments received during the discount period. In addition, volume discount schedules are apt to run afoul of the law if the largest discounts are actually available only to a very few large buyers.

The following discount schedule, made available to all purchasers, whether wholesale or retail, was held by the Supreme Court to be unlawfully discriminatory in the *Morton Salt Company* case:[5]

Purchases of "Blue Label" Salt	Per Case
Less-than-carload purchases	$1.60
Carload purchases	1.50
5,000-case purchases in any consecutive 12 months	1.40
50,000-case purchases in any consecutive 12 months	1.35

[5] *F.T.C. v. Morton Salt Co.,* 334 U. S. 37 (1948). The Federal Trade Commission has also consistently condemned the practice of allowing separate buyers to pool purchases in order to qualify for volume discounts. In addition, the commission has disapproved discounts based on the aggregate purchases of members of buying cooperatives, or on the combined purchases of several firms acting through buying agents. Similarly, discounts granted chain store organizations on the basis of aggregate purchases, rather than on the basis of the separate purchases of each unit, have been attacked successfully. See *Standard Brands, Inc.,* 30 F.T.C. 1117 (1940); *Simmons Co.,* 29 F.T.C. 727 (1939); *Sherwin-Williams Co.,* 36 F.T.C. 25 (1943); *John B. Stetson Co.,* F.T.C. Docket No. 5172 (1945); and the *Morton Salt* case.

It was shown that only five buyers (all chain grocery companies) bought sufficient quantities of the company's "Blue Label" salt in any consecutive 12 months to obtain the lowest price per case, and only 54 buyers, of a total of 4,040 buyers, were eligible for either volume discount. The company did not attempt to offer a cost-savings justification for its volume discounts; rather it contended that the discounts, being available to all buyers, were not discriminatory. The Supreme Court rejected the contention, pointing out that, since only a few chain buyers could qualify for the larger volume discount, these companies were able to sell salt at retail cheaper than wholesale purchasers could reasonably sell the same product to independent retailers in competition with the chains.

With reference to the carload discount, the Court recognized that such a discount might well have been justified by savings in cost if the company had proved (which it did not) that "the full amount of the discount is based on . . . actual savings in cost." This opinion is of utmost significance to business executives and accountants, since it may herald the beginning of a much more literal interpretation of the cost proviso of the Robinson-Patman Act than has hitherto been the case.

Establishing Quantity Discount Schedules.—Although the legal status of a particular seller's quantity discount schedule can be determined only with reference to all pertinent facts and current judicial opinion, certain general points pertaining to such schedules should be noted. The discount classes must not be unreasonably large or too few in number. The cost of serving customers within the same class must be substantially the same. The boundaries between classes must be reasonably placed. Finally, no one class may be granted a discount which is excessive as compared with other classes. These points are pertinent both to noncumulative quantity discounts and to cumulative or volume discounts. The hazards associated with use of the latter discounts must never be lost sight of, however. A statement on the establishment of equitable discount classes, made in 1938 by Robert E. Freer, former member and chairman of the Federal Trade Commission, merits repetition at this point. Mr. Freer stated: [6]

If the discount classes are broad, the costs of serving different customers within the same class will be dissimilar. An average of these costs probably will be unrepresentative of customers at the boundary of the class, and there is likely to be an indefensible discrimination between the largest buyers in one class and the smallest buyers in the next.

[6] Robert E. Freer, "Accounting Problems Under the Robinson-Patman Act," *Journal of Accountancy*, June, 1938, p. 484.

Sometimes, for example, a part of the seller's business consists of a very few small purchases which he accepts as a convenience to his customers at very high cost to himself. If, in preparing a quantity discount schedule, he includes in his lowest quantity bracket both these "nuisance" orders and the regular stock orders of his small customers, the effect is to charge these small customers with nearly the entire cost of the "nuisance" business, to raise the apparent cost of serving them, and to appear to justify for the larger customers a discount which is greater than the facts warrant. This is an example of a discount class which is too large.

Similarly, if the larger portion of the "nuisance" business is combined with the smaller portion of the commercially attractive business placed by small customers, the resulting class may not be too large, but its boundaries will be improperly located and there may be an unlawful discrimination between the smallest customers and the next smallest.

Determination of the size and boundaries of customer classes is in part a matter of discovering where and how the costs of doing business change most conspicuously. It depends, however, not merely upon a cost analysis, but also upon analysis of the market to discover what purchases originate in the same way and represent the same kind of transaction.

Given a reasonable system of discount classes, the determination of the maximum discount which can be justified by cost is a straightforward, but by no means simple, problem of cost accounting. In Congressional debate before the passage of the act, it was generally stated that the economies which arise merely from an increase in the total volume of business cannot be attributed to the last or the largest orders booked, nor used to justify special discounts upon these orders.

Marginal Cost Concept.—In many instances in the past, prices have been quoted to large buyers which covered only the additional direct costs entailed by such orders; or, in some cases, even less. The manufacturer has considered certain other benefits incident to the business of a mass distributor, such as enhanced prestige in the market, lower production costs generally as a result of increased volume, or the possibility of keeping workers better satisfied by regularity of employment. In bidding for these large orders, the producer has often been inclined to view this business as a potential addition to volume over and above that which he would otherwise receive. Therefore, he has not considered it imperative that the selling price of these large orders cover the full costs properly allocable to them. Instead, it has been considered sufficient that the prices quoted should cover the out-of-pocket costs, and possibly contribute something toward the general overhead.

The Robinson-Patman Act, as interpreted by the Commission, seems definitely to outlaw this kind of price making to the extent that it fails to reflect actual cost savings on a given order and is likely to have an injurious effect on competitive relationships. As the Senate Judiciary Committee stated in its report prior to the passage of the Act:

This [cost proviso] limits the differences in cost which may be honored in support of price differentials, to those marginal differences demonstrable as between the particular customers concerned in the discrimination. It is designed, among other things, to preclude the grant of a discrimination to a particular customer equal to the whole saving in cost resulting to the seller's entire volume of business as augmented by that customer's patronage; to preclude also differentials based on allocated or imputed, as distinguished from actual, differences in cost, representing particular facilities or departments which the favored customer may not have immediately utilized, but with which the seller cannot dispense in the general conduct of his business.

Problems of Cost Allocation.—The reference in the quotation above to allocated or imputed costs, as related to the immediate use or nonuse by a particular customer of facilities indispensable to the maintenance of a seller's business generally, introduces a number of perplexing problems. The reports both of the Senate and of the House Judiciary Committees indicated that it was the intent of the lawmakers that all costs of production and marketing be distributed among all transactions except where the justification for not so doing could be clearly demonstrated. It would seem that a cost defense based on an analysis of the effect on total costs of adding or dropping a particular order or account is insufficient to justify a price differential. An example of this is seen in the *Standard Oil* case in which the Federal Trade Commission rejected the company's cost justification of a price differential of 0.5 cents per gallon of gasoline allowed to a favored customer. Along with several other charges of deficiencies in evidence, the Commission stated that:[7]

Respondent attempted to segregate certain items of expense of an overhead nature as not being influenced by Ned's Auto Supply Company, on the theory that such expenses would not be appreciably influenced by the acquisition or loss of a single account, such as Ned's Auto Supply Company. The reason for not charging any of such items to the business of Ned's Auto Supply Company would apply equally to the business of any other single retail service station.

This same case provides a valuable commentary on the acceptability of methods of allocating certain items of expense only to those customers who actually use or require the services and facilities for which the expense items are incurred. The Commission charged that respondent attempted to allocate the costs of certain promotional sales work to all accounts other than Ned's Auto Supply Company on the theory that, being an established account, the latter did not require

[7] *In the matter of Standard Oil Company* (of Indiana), F.T.C. Docket No. 4389 (report and cease-and-desist order issued October 9, 1945). As noted previously, this case eventually reached the U. S. Supreme Court in 1951.

such services. This type of allocation was criticized by the Commission on the grounds that there were other established accounts that likewise would not require these services. Similar examples of unacceptable allocation procedures were cited as they concerned the cost of salesmen's calls and the cost of consumer advertising. Nothing in this case, however, would seem to forbid the apportionment of the expense of various distribution facilities and services against *only* the customers who use or require them. Such a principle of cost allocation was adopted by the Commission in the *Bird & Son, Inc.* case,[8] early in the history of the Robinson-Patman Act. It seems evident, nevertheless, that if certain customers are to be exempted from the apportionment of some costs, it is incumbent upon the seller to show that these customers are singularly different in certain respects from others and that the facilities or services in question do not benefit them in any way.

Thus far the problem of cost allocation has been considered on the tacit assumption that all marketing costs must be distributed for establishment of justifiable cost differentials. The Federal Trade Commission has shown, however, a willingness to accept cost allocations which exclude some indirect costs entirely. In the *Standard Oil* case, the Commission actually indicated a preference for partial allocation as contrasted with complete allocation dependent to a degree upon "arbitrary" methods of apportionment. The Commission charged that:

> In making this cost study the respondent did not limit its survey to cost differences which resulted from differing methods or quantities in which gasoline was sold or delivered to the two classes of customers nor was it limited to determining savings, if any, which accrued by reason of tank-car or transport-truck delivery as compared with tank-wagon delivery, but, instead, the respondent attempted to compare the cost of doing business with the one class as compared with the other by arbitrarily allocating all of respondent's costs of every nature which could be charged to the expense of doing business in the Detroit field, including Chicago general office costs allocated to that field.

The Commission's view expressed in this quotation would accordingly seem to be in harmony with the opinion advanced earlier in this book that complete allocation of distribution costs is, for managerial purposes, often less useful than allocation of only direct costs.

A warning as to inconsistency in the use of bases of cost allocation was also voiced in the *Standard Oil* case. The Commission asserted that:

> It further appears from respondent's cost study that direct-shipment expense has been allocated for the most part on the basis of effort, while the allocation

---

[8] *In the matter of Bird & Son, Inc., Bird Floor Covering Sales Corporation, Montgomery Ward & Co., Inc.,* F.T.C. Docket No. 2937 (complaint dismissed, July 17, 1937).

to the tank-wagon reseller channel has been made for the most part on the basis of gallonage except in accounts where allocation was made on the basis of effort in respondent's regular accounting procedure. The use of these two methods of allocation appears to be inconsistent, and the comparative results obtained do not properly reflect the difference in cost of sale and delivery between the tank-wagon and jobber channel.

Importance of Production Costs.—While the Robinson-Patman Act permits the use of differences in *production* costs as well as differences in *distribution* costs as a justification of price differentials, the former has not played an important part in cases to date. This is because production costs, in comparison with distribution costs, are less closely related to, and identifiable with, individual buyers and methods of sale and delivery.

Where goods are produced for stock, and orders filled from the stock room, there is no saving in the cost of manufacture resulting from serving any one customer as compared with any other. However, where goods are made to order, the conditions of production may provide a basis for a price differential. The cost of equipment, or adjustments in machinery, for example, may constitute direct costs attributable to a particular customer which tend to decline in terms of unit costs as that customer's purchases increase. Accordingly, price differentials may be granted, based on that fact.

It is also likely that, in many instances, ample cost differences can be found in distribution costs alone to justify price differentials, thereby precluding any need for similar production cost analysis.

Which Cost?—The procedure to be used in determining legitimate price differentials depends somewhat on the cost to be used as a test. The law permits differentials "resulting from the differing methods or quantities in which such commodities are to such purchasers sold or delivered." Must the cost, then, be the cost of specific transactions? Or may a more general cost be used? In applying the cost test, one of three bases might theoretically be employed:

1. The cost of the specific transactions under examination, or
2. General costs established in the industry for the type of transaction involved, or
3. The cost experienced by the particular manufacturer concerned, for the type of transaction under consideration.

The law prescribes no specific test, and the Congressional committee reports are not clear. Inference must be made from the few decisions of the Federal Trade Commission where cost examinations have been used.

If the cost of specific transactions were used as the basis, a most meticulous sort of record keeping would be necessary. This method would be impracticable in most cases. At the other extreme, a simpler and less expensive approach would be the development of standard costs within an industry for the various types of transactions involved. Even if such costs were acceptable, many difficulties would arise in determining what industry cost should be used. Should an average cost, a modal cost, a "reasonable" cost, or some other cost serve as a criterion?

It would seem that the proper cost to be used is that experienced by a particular concern, on the average, for the type of transaction under consideration. In the typical concern, the price structure should certainly be related to something more basic than a single transaction. Such an approach to distribution cost analysis has been used in the analysis methods suggested in the previous chapters of this book. Judging from the decisions of the Federal Trade Commission to date, it would appear that this view has been accepted by the Commission. In view of the practical difficulties of accounting under the Robinson-Patman Act, it has been unofficially indicated that the Commission may accept cost justifications based on average costs of serving typical classes of customers. The Commission probably would, however, accept such cost justifications only so long as good faith effort under current operating conditions was reflected.[9]

Cost Analysis Procedure Under the Robinson-Patman Act.—The question naturally arises as to what method of cost analysis procedure should be used in setting price and discount schedules which will conform to the requirements of the Act. Moreover, what procedure should be followed in preparing a defense before the Federal Trade Commission in cases where complaints are filed? In developing price schedules it must finally be determined what it costs to sell a given product to a particular customer under a set of prescribed circumstances, such as method of sale, size of order, and credit terms. If the same price is set for all customers to whom sales are made under substantially the same circumstances, full compliance is made with the Act. But if sales of the product are made to some customer under a different set of circumstances, a new cost must be determined and the price must be adjusted so that differentials to competing customers are not greater than differences in the cost. Otherwise, there is danger that one customer may complain of discriminatory treatment.

To illustrate, assume that in a particular case the difference in cost is the only consideration, other factors being the same. Product A is

---

[9] See John T. Haslett, "Price Discriminations and Their Justifications Under the Robinson-Patman Act of 1936," *Michigan Law Review*, February, 1948, p. 472.

sold to Adams at a total cost to make and sell of $100. The selling price is $110. Adams is a jobber who buys in small quantities at frequent intervals. Then the price must be $110 to all such competing jobbers whose transactions fall within the same set of circumstances. Now suppose that Product A is sold also to Brown, who is a competitor of Adams but who purchases in large quantities and at infrequent intervals. The total cost to make and sell to Brown is $92, or $8 less than to Adams. The selling price to Brown must then be not less than $102. Moreover, it must be not less than $102 to all other customers whose transactions fall within the same set of circumstances as those represented by Brown. If the price to Brown were $99, Adams could complain of illegal discrimination. If the price to Brown were set at $104, or only $6 below the price to Adams, Brown might claim discrimination but such discrimination would not be illegal as Brown could not prove injury to competition. The law in this case does not protect Brown. Brown's cost is $8 less than Adams' and the price to Brown must be not more than $8 less or $102; but the seller is not required by law to grant the full difference. He would be free to grant only $6 of the difference and therefore make a price to Brown of $104 or any amount between $110 and $102.

It appears, then, that customers must be classified into appropriate groups, in which circumstances of sale are substantially the same, and costs must be determined for each product for each such group. Prices must then be the same for all competing customers within a group, and, as between groups, the prices must not vary by more than the difference in costs.

For purposes of defense only, it may be unnecessary in some cases to carry the analysis to its full extent. For example, in the case above, if the price to Brown were set at $105 and Adams, who pays $110, were to complain of discrimination, it might be possible to show that the difference in one or two cost items alone, as between Adams and Brown, is sufficient to justify a price difference of $5. Here it might be unnecessary to actually determine the total cost to either Adams or Brown and it would be unnecessary to extend the analysis to other products or groups of customers since no one else has complained. In such a case, however, it would be necessary to show that there were no counterbalancing cost differences. Thus certain costs in selling to Brown might be $5 less than to Adams, but it would be necessary to show that other cost items were the same for both or would accentuate the differential.

The Robinson-Patman Act prescribes no particular procedure which is to be followed in making the necessary cost analysis, as between products and customers. To the extent that costs are directly related to particular customers, or customer groups, and to particular products, the analysis will present no great difficulty. Joint costs must be apportioned on such bases as would seem most reasonable, practicable, and equitable under the individual circumstances. It may be presumed that the Federal Trade Commission and the courts will continue to look to an intelligent balance of such factors. The direction which the analysis should take and the bases of allocation to be used must be appropriate to the circumstances of each case. Those acceptable in one case may not be applicable in another.

Accountants have long employed methods of direct and joint cost analysis, particularly in connection with production costs. It remains now for them to perfect this technique particularly as it relates to distribution costs. Methods of such analysis were discussed in Part I of this text.

Steps in Distribution Cost Analysis as Related to Robinson-Patman Act.—The method to be used in analyzing distribution costs, for purposes of price setting under the Robinson-Patman Act, depends largely upon the manner in which the distribution activity is organized. For example, concerns may organize their activities on the basis of channels of distribution, methods of sale, product lines, territories, etc. The sequence of steps to be followed in cost analysis will vary accordingly. The following outline is illustrative:

A. Sales organization and activity based primarily on CHANNELS OF DISTRIBUTION (for example, different salesmen and advertising methods employed in selling to large industrial customers and to jobbers)
1. Analysis by channels—to conform to basic sales organization
2. Subanalysis by size of orders or volume of customer purchases within each channel—to resolve customers into "conditions of sale" groups
3. Subanalysis by products within customer groups—to arrive at customer-product costs

   or

1. Analysis by channels—to conform to basic sales organization
2. Subanalysis by products within each channel
3. Subanalysis by size of orders or volume of customer purchases for each product—to resolve customers into "conditions of sale" groups and to reveal customer-product costs

B. Sales organization and activity based primarily on PRODUCTS (for example, different sales supervision, sales personnel, and advertising for different products)
1. Analysis by products—to conform to basic sales organization
2. Subanalysis of products by channels of distribution

3. Subanalysis of channels by size of orders or volume of customer purchases —to resolve customers into "conditions of sale" groups and to reveal customer-product costs

or

1. Analysis by products—to conform to basic sales organization
2. Subanalysis of products by size of orders or volume of customer purchases—to resolve customers into "conditions of sale" groups
3. Subanalysis of size of orders or volume of customer purchases by channels—to classify customers further by "conditions" and to reveal customer-product costs

C. Sales organization and activity based primarily on TERRITORIES (for example, separate warehousing, shipping, and selling facilities and administration for different territories)
1. Analysis by territories—to conform to basic sales organization
2. Subanalysis by products within each territory
3. Subanalysis of products by channels to resolve customers into "conditions of sale" groups and to reveal customer-product costs

or

1. Analysis by territories—to conform to basic sales organization
2. Subanalysis of territories by channels—to resolve customers into "conditions of sale" groups
3. Subanalysis of channels by products to arrive at customer-product costs

A note of warning is in point. The foregoing suggestion as to the sequence of steps which the distribution cost analysis may follow is purely illustrative and by no means complete. Almost any number of combinations of steps might be suggested. Moreover, less than three steps may be required. Many other factors may be injected, particularly in resolving customers into "conditions of sale" groups. The point to be emphasized is that some such sequence of steps must be selected in a particular concern, which will ultimately arrive at *customer-product costs*. To the extent that such costs differ, prices must differ if other conditions are present which subject the concern's transactions to the operation of the Robinson-Patman Act.

The task is not as difficult as it might appear. Once the proper method of analysis is established and the procedure developed, the cost differentials can be periodically determined as circumstances affecting the costs may require.

A question may be raised as to the period of time which the cost analysis should cover. In preparing a defense before the Federal Trade Commission, the analysis must cover the same period as that of the complaint unless it can be shown that a cost analysis of a different period is representative of the same conditions. The analysis for price-setting purposes is more or less of a continuous task and must be made frequently enough to reflect current conditions.

Cost Test an Optional Defense.—Price differentials which may lessen or injure competition or which may tend to create a monopoly are illegal if they make *more* than due allowance for differences in the cost of manufacture, sale, or delivery. However, if the price differentials can be shown to make only due allowance for the stipulated cost differences, the prices are lawful. Differences in cost, then, would appear to be one of the most important tests of price differentials. But the test is optional at the wish of the respondent. The Federal Trade Commission is not required to bring into the record the accounts of any given corporation against which a complaint is issued.[10] In fact, a complaint may be brought against a company, the case tried, and a cease-and-desist order issued without any reference to cost. If the price differential of the concern cannot be explained by its cost accounts, or other cost records, no question of accounting may even arise. However, if the cost of manufacture, sale, or delivery *will* explain the differential, then the respondent must take the initiative in presenting such data before the Commission, if a cost defense is to be given.

If the respondent does not wish to introduce cost data to justify this discrimination, he may use other defenses. For example, he may employ one or more of the following arguments for defensive purposes:

1. That the purchases involved were not in interstate commerce
2. That the discrimination did not involve goods of like grade and quality
3. That the discrimination was justified by changes in market conditions or the marketability of the goods
4. That the discrimination resulted from a good faith effort to meet an equally low price of a competitor

The first argument would attempt to show lack of jurisdiction of the Robinson-Patman Act for the transactions in question. The second argument, concerning goods of like grade and quality, would also serve as a bar to the establishment of a prima facie case of unlawful price discrimination. In connection with this argument it is of interest to inquire whether different brand names on otherwise identical goods may be sufficient to remove such goods from the classification of "like grade and quality." This question has not been definitively answered; however, current Federal Trade Commission complaints charge that goods so branded must be sold at the same price, even if part of the

---

[10] Freer, *op. cit.,* p. 480.

goods is sold under a purchaser's private brand.[11] The merits of the third and fourth arguments listed above have been discussed previously.

It will be noted that the list of noncost defenses does not include one based upon the inability or failure of the Commission to prove adverse effects upon competitive relationships. By sustaining the Commission in the *Morton Salt* case, the Supreme Court indicated that it will leave determination of the competitive effect of price discriminations entirely to the Commission's judgment. In this case the Court seems to have made a new and very literal interpretation of the Robinson-Patman Act which will sanction the prohibition of any discrimination if there is a *reasonable possibility* that it *may* adversely affect competition. Heretofore, the Court had required the Commission to show a reasonable *probability* of such an adverse effect. The doctrine of "reasonable possibility" obviously lessens considerably the Commission's burden of proof in Section 2(a) cases.

The Robinson-Patman Act in Relation to Accounting.—At the time of the passage of the Robinson-Patman Act it was confidently predicted that the cost proviso of Section 2(a) would stimulate extensive cost accounting developments in marketing. Even after two years of experience under the Act, Mr. Freer was encouraged to state that:[12]

It is my personal hope and belief that a by-product of the Robinson-Patman Act will be the development of a more adequate system of accounting for costs of distribution, capable of helping business men to be not only law-abiding, but also more efficient. The devices which have been used thus far to give the immediate knowledge of costs made desirable by the act have often proved to be inadequate.

Unfortunately, the hopes and forecasts embodied in Mr. Freer's statement have not as yet attained fruition. The Federal Trade Commission has been required to make only a few interpretations concerning acceptable cost accounting procedure for compliance with the Act. As a consequence, there are few specifically approved principles to serve as guides in a field of complex costing problems. The following excerpt from the Annual Report of the Federal Trade Commission for the fiscal year ended June 30, 1938, still has pertinent application.

Such cost accounting of distribution and the analysis of markets and market conditions which it requires are in the pioneering stage. Few, even of the large and important companies, have yet worked out and installed cost-accounting systems which, for purposes of defense under the Robinson-Patman Act, are

---

[11] For example, *B. F. Goodrich Co.*, F.T.C. Docket No. 5677 (pending); *Champion Spark Plug Co.*, F.T.C. Docket No. 3977 (pending); *U. S. Rubber Co.*, F.T.C. Docket No. 4972 (cease-and-desist order issued).

[12] Freer, *op. cit.*, p. 486.

sound and adequate in their conception and at the same time suitable and practicable for the everyday use of the individual business concern.

On the strength of very limited case experience, nevertheless, certain general observations may be made as to various aspects of the administration of the Robinson-Patman Act. These observations primarily are concerned with the nature and form of cost defenses prepared for presentation to the Federal Trade Commission.[13]

1. Elaborate cost studies should not be undertaken without prior consultation with representatives of the Commission in order to ascertain how complete and how detailed the cost studies must be. As noted previously, sample studies may be fully acceptable in some instances, provided that the sample is representative and, hence, that the results of the study are capable of extension to other segments of operation.

2. The method of presentation of cost data to the Commission is fully as important as the nature of the data. Explanation of techniques of allocation, for example, should be clearly and prominently presented, together with the *raison d'être* of such techniques.

3. Another point related to methods of presentation concerns sufficiency of evidence. In Robinson-Patman Act defenses it must always be remembered that the lawyer runs the case and the accountant is primarily his expert witness. The accountant must be fully aware of the legal requirements as to evidence if the accounting defense is to be of any value.

4. A respondent's own accounting methods, no matter of how long standing, will not necessarily be accepted by the Commission. It is certainly not true that methods thought to be satisfactory for managerial purposes in a particular company will necessarily be satisfactory for cost justifications under the Act.

5. Little reliance can be placed on authority in defense proceedings before the Commission. In one complicated case respondents employed accountants of highest reputation to verify the soundness of accounting theories and methods used. In addition, marketing experts testified that in their estimation the pricing schedules established by the company could have no substantial effect on competition. All this weight of authority made not the slightest dent in the Commission's skepticism.

6. Finally, as an over-all observation, it is evident that the Robinson-Patman Act has a great nuisance value. The cost of making a defense which may entail a heavy expenditure for special cost analyses is likely to induce respondents to accept the Commission's verdict without a real contest, even though they may be convinced that their cause is just.

It should be emphasized at this point that a grave responsibility still rests upon accountants to develop sensible and dependable methods of distribution cost analysis which will adequately serve in the just enforcement of this legislation. It is the accountants, not changing regu-

[13] Adapted primarily from Herbert F. Taggart, "The Standard Brands Case," *N.A.C.A. Bulletin,* October 15, 1939, pp. 195–262.

latory bodies, who are qualified by training and professional experience to lead the way in the development of fair and impartial methods. Private accounting executives and public practitioners must join in assuming this obligation or be remiss in their duty both to their own organizations and to the public.

C. Additional Federal and State Legislation

General Statement.—Numerous other laws pertaining to trade practice have been enacted in fairly recent years by federal and state governments. Some of these have no particular bearing on the subject of distribution costs but are worthy of brief note here as an indication of the trend and extent of regulatory measures. State laws modeled after the federal Robinson-Patman Act have been enacted in Idaho, Oregon, and Utah; whereas many other states have anti-discrimination laws less closely resembling the federal law. These apply, of course, to trade within the respective states.

The federal Wheeler-Lea Act was approved in 1938. It is an amendment to the Federal Trade Commission Act and amplifies and extends the power of the Commission. This amendment has three main provisions:

1. Whereas the Act formerly condemned "unfair methods of competition," it now condemns, in addition, "unfair or deceptive acts or practices in commerce." Previously action could be brought only by a competitor who claimed injury; now the Commission can act on its own initiative where injury to the public can be shown.
2. It provides that the Commission's cease-and-desist orders shall become effective after 60 days, unless appealed; that suits may be instituted in the District Courts; and that a civil penalty of $5,000 may be inflicted for each violation of the Commission's order after it becomes final.
3. In general it prohibits false advertising of food and drug products and even provides criminal penalties.

The Wool Products Labeling Act of 1939 also supplements the Federal Trade Commission Act. Approved in 1940, the Wool Act provides numerous safeguards for consumers and businessmen. The Fur Products Labeling Act, passed in August, 1951, is modeled after the Wool Act and is designed to prevent the use of fictitious names for fur and fur products.

Forty-five states have enacted laws which permit a manufacturer or his authorized distributor to stipulate a price below which his goods may not be resold by the buyer. In fact, the laws of some states permit the stipulation of the price at which the goods must be sold. These laws are usually referred to as resale price maintenance or fair trade acts. Since the stated intent is to protect the owners of brands and trademarks, this type of legislation pertains only to branded or trade-marked goods. It should be noted that such acts are permissive rather than mandatory in character; that is, the brand or trademark owner has the option as to whether or not he will place his goods under fair trade pricing protection. A novel feature of the typical state fair trade act is the so-called "nonsigner" clause, according to which even non-contracting parties are bound to observe the terms of resale price maintenance contracts, provided proper notification is given such parties.

The federal Miller-Tydings Act,[14] approved in 1937, had as its purpose the virtual elimination of trademarked goods, in open competition and distributed subject to state-approved vertical pricing agreements, from the jurisdiction of the antitrust laws. The efficacy of the Miller-Tydings Act in giving federal sanction to interstate shipments of fair-traded goods was severely lessened, however, by U. S. Supreme Court action in May, 1951. In the case of *Schwegmann Bros. et al. v. Calvert Distillers Corp.*,[15] the Court held that the Miller-Tydings Act was in-operative in so far as nonsigners of fair trade contracts were concerned. The severe blow thus dealt fair trade pricing was quickly parried by pas-sage of the McGuire Act in July of 1952. This Act is a direct amend-ment to the Federal Trade Commission Act instead of the Sherman Act and it expressly sanctions the extension of fair trade contracts to non-signers. In a number of other respects it is a stronger law than the Miller-Tydings Act, which was not repealed by the later Act.

D. State Unfair Trade Practices Acts

General Purpose of the Acts.—Of more interest to accountants than the various regulatory measures, mentioned in the preceding topic, are the state unfair practices acts. Resale price maintenance acts per-mit vertical control of prices when goods are branded and when the goods are of such a nature that list prices can be maintained. There are many areas, however, to which these conditions do not extend. More-over, price control under these laws requires the cooperation of the manufacturer. In an attempt to reach to other areas, some thirty states have now enacted unfair trade practices acts.

As a very general statement, these acts are mandatory measures which prohibit sales below cost and are intended primarily to prevent

---

[14] This Act is an amendment to the Sherman Act and, through specific mention, serves indirectly as an amendment to the Federal Trade Commission Act.

[15] 341 U. S. 384 (1951).

the use of loss-leaders. Whereas the fair trade laws apply vertically through a channel of distribution, the unfair practices acts cover a trade in a horizontal manner at each level of distribution. This legislation has been promoted chiefly by the trade associations, particularly in the wholesale grocery and drug trades. The interest of the accountant in these acts is immediately apparent. If sales cannot be made below cost, the question immediately arises as to what is to be included in the cost, and how is cost to be determined. Should it be construed as the purchase price, replacement cost, actual cost of the particular lot in question or average cost of numerous purchases? What overhead should be included and how should it be distributed as between different products, customers, and territories?

Sales Covered by the Acts.—The acts of ten states apply to *all* sales —producer, wholesaler, and retailer. The states are:

Arkansas	Oregon
California [16]	South Carolina
Colorado	Utah
Kentucky	Washington
Montana	Wyoming

In the remaining twenty states the acts apply only to the sales of wholesalers and retailers. In this group of states are:

Arizona [17]	New Hampshire
Connecticut	New Jersey [18]
Idaho	North Dakota
Kansas	Oklahoma
Louisiana	Pennsylvania
Maine	Rhode Island
Maryland	Tennessee
Massachusetts	Virginia
Minnesota	West Virginia
Nebraska	Wisconsin

Since no particular difficulties arise in connection with production costs, consideration will be given here only to the attempt of the acts to define costs at the wholesale and retail levels.

[16] The California Act has been held to be constitutional and not in conflict with the federal Sherman Act with reference to issues raised in the *Schwegmann Brothers* case, *supra.* See *People of the State of California v. Donald Gordon* (Calif. Dist. Ct. of App., 1951).

[17] Part of the Arizona Act has been held unconstitutional by the state supreme court. See *State of Arizona v. Walgreen Drug Co.* (Ariz. Sup. Ct., 1941).

[18] The New Jersey Act has been held unconstitutional by the state supreme court. See *State of New Jersey, on Complaint of Harry Lief v. Packard-Bamberger & Co., Inc.* (N. J. Sup. Ct., 1939).

The Cost Base.—In defining cost the acts set forth a cost base and then, with a few exceptions, designate certain elements of overhead to be added to the base. The resultant amount is the total cost below which sales are prohibited. Most of the acts further require the addition of freight and cartage charges in the computation of the cost base and permit deduction of all discounts except cash discounts. In each state law the cost base is defined in the same way for the wholesaler and the retailer. The cost bases found in the several acts may be classified as follows:

1. THE LOWER OF INVOICE OR REPLACEMENT COST. In twenty-seven states the cost base is prescribed as invoice cost or replacement cost, whichever is the lower. For example, the California law states that " 'cost' as applied to distribution means the invoice or replacement cost, whichever is lower, of the article or product to the distributor and vendor . . ." A similar provision is contained in the acts of each of the thirty states except New Jersey, Oregon, and South Carolina. With reference to replacement cost, a number of the acts require such cost to be figured as if goods were replaced within thirty days preceding the date of sale. The Montana law, as amended March 1, 1949, contains the provision that "as applied to distribution, 'cost' shall mean the invoice or replacement cost within ninety days prior to the date of sale and the quantity last purchased, whichever is lower. . . ."

The permissive use of a manufacturer's published list price and discounts as an alternate method of determining the cost base is a novel feature of the Minnesota Act. The Act reads:

The term "cost" as applied to the wholesale or retail vendor, means:

(1) The actual current delivered invoice or replacement cost, whichever is lower, not including customary cash discounts. . . . (2) Where a manufacturer publishes a list price and discounts, in determining such "cost" the manufacturer's published list price and discounts then currently in effect . . . shall be prima facie evidence of "cost."

2. REPLACEMENT COSTS. The Oregon and New Jersey laws define the cost base in terms of replacement cost exclusively. The former law states that "as applied to distribution, 'cost' shall mean the replacement cost of the article, product, or commodity to the distributor and vendor. . . ."

3. PURCHASE COST. The South Carolina Act merely prohibits the sale of an article "at less than the cost of such commodity bought in the open markets plus the freight and other charges to point of destination. . . ."

Addition of Overhead to Cost Base.—The various laws differ considerably as to the amount of overhead which must be added to the cost base. The requirements range from no overhead to all costs of doing business. Furthermore, the requirements for wholesalers are usually not the same as those for retailers. The provisions for the addition of overhead may be classified as follows:

1. No Provision for Overhead. The acts of five states—Arizona, North Dakota, South Carolina, Tennessee, and Utah—make no provision for the addition of overhead to the cost base of wholesalers' sales. Similarly, in New Jersey, North Dakota, and South Carolina, retailers are not required to add any markup for cost of doing business. The effect of these acts is to prohibit *predatory* loss-leader selling but not loss-leader selling. They provide a bottom for prices and a limitation of loss but they do not prevent all loss.

2. A Portion of Overhead. The majority of the state laws prohibit sales below the cost base plus a specified percentage of the cost base, unless the distributor can prove that his own cost of doing business is less than the stipulated percentage. These laws recognize the difficulty of compliance with, or enforcement of, a provision requiring addition of total overhead. At the wholesale level, a 2% markup is required in the following sixteen states: Connecticut, Idaho, Kansas, Louisiana, Maine, Maryland, Massachusetts, Nebraska, New Hampshire, New Jersey, Oklahoma, Pennsylvania, Rhode Island, Virginia, West Virginia, and Wisconsin. At the retail level, various minimum percentages are found. The laws of fourteen states require the retailer to add a 6% markup to his basic cost. The states with this requirement are Connecticut, Idaho, Kansas, Louisiana,[19] Maine, Massachusetts, Nebraska, New Hampshire, Oklahoma, Rhode Island, Tennessee, Utah, Virginia, and Wisconsin. In West Virginia, however, the markup must be at least 7%; and in Arizona, at least 12%. The Maryland law requires only a 5% markup; the Pennsylvania law, only 4%.

3. Total Overhead. The acts of nine states prohibit sales below the sum of the cost base and total overhead. These acts apply to wholesalers and retailers alike. In most of these state laws the items to be included as overhead are specifically enumerated in spite of an all-inclusive clause which defines overhead as *"all* costs of doing business." For example, the California law reads:

---

[19] The Louisiana law has been amended to provide that both wholesale *and* retail markups should be utilized in determining retailer cost in those cases in which the retailer buys directly from the manufacturer and receives the wholesaler's discount.

. . . all costs of doing business incurred in the conduct of such business and must include without limitation the following items of expense: labor (including salaries of executives and officers), rent, interest on borrowed capital, depreciation, selling cost, maintenance of equipment, delivery costs, credit losses, all types of licenses, taxes, insurance and advertising.

The states included in this group are Arkansas, California, Colorado, Kentucky, Minnesota, Montana, Oregon, Washington, and Wyoming. The laws of most of these states do not indicate the basis upon which overhead is to be apportioned or distributed to individual commodities or the period of time which should be used in establishing an overhead percentage rate. An exception to this is found in the Minnesota Act which reads:

The "cost of doing business" or "overhead expense" is defined as all current costs of doing business incurred in the conduct of such business . . . during the calendar year or the 12 months immediately preceding any alleged violation . . . ; or in the event any retailer or wholesaler shall have been engaged in business within the state for a shorter period of time, then such cost for such period of time immediately preceding any alleged violation thereof shall be prima facie evidence of "cost."

A somewhat similar provision is found in the Oregon law. It appears probable that most legislatures had in mind an average rate of overhead for all commodities taken together and that the average rate should be based on some reasonable period of time immediately preceding the complaint.

The prohibition of sales below the sum of the base cost and total overhead is obviously intended to prevent any type of leader selling. Theoretically, no item can be sold for less than its purchase price (or production cost) and the total cost of selling. Practically, such legislation has not proved highly effective.

Cost Survey Clause.—The acts of the various states contain certain other provisions relative to cost. Included in the acts of nine states is a so-called *cost survey* clause. For example, the California Act contains this statement:

. . . where a particular trade or industry, of which a person complained against is a member, has an established cost survey for the locality and vicinity in which the offense is committed, that cost survey is competent evidence to be used in proving the costs of such person.

The general intent of this clause is to permit trade associations to establish overhead markup rates which will be accepted as competent evidence in complaints. The acts do not specify what is meant by a *cost survey* and there appears to be considerable question as to its legal validity.[20] A seller can, of course, justify prices below minimums established by survey if he has accurate and continuous records to show that his own costs are lower than those prevailing in his vicinity.

Other Provisions of the Acts.—While the acts are directed on the whole against geographic price discrimination; predatory price cutting; and the limiting, or elimination of, leader selling; they contain numerous other prohibitions, such as false and deceptive advertising, secret rebates, and special services, which injure competitors, tend to destroy competition, and in general violate the spirit of the acts. On the other hand, numerous provisions are included which make the acts inapplicable to sales made in good faith to meet competition, sales of perishable or seasonal goods, genuine clearance and liquidation sales, sales to charity, court orders, etc.[21]

Penalties found in the acts are both civil and criminal and include: "injunctive relief," voiding of contracts, personal liability of officers and directors, revocation of charter, ouster of corporation, treble damages, fines, and imprisonment.

Significance of the Acts.—It will be apparent to every accounting and marketing executive, from a brief review of these acts, that many questions must arise as to their interpretation. List prices, discount terms, replacement cost, and even purchase price are subject to many different interpretations. Overhead may vary greatly under varying circumstances. Under such legislation there is added necessity for complete distribution cost analysis.

While the authors share, with many others, some grave doubt as to the political and economic expediency of price-setting legislation, a discussion of such views is not appropriate here. So long as such measures are on the statute books, accounting and marketing executives must attempt to interpret them fairly and lend honest effort to their enforcement. As a concluding word, it is probably fair to say that the concern which follows no trade practices which it would not consider as fair, were it placed in the position of competitors or the public, has little to fear from restrictive measures so far imposed.

[20] Cost plus 8%, as determined by a survey of the grocery trade in the Los Angeles area, was approved by the California courts. In Colorado, however, members of a grocers' association were successfully prosecuted by the United States Attorney General's office because they made a "survey" by *voting* cost plus 12%.

[21] For further information see Betty Bock, *Small Business and Regulation of Pricing Practices*, U. S. Department of Commerce, Economic (Small Business) Series No. 61 (Washington, D. C.: Government Printing Office, 1947), pp. 26–27.

APPENDIX

ANTI–DISCRIMINATION ACTS

SECTION 2 OF CLAYTON ACT AS AMENDED

SEC. 2. DISCRIMINATING IN PRICE, SERVICE, OR FACILITIES.[1] (49 Stat. 1526; 15 U.S.C.A., sec. 13, as amended.)

SEC. 2. (a) That it shall be unlawful for any person engaged in commerce, in the course of such commerce, either directly or indirectly, to discriminate in price between different purchasers of commodities of like grade and quality, where either or any of the purchases involved in such discrimination are in commerce, where such commodities are sold for use, consumption, or resale within the United States or any Territory thereof or the District of Columbia or any insular possession or other place under the jurisdiction of the United States, and where the effect of such discrimination may be substantially to lessen competition or tend to create a monopoly in any line of commerce, or to injure, destroy, or prevent competition with any person who either grants or knowingly receives the benefit of such discrimination, or with customers of either of them: *Provided,* That nothing herein contained shall prevent differentials which make only due allowance for differences in the cost of manufacture, sale, or delivery resulting from the differing methods or quantities in which such commodities are to such purchasers sold or delivered: *Provided, however,* That the Federal Trade Commission may, after due investigation and hearing to all interested parties, fix and establish quantity limits, and revise the same as it finds necessary, as to particular commodities or classes of commodities, where it finds that available purchasers in greater quantities are so few as to render differentials on account thereof unjustly discriminatory or promotive of monopoly in any line of commerce; and the foregoing shall then not be construed to permit differentials based on differences in quantities greater than those so fixed and established. *And provided further,* That nothing herein contained shall prevent persons engaged in selling goods, wares, or merchandise in commerce from selecting their own customers in bona fide transactions and not in restraint of trade: *And provided further,* That nothing herein contained shall prevent price changes from time to time where in response to changing conditions affecting the market for or the marketability of the goods concerned, such as but not limited to actual or imminent deterioration of perishable goods, obsolescence of seasonal goods, distress sales under court process, or sales in good faith in discontinuance of business in the goods concerned.

(b) Upon proof being made, at any hearing on a complaint under this section, that there has been discrimination in price or services or facilities furnished,

[1] This section of the Clayton Act contains the provisions of the Robinson-Patman Anti-discrimination Act, approved June 19, 1936, amending Section 2 of the original Clayton Act, approved Oct. 15, 1914.

the burden of rebutting the prima-facie case thus made by showing justification shall be upon the person charged with a violation of this section, and unless justification shall be affirmatively shown, the Commission is authorized to issue an order terminating the discrimination: *Provided, however,* That nothing herein contained shall prevent a seller rebutting the prima-facie case thus made by showing that his lower price or the furnishing of services or facilities to any purchaser or purchasers was made in good faith to meet an equally low price of a competitor, or the services or facilities furnished by a competitor.

[1527] (c) That it shall be unlawful for any person engaged in commerce, in the course of such commerce, to pay or grant, or to receive or accept, anything of value as a commission, brokerage, or other compensation, or any allowance or discount in lieu thereof, except for services rendered in connection with the sale or purchase of goods, wares, or merchandise, either to the other party to such a transaction or to an agent, representative, or other intermediary therein where such intermediary is acting in fact for or in behalf, or is subject to the direct or indirect control, of any party to such a transaction other than the person by whom such compensation is so granted or paid.

(d) That it shall be unlawful for any person engaged in commerce to pay or contract for the payment of anything of value to or for the benefit of a customer of such person in the course of such commerce as compensation or in consideration for any services or facilities furnished by or through such customer in connection with the processing, handling, sale, or offering for sale of any products or commodities manufactured, sold, or offered for sale by such person, unless such payment or consideration is available on proportionally equal terms to all other customers competing in the distribution of such products or commodities.

(e) That it shall be unlawful for any person to discriminate in favor of one purchaser against another purchaser or purchasers of a commodity bought for resale, with or without processing, by contracting to furnish or furnishing, or by contributing to the furnishing of, any services or facilities connected with the processing, handling, sale, or offering for sale of such commodity so purchased upon terms not accorded to all purchasers on proportionally equal terms.

(f) That it shall be unlawful for any person engaged in commerce, in the course of such commerce, knowingly to induce or receive a discrimination in price which is prohibited by this section.

ROBINSON–PATMAN ANTI–DISCRIMINATION ACT

[Public—No. 692—74th Congress]

[H. R. 8442]

An Act to amend section 2 of the Act entitled "An Act to supplement existing laws against unlawful restraints and monopolies, and for other purposes," approved October 15, 1914, as amended (U.S.C., title 15, sec. 13), and for other purposes.

DISCRIMINATING IN PRICE, SERVICE, OR FACILITIES. (49 Stat. 1526; 15 U.S.C.A., sec. 13.)

Be it enacted by the Senate and House of Representatives of the United States of America in Congress assembled, That section 2 of the Act entitled

"An Act to supplement existing laws against unlawful restraints and monopolies, and for other purposes," approved October 15, 1914, as amended (U.S.C., title 15, sec. 13), is amended to read as follows:

"Sec. 2. (a) That it shall be unlawful for any person engaged in commerce" (etc., as published *supra* p. 51 as the text of sec. 2, namely, subparagraphs (a) to (f), inclusive, ending with the words "which is prohibited by this section").

Sec. 2. Rights, Litigation, or Orders of Commission under Sec. 2 of Act of Oct. 15, 1914. (49 Stat. 1527.)

Sec. 2. That nothing herein contained shall affect rights of action arising, or litigation pending, or orders of the Federal Trade Commission issued and in effect or pending on review, based on section 2 of said Act of October 15, 1914, prior to the effective date of this amendatory Act: *Provided,* That where, prior to the effective date of this amendatory Act, the Federal Trade Commission has issued an order requiring any person to cease and desist from a violation of section 2 of said Act of October 15, 1914, and such order is pending on review or is in effect, either as issued or as affirmed or modified by a court of competent jurisdiction, and the Commission shall have reason to believe that such person has committed, used or carried on, since the effective date of this amendatory Act, or is committing, using, or carrying on, any act, practice or method in violation of any of the provisions of said section 2 as amended by this Act, it may reopen such original proceeding and may issue and serve upon such person its complaint, supplementary to the original complaint, stating its charges in that respect. Thereupon the same proceedings shall be had upon such supplementary complaint as provided in section 11 of said Act of October 15, 1914. If upon such hearing the Commission shall be of the opinion that any act, practice, or method charged in said supplementary complaint has been committed, used, or carried on since the effective date of this amendatory Act, or is being committed, used or carried on, in violation of said section 2 as amended by this Act, it shall make a report in writing in which it shall state its findings as to the facts and shall issue and serve upon such person its order modifying or amending [1528] its original order to include any additional violations of law so found. Thereafter the provisions of section 11 of said Act of October 15, 1914, as to review and enforcement of orders of the Commission shall in all things apply to such modified or amended order. If upon review as provided in said section 11 the court shall set aside such modified or amended order, the original order shall not be affected thereby, but it shall be and remain in force and effect as fully and to the same extent as if such supplementary proceedings had not been taken.

Sec. 3. Discounts, Rebates, Allowances, Discriminating Against Recipient's Competitors; and Place Discrimination and Sale or Offer at Unreasonably Low Prices to Destroy or Eliminate Competition. (49 Stat. 1528; 15 U.S.C.A., sec. 13a.)

Sec. 3. It shall be unlawful for any person engaged in commerce, in the course of such commerce, to be a party to, or assist in, any transaction of sale, or contract to sell, which discriminates to his knowledge against competitors of the purchaser, in that, any discount, rebate, allowance, or advertising service charge is granted to the purchaser over and above any discount, rebate, allowance, or advertising service charge available at the time of such transaction to said competitors in respect of a sale of goods of like grade, quality, and quantity; to sell, or contract to sell, goods in any part of the United States at prices lower than those exacted by said person elsewhere in the United States for the purpose of destroying competition, or eliminating a competitor in such part of the United States; or, to sell, or contract to sell, goods at unreasonably low prices for the purpose of destroying competition or eliminating a competitor.

Any person violating any of the provisions of this section shall, upon conviction thereof, be fined not more than $5,000 or imprisoned not more than one year, or both.

SEC. 4. COOPERATIVES AND SCHOOL AND SIMILAR EXEMPTIONS.[2] (49 Stat. 1528; 15 U.S.C.A., sec. 13b.)

SEC. 4. Nothing in this Act shall prevent a cooperative association from returning to its members, producers, or consumers the whole, or any part of, the net earnings or surplus resulting from its trading operations, in proportion to their purchases or sales from, to, or through the association.

Approved, June 19, 1936.

---

[2] By Public No. 550, 75th Congress, Chapter 283, Third Session (H. R. 8148), approved May 26, 1938, it was further provided "That nothing in the Act approved June 19, 1936 (Public, Numbered 692, Seventy-fourth Congress, second session), known as the Robinson-Patman Anti-discrimination Act, shall apply to purchases of their supplies for their own use by schools, colleges, universities, public libraries, churches, hospitals, and charitable institutions not operated for profit."

SELECTED BIBLIOGRAPHY

BOOKS

Distribution Cost Analysis and Accounting

CASTENHOLZ, WILLIAM B. *The Control of Distribution Costs and Sales.* New York: Harper & Bros., 1930.

CULLITON, JAMES W. *The Management of Marketing Costs.* Boston: Division of Research, Graduate School of Business Administration, Harvard University, 1948.

HECKERT, J. BROOKS, and STONE, IRVING J. *Wholesale Accounting and Control.* New York: McGraw-Hill Book Co., Inc., 1935.

HILGERT, JOSEPH R. *Cost Accounting for Sales.* New York: The Ronald Press Co., 1926.

LONGMAN, DONALD R. *Distribution Cost Analysis.* New York: Harper & Bros., 1941.

MINER, ROBERT B. *Trends and Variations in Marketing Costs.* Unpublished Doctor's dissertation, Ohio State University, 1948.

Standard Expense Accounting Manual for Department Stores and Specialty Stores. New York: Controllers' Congress, National Retail Dry Goods Association, 1948.

Marketing Management and Analysis

BECKMAN, THEODORE N., and ENGLE, NATHANAEL H. *Wholesaling Principles and Practice,* rev. ed., rev. printing. New York: The Ronald Press Co., 1950, especially chaps. xxviii and xxix.

BROWN, LYNDON O. *Marketing and Distribution Research.* New York: The Ronald Press Co., 1949, especially chaps. vi–ix.

CANFIELD, BERTRAND R. *Sales Administration Principles and Problems,* rev. ed. New York: Prentice-Hall, Inc., 1947, especially chap. xx.

CRISP, RICHARD D. *How to Reduce Distribution Costs.* New York: Funk & Wagnalls Co. in association with *Modern Industry* magazine, 1948.

DAVIS, JAMES H. *Increasing Wholesale Drug Salesmen's Effectiveness.* Columbus, Ohio: Bureau of Business Research, Ohio State University, 1948.

DUNCAN, DELBERT J., and PHILLIPS, CHARLES F. *Retailing Principles and Methods,* rev. ed. Chicago: Richard D. Irwin, Inc., 1949, especially pp. 572–87.

EASTWOOD, ROBERT PARKER. *Sales Control by Quantitative Methods.* New York: Columbia University Press, 1940.

MAYNARD, HAROLD H., and NOLEN, HERMAN C. *Sales Management,* rev. ed. New York: The Ronald Press Co., 1950, especially chaps. xxviii–xxxi.

Cost Accounting

BLOCKER, JOHN G. *Cost Accounting,* 2d ed. New York: McGraw-Hill Book Co., Inc., 1948, especially chaps. xxii–xxv, and xxix.

DEVINE, CARL T. *Cost Accounting and Analysis.* New York: The Macmillan Co., 1950, especially chaps. xxix, xxxvii, and xxxviii.

GREER, HOWARD C., and WILLCOX, RUSSELL S. *Problems in Cost Accounting.* New York: McGraw-Hill Book Co., Inc., 1931, especially Part 5, Sec. E.

LAWRENCE, W. B. *Cost Accounting,* 3d ed. New York: Prentice-Hall, Inc., 1946, especially chaps. xx and xxi.

NEUNER, JOHN J. W. *Cost Accounting Principles and Practice.* 3d ed. Chicago: Richard D. Irwin, Inc., 1947, especially chaps. xxi–xxiv.

Van Sickle, Clarence L. *Cost Accounting.* New York: Harper & Bros., 1938, especially Part 7.

Budgeting

Heckert, J. Brooks. *Business Budgeting and Control.* New York: The Ronald Press Co., 1946, especially chaps. xii–xvii.

PERIODICAL ARTICLES

Beckett, John A. "The Art and the Science of Distribution Costing," *N.A.C.A. Bulletin,* XXXII, No. 8 (April, 1951), pp. 893–906.

Greer, Howard C. "Accounting as an Aid to a Sound Distribution Program," National Association of Cost Accountants, *Proceedings of the Twenty-ninth International Cost Conference* (1948), pp. 160–78.

Hollander, Sidney, Jr. "A Rationale for Advertising Expenditures,"*Harvard Business Review,* XXVII, No. 1 (January, 1949), pp. 79–87.

Kelley, E. W. "Distribution Cost Control—and Beyond," *N.A.C.A. Bulletin,* XXXII, No. 8 (April, 1951), pp. 907–22.

Research Series No. 19, "Assignment of Nonmanufacturing Costs for Managerial Decisions," *N.A.C.A. Bulletin,* XXXII, No. 9, Sec. 4 (May, 1951).

Research Series No. 20, "The Assignment of Nonmanufacturing Costs to Products," *N.A.C.A. Bulletin,* XXXII, No. 12, Sec. 4 (August, 1951).

Research Series No. 21, "The Assignment of Nonmanufacturing Costs to Territories and Other Segments," *N.A.C.A. Bulletin,* XXXIII, No. 4, Sec. 3 (December, 1951).

Watson, Robert H. "Bases for Allocating Distribution Costs," *Journal of Marketing,* XVI, No. 1 (July, 1951), pp. 29–42.

GOVERNMENT PUBLICATIONS

Federal Trade Commission. *Case Studies in Distribution Cost Accounting for Manufacturing and Wholesaling.* Washington, D. C.: Government Printing Office, 1941.

Meserole, William H., and Sevin, Charles H. *Effective Grocery Wholesaling,* Economic Series No. 14, Bureau of Foreign and Domestic Commerce, U. S. Department of Commerce. Washington, D. C.: Government Printing Office, 1941.

Sevin, Charles H. *Distribution Cost Analysis,* Economic Series No. 50, Bureau of Foreign and Domestic Commerce, U. S. Department of Commerce. Washington, D. C.: Government Printing Office, 1946.

———. *How Manufacturers Reduce Their Distribution Costs,* Economic Series No. 72, Office of Domestic Commerce, U. S. Department of Commerce. Washington, D. C.: Government Printing Office, 1948.

Taggart, H. F. *Distribution Cost Accounting for Wholesaling,* Domestic Commerce Series No. 106, Bureau of Foreign and Domestic Commerce, U. S. Department of Commerce. Washington, D. C.: Government Printing Office, 1939.

INDEX